Reforming Capitalism

Routledge Studies in Business Ethics

Reforming Capitalism

The Scientific Worldview and Business

Rogene A. Buchholz

 Routledge
Taylor & Francis Group

LONDON AND NEW YORK

First published 2012 by Routledge

2 Park Square, Milton Park, Abingdon, Oxon OX14 4RN
711 Third Avenue, New York, NY 10017, USA

Routledge is an imprint of the Taylor & Francis Group, an informa business

First issued in paperback 2017

Library of Congress Cataloging-in-Publication Data
Buchholz, Rogene A.
   Reforming capitalism : the scientific worldview and business / by
Rogene A. Buchholz. — 1st ed.
      p. cm. — (Routledge studies in business ethics ; 5)
   Includes bibliographical references and index.
   1. Business education.   2. Science—Moral and ethical aspects.
3. Pragmatism.   4. Philosophy, American.   5. Social responsibility
of business.   I. Title.
   HF1106.B74 2011
   174'.4—dc23
   2011040879

ISBN13: 978-0-415-51738-6 (hbk)
ISBN13: 978-1-138-11837-9 (pbk)

Typeset in Sabon
by IBT Global.

This book is dedicated to my wife Sandra B. Rosenthal (Sandy) who is not only the love of my life but also my intellectual companion who taught me most everything I know about classical American pragmatism and its relevance to business and management.

Contents

Acknowledgments

This book would not have been possible were it not for the person to whom the book is dedicated. My wife, Sandra B. Rosenthal, introduced me to classical American pragmatism and has helped me to think more philosophically in general. We have had many inspirational discussions about philosophical issues in relation to business and management and have collaborated on numerous papers and lectures which we have jointly presented both in the United States and abroad. We have published over forty articles together in the areas of business ethics and environmental ethics and have coauthored a book published by Oxford University Press entitled *Rethinking Business Ethics: A Pragmatic Approach* as part of the Ruffin Series in Business Ethics from which I rewrote some material for portions of this book. Classical American pragmatism provided the intellectual foundations for a new view of science which forms the basis for reforming capitalism and the business system. For all of her contributions to my life, I am eternally grateful.

This book was also made possible by William C. Frederick, who was my mentor while I was studying for my doctorate at the University of Pittsburgh and has been a continual source for new insights into the nature of corporate social responsibility and business ethics. Throughout my career I have also learned a great deal from my interactions with colleagues in the field, many of whom have been the best friends one could hope for, and from my many students at all the schools where I have taught. Both my colleagues and students have been a continual source of inspiration and encouragement for all my efforts.

In addition I would also like to thank Warren Bennis and James O'Toole for writing their article that appeared in the *Harvard Business Review* that criticized management education for a wholesale adoption of the scientific model and advocated the adoption of a more professional approach to business education. This article set me to thinking about management as a profession and what it would take to implement this vision. Thus I came to the realization that it would take no less than a rethinking and a reforming of capitalism for management to become a profession in the best sense of the word which provided the motivation for writing this book about the influence of the scientific worldview on our understanding of business and capitalism and my previous one on community and responsibility in business.

Since I retired I have been auditing philosophy classes at the University of Colorado at Denver, which has broadened my horizons and introduced me to new ways of thinking. In particular I would like to thank Myra Bookman, Maria Talero, and Chad Kautzer, who taught classes that I audited which gave me new ideas about capitalism and introduced me to philosophical writings that were relevant to this book. It has been great fun to audit these courses and have the privilege of interacting with these faculty and the students in the classes I audited. It is like going back to school without having to write papers or take exams, the best of all possible worlds.

Robert W. Kolb, the Frank W. Considine Chair in Applied Ethics at Loyola University Chicago, is owed a great many thanks for introducing me to Laura D. H. Stearns, my editor at Routledge Research of the Taylor & Francis Group, who took an interest in the book and guided it through the review process. She was a great pleasure to work with and deserves many thanks for her efforts. Thanks are also due to Stacy Noto, editorial assistant with Routledge Research and Eleanor Chan at IBT Global.

Finally, I would like to thank three anonymous reviewers who gave the book a positive response and made many suggestions for improvement that were taken into account in a revision of the book. Their efforts are greatly appreciated and their suggestions made for a much better book.

Excerpts were rewritten from the following publication with kind permission from Springer Science+Business Media.

Journal of Business Ethics, The Unholy Alliance of Business and Science, 2008, 199–206, Rogene A. Buchholz and Sandra B. Rosenthal. Copyright Springer.

Excerpts were also rewritten from the following book with the kind permission of Oxford University Press.

Sandra B. Rosenthal and Rogene A. Buchholz, *Rethinking Business Ethics*. New York: Oxford University Press, 2000.

Excerpts were also rewritten form my first book with Routledge with the kind permission of Taylor & Francis Group.

Rogene A. Buchholz, *Rethinking Capitalism: Community and Responsibility in Business*. New York: Routledge, 2009.

Introduction

This book is a companion piece to an earlier book I wrote about rethinking the philosophical foundations of capitalism.[1] Both books grew out of an article that appeared in the *Harvard Business Review* in 2005 in which Warren Bennis and James O'Toole, two management professors who were at the University of Southern California at the time the article was written, analyzed the reasons for what they believed was the failure of business schools to adequately prepare their graduates for the world of business.[2] The actual cause of this failure, they believed, could be traced to a dramatic shift in the culture of business schools that had taken place over the past several decades.

Many leading business schools had come to measure their success solely by the rigor of their scientific research rather than in terms of the competence of their graduates or how well faculties understood important drivers of business performance. This scientific model, they argued, is predicated on the faulty assumption that business is an academic discipline like chemistry or geology, when in fact it is a profession akin to medicine and the law. Business schools should be professional schools, and this distinction between a profession and an academic discipline is crucial; and no curricular reforms would work, in their opinion, until the scientific model is replaced by a model that is more appropriate to the special requirements of a profession.

As a result of this article, I was motivated to write a book on what it would mean for management to become a true profession akin to law and medicine, and made the point that it would involve no less than a rethinking of the philosophical foundations of capitalism. The traditional understanding of capitalism, I argued, is based on a philosophy of individualism and rights which informs the way we think about the responsibilities of business to society and the role of management. This philosophy must be broadened to include community and responsibility, but such a broadening must start with a definition of the self that is not individualistic in nature. Thus I presented a different view of the self that is social in nature and based on the social context in which it emerges, and then traced out the implications of this view of the self for capitalism and other aspects of the corporation, and finally what it would mean for the practice of management.

In the course of writing this book about management and the adoption of a professional model, I wondered why the scientific model had come to be the dominant paradigm in schools of business and management and why business education came to see itself as an academic discipline. Thus I came to see that there were really two interrelated parts to the argument of Bennis and O'Toole: one dealing with management as a profession and the other related to the scientific aspects of business and management. Thus in this book I want to discuss the way science influences how we think about business organizations and their purpose in society and how this contributes to the problems Bennis and O'Toole see with management education.

There have been many criticisms about the relevance of management research to the actual practice of management over the years, and organizations like the Academy of Management have responded to this criticism by establishing new journals, which in the Academy's case is called *Perspectives,* that are akin to the *Harvard Business Review* and publishes articles that are more practitioner oriented. Yet it remains a fact of life for faculty in schools of business and management that publication in these kinds of journals, particularly in the better schools, does not count for promotion and tenure. There is a fairly narrow set of journals in the management field that are considered to be the best as far as scientific research is concerned, and publication in these journals is what every faculty member interested in getting ahead seeks to accomplish. The scientific paradigm reigns supreme in terms of promotion and tenure decisions. While faculty are supposed to strive for excellence in teaching and provide a certain level of service to the school and university in the form of committee assignments, etc., in the final analysis it is research publications that count.

In response to the financial crisis of 2008–2009, there was renewed criticism of business schools, particularly given the fact that the top schools routinely sent more that 40 percent of their graduates into the financial industry. Some of the these criticisms focused on the scientific orientation claiming that business schools had become too scientific and detached from real-world concerns. Others said that students in these schools were taught to oversimplify management problems and come up with hasty solutions to more complicated problems that should have taken more time and thought. Still others contended that students received a limited and distorted view of their role in society and that they graduated with a focus on maximizing shareholder value with only a limited understanding of social and ethical factors that are essential to business leadership, a criticism that is germane to my earlier book dealing with management as a profession.[3]

Science serves many purposes in business organizations as well as in business-school education. It is used to enculturate students to a certain way of thinking about the world that is then perpetuated in business organizations. Science is much more than just a method to gain knowledge about business problems in the hopes of finding a solution. It is also something of an ideology that provides a rationale for the things business does and a justification for its purposes in our society. It is a worldview that informs our understanding of what we are as a society and what we hope to attain, and since business and its activities are so much a part of that society it is important for business to maintain this worldview in business-school education and train students to accept its legitimacy.

The first part of the book will then discuss the rise of modern science and its major characteristics. It is this traditional view of science that is the paradigm operative in business-school education and forms the basis of the scientific culture in which business-school students are enculturated. The book will then go on to discuss how this traditional understanding of science affects an understanding of ethics and values and the difficulties this presents in incorporating ethical and moral considerations into business education because of the fact/value dichotomy and its corollary of value-free decision making. This leads into a discussion about economics as an academic discipline and the scientific foundation this provides for business activities. The book will then take a look at how the scientific worldview affects the way government is understood and the implications of this view for business organizations, the culture that is created by a scientific and technological approach to life, and the way nature is viewed and used by business organizations.

The second part of the book will then use insights contained in classical American pragmatism to show how a different way of thinking about science will lead us to a different understanding of our world and how it operates. By classical American pragmatism I mean a philosophical school of thought, not the traditional practical attitude to which pragmatism usually refers. This philosophy is little understood and not widely taught, yet it contains insights that point the way to a different way of understanding science and its relationship to business and business education. This understanding of science has implications for the way the multiple environments of business are understood and the way business relates to them. These multiple contexts include the moral, economic, political, cultural, and natural environments. Business is embedded in these environments and how it relates to them has profound implications for the society in which business functions.

The last part of the book, then, will involve a discussion of how the scientific worldview informs our understanding of corporations and their role in society. Another chapter will focus on science as a method of inquiry and describe how the scientific method came to be dominant in business-school education and the way it is used and the purposes it serves in the educational process as well as business organizations. Science embeds in students a certain way of understanding their role in society that was evident in the recent financial crisis; thus a chapter is devoted to this situation. The last chapter will discuss a new model for management education that is based on an ethic of service that it is argued should permeate business organizations and replace the dominant scientific paradigm.

This book, thus, looks at the other half of the Bennis and O'Toole argument and discusses the scientific worldview that undergirds business and society and helps create the problem they see with management education and also causes problems in the larger society that were all too evident in the financial crisis the country recently experienced. The scientific worldview involves a certain way of looking at the world of business and its relation to the multiple environments in which it is embedded. This kind of thinking is pervasive in our society and informs how we understand morals, economics, politics, culture, nature, and all the rest of our lives. While scientific thinking has made it possible to manipulate our world and has led to technologies that have made our lies easier and more fulfilling, it has also limited our options and cut us off from a richer understanding of our world as well as causing problems that we have not as yet been able to resolve.

Part I

The Traditional Scientific Worldview

1   The Rise of Modern Science and Its Characteristics

We view the world in a certain manner that enables us to live in the world and work out some kind of meaningful existence. The way we think about the world reflects the dominant intellectual influences of our time which in our country and Western countries in general are largely scientific and technological in nature. This scientific and technological culture we live in involves a certain way of viewing the world that shapes our language and concepts and the way we relate to the world. This way of thinking influences everything we do and is reflected in every aspect of our lives including ethics, economics, politics, culture and the way we relate to nature. In this kind of world, the tools and techniques developed by science and technology are used to manipulate and shape the natural world in our interests. This manipulation is based on a certain understanding of the way in which the world works and functions.

This scientific worldview is based on the assumption that the world is made up of individual elements that relate to each other through laws that can be discovered in scientific inquiry. The behavior of the world is not random but operates according to laws that function in nature which produce regularities that can be counted on to continue. These laws allow us to send shuttles into space to dock with the international space station and land people on the moon. They enabled us to develop the atomic bomb and nuclear power plants. They exist in all parts of our physical world and form the basis of our ability to understand how the physical world works and allow us to manipulate it to accomplish our own goals and objectives.

Science deals with the natural world and involves a search for natural causes and explanations of things that happen in the world. It does not deal with supernatural explanations or beliefs but concerns itself solely with the natural world and assumes that everything can be explained on the basis of natural causes without an appeal to the supernatural. Science is materialistic in assuming that there is a real external world out there that can be accessed through the scientific method. Science is a way of knowing this reality; it involves a method that systematically investigates and organizes aspects of this reality that we can access through our senses. Knowledge that comes to us in other ways is not scientific knowledge.

The mythological worldview that science largely, but not completely, replaced consisted of a collection of stories that expressed the beliefs of a particular culture relative to the world in which they lived. For thousands of years people associated objects in the sky, the earth, and aspects of their physical world with supernatural beings. Myths often tell the story of ancestors, heroes, and gods or goddesses with special powers over the world and human existence. These stories sometimes contain mythical characters such as mermaids, unicorns, dragons, or angels that play certain roles in the stories. Myths were used to explain certain things that happened in the world and provided an understanding of complex natural phenomena that helped people cope with their existence.

Nature can be terrifying to humans. Imagine how primeval forests appeared to early peoples who populated the earth. These forests contained many unknowns such as animals and other things that posed a threat to human existence, much the same as jungles appear to us in today's world. There were hurricanes, tornados, earthquakes, floods, volcanic eruptions, and other forces in nature that posed major threats just as they do today. And there were diseases that could strike at any time and wipe out many people, as they can today. Nature can be quite terrifying and arbitrary and beyond the control of humans.

Mythology helped people cope with this tenuous existence and provided a means of understanding what was happening in their world. The idea of God, for example, puts nature under the control of a supernatural being. One can appeal to this being through prayer or other means to look favorably upon the petitioner. This helps reduce some of the anxiety involved in living in such an uncertain world. Science, on the other hand, demythologizes nature and provides another way of understanding the world that allows for greater control and manipulation of nature to reduce the anxiety and make it less terrifying. Science gives us the means to predict where hurricanes might strike so we can prepare for them. It allows us to develop medicines to combat diseases that threaten to wipe out vast numbers of people. It enables us to understand how tornados form and predict where they might develop.

This scientific worldview did not develop and win adherents overnight but had to struggle against the worldview of other authoritative entities in society. For example, based on Aristotelian philosophy it was believed that the sun and other planets revolved around the earth and that human beings and the earth they lived on were the center of the universe. This belief was perpetuated by the church, which placed its considerable authority behind such a view of the universe. Leading intellectual figures of the time supported the assumption that the earth was the motionless center of a system around which the sun and planets revolved. As observations began to be made about the movements of the planets and the sun, elaborate and complicated theories had to be invented to explain the observed irregularities of their rotation based on an earth-centered assumption.[1]

None of these explanations proved to be satisfactory, however, and they made less and less sense as time went on and became unworkable.[2] Finally, the only thing that did make sense was to abandon the old worldview about an earth-centered solar system and accept the view that the earth and other planets revolved around the sun instead. In attempting to develop an astronomical theory that would more accurately reflect the actual position of celestial bodies, Copernicus had to challenge the traditional view of the universe. In the Copernican system, the earth was not the center of the universe or even of our own solar system. Such a view constituted no less than a scientific revolution or paradigm shift and eventually became the accepted way of viewing the universe.[3]

Such changes in thinking do not come easily, however, and the early scientists who developed these new theories did so at considerable personal cost to themselves because of opposition from church authorities.[4] It took courage to publish these new ideas, especially when they challenged both Aristotelian physics and Holy Scripture. Church authorities officially banned the Copernican worldview in 1616 when his book, *On the Revolution*, was put on the Index of Forbidden Books by the Congregation of the Index.[5] When Galileo came along and made observations through a crude telescope that convinced him that the Copernican model of the universe had to be the true picture, the church commanded Galileo to abandon such a worldview and support the traditional assumptions about the earth and its place in the universe. While Galileo tried to comply with conditions laid down by the Pope, he simply could not make a convincing case for the traditional worldview and was eventually brought before the Inquisition and sentenced to house arrest.[6]

But the damage had been done. It was widely perceived that science had demonstrated new truths about the universe through observation which could not be erased by religious dogma based on outdated philosophies. The church eventually had to reconcile itself to the results of scientific observation, which rapidly became the new authority in such matters. From these beginnings, science went on to become the established authority in matters pertaining to the physical universe and eventually was extended into other fields such as medicine, biology, geology, and on into the social sciences such as economics, political science, and sociology. Science thus became the basis for a new worldview of everything, not just the physical universe. The implications of the Copernican Revolution, as it has been called, thus affected far more than astronomy, according to Thomas S. Kuhn, ultimately affecting not only science but also philosophy, religion, and social theory.[7]

Initiated as a narrowly technical, highly mathematical revision of classical astronomy, the Copernican theory became one focus for the tremendous controversies in religion, in philosophy, and in social theory, which, during the two centuries following the discovery of America, set the tenor of the modern mind. Men who believed that their terrestrial home was only a planet circulating blindly about one of an infinity of stars evaluated their place in the cosmic scheme quite differently than had their predecessors who saw the earth as the unique and focal center of God's creation. The Copernican Revolution was therefore also part of a transition of man's sense of values.[8]

This scientific revolution involved a change in ways of securing our beliefs about the natural world. The philosophical basis for this revolution stressed the role that the experimental method played in the development of scientific theories and held that the universe was a mechanical system that could be described by mathematical laws that could be discovered through scientific observation. According to Steven Shapin, a professor of sociology at the University of California, San Diego, there were four inter-related aspects of this revolution: (1) the mechanization of nature, (2) the depersonalization of natural knowledge, (3) the attempted mechanization of knowledge, i.e., following explicitly formulated rules of method in producing knowledge to eliminate the effects of human interests and passions, and, (4) "the aspiration to use the resulting reformed natural knowledge to achieve moral, social, and political ends, the condition of which was agreement that the knowledge in question truly was benign, powerful, and above all *disinterested*."[9]

Reasoning was made subject to the findings of reliable observation conducted according to the rigors of accepted scientific methodology and mathematically disciplined thinking. What counted was reliably constituted observation of nature, not tradition or religious authority. Adherents of the scientific revolution were encouraged to believe what they saw with their own eyes rather than adhering to accepted tradition. This empirical content rested not just on direct observation of what went on in the world naturally, however, but also on artificially and purposefully contrived experiments which produced phenomena that might not be observed easily or at all in the normal course of nature.[10]

Principles related to the physical world rest on empirical claims that support hypotheses about the way the world is constituted. Scientific method is an inductive and empirically grounded procedure; it proceeds from accumulated knowledge of particulars (observational and experimental facts) to causal knowledge and general truths about nature.[11] The foundation of scientific knowledge is facts discovered in the course of scientific investigation, and these facts are established by reliable observation or experiment guided by hypotheses. These facts had to be guaranteed as authentic and protected from contamination by other less certain items of knowledge, hence the importance of adhering to a rigorous methodology. "A factually grounded approach to knowledge held out the prospect of a well-founded certainty and a well-conceived approach to knowledge of nature's underlying causal structure."[12]

Science, according to Timothy Ferris, an emeritus professor at the University of California, is inherently antiauthoritarian. Scientific propositions must be subject to experimental method and tested according to the rules of scientific procedure. If a proposition repeatedly fails such testing it is dropped from further consideration regardless of who supports it and how much it may have made sense. Science is self-correcting as the results of such tests are subject to being replicated by other scientists, and if a new discovery cannot be replicated, the results are not considered to be valid.[13] In this manner, cold fusion, which was supposedly discovered by two scientists at the University of Utah in 1989, were found to be a hoax because it could not be replicated by other scientists.

Science also utilized mathematics because nature was believed to be mathematical in structure. Scientific investigation of physical phenomena tried to make sense of physical evidence gathered from observation and experiments by establishing formal mathematical patterns that were believed to underlie and give rise to the natural world. Nature was believed to follow laws that were mathematical in form and that could be expressed in the language of mathematics. Newton, in fact, was concerned with the certainty of mathematical demonstration insofar as it could be legitimately attained in physical inquiry. Physical theories that could be mathematically expressed that were also supported by legitimate empirical observation or experiment could be spoken of with absolute confidence.[14] Thus science was able to establish itself as the new authority with respect to the physical world, an authority that was eventually extended into the social realm and into human behavior itself.

Religion has not accepted this new worldview without difficulty. Galileo, for example, was not formally let off the hook by the Catholic Church until just a few short years ago in an official statement. Fundamentalist religions have still not accepted theories of evolution and battles between creationists and evolutionists continue in today's world. But when push comes to shove, science usually wins out with regard to our understanding our world and developing solutions to problems simply because it makes better sense to most people and works better in solving problems. Scientific thinking dominates or world and shapes our perception of what the world is like and enables us to manipulate it in our interests through the development of new technologies.

Philosophy had to come to terms with the scientific worldview and incorporate modern science in its understanding of the world. It was René Descartes, a French philosopher who lived in the first half of the seventeenth century, who embodied this worldview in his philosophy. The body, for Descartes, was a mechanical entity that could be worked on and understood in a scientific sense. But Descartes did not want to reduce the mind to this state, so he located the mind outside of nature. This action created a mind-body dualism where the mind became something separate from the body located in some nonmaterial realm. As Steven Shapin states, the mind was not a mechanical entity and could not be accounted for in this manner.

> For human beings, however, the scope of mechanical accounts was crucially limited. Explanations of the human *body* were, for Descartes, not the same thing as explanations of human *beings*, for there was something about human beings that could not be comprehended by and account for the body's matter and motion. We do not *feel* ourselves to be machines, and Descartes agreed that we are not. We feel ourselves to exercise will, to have purposes, to move our bodies in response to our purposes, to be conscious, to make moral evaluations, to deliberate and to reason (that is, to *think*), and to express the results of our thoughts in language—none of which Descartes reckoned that machines or animals can do.[15]

For Descartes, the *I* with its characteristics was a self-contained entity, a thing that thinks outside of nature and beyond the realm of scientific study. The material world is other than the *I* and can be observed and studied by science. Human beings thus have a dual nature. Their bodies are like machines and can be accounted for by matter in motion. But they also have a mind which can not be accounted for in this manner. The world itself thus is made up of two different realms, that of matter and that of mind, and it is only in human beings that these two realms meet. Exactly how mind and matter meet in the human being remained something of a mystery. The body is extended in space but the mind is not so extended. However, if the mind is not extended into space, then where is it located? And how do the two realms make contact with each other?[16]

This mind-body dualism and the dichotomies that came with it such as the split between the spiritual and material world and the subject-object dichotomy have plagued philosophy ever since as philosophers have been struggling with these issue for centuries. Those scientists who wanted to reject dualism and study the mind as an object had to treat it as part of scientifically defined nature and so the mind in modern times has been reduced to the brain, which can be scientifically studied as some kind of a mechanical entity. Things like love, ethics, freedom, etc., have become nothing more than neurons firing in certain parts of the brain that can be observed with modern technology.[17]

Nature as a whole came to be viewed as a machine that was considered to be wholly intelligible. There was nothing mysterious or magical about a machine. It operated according to universal laws and there was nothing capricious about the uniformities that were observed in nature. The machine metaphor was a "model of the form and scope that human knowledge of nature might properly have and of how human accounts of nature might properly be framed."[18] Matter was considered to be passive and inert, and while there were complexities in nature, these were not the result of purpose and design. This mechanical account of nature was in opposition to a tradition that saw purpose or intention in nature.

This classical vision of a machinelike world governed entirely by universal mathematical laws has no room for spontaneity or freedom. The world of nature is seen as an automatic machine with no soul, no spontaneous life, and no purposes of its own.[19] This desacralized, soulless vision of nature became the foundation for modern science and established itself as the reigning paradigm in the scientific revolution of the seventeenth century.[20] Nature came to be regarded as dead matter subject only to mechanical forces and governed by mathematical laws. The whole course of nature was thought to be determined because everything was believed to carry on inexorably and mechanically and was in principle completely predictable. The whole of nature was thought to be essentially knowable to the mathematical reason of scientists.[21]

Science thus views the world as a closed system that operates according to mechanical laws that can be expressed in mathematical terms. This worldview produces a quantitatively characterized universe that constitutes the way we perceive the world and the kind of sensibilities we develop as human beings. Knowledge becomes the building up of a storehouse of so-called objective facts gleaned from scientific studies. The way to know the world is through such studies that are based on a spectator theory of knowledge where the researcher is only an observer of what's there in nature. The scientific approach to reality is one of breaking the whole of life down into its component parts in the interests of understanding how the world works so as to be able to manipulate those parts and shape the world to our advantage.

CHARACTERISTICS OF THE SCIENTIFIC WORLDVIEW

The way science operates is to reduce everything to its most fundamental elements on the assumption that everything that exists in the natural world can be explained through the interactions of a small number of simple elements whose behavior is governed by physical laws pertaining to those elements. This method is most often referred to as *reductionism*, which has been defined as "the endeavor of understanding any object of inquiry, such as physical objects, situations, phenomena, explanations, theories, concepts, language, and so forth, by specifying the elements that constitute it . . . The whole does not impart meaning to the parts, but rather, the parts are the meaning of the whole. The study of anything must be the study of its parts."[22]

While reductionism can be traced back before the rise of modern science, it was with the development of classical physics, which incorporated the method of understanding an object of inquiry by analyzing its constituent elements, that reductionism emerged into its full significance. Classical physics views the universe as composed of discrete particles that operate mechanistically and deterministically following universal laws of motion and gravity.[23] Thus in particle physics, for example, the search is on for the fundamental building blocks of the universe, and physicists have gone way beyond protons, neutrons, and electrons, which some of us were brought up to believe made up the atom, to leptons and quarks, combinations of which make up all the matter we can see and touch. These particles interact by exchanging bosons, which along with gluons and photons are called force carriers that regulate three of the four fundamental forces of the universe. This so-called standard model of particle physics is thought to be the best way to get at the fundamental elements and forces that make up physical matter.[24]

In medical science, the human body is broken up into various systems such as the skeletal system, the muscular system, the nervous system, the circulatory system, the digestive system, the respiratory system, and so on, and each system is composed of various parts such as different kinds of bones, muscles, nerves, the heart and blood vessels, the digestive organs, and respiratory organs such as lungs. Doctors specialize in these different areas of the body, and if an internist cannot diagnose or heal our ailment, he or she will refer us to one of these specialists. The body is considered to be a mechanical and chemical system that can be examined and manipulated to make it function better.

In neuroscience, human behavior is studied by looking at what parts of the brain are stimulated by certain human activities. The assumption behind this research is that everything can be reduced to neurons firing in certain parts of the brain. As stated by Nobel laureate Francis Crick, "You, your joys and your sorrows, your memories and your ambitions, your sense of personal identity and free will, are in fact not more than the behavior of a vast assembly of nerve cells and their associated molecules."[25] Since there are more than 100 billion neurons in the human body and each neuron is connected to hundreds of thousands of other neurons and each can fire signals hundreds of times a second across about 100 trillion synapses, understanding the human brain in this fashion is a daunting task.

In the social sciences, human behavior is studied in a reductionist manner in that individual components of human and social behavior are identified and related to each other through some kind of statistical process to see if there are significant relationships. Variables that relate to the phenomenon under investigation are specified, and data collected on these variables are then analyzed with statistical methods to determine if there are relationships between these variables that can describe the behavior under examination and that can then be used to predict future behavior. Thus the whole is broken down into various parts and these parts are then examined for relationships with each other that can be expressed in statistical terms related to the behavioral process under investigation.

Each scientific area has its own methods to investigate problems in a scientific manner. Thus our knowledge of the world is broken up into different fields of study that have separate scholars, journals, and conferences as well as standards. Science has become specialized to the extent that people in one field of study cannot really talk and understand what is going on in other fields. In the natural sciences there are different kinds of physical scientists, some looking for smaller and smaller particles in a search for the basic building blocks of the universe while other deal with larger natural structures such as the universe itself. In the social sciences there are economics, sociology, and political science all looking at various aspects of human behavior in different contexts.

Such a process has greatly increased our knowledge of particular areas of interest, but it has also led to a fragmentation of knowledge and a loss of the whole picture. It seems impossible to fit all this knowledge together in some unified theory of everything and so the world remains fragmented in our thinking. Some attempts have been made to link fields together as in organizations that have a hyphen in their name such as socio-economics and astro-physics, but such hyphenated efforts do not really do the job of uniting knowledge into some kind of meaningful whole. It seems that over time science is becoming more and more specialized with each specialization building its own knowledge base ever larger, a base that has to be learned by anyone entering the field.

The ultimate task of reductionism, however, is to unite these different fields of knowledge by showing that they stem from a common ground. Paul Oppenheim and Hilary Putnam, for example, look towards a unity of the sciences through a reductive process and state that "the assumption that unitary science can be attained through cumulative micro-reduction recommends itself as a working hypothesis."[26] What they mean by this is that there is at least a possibility that all science may one day be reduced to the elementary particles of microphysics. The different reductive levels that they employ start with social groups and proceed downward through multicellular living things, cells, molecules, atoms, and finally elementary particles.[27] They cite numerous examples where success in this reductionistic process has already been attained and mention other possibilities to show where this process may be applied.

> It is not absurd to suppose that psychological laws may eventually be explained in terms of the behavior of individual neurons in the brain; that the behavior of individual cells—including neurons—may eventually be explained in terms of their biochemical composition; and that the behavior of molecules—including the macromolecules that make up living cells—may eventually be explained in terms of atomic physics.[28]

Thus everything is reduced to the fundamental particles of atomic physics. This is the ultimate goal of reductionism: that we can understand everything about the universe and human beings by understanding how the so-called fundamental building blocks of nature relate to each other. Human beings become nothing more that a bunch of subatomic particles that behave in certain ways that science can discover. Questions can be raised, however, as to whether this is a satisfactory way of dealing with human behavior and whether such reductionism can even adequately explain the natural world. There have been complications at the subatomic level with the development of quantum mechanics mentioned in the next section that makes even our understanding of particle behavior problematic.

Classical science is thus *atomistic* in looking for individual components that make up nature and then tries to understand how these components relate to each other through some mechanistic process. This view of nature also pervades the social sciences, where individual components of human behavior are identified and then related to each other through some statistical process to see if there are significant relationships. The reductionistic process thus forces us to think in terms of individual atoms and look for mechanisms through which these atoms relate to each other. In a philosophical sense this is called atomic individualism and it results in a view of society as a collection of independent self-sufficient individuals. Each person is like an atom and we are what we are regardless of the social context. The society is simply the sum of these individualistic atomistic humans which provide the substance of society.

The term *atomism* comes from the Greek word *atoma*, which means things that cannot be cut or divided. Supposedly this philosophy originated with Democritus in 460 BCE and can be summarized in four propositions: (1) all bodies are composed of atoms and spaces between the atoms, (2) atoms are eternal, indivisible, infinite in number, and homogeneous in nature; all differences in bodies are due to a difference in the size, shape, or location of the atoms, (3) there is no purpose or design in nature, and in this sense all is ruled by chance, and (4) all activity is reduced to local motion.[29] With the rise of modern science, this philosophical conception of reality was applied to physics and became the basis of most of the sciences. Matter is not continuous but is considered to be atomically constituted.

Furthermore, these atoms were believed to be fixed and unchanging, and while they may change their position in space, they are unchangeable as far as their own being is concerned. An atom may change its direction and velocity of motion so that its relationship to other things is changed, but all this is external to its internal being, which does not change. Changes that occur are between substances and these changes do not affect the atom's inner nature. The atom has no potentialities to become something else; it has no development or history of change. It is what it is and is the same yesterday, today, and forever. These immutable entities are the objects of any true knowledge of nature because they have the characteristic of a fixed certitude that is unchanging.[30]

Science thus deals with *discretes*: it breaks up space and time into discrete elements so space can be measured and time broken into identifiable units. We experience space as continuous, yet when we measure it for whatever purpose we break it into parts that can be dealt with individually. Land, for example, is a continuous thing, but when we break it into lots we are able to allocate it for individual usage. This creates problems at a conceptual level, however, as with Zeno's paradox.[31] Time is broken up into hours and minutes and seconds so we can organize our day and accomplish certain goals within time; patterns of human activity became regulated according to a mechanical conception of time rather that the rhythms of human life or natural seasons. But this creates the problems as to what holds all these minutes and seconds together and makes a continuous day or year or lifetime.

One of the most important characteristics of the scientific approach is its use of *quantitative* procedures to support its findings and identify what is considered to be true knowledge. Mathematics is considered to be the language of nature and the only knowledge worth considering from a scientific perspective is that which can be quantified and mathematized in some manner to arrive at a scientific conclusion. What lies outside the domain of science and cannot be quantified or mathematized is considered to be merely opinion, speculation, belief, feeling, or superstition. Quantification crowds out so-called subjective impressions since the reality science deals with is objectified and mathematized. Experience or common sense becomes disconnected from knowledge and becomes purely subjective in nature. There is no place for the sacred, for religious experience, or for the spiritual realm in a purely mathematical worldview. According to Christopher Dawson, writing in *Progress and Religion:*

> From the 17th century onwards, the modern scientific movement has been based on the mechanistic view of nature which regards the world as a closed material order moved by purely mechanical and mathematical laws. All the aspects of reality which could not be reduced to mathematical terms . . . were treated as mere subjective impressions of the mind.[32]

Quantification involves measurement as quantitative attributes are those it is possible to measure in some fashion. Physical quantities that can be measured include distance, mass, and time, while many attributes in the social sciences such as beliefs and values can also be studied as quantifiable properties. The assumption is that these properties have a quantitative structure where some kind of measurement can be made that will capture the reality of the property. Measurement is critical to quantitative research because it provides a connection between empirical observation of discrete entities and a mathematical expression of quantitative relationships between them.

A final characteristic of the scientific worldview is *determinism*, the idea that every event in the world, which includes human events and actions as well as events in the physical world, is causally determined by an unbroken chain of prior occurrences. If all of reality can be reduced to fundamental atoms, the behavior of which is governed by mathematical laws, then if we have complete knowledge of physical matter and all of the laws governing that matter, we should be able to compute every physical event that will ever occur in the world. All these events are predetermined by the nature of physical matter at a given point in time and the laws that govern the behavior of that matter. As John Dewey states:

> The fundamental principle of the mechanical philosophy of nature is that it is possible to determine exactly (in principle if not in actual practice) both the position and velocity of any body. Knowing this for each particle which enters into any change, as a motion, it is possible to calculate mathematically, that is exactly, just what will happen. The laws or physical equations that express the relations of the particles and bodies under different conditions are then assumed to be a "governing" framework on nature to which all particular phenomena conform . . . The philosophy in question assumed that these positions and velocities are there in nature independent of our knowing, or our experiments and observations, and that we have scientific knowledge in the degree in which we ascertain them exactly. The future and the past belong to the same completely determinate and fixed scheme. Observations, when correctly conducted, merely register this fixed state of changes according to laws of objects whose essential properties are fixed.[33]

This idea of determinism finds in way into many areas of our existence. In biology it leads to the belief that all human behavior is fixed by our genetic endowment. In neuroscience it leads to the notion that human behavior is determined by neurons firing in certain parts of the brain, which in turn is determined by certain chemicals or lack thereof in the body. Environmental determinism holds that the physical environment determines the kind of culture people develop and the values that they believe in most strongly. Technological determinism is the belief that the technology we employ has certain outcomes that cannot be changed by any actions humans may take to alter those outcomes.

Determinism is related to prediction as strict determinism leads to perfect predictability. If we know all we need to know about the initial conditions regarding the nature of physical matter and the laws that govern the behavior of that matter, then obviously we can predict with perfect accuracy what will happen in the future. Lack of perfect predictability, however, does not mean lack of determinism. It may be that we simply do not have all the information we need to make such a prediction. We do not know everything we need to know about the initial conditions or about the laws of nature, which implies that sometime in the future, when more research has been done, we may have such information and be able to make such predictions.

This idea of determinism obviously conflicts with notions about free will and human freedom. While we may like to think that humans have free will to make decisions about their future, if determinism is true then we may not have this kind of freedom, in particular the freedom to have done otherwise given certain past states of affairs or initial conditions. This debate about determinism and human freedom has gone on for some time in philosophy and there have been some creative attempts to resolve this problem.[34] The traditional way of dealing with this problem, however, continues the dualism of Cartesian philosophy, which made a separation between mind and matter. The mind was placed outside of nature and thus the uncertain and indeterminate were considered to be only subjective impressions of the mind and had no objective reality. According to John Dewey, this contrast between the doubtful and the determinate became one of the chief marks by which the subjective and objective were placed in opposition to each other.[35]

Our ability to land rovers on Mars and send satellites into space based on our knowledge of the laws of motion governing the behavior of bodies in our solar system provides strong evidence to support a deterministic view of the universe. As long as we get things right, we have confidence that the universe will act as it always has and our satellites will go where they are supposed to and do what has been planned. However, there have been relatively new developments in science itself that have raised questions about the idea of strict determinism as well as other aspects of the classical scientific worldview and have made the case for a probabilistic view of the universe, particularly at the subatomic level.

NEW DEVELOPMENTS IN SCIENCE

There have been new developments in science, many taking place in recent years that have modified or perhaps even radically challenged the classical view of science and the characteristics of its worldview. The first such development came from quantum theory, which held that the energy in all heat, light, and radio waves existed in the form of tiny, discrete amounts called quanta. In classical physics, all changes in energy levels and light were conceptualized as continuous. Quantum theory introduced discreteness into this picture and for a while the orbits of electrons were believed to be another example of an unexplainable discontinuity in nature until an alternative view was discovered where atoms acted like waves, not particles, and this conception could then explain the orbits of electrons better than classical physics.[36]

There were now two radically different concepts of the atom that could not immediately be reconciled. Was the electron a wave or a particle?[37] This led to Werner Heisenberg's principle of uncertainty, which, along with Bohr's principle of complementarity, established the internal consistency of quantum theory.[38] Heisenberg theorized that the mere fact of observing an object inevitably changes its location, and it is therefore impossible to know where it really is; and furthermore, the more you know about the particle's position, the less you are able to know about its speed and direction; and the more you know about a particle's speed and direction, the less you can know about where it is located at any given time. Thus it is fundamentally impossible to know both a subatomic particle's exact speed of movement and its exact position at the same time.[39]

This insight challenged the classical view of nature as an independent reality apart from any observation that could be known objectively through the methods of science. What we see, according to Heisenberg, depended on the conceptual net we used to capture nature and the context surrounding the observation. The observation itself affects what is observed and thus subjectivity enters into the experiments we conduct. As Heisenberg himself puts it: "This again emphasizes a subjective element in the description of atomic events, since the measuring device has been constructed by the observer, and we have to remember that what we observe is not nature itself but nature exposed to our method of questioning. Our scientific work in physics consists in asking questions about nature in the language that we possess and trying to get an answer from experiment by the means at our disposal."[40]

Thus Heisenberg saw that the electron was a particle whose position and velocity could only be expressed as a probability. The classical view of Newtonian determinism, which claimed that all events could be described with infinite precision, was now replaced by probabilities, and science moved from a world of fixed rules and laws to a world of chance and uncertainty. Heisenberg challenged the premise of the classical view by asserting that we cannot know the present in all its details as a matter of principle. And if we cannot know the initial conditions in all their detail, the future becomes unpredictable.[41]

This view of how the world of subatomic particles acted was resisted by those who trusted in the certainties of a Newtonian universe and even had religious implications in that it challenged God's omniscience. If God cannot know where the electron is, then he cannot know what will happen in the future and free will is introduced into our world.[42] Matter is thus changing all the time because of its interaction with the act of observing and a subjective element is introduced into the very heart of the notion of an objective nature that is independent of our existence. For many, according to John Dewey, this seemed to make the universe unintelligible and arbitrary.

> The idea of a universal reign of law, based on properties immutably inhering in things and of such a nature as to be capable of exact mathematical statement, was a sublime idea. It displaced once for all the notion of a world in which the unaccountable and the mysterious have the first and last word, a world in which they constantly insert themselves. It established the idea of regularity and uniformity in place of

the casual and sporadic. It gave men inspiration and guidance in seeking for uniformities and constancies where only irregular diversity was experienced. The ideal extended itself from the inanimate world to the animate and then to social affairs. It became, it may be fairly said, the great article of faith in the creed of scientific men. From this point of view, the principle of indeterminacy seems like an intellectual catastrophe. In compelling surrender of the doctrine of exact and immutable laws describing the fixed antecedent properties of things, it seems to involve abandonment of the idea that the world is fundamentally intelligible. A universe in which fixed laws do not make possible exact predictions seems from the older standpoint to be a world in which disorder reigns.[43]

The view of the passive scientific observer is thus challenged by a view of science as participatory. The scientific observer is involved in what is being observed as quantum theory discovered. What is being looked for and the way it is looked at affects what is found by the scientist. The expectations of the experimenter affect what is observed and the eventual outcome of the experiment. There is more of participatory sense on the part of some scientists, that our knowledge of nature is not entirely objective and that there is no such thing as unobtrusive measures or experiments that do not affect that which is being observed.[44] In spite of the objections to this view of nature, quantum theory has gone on to become the basis for many scientific and technological advances of recent origin.

New understandings in the complexity sciences that draw attention to the interactive effects and emergent properties of living systems also challenge the mechanistic paradigm of classical science. This approach is nonlinear in nature and provides a way of going beyond the limits of reductionism. The basic building blocks of nature cannot exist or be understood, so it is argued, apart from the cognitive context that frames their relationships.[45] Such scientists claim that we are living through a period of change in the natural sciences that involves a paradigm shift from the idea of nature as inanimate and mechanical to a new understanding of nature as organic and alive.[46] The world cannot be fully explained by just looking at its parts, but is holistic and difficult to comprehend by classical scientific analysis.[47]

In the area of cosmology, the idea of the cosmos as a machine has given way in some instances to the image of the cosmos as a living organism. The big bang theory holds that the universe began with a singularity as small as the point of a pencil and has been expanding ever since this singular beginning. The discovery that the universe was expanding at all points, that everything was moving away from everything else, was a major change in thinking from the idea of a steady state universe. As the universe expands, a succession of new structures and forms appear that are nothing like a machine but more like the way an embryo develops or a tree that grows from a small seed. Thus cosmology has adopted an image of a developing organism as opposed to a machine that operates according to universal laws of motion.[48]

The doctrine that everything is determinate and in principle predictable began to be questioned by quantum theory; it has also been challenged by the development of chaos theory, and chaotic dynamics has made the old idea of determinism untenable not just in the quantum realm but in the predicting of weather, the development of spreading waves, and in most other natural systems.[49] The idea that very small changes in a system can have large and unexpected consequences is a fundamental tenant of chaos theory. Chaos and indeterminism have introduced a greater sense of freedom and spontaneity into nature than anything that prevailed for more than three centuries, when science was under the spell of classical determinism.[50]

These and other developments in the scientific community are leading to a shift in worldview to some kind of a postmechanistic state where the universe and the earth are an organism that is growing and changing, and even the laws that govern the behavior of more fundamental elements that make up the universe may be changing and evolving. However, these developments have not filtered down to other sciences, let alone the average person in society. The classical scientific worldview, with its characteristics of reductionism, atomic individualism, discreteness, its quantitative approach, and its deterministic outlook, has pervaded everything in our society and created a certain kind of consciousness that makes us look at everything through these kinds of glasses.[51]

Most of us still live in a world of scientific objectivity where things happen in front of an observing and detached scientist. The idea that scientists are somehow disembodied and not bodily or emotionally involved in what they are doing is still the dominant scientific paradigm.[52] The idea that nature may be a living organism has been largely relegated to the realm of subjective experience and private life, while mechanistic attitudes have been given scientific authority.[53] Thus the traditional or classical scientific worldview is alive and well in our society and constitutes the way most people think about most aspects of life. And a quick glance at any of the articles in a leading journal of management research, such as the *Academy of Management Journal*, will show that this classical view with its operative characteristics is the dominant paradigm in management research.

The following chapters of this the book will show how this worldview and its way of thinking about the world have pervaded our understanding of economics and politics as well as culture and nature. This way of thinking influences the way we deal with problems and determines the options we have available to deal with these problems. It influences the way we treat each other and the way we relate to the world in which we live. It shapes our view of reality and the way we understand ourselves and the way we live our daily lives and provide for our existence. First, we will look at the moral and ethical environment and show how science undermines values because of the fact/value dichotomy, which makes it difficult for ethics and morals to have a significant impact on business organizations.

2   Values and Ethics

The scientific worldview has an impact on values related to what goals are worth pursuing in life and what one ought to do in order to live an ethical life and create an ethical society. Value questions related to what one ought to do to be moral are terribly important in any society and yet science has reduced those questions to the realm of subjectivity . With its emphasis on the material world as the source of true knowledge, science has undermined the status of value in our world. Value statements do not have any kind of objectivity and have been reduced to matters of opinion where there is no scientific standard to judge one opinion better than another. Values are seen to be noncognitive in nature, which leaves values floating in a never-never land where there is no foundation that would give value statements about what is good in life and what activities one ought to pursue to be a moral person some kind of validity. Science investigates and describes what is and establishes certain facts about our world and there is no way to get from these facts to a determination of what is ethical, from an is to an ought as it is often stated in the literature.

THE FACT-VALUE DISTINCTION

This problem of the distinction between facts and values has existed in philosophy for several centuries. Other ways of stating the problem such as the difference between objective and subjective approaches, the is versus the ought, and descriptive versus prescriptive statements have also appeared. These distinctions all get at the same problem and involve questions about the seriousness with which normative or ought statements should be taken. Are ethical oughts in any way scientific or empirical propositions that say something significant about the world in which we live or are they merely matters of opinion? Do ought statements relate in any significant way to factual claims that are the subject matter of scientific endeavors? Can normative claims be made about how life ought to be lived that have a firm foundation in a scientific and technological culture?

Descriptive claims deal with matters of "fact" and attempt to make clear the way things work in the natural world and attempt to describe this reality. Such statements are the purview of science in its attempt to objectively analyze the natural world by identifying important variables and establishing relationships between these variables in the form of natural laws to further understand the way the world works and functions. Prescriptive statements, on the other hand, deal with questions of value and prescribe the way things should be in order to live a "good" life or promote human welfare and fulfillment. Values relate to the importance, merit, or worth of some entity and are believed to be inherently subjective representing opinions about what is good or valuable. Given this assumption, if values cannot be reduced to facts, if there is a fact-value distinction, then objective morality becomes impossible.

The implications of this fact-value distinction for traditional ethical theories can be seen in Bentham's utilitarian position.[1] The fact-value distinction is completely ignored by Bentham in his position, for he slides back and forth between the factual claim that individuals *are* motivated by pleasure and the normative claim that individuals *ought to be* motivated by pleasure. The unexpressed assumption that runs through his position is that the supposed truth of hedonism as a psychological theory about the way individuals behave is an automatic justification for the moral claim about the way individuals ought to behave. This assumption cannot be scientifically proven and thus his entire theory can be dismissed from a scientific perspective as having no validity for making normative claims about how people ought to behave.

John Stuart Mill, a utilitarian writing after Bentham, tried to prove explicitly that the "ought" claim could be derived from the "is" claim but was ultimately shown to have failed in this endeavor. The claim that the production of pleasure is good is a normative claim having no more or no less justification in factual evidence than any other normative claim and must be judged like all other normative claims. For example, even if psychological hedonism was a "proven" scientific fact, a moral philosopher could well claim that though we are motivated by pleasure we ought not to be, for the human being has the ability to transcend such inclinations and be motivated by a higher moral calling.[2]

Further problems for prescriptive statements came from David Hume, who argued that descriptive statements cannot provide adequate grounds for validly and cogently reaching prescriptive statements. A prescriptive conclusion cannot be validly drawn from premises that are entirely descriptive.[3] To take a current example, medical science can establish scientific grounds for believing that cigarette smoke harms people who breathe in the smoke, whether they are actually smoking themselves or sitting in a smoke-filled room and inhaling secondhand smoke. But such a "factual" statement does not lead to the conclusion that nonsmoking areas ought to be established in all public places to protect the health of people who do not smoke. This prescriptive statement would have to be established on other grounds.

G. E. Moore, known for his formulation of the naturalistic fallacy, also attacked the attempt by empiricists to define moral goodness in terms of anything sensible. He argued that a normative concept such as the morally good cannot be equated with pleasure or any other sensible or "natural" quality for the two are never identical in meaning. Value predicates are never identical in meaning with factual predicates. No list of what is the case could ever determine what ought to be the case. Therefore no factual term entails a value term and no factual judgment entails a value judgment. There is a complete separation between facts and values, and naturalism, which holds that value judgments are a species of factual judgments, is mistaken.[4] Values are grasped by a non-natural intuition.

While not necessarily his view, the complete separation of fact and value that Moore advocates can lead one to hold a view that ethics is noncognitive in nature, that neither ethics nor moral philosophy has the status of genuine knowledge. In this view, ethics consists solely of opinions that express our likes or dislikes, our preference or predilections, our wishes and aversions. This is the position taken by A. J. Ayer, who holds that if statements of value cannot be reduced to statements of fact, then value claims are meaningless, for any meaningful claim must be reducible to sensible facts. Our guides to action, our praises and condemnations, are merely emotive. Statements of what ought to be are unverifiable because they do not express genuine propositions about the world.[5]

The separation of facts from values has led some people to adopt either a form of noncognitivism with regard to ethics or some form of relativism. The first approach holds that ethical expressions, such as "lying is wrong," do not express factual claims or beliefs. They are neither true nor false and there are no objective facts that can be used to verify their truth or falsehood. Such statements are often held to be either expressions of emotional approval or disapproval or nonfactual speech that can work as if it was cognitive. Ethical relativism holds that there are no universally valid moral principles and that morality is purely conventional. Cultural relativism holds that moral claims are valid if they conform to the particular culture in which one is located, while individual relativism holds that moral claims are validated on the basis of individual choice and therefore one choice is as good as another.[6]

The fact-value distinction in a broad sense leads to the view that facts are not action guiding in the sense of indicating that something ought to be done or valued. They are descriptions or causal explanations of human or natural phenomena. Value judgments, on the other hand, do have an action-guiding function and commend or condemn particular courses of action, but do not have an empirical or objective basis from with to make any claims to validity beyond the individual making the judgment. What makes one person's judgment better than another's cannot be determined on a scientific basis and thus a person committed to the scientific worldview finds the whole of ethics and morals very unsatisfying. These attacks on ethics and morals are responsible for much of the skepticism about the objective truth of moral philosophy that became prevalent in modern society.

This situation leads to extreme positions with respect to values and morality. At one extreme are those who accept the view that moral philosophy is not a body of genuine knowledge, that judgments of value or prescriptive claims about what ought to be done are neither true nor false. They express nothing but our personal preferences, our likes and dislikes, in other words, our subjective feelings about the objects or actions in question. Moral judgments are mere opinion concerning which there is no point discussing and no way of investigating a moral proposition to determine its validity. Descriptive statements are the only kind of statements that can be examined by the scientific method to determine their truth value. Hence ethical statements are relative to the individual or a culture and are based on his or her subjective feelings or the traditions of a particular culture.

At the opposite extreme are those who believe there are objective standards of right and wrong that can be applied to what ought to be done or what ought not to be done in specific circumstances. They feel secure in a dogmatic assertion that the existence of objective moral standards and values is incontrovertible. People who enunciate this view claim an authority to make moral judgments and expect them to be accepted by others on the basis of this claimed authority. Again, there is nothing to discuss or examine as far as prescriptive claims are concerned because adherents to this view claim to be speaking absolute truth that need not be validated by external criteria. These claims about morality lie in the realm of pure reason for the secularist, or are revealed by God in Scripture for those claiming a religious authority. In either case, these standards are handed down from on high, so to speak, and do not arise out of everyday experience.[7]

IMPLICATIONS FOR BUSINESS ETHICS

Business ethics finds itself caught in this fact-value dichotomy. For the most part, scholars who are interested in business ethics seem to have split into two camps talking about two kinds of business ethics, the normative and the empirical. The former is considered to be a prescriptive approach and the latter an explanatory or descriptive approach. Normative business ethics is the domain of philosophers and theologians, while empirical business ethics is considered to be the domain of management consultants and business-school professors. Scholars who represent these different domains are said to be guided by different theories, assumptions, and norms which often result in misunderstanding or lack of appreciation for each other's endeavors.

The normative approach is rooted in philosophy and the liberal arts and focuses its attention on questions of what ought to be and how individuals or business organizations ought to behave in order to be ethical. The empirical approach is rooted in management and the social sciences and is generally concerned with questions of what is, assuming that the organizational world is objective and "out there" awaiting impartial exploration and discovery. Empiricists answer questions of what is by attempting to describe, explain, or predict phenomena in the organizational world by using the agreed-upon methodologies of their social scientific training. They may look at things like what ethical standards are operative in a given organization without making any judgments as to the moral quality of these standards.

The social scientist may devalue the philosopher's moral judgments because these judgments cannot be understood in empirical terms and cannot be verified by scientific methodology or be used to predict or explain individual or organizational behavior. The social scientist's statements about morality, on the other hand, are seen to be of little value to the philosopher because such statements do not address the essential questions of right and wrong. Normative ethical theories involve standards by which the propriety of certain practices in the business world can be evaluated. In contrast, the empirical approach focuses on identifying definable and measurable factors within the individual psyches and social contexts that influence individual and organizational ethical behavior.[8]

Gary Weaver and Linda Trevino have described three conceptions of the relationship between normative and empirical business ethics. The first, what they call the parallel relationship, rejects any efforts to link normative and empirical inquiry for both conceptual and practical reasons. The second conception, called the symbiotic relationship, supports a practical relationship in which the two domains may rely on each other for guidance in setting agendas or in applying the results of their conceptually and methodologically distinct inquiries. Information from each type of business ethics inquiry is potentially relevant to the pursuit and application of the other form of inquiry. The third conception, a full-fledged theoretical integration, countenances a deeper merging of distinct forms of inquiry involving alterations or combinations of theory, assumptions, and methodology, a task the authors believe few people in the field are equipped to even attempt, let alone resolve.[9]

Diane Swanson argues that this dichotomy between the normative and descriptive also exists in the field of business and society, stating that the normative, which consists of what corporations should or should not do, and the descriptive, regarding what corporations do or can do, have not been satisfactorily blended into one theoretical perspective, and until these two dimensions are integrated, a coherent theory of business and society will not be developed. She proposes a strategy of value attunement which she suggests holds the potential for a normative-descriptive unification, which has advantages for theory-building in moving inquiry beyond the problems that are posed by the lack of integration.[10]

B. Victor and C. W. Stephens call for a unification of the two domains, arguing that ignoring the descriptive aspects of moral behavior in a business context is to risk unreal philosophy, and ignoring the normative aspects is to risk amoral social science.[11] Tom Donaldson and Tom Dunfee develop an integrative social-contracts theory that incorporates empirical findings as part of a contractarian process of making normative judgments. These two authors seek to put the "ought" and the "is" in symbiotic harmony that requires the cooperation of both empirical and normative research in rendering ultimate value judgments.[12]

None of these suggestions seem to be a satisfactory solution to the problem because they lack a philosophical basis for accomplishing this unification. There seems to be no position where ethical or normative statements can be validated by experience and have some connection with the way the world is as described by scientific endeavors. One is forced to choose between these positions and this choice will most likely reflect one's personal beliefs and the context in which one is located. In a business school or business organization that adheres to a scientific orientation towards the world, where empirical data are collected and analyzed to solve business problems, the empirical approach to business ethics is more likely to be accepted. Schools of business and management that are dominated by a scientific or quantitative approach often do not find normative analysis very useful in dealing with business problems and are more comfortable with a value-free decision-making process.

In any event, the scientific worldview and its approach to knowledge has undermined a firm foundation for values and ethics and has largely been responsible for creating ethical confusion in our society. Many people cannot recognize a moral issue when they see one, let alone being able to speak intelligently about an issue from a moral point of view. Many tend to see business ethics as an oxymoron, meaning that business is an amoral institution that operates according to its own set of principles rooted in the science of economics. Ethics and morals simply have no application to business decisions, which are made on the basis of what is economically best for the organization. Business operates on a scientific model where the laws of supply and demand regulate business behavior and the ethical obligations of business are exhausted if they adhere to economic or market principles.

MORAL PLURALISM

This problem that science creates for business ethics has resulted in a fragmentation of ethics into different theoretical approaches. There is no comprehensive theory that applies to all aspects of business and human behavior. The usual approach to ethical theory in business is to present either in cursory form or sometimes in greater detail the theory of utilitarianism based on the writings of Jeremy Bentham and John Stuart Mill as representative of a more general class of what was called teleological ethics and Kantian ethical theory related to the categorical imperative as representative of the deontological approach to ethical decision making. Certain notions of justice are also usually considered, such as the egalitarianism of John Rawls and the opposing libertarianism of Robert Nozick. A discussion of rights is also usually included and sometimes a variation of virtue theory.

This approach to ethical theory leaves one with a kind of ethical smorgasbord in which one can choose from various theories that are supposed to shed some light on the ethical problems under consideration and lead to a justifiable decision. But students and practitioners were never told exactly how to decide which theory to apply in a given situation, what guidelines to use in applying these different theories, what criteria to determine which theory is best for a given situation, and what to do if the application of different theories resulted in totally different courses of action. The authors of the leading textbooks in business ethics seemed to recognize this problem, but do not know how to deal with it in a satisfactory fashion. For example, after presenting the theories of consequentialism, deontology, and what they called human-nature ethics—what could be seen as a variation of virtue ethics—Tom Donaldson and Patricia Werhane state:

> Indeed, these three methods of moral reasoning are sufficiently broad that each is applicable to the full range of problems confronting human moral experience. The question of which method, if any, is superior to the others must be *left for another time*. The intention of this essay is not to substitute for a thorough study of traditional ethical theories—something for which there is no substitute—but to introduce the reader to basic modes of ethical reasoning that will help analyze the ethical problems in business that arise in the remainder of the book.[13]

Manuel Velasquez states the problem in the following manner:

> Our morality, therefore, contains three main kinds of moral considerations, each of which emphasizes certain morally important aspects of our behavior, but no one of which captures all the factors that must be taken into account in making moral judgments. Utilitarian standards consider only the aggregate social welfare but ignore the individual and how that welfare is distributed. Moral rights consider the individual but discount both aggregate well-being and distributive considerations. Standards of justice consider distributive issues but they ignore aggregate social welfare and the individual as such. These three kinds of moral considerations do not seem to be reducible to each other yet all three seem to be necessary parts of our

morality. That is, there are some moral problems for which utilitarian considerations are decisive, while for other problems the decisive considerations are either the rights of individual or the justice of the distributions involved . . . We have at this time no comprehensive moral theory capable of determining precisely when utilitarian considerations become "sufficiently large" to outweigh narrow infringements on a conflicting right or standard of justice, or when considerations of justice become "important enough" to outweigh infringements on conflicting rights. Moral philosophers have been unable to agree on any absolute rules for making such judgments. There are, however, a number of rough criteria that can guide us in these matters . . . But these criteria remain rough and intuitive. *They lie at the edges of the light that ethics can shed on moral reasoning.* [14]

These statements seem to be making a virtue of a necessity and beg the questions posed earlier. In none of these theories can there be guidance in deciding when to use a particular theory, for each theory is self-enclosed or absolute. No principle or rule can provide any guidance for the moral reasoning that underlies the choice among the various principles or rules. What, then, determines the decision as to which theory is appropriate in a given situation? The basis for this choice, which now becomes the heart of moral reasoning, the very foundation for moral decision making, remains mysterious and outside the realm of philosophical illumination.

The litany of conflicting theories and principles, each of which was initially meant as a universal approach to ethical problems, gives conflicting signals to people in positions of responsibility in business or other organizations. Shifting between utilitarianism and the categorical imperative or between theories of justice and rights involves at best an unreflective or shallow commitment to ethics and a moral point of view. These theories cannot be applied or ignored at will as the situation may seem to dictate because each of them involves commitment to the philosophical framework on which it is based, and these frameworks are often in conflict. The philosophical framework on which Kant's deontological ethics is based is radically different from the philosophical framework on which utilitarianism is based. To be a Kantian at one time and a Benthamite at another is to shift philosophical frameworks at will. This shifting has been called, quite aptly, "metaphysical musical chairs." [15]

What we are really dealing with in all these instances is moral pluralism, which is the view that no single moral principle or overarching theory of what is right can be appropriately applied in all ethically problematic situations. There is no one unifying principle from which lesser principles can be derived. Different moral theories are possible depending upon which values or principles are included. According to moral pluralism, none of these theories provide guidance in deciding when to use a particular theory, for each theory is self-enclosed or absolute; no principle or rule can provide any guidance for the moral reasoning that underlies the choice among the various principles or rules of different theories.

A reductionistic way of dealing with this problem is presented by Collins and O'Rourke, who wrote a casebook dealing with ethical issues in business.[16] The cases in the book are to be analyzed by asking the following six questions of each policy option: (1) Who are all the people affected by the action (stakeholder analysis)? (2) Is the action beneficial to me (egoism)? (3) Is the action supported by the social group (social-group relativism)? (4) Is the action supported by national laws (cultural relativism)? (5) Is the action for the greatest good of the greatest number of people affected by it (utilitarianism)? And (6) Are the motives behind the action based on truthfulness and respect/integrity toward each stakeholder (deontology)?

After this analysis, the decision-making model used to choose the best policy option from an ethical point of view consists of the following: (1) If the answers to questions 2–6 are all yes, do it; (2) If the answers to questions 2–6 are all no, do not do it; (3) If the answers to questions 2–6 are mixed, amend your decision; (4) If answers to questions 5 and 6 are yes, this is the most ethical decision but you may need to amend your decision in consideration of any no answers to questions 2–4; (5) If answers to questions 5 and 6 are no, this is the least ethical action but you may need to amend the decision in consideration of any yes answers to questions 2–4; (6) If the answers to questions 5 and 6 are mixed, this is moderately ethical and the decisions should take into account any no answer to questions 2–4.

The shortcomings of this approach to ethical decision making should be obvious. It reduces ethics to a mechanical process. Yet there are many proposals of this sort that reduce ethical decision making to outlining certain steps that are to be followed in a mechanical fashion. Some proposals even go so far as to flowchart ethical decision making like a computer diagram. These approaches are all part of the reductionistic process that treats ethics as something objective that can be considered apart from the decision maker and has an independent reality of its own rather than considering ethics a way of life that involves the whole person. Reductionistic approaches see ethics as a series of steps to be followed or principles to be applied in a mechanistic fashion rather than as a life to be lived with a commitment to an ethical point of view.

What we are left with in business ethics is thus a litany of theories no one of which provides a comprehensive ethic that can shape the behavior of people in our society. Business ethics is largely "sold" on the basis of its contribution to the "bottom line," that good ethics is good business, that being ethical will somehow lead to greater profits for the organization either in the positive sense of creating a more functional organization that can successfully compete in the marketplace or in the negative sense of avoiding lawsuits that stem from unethical behavior. Ethics is subservient to economics and it is economic considerations that are paramount in management decision making. The behavior of people is largely shaped by economic considerations and business ethics has to shape itself to be consistent with this dominant value system.

INDIVIDUALISM

Traditional ethical theory is shot through with individualism, as the long-standing nonrelational view of the self, the self as an isolatable building block of community, dominates the ethical tradition. The conflict between the individual and community is manifested in the different approaches of Bentham and Kant to ethical decision making. The utilitarianism of Bentham assumes that the whole is no more than the sum of the parts; one adds up the cost and benefits of particular courses of action in whatever units are appropriate to arrive at a decision that will create the greatest amount of social welfare however this is defined. Kant stresses the autonomy of the individual as against aggregate social welfare and holds that certain principles are to be adhered to with no exceptions regardless of the consequences. Rights are often used to protect the individual from being oppressed because of utilitarian considerations. Contemporary views of justice as diverse as that of Rawls and Nozick both presuppose an individual self that can be considered theoretically in isolation from, and prior to, a community.[17]

For example, the principles of justice that Rawls advocates are based on a social contract agreed to by members of society in a so-called original position. This original position is something of an intellectual exercise to show how principles of justice can be derived in an impartial and unbiased manner. In this exercise, principles of justice are worked out behind a so-called veil of ignorance where the members of a society do not know their race, social standing, economic resources, gender, or anything else of a concrete nature about themselves. Without this kind of knowledge they are then supposedly free from particular kinds of interests that they would be prone to protect if they had this kind of knowledge. Since they do not know what their station of role in society will be, it is assumed that they can come to a more just agreement regarding the rules they want to live by when they step out from behind this veil of ignorance and take their place in society. This agreement is thus worked out by atomic individuals prior to their membership in any kind of society. Rawls's position is rooted in the self-interest-driven principles of abstract justice formed by atomic presocial individuals operating behind a veil of ignorance. This position emphasizes the primacy of the individual and assumes that individual units are prior to and can exist independently of any kind of social or community relationships.

People may form social contracts in order to function together, but these contracts are generally formed on the basis of individualism, because such contracts are agreed to by individuals prior to or apart from their existence in society. While peripheral ties may be established when antecedent individuals enter into contracts with one another through government or other means of collective activity in order to more readily secure their individualistic goals, these bonds cannot root them in any ongoing endeavor which is more than the sum of their separate selves, separate wills, and separate egoistic desires. True community is not possible when one starts from a position of what can be called atomic individualism, where the individual is considered to be an atom much like an atomistic particle in physics.

Ethics is undermined, then, by science in a variety of ways, including the fact-value problem, moral pluralism, and atomic individualism. We tend to think of ethics as something out there, some independent body of principles to which we must adhere in order to be ethical. Scientific method cannot be used to verify which principles are the right ones, since ethics and values are matters of opinion. There is no way to establish, apart from an appeal to some secular or religious authority, the ethical way to act in a given situation, so one is free to pick and choose which ethical theory to apply or which steps to follow. Ethical confusion abounds, which results in something of an amoral society where science dominates and we look to scientific principles to tell us the right thing to do when confronted with a decision that has ethical dimensions. A scientific worldview holds that education can and should be value-free and scientists can and should conduct value-free research that is completely objective in nature. Thus values and ethics are highly problematic in a scientific and technological world. John Dewey states the problem in the following manner:

> It is more or less commonplace to speak of the crisis which has been caused by the progress of the natural sciences in the last few centuries. The crisis is due, it is asserted, to the incompatibility between the conclusions of natural science about the world in which we live and the realm of higher values, of ideal and spiritual qualities, which get no support from natural science. The new science, it is said, has stripped the world of the qualities which made it beautiful and congenial to men; has deprived nature of all aspiration toward ends, all preference for accomplishing the good, and presented nature to us as a scene of indifferent particles acting according to mathematical and mechanical laws . . . philosophers have been troubled by the gap in kind which exists between the fundamental principles of the natural world and the reality of the values according to which mankind is to regulate its life.[18]

When the subject matter of science became exclusively physical and mechanistic and science took over the domain of the natural world, according to John Dewey, the dualistic opposition of matter and spirit arose, the split of nature from ultimate ends and goods and values worth pursuing. Concerns about qualities and purposes of life were excluded from nature by science and had to become rooted in the realm of the spiritual, which was considered to be above nature but yet was its source and foundation. The tension created by these oppositions gave rise to all the characteristic problems of modern philosophy. There was a necessary connection between nature and spirit, yet philosophy could be neither frankly naturalistic and give up the spiritual realm nor fully spiritual and disregard the conclusions of modern science. Since human beings were on the one hand a part of nature and on the other hand a member of the realm of the spirit, all problems of philosophy came to focus on this double nature. This dual nature is nowhere more evident than in the science of economics.[19]

3 Economics

Economics is generally considered to be the queen of the social sciences as it supposedly deals with its subject matter in a more rigorous and analytical method than some of the other social sciences. Economics as a social science is concerned with the production, distribution, and consumption of goods and services produced in society. The term *economic* comes from the Greek *oikos* and *nomos*, which mean, respectively, house and manage, thus referring to way in which a household is managed regarding the provision of food and shelter and other necessities necessary to run a successful household. For much of human history, household management was the important economic task as there were no such things as factories and business organizations to produce goods and services.

The rise of modern science resulted in many technological innovations that made the industrial revolution possible. The development of the factory system and the emergence of markets for the goods these factories produced brought about a revolution in the manner in which people provided for themselves. They worked in factories rather than in the fields and purchased goods in stores with money they earned rather than bartering with merchants. New classes were formed that reflected these changes. There were factory owners and entrepreneurs who benefited greatly from the new economic order that was developing, and wage workers who were subject to the demands of the new capitalistic system. Things were changing drastically and there was a need to understand what was happening in something of a scientific manner.

The so-called classical school of economics arose from this need to understand and describe these developing relations. The Scottish philosopher Adam Smith was the most prominent of these early economists, and in his book *The Wealth of Nations* defined wealth as the goods and services produced by a society which was a much different conception of wealth than was true in a mercantilist view of economic relations. Smith was interested in describing how this wealth was created in a factory system based on the specialization of labor and the role played by capital and markets. He identified self-interest as the driving force of this capitalistic system and through the metaphor of the *invisible hand* showed how this self-interest is directed by a self-regulating market system to the good of society as a whole.

> As every individual, therefore, endeavours as much as he can both to employ his capital in the support of domestic industry, and so to direct that industry that its produce may be of the greatest value; every individual necessarily labours to render the annual revenue of the society as great as he can. He generally, indeed, neither intends to promote the public interest, nor knows how much he is promoting it. By preferring the support of domestic to that of foreign industry, he intends only his own security; and by directing that industry in such a manner as its produce may be of the greatest value, he intends only his own gain, and he is in this, as in many other cases, led by an invisible hand to promote an end which was no part of his intention. Nor is it always the worse for the society that it was no part of it. By pursuing his own interest he frequently promotes that of the society more effectually than when he really intends to promote it.[1]

Thus it was Adam Smith who, whether it was intended or not, made this feature of capitalistic societies into a virtue with the claim that the pursuit of economic self-interest led to the public good by increasing the wealth of nations through the production of more and more goods and services. Smith, however, did not advocate the pursuit of self-interest in a moral vacuum. In *The Theory of Moral Sentiments*, he stressed the role of sympathy and benevolence in creating a cohesive society. It seems clear that Smith assumed that the free pursuit by individuals of their own self-interest would serve the public good only if it occurred in a society that was morally disciplined in this regard. In this moral context, social cooperation and cohesiveness would be further advanced by the pursuit of self-interest. Given the division of labor and the enhancement of productivity this division brought about it, would be in everyone's self-interest to engage in mutually advantageous cooperative economic transactions. Thus self-interest was viewed in the context of certain background moral conditions that would direct it in the interests of the whole.[2]

This image of the "invisible hand" is a metaphor for the socially positive unintended consequences of the market, through which the economic self-interest of individuals is channeled into collective benefits for the society as a whole. Over time, this view of the market as a mechanism for directing self-interest for the social good took precedence over his view of moral sentiments as necessary background conditions for this to take place.[3] When taken out of context, the market itself offered individuals the rationale that their own self-interest expressed in a system of free and open competition would be sufficient to further the economic interests of society as a whole. The invisible hand of the free market could on its own ensure an outcome which exploited the benefits of market exchange to the mutual advantage of all the participants in the market.

This proved to be a morally attractive outcome that was brought about by individual freedom without the need for government intervention and the explicit need for moral considerations. Self-interest and competition were shown to be positively beneficial, and a system of natural liberty for individuals to pursue their own interests was shown to be compatible with the good of society as a whole. One did not need to worry about the outcome of these self-interested actions nor did anyone need to concern themselves with the moral implications of these actions. This was indeed a system that captured the imagination of people and warranted their allegiance. While *The Theory of Moral Sentiments* emphasized the role of sympathy, imagination, desire for approval and benevolence in forming socializing attitudes and creating a cohesive society, *The Wealth of Nations* stressed the importance of self-interest as the driving force behind the development of cooperation and mutual dependence in society.[4]

What lies behind this view of the economy is the idea that the economy is a machine, a view which comes directly from the classical scientific worldview as described in a previous chapter. The unregulated market will lead to an efficient allocation of resources that will benefit society as a whole and any interference with this mechanism will only lessen the creation of economic wealth. As Smith himself put it, "The extension of trade and manufactures, are noble and magnificent objects . . . We take pleasure in beholding the perfection of so beautiful and grand a system, and we are uneasy till we remove any obstructions that can in the least disturb or encumber the regularity of it motions."[5] These obstructions in modern parlance include government regulation, business taxes, restrictions on international trade, and similar measures all of which create a drag on the creation of economic wealth.

Thus we have the view of a system driven by self-interest that allocates resources to their most efficient uses. Competition assures that any one producer will not be able to create a monopoly that can control market outcomes to favor that producer. Manufacturers are driven by the profit motive to produce things people want in an efficient manner to beat the competition. Resources will be distributed according people's preferences as expressed through the market mechanism, as it is often called. Perfectly functioning free markets will lead to an efficient outcome for society. There is no need for ethical considerations to enter into market deliberations as they are not applicable to a system that functions as a machine with laws that govern its behavior analogous to the laws that govern the physical world. People participating in this system need have no moral or social intentions such as social responsibility that would only gum up the works and lead to a less satisfactory outcome for society. According to Richard Bronk, writing in *Progress and the Invisible Hand*:

From the time Adam Smith published *The Wealth of Nations*, which examined the origins of wealth creation, the liberal free market he espoused has been seen to deliver an indefinite augmentation of wealth and living standards. Such economic growth has succeeded in making belief in perpetual progress in welfare, if not happiness, the dominant faith of modern man. Moreover, the modern liberal economy has seemed not only to promise the morally attractive outcome of maximizing the welfare of society as a whole, but to do so without even requiring individuals to have consciously moral or social intentions. For the 'invisible hand' of the market is seen to lead to the most efficient satisfaction of the wants of different market participants, and in this sense to maximize the social good, merely by harnessing the selfish desires of individuals to further their own ends.[6]

Economics as an academic discipline reflects this view of the economy as a machine. It deals with the laws of supply and demand, the law of diminishing returns, and the like, describing these as inexorable laws that govern the workings of the economy. Modern economics has gone more and more quantitative in recent decades, using calculus and other mathematical methods to describe how these laws function in allocating resources to their most efficient uses. Thus economics reflects all the characteristics of classical science, including reductionism, atomism, discreteness, a quantitative orientation, and determinism. It has no need for ethical considerations, according to Julie A. Nelson, as are these are only subjective impressions of the mind that have no bearing on the mechanical working of the economy.

> The separation of economics from ethics now seems entirely natural to many people. To my mainstream economist colleagues, economics is a positive science that seeks to understand the mechanisms underlying economic systems. Ethics, to them, seems like a soft, subjective topic, necessarily encompassing value judgments and ambiguity. Ethics is not, in their perception, a "hard" field, like their own, which starts with objective, "value-free" premises and then logically derives clear, precise, and defensible results. Most economists believe that economic science can proceed just fine without attention to ethics.[7]

Economics reduces nature, in this case human nature, to the self-interested individual who maximizes his or her return on their investments or maximizes his or her satisfaction in consumer purchases. This so-called rational economic man or woman is soulless and uncaring about other human beings in an endless quest for profit or for an ever-increasing variety and quantity of goods and services available on the market. Economics treats these humans as atomistic with no sense of belonging to a larger community where the whole is more than the sum of the parts. It deals with discrete products that can be bought and sold on the market. Economics has become highly quantitative, with mathematics being the language employed to express the laws that govern economic behavior. And finally, it is deterministic in being able to predict human behavior and manipulate it to accomplish the goals of the organization or society.

Economics thus assumes that society is nothing but the aggregation of atomistic individuals so that there are no social objectives to individual decisions.[8] The economy and economic activity are envisioned as separate realms of human activity that can be studied outside of their social and political contexts and have an existence separate from the rest of people's lives. Thus one of the important accomplishments of economics has been to distinguish the economy as a separate realm of human activity and then see it as managed by an automatic mechanism that is both self-adjusting and socially rational, even though no rational thought is involved in its operation. Conscious direction of the economy is not only unnecessary but inappropriate and destructive. Through the competition among self-interested parties, the narrow self-seeking that motivates these individuals is canceled out and an outcome intended by none of these participants emerges. This outcome is supposedly rational in the sense of minimizing costs and using scarce resources efficiently in satisfying the aggregate preferences of the population.

MARKET SYSTEMS

When market societies came into existence, they replaced the traditional social systems that had been in place and served to prescribe roles and functions for people in society. Economic activity had always been subordinated to the social system and was merely a part of a larger social reality that gave people a sense of identity and belonging. But market systems and the market principle took over and became social systems in and of themselves and other aspects of social life became subordinated to market duties and roles. The market itself became the primary manner in which society organized itself and the roles of producer and consumer, along with other economic roles, became the most important roles in society.[9] These roles became objectified within this economic worldview and moral considerations were undermined. The market system has no moral grounding and operates according to its own scientific laws quite apart from moral and ethical considerations. The economy has become an end in itself and takes on a life of its own isolated from its social and moral context subject only to the "laws" of the market. As stated by Bob Goudzwaard, writing in *Capitalism and Progress: A Diagnosis of Western Society:*

> Objectification of people can occur with reference to employees (who are accordingly plugged into the production process as mere suppliers

of almost infinitely divisible units of labor), as well as reference to consumers. Consumers are made into objects when they are manipulated by marketing techniques as just so many bundles of psychic impressions and motivations. The mark of objectification is that people are no longer treated as bearers of responsibilities. A business enterprise, for example, treats a consumer as an object when it no longer appeals to his sense of responsibility, but instead attempts to overrule or manipulate his choice. Employees, similarly, can be reduced to objects by the minimization or destruction of the possibility of making responsible choices of their own. Morality is always a matter of the recognition of other people's responsibilities.[10]

The market is the principle means by which modern Western societies organize themselves to provide goods and services people need to live and enhance their material welfare. The market system is an economic arrangement where economic wealth is created based upon private ownership of the means of production. Every society has to make decisions about what to produce as far as goods and services are concerned, in what quantities they are produced, and how they are disturbed in the society. In a market-oriented society these decisions are made by individuals acting in their self-interest, and the market aggregates these individual decisions into a collective demand schedule that is responded to by productive organizations. The productive mechanism, then, has to meet the preferences of individual consumers who express their values by the decisions they make about the purchase of products and services that are available in the marketplace.

In a socialistic society such as the former Soviet Union these decisions were made by a planning agency based on some scientific or quasi-scientific assessment of the needs of people weighed against other needs of society for military goods and services, for example. The demand schedule that faced productive organizations was put together through a bureaucratic process rather than a free market, and they were given quotas to meet as far as production of goods and services was concerned. While consumers still had a choice to make relative to the goods and services that were available, these choices did not affect the kinds of goods and services that were available nor the quantities that were produced. The distribution principle was to expect every person in society to produce according to their ability and to receive goods and services according to their needs, and prices were set by the bureaucracy that was supposedly consistent with this principle.

While having great ideological appeal, these systems did not work out well in practice, and recent decades have seen the abandonment of socialistic systems throughout much of the world and the adoption of some kind of market system. The socialistic system in many countries degenerated into a state-run economy where the bureaucracy that made economic and political decisions made sure their needs were adequately taken care of while the rest of the population suffered in relative poverty.

The self-interest principle apparently was alive and well in these countries but played itself out in ways that were not very productive for the society as a whole.

In a free-market society, at least in theory, self-interest is harnessed to serve the greater good, as the energies people expend in the pursuit of their own interests are coordinated by the market mechanism to create economic wealth for the society as a whole. The fact that socialistic systems have been largely abandoned gives ample testimony to the superiority of market systems in producing a greater economic product for the citizens of a society to enjoy than socialistic systems. It seem rather clear that socialistic systems were held together more by force than by consent of the people, and once that force was removed or at least was less of a threat, a change to some kind of market system seemed inevitable.

At the heart of a market system is an exchange process where goods and services are traded between the parties to a particular transaction. In a strictly barter type of situation where money is not involved, goods and services are exchanged directly for other goods and services. Where money is used, it serves as an intermediate store of value in that goods and services are exchanged for money and then the same money can be used to purchase other goods and services immediately or at some time in the future. Money has little or no value in and of itself, but is valued for what it represents as purchasing power. It is money that enables us to get other people to do things for us we either cannot or do not want to do for ourselves. The use of money greatly facilitates exchange over a barter type of economy and greatly increases the number of exchange transactions that are possible.

In the market system, all kind of exchanges between people and institutions are continually taking place. Decisions as to whether or not to exchange one thing for another are made by individuals and institutions acting in their own self-interest as defined by them and based on the particular value they attach to the entities being traded. That is, people decide whether the item they are considering purchasing is of sufficient value to them to warrant the sacrifice of something they already have that is of value. Exchanges will not normally take place unless there is an increase of value to both parties to the exchange. Thus the exchange process usually results in a positive-sum game as both parties believe themselves to be better off because of the exchange.

Based on these individual decisions in the market, then, resources are allocated according to the preferences of individuals for one kind of merchandise over another, one job over another, the stock of one corporation over others, and so forth, across the entire range of choices the market offers. The values that eventually come to be associated with particular goods and services and the decisions that are made with respect to the allocation of resources for the production and distribution of these goods and services are based on this exchange process. Thus the values that guide the process are exchange or market values rather than values based on use of the particular entity or the labor involved in its production.

The nature of the goods and services that are traded in the market makes such exchange possible. These goods and services are private in the sense that they can be purchased and used by individual persons or institutions. They become the private property of the persons who attain them and are of such a nature that they do not have to be shared with anyone else. The goods and services exchanged in the market are thus *discrete* and divisible into individual units that can be totally consumed and enjoyed by the people or institutions who obtain the property rights to these goods and services. Property rights can be assigned to these goods and services because of their *discreteness* and divisibility into individual units that can be privately owned and consumed.

The value of all these *discrete* entities that are exchanged in the market system are able to be *quantified* in common units that stem from an underlying economic value system. The worth of an individual's labor, the worth of a particular product or service, the worth of a share of stock can all be expressed in economic terms. This is not to suggest that the fundamental value of everything is economic in nature. One might value a particular piece of residential property because of the view it commands of the surrounding countryside, thus making the aesthetic value of the property of primary concern. But in order for exchange to take place where money is involved, these other values have to be *reduced* to economic values and *quantified* accordingly.

This economic value system thus serves as a common denominator in that the worth of everything can be expressed in a common unit of exchange such as dollars and cents in our society. The terms on which a good or service can be acquired in the marketplace reflect the collectivization of numerous people's evaluations of the worth of that good or service to themselves. This commonality facilitates the exchange process and makes it possible for individuals to make decisions much easier than if such a common denominator were not available. People who travel to foreign countries know the difficulty involved in translating a foreign currency into dollars in order to get a sense of the worth of the good or service under consideration.

This common value system allows a society to allocate its resources according to the collective preferences of its members. All the diverse values that people hold in relation to private goods and services are aggregated through the market system into a collective demand schedule that faces productive institutions. If a particular product is not valued very highly by people, aggregate demand for that product will not be very high and its price will have to be low in order for it to be sold, if it can be sold at all. Thus not many resources will be used for its production and it may eventually disappear from the market altogether. Resources will go where the price, wage or salary, or return on investment is the highest, all other things being equal, and are thus allocated to their most productive use where they can be combined to produce the greatest wealth for society in comparison with other alternatives.

People are free in a market economy to use their property, choose their occupation, and strive for economic gain in any way they choose, subject, of course, to limitations that may be necessary to protect the right of all people to do the same thing. The market economy is believed to support a system of natural liberty that gives people the greatest freedom of choice and action. Society, however, may place limitations on the use of property because of moral standards or safety and environmental concerns if these are believed important enough to override market forces. However, these should be kept to a minimum and a strict libertarian approach to the use of property would oppose any type of such restrictions.

The pursuit of self-interest is assumed to be a universal principle of human behavior with a powerful advantage, as far as motivation is concerned, over other forms of human behavior. The pursuit of one's own interests is believed to elicit far more energy and creativity from human beings that would the pursuit of other interests like those of the state, especially under coercive conditions. It is difficult to sustain a high level of motivation if much of the effort one expends goes for the benefit of other people or some institutional entity like the state. This self-interest principle has proven to be true in many instances where the state has tried to collectivize economic activities.

Atomistic thinking consistent with the scientific worldview pervades our understanding of the way in which market systems function. In traditional economic theory, people are seen as atomic units who have individual preferences for certain goods and services. Those who participate in the market do so as individuals disconnected from any larger sense of community. These individuals are encouraged to pursue their own interests, not the interests of others or the interests of the whole community. These individual preferences are aggregated into a collective demand schedule that faces the productive units of society that respond out of a desire to make a profit. Self-interest is assumed to be a powerful motivating force to get people to produce and consume to keep the system going.

Within the market system, the definition of self-interest is not completely arbitrary, depending on the whims of each individual. People are assumed to be rational economic actors and their behavior is *reduced* to economic considerations. If one is engaged in some aspect of the productive process, economic rationality dictates that self-interest consists of maximizing one's economic return on one's investment. Consumers are assumed to maximize satisfaction to themselves through their purchases of goods and services in the marketplace. Sellers of labor are expected to obtain the most advantageous terms for themselves in bargaining with their employer. Investors are expected to maximize their returns in the stock market.

While self-interest may drive the system, it is competition that keeps it under control. Individual producers and consumers are like *atoms* that bump into each other in the marketplace and competition is the mechanism that keeps this process from getting out of hand and becoming self-destructive. No single producer or consumer can come to dominate the marketplace and begin to dictate the terms of trade to everyone else. Competition prevents any individual producer from getting too large and driving everyone else out of business so that they would have the power to set whatever price they wanted subject only to general economic conditions, not to competitive conditions in the markets they are serving.

Competition thus acts as a mechanical regulator in keeping individual producers in check and preventing any one producer from dominating the rest to the detriment of the consumer. Competition assures that producers continually respond to the forces of supply and demand and consumers are thus assured of the lowest prices and the best quality goods that can be made available. If any one competitor begins to dominate a market, someone else is supposed to step in and provide competition to limit the power of the would-be monopolist. This clash of individual atoms on the marketplace regulated by competition is supposed to result in a greater good for society than any other economic arrangement.

Based on this economic rationality, resources are allocated in a market system by an invisible hand. This is something of a mythological concept but one that is a crucial metaphor in thinking about a market system. There is no supreme authority in government that makes decisions for the society as a whole about what goods and services get produced and in what quantities and allocates resources according to some overall plan for the economy. These decisions are made by individuals who participate in the marketplace and express their preferences based on an assessment of their own self-interest. These preferences are aggregated by the market to elicit a response from the productive institutions of society to supply the goods and services desired.

The invisible hand consists of the forces of supply and demand that result from the aggregation of these individual decisions. Resources are allocated to their most productive use as defined by individuals collectively. Society as a whole benefits more from this kind of a resource allocation process than if someone were to consciously try to determine the best interests of society. Pursuit of one's own self-interested ends without outside interference is believed to result in the greatest good for the greatest number of people. The invisible hand assures that everyone's needs are taken care of through an increase in the size of the pie that can be divided among members of society. Thus the market system is given a utilitarian justification as far as ethics in concerned.

What drives the productive institutions of society is the quest for profits, as profits are the lifeblood of a business organization and without them a business organization cannot normally survive. Profits are a reward to the business or entrepreneur for the risks that have been taken in producing a good or service for the market. If the management of a business organization guesses wrong and produces something people do not want and cannot be persuaded to buy, no rewards will be received for this effort and the product eventually will be removed from the market. Resources must also be combined efficiently so as to meet or beat the competition in producing a product or service for which there is a demand. Some companies may be able to pay lower wages or employ a more efficient technology or have some other competitive advantage. Thus a lower price can be charged and high-cost producers are driven from the market. This effort is rewarded with increased profits as society benefits from having its resources used more efficiently.

The ultimate objective of all this economic activity is to continually increase the wealth of the nation through economic growth. There are no biophysical limits to economic growth and it is assumed it can continue forever in a linear fashion. Growth is measured in a *quantitative* fashion by aggregating all the goods and services produced and expressing this percentage figure every quarter indicating whether the economy has grown or is in a recession or depression. It is assumed that this quantification says something important about the society and its well-being, and if growth is negative for any quarter steps are taken to stimulate the economy so it can continue growing. More and more economic growth is taken as resulting in a better society and thus a measure of quantity is assumed to be a surrogate for the quality of life that exists in that society.[11]

MARKETS AND THE ENVIRONMENT

It should be quite evident after this exposition that the market is infused with scientific reductionism, atomism, discretes, and other aspects of the scientific worldview. This process works well in providing for people's needs for goods and services that can be exchanged on the market. But we live in a world where there are environmental considerations that need to be taken into account, and a marketplace that deals only with discrete entities and is based on atomism cannot deal with environmental entities. The environment in which people produce and consume goods and services is continuous and cannot be broken down into discrete items to be exchanged on the marketplace.

Air, for example, is continuous and not discrete, and thus cannot be exchanged on the marketplace. Since there is nothing to be exchanged, the value of the environment or any of its components cannot be determined through a market process. People cannot take a piece of dirty air, for example, and exchange it for a piece of clean air on the market. Air is not divisible and for all practical purposes one cannot buy a certain amount of clean air on the marketplace to enjoy privately. If a society deems clean air important enough to spend some money for its provision, government has to pass laws establishing standards relative to how much of a certain pollutant is legally allowable and then enforce those laws through some enforcement mechanism. Government decides how much clean air to provide for all its citizens and each citizen then enjoys roughly the same amount depending on how close they may live to a freeway or an electric utility or factory that pollutes the air to the extent legally allowed. Citizens pay for this clean air either through increased taxes or through increased prices for products that reflect the additional expenses producers have to pay to comply with pollution standards.

Some might want to argue even if clean air cannot be purchased directly, environmental goods of this nature could still be provided through market-place transactions. Suppose, for example, the market offered a consumer a choice of two automobiles in a dealer's showroom that are identical in all respects, even as to gas mileage. The only difference is that one car has pollution control equipment to reduce emissions of pollutants from the exhaust while the other car has no such equipment. The car with the pollution control equipment sells for $500 more than the other.

If a person values clean air it could be argued that he or she would choose the more expensive car to reduce air pollution. However, such a decision would be totally irrational from a strictly economic point of view. The impact that one car out of all the millions on the road will have on air pollution is infinitesimal; it cannot even be measured. Because air is continuous and the common property of everyone, there is no relationship in this kind of an individual decision between costs and benefits. One would be getting nothing for one's money unless one could assume that many other people would make the same decision. Such actions assume a common value for clean air that is difficult to implement in a market context where value is determined through an exchange process. Thus the market never offers consumers this kind of choice. Automobile manufacturers know that pollution control equipment won't sell in an unregulated market.

Moreover, there is another side to the coin. If enough people in a given area did buy the more expensive car for some reason so that the air was significantly cleaner, there would be a powerful incentive for others to be free riders. Again, the impact of any one car would not alter the character of the air over a given region. One would be tempted to buy the polluting car for a cheaper price and be a free rider by enjoying the same amount of clean air as everyone else and not paying a cent for its provision. There is thus a kind of double whammy effect on the ability of the market mechanism to respond to environmental concerns that renders it ineffective as far as these common goods are concerned.

Some call this inability of market systems to respond to environmental pollution and degradation a market failure, but to use this term is not entirely accurate. Market systems were not designed to respond to continuous entities and factor in environmental costs, and it is not fair to blame the system for not doing something for which it was not designed. Property rights are not appropriately assigned as regards the environment and nature often lacks a discrete owner to look after its interests. The rights of nature can be violated by market exchanges, and as a common property resource, nature can be overused and degraded in a manner that adversely affects human existence.

The natural environment is continuous, for the air we breath and the ozone layer that protects us from the ultraviolet rays of the sun, as well as the climate as a whole, cannot be divided into discrete units that can be owned by someone and then bought and sold on the marketplace. They are common property and are of benefit to humankind as a whole, not just for those who can afford them. While land can be divided into parcels that can then be bought and sold on the market, this is a violation of its continuous nature and is another example of scientific reductionism applied to nature. Native Americans had no sense of property rights and did not believe they owned the land that sustained them. Instead, they believed they belonged to the land. They erected no fences to protect private property but left the land in its continuous state, and thus had no legal claim to the land when European settlers began to take the land for themselves.

Environmental degradation and pollution are external to normal market processes and are not taken into account in the price mechanism unless these costs are determined by some other process and imposed on the market system. The market system by itself cannot determine the value of the environment and quantify the price of clean air or the value of preserving a wilderness area in its natural state. These decisions have to be made through some other process and imposed on the market system in order for these values to be internalized and reflect themselves in market decisions. The ecological functions of the environment have no value as far as the market is concerned. It is only their economic utility or instrumental value that is of importance in a market economy.

Market systems evolved to serve human needs and interests; they are not constructed to protect the environment. The environment is considered to be an objective entity quite differentiated from the self and is treated as a source of raw materials to be used in the production process and as a bottomless sink in which to dispose of waste materials left over from the consumption of goods and services. The environment has no value in and of itself but is only worth something as it can be used to serve some human purpose such as enhancing living standards through the creation of more and more economic wealth. Market systems are limited in their scope and cannot be used to determine the value of the environment in itself or most of its components.

A tree in the Amazon rain forest, for example, has no value as far as its ecological functions are concerned. It has value only when it is cut down for timber products or to clear land for planting crops or used as grazing space for cattle. In some limited cases, the trees may be left standing if they provide fruits and nuts or may eventually have some kind of medicinal value in providing a cure for some disease. But the ecological value of the rain forest in terms of providing the world with a carbon sink and contributing to the diversity of plant and animal life has no economic value. From a strictly economic point of view, the forest has no value in its natural state and must be cut down and made into something useful for humans or left standing as long as it can be economically productive in some other sense.

The same is true of wetlands, which cover vast areas of some parts of the world, both along coastal and inland areas. These wetlands perform valuable ecological functions, yet from an economic point of view they only have value because they contain certain resources such as gas and oil that can be exploited or can be filled in to provide land area for residential or commercial development. Most people probably consider wetland areas as wasteland and fail to appreciate the ecological functions they perform such as providing a habitat for fish and wildlife and acting as water reservoirs to prevent flooding. They also filter out pollutants from the water and act as a buffer to reduce the effect of hurricanes.

In some cases the market may be able to be used for some of these determinations. A good example is the cap-and-trade system that is being advocated for control of carbon dioxide emissions that are believed to be the major culprit in global warming or climate change.[12] If the climate can be stabilized, at least to some extent, this again is a good thing because climate change on the scale forecasted by some scientists will result in major expenses for most societies as they cope with rising sea levels, drought conditions, the collapse of some industries dependent on a stable climate, and other effects that have been predicted. Again, this is not a public good that can be bought and sold on the market in an ordinary manner because climate change is not divisible into private property. But the market can be used for some of the decisions that have to be made about dealing with global warming.

Taking a look at the cap-and-trade system that was implemented several years ago to control sulfur dioxide emissions will help in understanding how the market is used in this regard. Sulfur dioxide was the major culprit in causing acid rain which became a major problem in many parts of the country. Before the 1970 Clean Air Act, sulfur dioxide emissions in the United States were increasing dramatically and were traceable to the burning of fossil fuels in power plants and factories. By 1986 annual sulfur dioxide emissions had declined by 21 percent but even more reductions were needed to solve the problem.[13]

The 1990 Clean Air Act contained provisions for large reductions in emissions of sulfur dioxide. By the year 2000 sulfur dioxide emissions were to be reduced nationwide by 10 million tons below 1980 levels, a 40 percent decrease. These reductions were to be obtained through a program of emission allowances where each utility could "trade and bank" its allowable emissions. Power plants covered by the program were to be issued allowances that were each worth one ton of sulfur dioxide released from smokestacks during a specified year. To obtain reduction in sulfur dioxide pollution, these allowances were to be set below the current level of sulfur dioxide releases. Plants could release only as much sulfur dioxide as they had allowances to cover. If a plant expected to release more sulfur dioxide than it had in allowances, it had to buy allowances from plants that reduced their releases below their number of allowances and therefore had them to sell or trade. These allowances were to be bought and sold nationwide, with stiff penalties for plants that released more pollutants than their allowances covered.[14]

The first trade under the program took place in 1992 when Wisconsin Power & Light agreed to sell pollution credits to the Tennessee Valley Authority and the Duquesne Light Company of Pittsburgh.[15] The Chicago Board of Trade began offering futures contracts on sulfur dioxide credits in 1993 and hoped to become the pollution clearinghouse for the nation, but a vibrant off-exchange pollution-rights market also developed.[16]

In its 2003 progress report, the Environmental Protection Agency reported that in 2003 there were 10.6 million tons of sulfur dioxide emissions, which represented a 38 percent reduction from 1980 levels. The program was thus on target to reach its goal of 8.95 million tons by 2010. The electric power industry had achieved nearly 100 percent compliance with the requirements of the program as only one unit had emissions exceeding the sulfur dioxide allowances that it held. The report also indicated that over the last decade sulfur dioxide and sulfate levels were down more than 40 and 30 percent, respectively, in the eastern part of the country and that there were signs of recovery in acidified lakes and streams in the Adirondacks, the northern Appalachian Plateau, and the upper Midwest. These signs included lower concentrations of sulfates, nitrates, and improvement in acid-neutralizing capacity.[17]

This cap-and-trade program allows sources to select their own compliance strategy rather than having this dictated by the federal government with a command-and-control approach. They can use coal containing less sulfur, wash the coal, or use devices called scrubbers to chemically remove pollutants from the gases leaving smokestacks. They can also use a cleaner burning fuel like natural gas or reassign some of their energy production from dirtier units to cleaner ones. Sources may also reduce their electricity generation by adopting conservation or efficiency measures or switch to alternative energy sources such as wind power or solar energy.

It is important to note, however, what the market does and does not do in these situations. The market does not make the decision to reduce emissions of sulfur dioxide or carbon dioxide. These decisions are made by the government; they are public-policy decisions that are made by a public body accountable to the citizens. The government also decides what level or standard to set regarding the overall amount of these pollutants that are allowable in a certain time frame. Thus the government makes the decisions about what to produce and the quantities involved, i.e., how free the air should be of these pollutants based on the best scientific evidence relative to the objectives of reducing acid rain to minimize the destruction it was causing and slowing climate change to manageable levels. The government creates a market for pollution credits that it issues and the market is only used to promote a more cost-efficient way to reduce these pollutants by allowing greater freedom for companies to develop their own way of meeting the standards.

The problem is one of placing an appropriate value on nature so that it can be reflected in market decisions. An interesting attempt to quantify nature appeared in the effort of an international collection of economists, ecologists, and geographers from twelve prestigious universities and laboratories in three nations to place a dollar value on nature. In an article that appeared in the May 15, 1997, issue of *Nature*, these experts estimated that the economic value of the biosphere's essential "ecosystem services" such as climate regulation, soil formation, food production, flood control, and water supply averages about $33 trillion annually. To put this number in perspective, the value of the output of the total world economy each year is $18 trillion.[18]

The reactions to this effort were interesting. Some conservationists saw some positive value in this effort in that putting a dollar figure on what is likely to be destroyed over the next few years if we do not change our ways is a useful tactic to argue for greater conservation efforts. Some argued that it succeeds in speaking in a language that business might begin to hear regarding the value of what we collectively, and thoughtlessly, are destroying. Others, however, felt differently. When asked to comment on this nature-valuation effort, an ecologist by the name of David Ehrenfeld said that "I am afraid that I don't see much hope for a civilization so stupid that it demands a quantitative estimate of its own umbilical cord."[19]

Such quantification only further objectifies nature and leaves out our experience with nature and our so-called subjective relationship with the world. If nature has to be quantified for us to have a sense of its value, then we have lost any real connection with nature and see it as well as ourselves as nothing more than another object in a quantified universe. Our spiritual and emotional connections to the source and substance of our very being are no less real and no less important for the fact that they cannot be quantified. They are no less a part of what it means to be a human being living in a finite world. As stated in one comment on the subject of valuing the environment, "Put me in a redrock canyon and let me watch a mule dear moving beneath the dappled shadow of a cottonwood grove, and I do not need to be told how much what I see and feel there is worth: it is worth nothing—and everything."[20]

Robert Nadeau, who teaches environmental science and public policy at George Mason University, argues that unscientific assumptions in economic theory are undermining efforts to deal with environmental problems. These assumptions include: (1) the market system is a closed circular flow between production and consumption with no inlets or outlets; (2) natural resources exist in a domain that is separate and distinct from a closed market system, and the economic value of these resources can by determined only by the dynamics that operate within this system; (3) the costs of damage to the external natural environment must be treated as costs that lie outside the closed market system or as costs that cannot be included in the pricing mechanisms that operate within the system; (4) the external resources of nature are largely inexhaustible, and those that are not can be replaced by other resources or by technologies that minimize the use of the exhaustible resources or that rely on other resources; and (5) there are no biophysical limits to the growth of market systems.[21]

He goes on to argue that neoclassical economic theory can no longer be regarded as useful even in pragmatic or utilitarian terms to solve environmental problems because it fails to allow economic activities to be coordinated in an environmentally responsible manner. Neoclassical theory does not acknowledge the costs of environmental problems and the limits to economic growth and constitutes one of the greatest barriers to combating climate change and other threats to the planet. New theories need to be devised, according to Nadeau, that take all the realities of the global system into account.

Natural resources that are continuous in nature exist in a separate domain that is separate and distinct from the market system and their economic value is difficult to determine. Science plays a crucial role in determining the standards that should be adhered to in order to protect and promote human health, standards related to clean air and water, exposure to toxic wastes and ultraviolet radiation, and keeping the earth's temperature in bounds. But science is subject to a great deal of uncertainty, which those opposed to such standards use to their advantage, and the findings of scientific studies can be altered by decision makers to suit their political and ideological interests.[22] Setting reasonable standards that adequately protect humans and the environment and are acceptable as far as their cost is concerned is one of the most difficult problems modern industrial societies face in today's world and neoclassical economics seems to offer no solution.

THE MARKET AND SOCIETY

The emergence of laissez-faire capitalism turned human and social relations around and altered the relationship of humans with nature. Whereas, in earlier times, economic relations were embedded in and secondary to their broader social context, market systems actually embedded social relations into the economic system. The evolution of market-oriented societies occurred through the transformation of humans, capital, and nature, the so-called factors of production, into fictitious economic commodities that could be bought and sold on the market. While such fictionalizing of economic elements of things that are fundamentally social and moral ushered in a period of production of goods and services never before experienced, it also set loose forces that caused social, political, and environmental dislocation of an unparalleled nature.

These dislocations eventually became of concern to society and questions began to be raised about the traditional view of business and its relationship to society. Business was not just embedded in a market-oriented economy, it was argued, but also in society and had responsibilities to that society. The problems that society was experiencing, such as pollution, unsafe workplaces, discrimination, and unsafe products, were in large part created by the drive for efficiency in the marketplace. For example, in seeking to maximize profits and disposing of its waste material as cheaply as possible, business was causing some serious pollution problems regarding air and water. By always hiring the best-qualified person for a job opening is was helping to perpetuate the effects of discrimination against minorities and women.

People in society began to believe that cleaning up pollution, providing safer workplaces, producing products that were safe to use, promoting equal opportunity, and attempting to eliminate poverty in our society had something to do with promoting human welfare and creating a "good" society. Thus a gap developed between the social expectations of society and the social performance of business and the idea of social responsibility began to take hold in society: the idea that business was not only an economic institution but also a social institution with social impacts that needed to be taken into account. Business had a broader constituency to serve than just stockholders, and values other than just economic values needed to be taken into account.

Much effort was devoted to convincing management to take these social responsibilities seriously. Arguments were made that it was in the long-run self-interest of business to help society solve some of its most pressing social problems. Business could not remain a viable organization in a society that was deteriorating. Business could also gain a better public image by being socially responsible and in this way gain more customers and provide more of an incentive for investors to put their money in the company. Other arguments had to do with the avoidance of government regulation; that by being socially responsible and effectively responding to the changing social expectations of society business might be able to eliminate the necessity of onerous government regulations that would affect its profits and other aspects of business performance.

A great deal of research was done to help management redesign corporate organizations and develop policies and practices that would enable corporations to respond to the social expectations of society more effectively and measure their social performance. These efforts were hampered, however, by the lack of a solid social and moral philosophy that embedded business firmly in society and reversed the relations between the economy and the larger society that market systems brought about. Business and society were considered to be two separable and discrete entities reflecting the philosophical position of atomic individualism that is part of the scientific worldview. Institutions such as business were considered to be isolatable entities that have well-defined boundaries that can be considered as separate from their surroundings and are not an integral part of the society in which they function. As stated by Robert C. Solomon:

> The notion of responsibility is very much a part of the . . . individualism that I am attacking as inadequate, and the classical arguments for "the social responsibilities of business" all too often fall in the trap of beginning with the assumption of the corporation as an autonomous, independent entity, which then needs to consider its obligations to the surrounding community. But corporations, like individuals, are part and parcel of the communities that created them, and the responsibilities that they bear are not products of argument or implicit contracts but intrinsic to their very existence as social entities.[23]

Many advocates of social responsibility reflected this atomistic worldview and did not take into account the competitive environment in which corporations function and treated the corporation as an isolated entity that had unlimited ability to engage in unilateral social action. But it was increasingly recognized that corporations are severely limited in their ability to respond to social problems. If a firm unilaterally engages in social action that increases its costs and prices, it will place itself at a competitive disadvantage relative to other firms in the industry that may not be concerned about being socially responsible. Neil W. Chanberlain stated the problem in this manner:

> Every business is . . . in effect, "trapped" in the business system is has helped to create. It is incapable, as an individual unit, of transcending that system . . . the dream of the socially responsible corporation that, replicated over and over again can transform our society is illusory . . . Because their aggregate power is not unified, not truly collective, not organized, they [corporations] have no way, even if they wished, of redirecting that power to meet the most pressing needs of society . . . Such redirecting could only occur through the intermediate agency of government rewriting the rules under which all corporations operate.[24]

The debate about social responsibility never took this institutional context of corporations seriously. Concerted action to solve social problems is not feasible in a competitive system unless all competitors pursue roughly the same policy on the same problems. However, the proponents of social responsibility produced no clear and generally accepted moral theory that would impose upon business an obligation to work for social betterment. Ascribing social responsibility to corporations does not necessarily imply that they are moral agents that are then responsible for their social impacts. The various arguments that were used to try to impose this obligation, such as enlightened self-interest, responsible use of power, and the like, tried to link moral behavior to business performance. Little was accomplished, however, by way of developing acceptable support for the notion of social responsibility that was rooted in something other than the traditional scientific worldview.

The bottom line for business remained intact. Business had no moral responsibility other than to make as much money as it could for individual shareholders because they were the property owners. Business had no responsibility to help a collective entity such as society solve its social problems. Such a responsibility is not built into the system; it is not measurable; it is not something that business is required to report on to its shareholders. It became an illusion to think that the notion of social responsibility could make a significant difference in getting business to clean up its pollution, to hire minorities and women and treat them equally, and to have consumer protection in mind rather than profits.[25]

Another effort to describe and analyze the corporation's relationship to society and deal with the dislocations caused by market systems is stakeholder theory. While there are many definitions of stakeholder theory, each version stands for the same principle, namely that corporations should heed the needs, interests, and influence of those affected by their policies and operations. A typical definition is that of Carroll, who holds that a stakeholder may be thought of as "any individual or group who can affect or is affected by the actions, decisions, policies, practices, or goals of the organization."[26] A stakeholder, then, is an individual or group that has some kind of stake in what business does and may also affect the organization in some fashion.

The typical stakeholders are considered to be consumers, suppliers, government, competitors, communities, employees, and of course stockholders. However, the stakeholder map of any given corporation with respect to a given issue can become quite complicated. Stakeholder management involves taking the interests and concerns of these various groups and individuals into account in arriving at a management decision, and in this way, the responsibilities of business will be broadened to include other constituencies besides those of stockholders alone.

The theory assumes that stakeholders are isolatable, individual entities that are clearly identifiable by management and that their interests can be taken into account in the decision-making process. Complications arise when the same person may be a member of several stakeholder groups. An employee, for example, may also be a consumer of the company's products and thus have different interests as a member of two different stakeholder groups. While such complications are acknowledged, they are not given due credence in applying the theory. Each stakeholder is assumed to have identifiable interests that must be taken into account by a manager in arriving at a responsible decision.

Wicks, Gilbert, and Freeman, the latter having done the seminal work on the stakeholder concept, recognize the problem of atomism in stakeholder theory. The authors write about the celebration of the individual and the respect for personal freedom which characterizes the post-Enlightenment West, particularly the United States with its image of the self-sufficient pioneer. They then go on to describe the problem of atomic individualism and show how it is embedded in definitions of stakeholder theory.

> One of the assumptions in this worldview is that the "self" is fundamentally isolatable from other selves and from its larger context. Persons exist as discrete beings who are captured independent of the relationships they have with others. While language, community, and relationships all affect the self, they are seen as external to and bounded off from the individual who is both autonomous from and ontologically prior to these elements of context. The parallel in business is that the corporation is best seen as an autonomous agent, separate from its suppliers, consumers, external environment, etc. Here too, while the larger market forces and business environment have a large impact on a given firm, it is nonetheless the individual corporation which has prominence in discussions about strategy and preeminence in where we locate agency.
>
> In terms of how we understand stakeholders, they are people who affect or are affected by the corporation, but they are not integral to its basic identity. This is reflected in the understanding of stakeholders offered by a number of authors . . . These definitions all share the implicit premise that the basic identity of the firm is defined independent of, and separate from, its stakeholders. The macro level view of the world of business is seen as a collection of atoms, each of which is colliding with other atoms in a mechanistic process representative of the interactions and transactions of various firms.[27]

Thus several scholars recognize the assumption of atomic individualism which is embedded in definitions of stakeholder theory and this assumption reflects the scientific worldview. This assumption is seen as a problem that needs to be addressed for the field to move forward. Stakeholder theory has been widely employed to describe the business-society relationship and broaden the responsibilities of business, but efforts to further develop this concept and apply it to business and society continue to be plagued by this problem.

Finally, the social responsibilities of business have also been expressed in terms of a changing contract between business and society.[28] The old contract between business and society was based on the view that economic growth was the source of all progress, social as well as economic. The engine providing this economic growth was considered to be the drive for profits by competitive private enterprise. The basic mission of business was thus to produce goods and services at a profit and in doing this business was making its maximum contribution to society and being socially responsible.[29]

The new contract is based on the view that the single-minded pursuit of economic growth produced detrimental side effects or dislocations that imposed social costs on society, and did not necessarily lead to social progress, but instead led to a deteriorating physical environment, unsafe workplaces, discrimination against certain groups in society, and other social problems. This new contract between business and society involved the reduction of these social costs of business through impressing upon business the idea that it has an obligation to work for social and well as economic betterment. This idea was expressed by the Committee for Economic Development as follows:

> Today it is clear that the terms of the contract between society and business are, in fact, changing in substantial and important ways. Business is being asked to assume broader responsibilities to society than ever before and to serve a wider range of human values. Business enterprises, in effect, are being asked to contribute more to the quality of American life than just supplying quantities of goods and services.[30]

The changing terms of the contract are to be found in the laws and regulations that society has established as the legal framework within which a business must operate and through shared understandings that prevail as to each group's expectations of the other. The social contract is a set of understandings that characterize the relationship between business and society, and the changes in this contract that have taken place over the past several decades are the direct outgrowth of the increased importance of the social environment of business. The "rules of the game" have been changed through laws and regulations that have been passed relating to social issues such as pollution and discrimination.

Subsequent formulations of the social-contract notion emphasized a broad range of responsibilities related to consumers and employees and the responsibilities of multinational corporations to home and host countries.[31] But all of these efforts are plagued by the same problems that underlie social responsibility and stakeholder theory. Social-contract theory assumes that there are two distinct and discrete parties to the contract, namely business and society, which are separable entities with conflicting interests. These conflicts have to be worked out in some fashion through a negotiation process so a mutual agreement can be reached that is satisfactory to both parties. This process does not recognize the embeddedness of business in society nor does it overcome the atomistic view of science.

These efforts to develop new models of the business-society relationship have attempted to broaden our understanding of market systems and relate market systems to the social system from which they became separated. They contain within them a relational view of the corporation and society that goes beyond the economic roles of business as prescribed by market approaches. They have attempted to make the case that corporations have a broader constituency to serve than just stockholders and that they serve a wider range of values than just the economic values that are part of a market outlook. These efforts attempted to establish the notion that corporations have a moral responsibility to society that goes beyond the production of goods and services at a profit.

Nonetheless, these efforts are victimized by the same scientific worldview that afflicts traditional economic approaches. The assumption that the corporation is an autonomous agent within society and that a society is no more than the sum of the parts of which it is comprised undermines these efforts. This whole way of thinking about the business-society relationship is permeated by the problems of atomism and reductionistic thinking that is part and parcel of the scientific worldview. There is no way to get at a true community that has an existence and purposes apart from the individuals that are members of that community.

If society is seen as nothing more than the sum of its parts, society bounces back and forth between an emphasis on individual rights and community needs, between a celebration of pluralism and the need for common goals and interests. Once an institution is taken as an isolatable unit, then the institution and society become pitted against each other in an ultimately irreconcilable tension. Nothing binds institutions and society together except self-interest, which makes it difficult to arrive at mutually satisfactory solutions to social problems. If one starts with atomic bits of this sort, there is no way to get a true sense of community or society and develop a relationship that is anything more than mechanistic in nature. The relationship between business and society is largely emptied of any meaningful moral content because of the scientific worldview.

4 Politics

Some sense of community is important for a society in order for people to agree on common courses of action to deal with problems that can't be handled on an individual basis through the market. People have to agree on things that are good for all members of the community or the community as a whole, things like clean air and water, for example, or national defense. When individuals bump into each other, or in other words when the interests of individuals clash such that not everyone can do as they please, compromises have to be reached that are going to affect these individual interests. There has to be some sense of the common good and a willingness to sacrifice individual interests for the good of the whole community for common problems to be addressed.

Political systems exist to help people reach these compromises and adjudicate differences in the interests of preserving order and preventing people from going to war with each other to preserve their interests. Some people may have to sacrifice their individual desires for this to happen; thus any institution that represents the whole society such as government is seen as a necessary activity that has to encroach on individual interests to keep the whole society functioning. The state is often seen in a negative sense as a necessary evil in a society that celebrates the individual, like the United States, and not as something positive that has useful functions to perform in society. Yet the state, as Aristotle said centuries ago, aims at the highest good to a greater degree than any other institution in society.

> Every state is a community of some kind, and every community is established with a view to some good; for mankind always act in order to obtain that which they think good. But, if all communities aim at some good, the state or political community, which is the highest of all, and which embraces all the rest, aims at good in a greater degree than any other, and at the highest good.[1]

A scientific worldview undermines these notions of a common good and a sense of the whole that the notion of community involves. When atomic individualism is taken as a basic assumption regarding beliefs about the individual in the sense that the individual is believed to be the basic building block of society in a reductionistic sense, a true community can never be reached. When individuals are seen as the basic building block of society, society is comprised of nothing more than individual egos clashing with each other much like atoms that bump into each other in the physical universe. Whatever sense of community that may develop is nothing more that the sum of these individuals and their interests, these egoistic desires and drives that are rooted in the individual.

THE INDIVIDUAL VERSUS THE COMMUNITY

Alasdair MacIntyre believes that the United States may well be founded on incompatible moral and social ideals; on the one hand, a communitarian vision of a common "telos," and on the other hand, an ideal of individualism and pluralism. Thus he holds that "We inhabit a kind of polity whose moral order requires systematic incoherence in the form of public allegiance to mutually inconsistent sets of principles."[2] Thus it is difficult for Americans to see both individual responsibility and responsibility to the community as part of the same moral matrix. We tend to focus on one or the other of these poles and all too often community interests or the common good is pitted against the rights and freedoms of the individual. Anything the government does in the interests of promoting the good of the whole society is seen as an encroachment on the sacred right of individuals to be free to do as they please.

This dichotomy is at work in many policy areas where there are clashes between community and individual interests. The Environmental Protection Agency (EPA) sees its role as protecting the environment and public health by regulating certain pollutants that are believed to harm people and working to preserve certain parts of our environment. It issues regulations that have to do with wetlands preservation, for example, which are rapidly disappearing in some parts of the country. This is seen to be a problem because wetlands perform many valuable functions and are necessary for wildlife preservation. These regulations prevent farmers and developers from using parts of their land that are defined as wetlands for agricultural and commercial purposes in order to keep the wetlands they own from being destroyed. Their individual right to use property in their own interests is interfered with in the interests of the environment or common good. These clashes are seen as pitting the individual against the community with the government representing community interests and the common good.

This long-standing tug-of-war between public and private interests is best reflected in the ongoing debate between libertarianism and communitarianism. Libertarianism is based on the assumption that an appropriate comprehension of social reality necessitates an entirely individualistic orientation. The philosophy of a free society is constructed from the concept of humans as autonomous beings whose actions are the product of choice and purpose. Any attempt to abridge this individual autonomy by coercive activity, which is most often used by the state, destroys the separateness and identity of the individual human being and makes humans a means to be used for the end of some social and collective good. While recognizing the need for law and morality to place limits on the autonomy of the individual, libertarians argue that law and morality should be limited to enforcing the equal right of each individual to pursue his or her own interest. According to John Hospers, libertarianism entails

> the liberty of each person to live according to his own choices, provided that he does not attempt to coerce others, and prevent them from living according to their choices. Libertarians hold this to be an inalienable right of man; thus, libertarianism represents a total commitment to the concept of individual rights.[3]

Communitarianism, on the other hand, challenges the primacy of the unfettered individual and tries to temper the excesses of American individuality in the interests of the larger society. According to this philosophy, the preservation of individual liberty depends on the active maintenance of the institutions of civil society; thus the rights of the individual must be balanced with the responsibilities to the needs of community. The community is more than just the sum of the individuals in that community, and people have a social obligation to preserve common values and ideals that go beyond the self-interest of individuals. An understanding of the general welfare or common good must take group interests and identities into account while standing apart as more than their aggregate.

This debate between libertarianism and communitarianism is relevant to much of the contemporary discussion of social and moral philosophy, to say nothing of policy debates over the appropriate way to address specific problems in society. These debates traditionally pit individual identity against group conformity, individual rights against community interests: dichotomies that often lead to impasses that are difficult to resolve. Contemporary communitarianism supposedly is presenting a new way to understand the relation between the individual and community. According to Amitai Etzioni, founder of a new communitarian movement in America:

> The term highlights the assumption that individuals act within a social context, that this context is not reducible to individual acts, and most significantly, that the social context is not necessarily or wholly imposed. Instead, the social context is, to a significant extent, perceived as a legitimate and integral part of one's existence, a We, a whole of which the individuals are constituent elements.[4]

Thus a view of the self as an atomic unit is denied in Etzioni's reference to the social context as irreducible to the acts of individuals. But it is the atomic view of the self which is still operative in individualism and its ongoing interpretation of community as simply a collection of individuals, an interpretation which provides the basis for its attack on communitarianism as reducible to collectivism and majoritarianism. The communitarian movement in America has not made significant inroads into how we think of ourselves in relation to the larger whole in part because it does not have a strong philosophical underpinning. Individualism remains alive and well in American society and is reflected in the way our democracy functions.

CONTEMPORARY DEMOCRACY

Michael Sandel, writing in *Democracy's Discontent: America in Search of a Public Philosophy*, states that there are two concerns that lie as the heart of the public's discontent with democracy. One is the fear that individually and collectively, Americans are losing control of the forces that govern their lives, and the other is the sense that from family to neighborhood to nation the moral fabric of community is unraveling. These two fears, the loss of self-government and the erosion of community, define the anxiety of the nation. He goes on to say that American politics is ill equipped to allay this discontent; that it cannot speak convincingly about self-government and community in a manner that connects with the prevailing public philosophy in American society.[5]

The political philosophy by which Americans live, says Sandel, is a certain version of liberal political theory whose central idea is that government should be neutral toward the moral and religious views its citizens espouse. Since people disagree about the best way to live in a pluralistic society such as ours, government should not affirm in law any particular vision of the good life. "Instead it should provide a framework of rights that respect persons as free and independent selves, capable of choosing their own values and ends. Since this liberalism asserts the priority of fair procedures over particular ends, the public life it informs might be called the procedural republic."[6]

This political philosophy replaced a rival public philosophy that Sandel calls a version of republican political theory. In this philosophy, sharing in self-rule means deliberating with fellow citizens about the common good and helping to shape the destiny of the political community. This deliberation requires knowledge of public affairs, a sense of belonging, and a concern for the whole, a moral bond with the community whose fate is at stake. In contrast to liberal philosophy, republican politics cannot be neural toward the values and ends its citizens espouse.[7]

In recent decades, according to Sandel, the civic or formative aspect of our politics has largely given way to the liberalism that conceives of persons as free and independent selves that are unencumbered by any moral or civic ties related to community. Liberal political theory does not see political life as concerned with the highest ends or with the moral excellence of its citizens. Rather than promoting a particular conception of the good life, liberal political theory insists on toleration, fair procedures, respect for individual rights, and values that respect people's freedom to choose their own ends. But Sandel asks a critical question about this philosophy. "If liberal ideals cannot be defended in the name of the highest human good, then in what does their moral basis consist?"[8] Sandel sees a problem here in that the moral basis for democracy has been eroded by the liberal conception of government.

> For despite its appeal, the liberal vision of freedom lacks the civic resources to sustain self-government. This defect ill-equips it to address the sense of disempowerment that afflicts our public life. The public philosophy by which we live cannot secure the liberty it promises, because it cannot inspire the sense of community and civic engagement that liberty requires.[9]

Again, one can see at work in this philosophy the scientific worldview with its reductionism and atomism that leads to the erosion of a moral basis for democracy. Society is seen as a collection of individuals that have their own ends and government exists to assure that people have the freedom to choose these ends without undue interference. Government should not promote any particular conception of the good life or seek to promote the common good, which is presumed to be a fiction. The government is in some sense a political marketplace that simply coordinates supply and demand for the goods and services government supplies (public goods and services), the same as the economic marketplace coordinates the supply and demand for private goods and services. Government becomes a free-for-all of competitive interests who seek to use government in their own interests with no concern for the public or common good.[10] Michael J. Lerner, writing in the *Politics of Meaning*, states the problem in the following manner:

> Ever since the rise of market societies helped displace spiritually based conceptions of human life, Western thought has been shaped by the view that human beings are isolated monads whose highest goal is individual fulfillment in a universe designed for this self-indulgent purpose. The geocentricism and arrogance of many strains of contemporary Western thought reflect and help perpetuate a social reality in which human beings are separated from one another and from the larger spiritual reality of the universe. We each have to come to see ourselves as the center of reality, and then to wonder how we could ever connect with others or be part of a real community.[11]

The way the government currently operates reflects this atomism where individual interests are adjudicated and compromises are reached between different interests that clash in the political marketplace. Government is seen as a collection of individuals and interest groups rather than as something that represents and helps create a true community. Rather than having a holistic or organic view of government that is concerned with building or maintaining a sense of community and the public good, government is more often seen as a clash of individual interests that are out to use the public treasury to advance their own causes or interests. The purpose of government is to work out some kind of compromise between these competing interests through the process of negotiation so that a decision can get made and a course of action taken with respect to a particular problem.

The tendency to view government as nothing more than atomic individuals or groups that clash in a political setting is a prevailing tendency. Groups from business organizations to universities have their lobbyists in Washington to argue their cause before the appropriate committees or government officials in the hopes of getting something to advance their interests, whether it is to get a bill passed or some money to fund a research program or whatever else the government can provide. If there is something called the public interest, it is understood as a balance or compromise between a multitude of individual or group interests. The idea that there is some kind of common good or something called community interests that goes beyond this balancing of special or individual interests does not seem to have much political credibility.

The government cannot seem to develop a plan to deal with specific problems or think long-range in regard to some of the issues facing the nation. For decades politicians have been advocating an energy policy to reduce our dependence on foreign oil and produce fewer greenhouse gases that contribute to global warming. It is a feature of almost every campaign and the notion of energy independence is a rallying cry tapping into American values of independence and self-reliance. But we are no closer to a real energy policy despite all this rhetoric. We don't know what an overall energy policy would look like and have no idea of how to think holistically about the nation's energy future. All we can do is respond to the lobbying of private interests and promote the latest fad by providing subsidies for certain technologies that happen to be in vogue.

The health-care debate that took place in 2009–2010 also reflects this problem. The bill that eventually emerged is a hodgepodge of special interests where compromises had to be reached to get the bill passed. The public option, along with other provisions in the original bill that may have been beneficial, were dropped because of the opposition of the health-insurance industry and other factions in society. The basic question about health care was never asked or answered, that question being whether health care is a private or public good. However that question is answered, the rest follows. What we have is a bill that tries to have it both ways. People have been given new rights not to be denied coverage because of preexisting conditions or to have their insurance dropped when they get ill, but everyone is also required to have health insurance in order for the system to be afford-able. The private health-insurance industry will provide this coverage and will be given a larger clientele to serve with the opportunity of making more money so the bill may end up serving private interests to a greater extent than the public interest.[12]

Many people were not happy with this bill and with government involve-ment with health care in general. Protests were held all over the country and the Republicans, none of whom voted for the bill, promised to repeal it if they were able to take over Congress and wield enough power. The attorneys general of several states also challenged the bill because of it alleged unconstitutionality as encroaching on individual freedom of choice by requiring all citizens to have health insurance subject to fines if they refused. This provision will be ruled on by the Supreme Court in the near future.The process by which the bill was finally passed was seen to be cor-rupt and many people were disgusted with government because of all the deals that had to be cut to get it passed. The bill that finally passed did not seem to reflect a common interest in improving our health-care system but was an amalgam of private interests that did not please anyone. Aristotle again had a word for this several centuries ago.

> The true forms of government, therefore, are those in which the one, or the few, or the many, govern with a view to the common interest; but governments which rule with a view to the private interest, whether of the one, of the few, or the many, are perversions.[13]

Jeffrey Sachs, director of the Earth Institute at Columbia University and a Nobel Prize winner, has stated that the actual health consequences of the bill were never reviewed or debated coherently. The legislative process was driven by political and lobbying considerations without the input of experts, who were never invited to comment or debate about the legislation, which would have helped the public and politicians understand the issues, and without the informed participation of the American people, leaving the public at large with "little basis for reaction other than the gut instincts and fearful sentiments fanned by talk-show hosts." Commenting on the public-policy process in general, he further states that ". . . a systematic vetting of policy options, with recognized experts and the public comment-ing and debating, will vastly improve on our current policy performance, in which we often fly blind or hand the controls over to narrow interests and viewpoints." [14]

Science does not provide us with a view of reality where the community and the individual are inextricably intertwined and in some sense consti-tute each other so that community does not stem from some relationship of individuals but is a reality present in the very nature of individuals. With-out this sense of community, government cannot develop a vision of what a good society would look like and work toward that end in developing an energy policy or health policy or any other holistic policy for that matter. It can only respond to individual and group interests and deal with whatever emerges from this kind of political marketplace.

INDIVIDUALISM AND RIGHTS

The problem is an individualistic philosophy that informs our understanding of government and the assumption that rights are inherent in individuals rather than the community. Individualism has been a key idea in Western societies for many centuries and is one of those unexamined assumptions about the way the world is constituted. Individualism is the idea that people are individual selves that are quite distinguishable from other selves and can be defined apart from any social context. The individual is held to be the primary unit of reality and the ultimate standard of value. Every person is an end in himself or herself and no person's interests should be sacrificed for the sake of anothers in some utilitarian context where the greater good would override individual interests. While societies and other collective entities such as business organizations exist, they are nothing more than a collection of the individuals in them, not something over and above them. Organizations thus derive their being from the individuals who choose to become part of them and comprise their membership.

We are thought to be like atoms that are traveling around the world bumping up against other atoms or individuals in the course of our existence. As individual selves we are by and large alone in the world and in competition with other selves for the resources of society. We create institutions such as business and enter into contracts in order to survive and provide for our needs through some form of cooperative endeavor. But most of these institutional and contractual relationships are instrumental in that we relate to other people only because they can do something for us and provide us with something we need for our existence. We are not linked to people except through these external ties that can never lead to a true community.

Within this philosophy of individualism there is nothing but these external links to bind people and institutions together. Self-interested individuals and institutions that have separate wills and desires are constantly colliding like atoms in space; hence this philosophy of individualism is sometimes called atomic individualism. To minimize the collisions and reduce conflict, people and institutions may come together on occasion to work out these differences and establish some sort of relationship. But while peripheral ties may be established when antecedent individuals enter into contract with one another or come together to more readily secure their own individualistic goals, these kinds of bonds cannot root them in any ongoing endeavor which is more than the sum of their separate selves, separate wills, and separate egoistic desires. There is never any possibility of developing a true community or society based upon a sense of responsibility for each other.

If the community is seen as nothing more than the sum of its parts, society bounces back and forth between an emphasis on individual rights and community needs, between a celebration of diversity and the need for common goals and interests. Once the individual is taken as an isolatable unit, the individual and the community become pitted against each other in an ultimately irreconcilable tension. This tension between the individual and community causes a great deal of difficulty in arriving at mutually satisfactory solutions to social and political problems. Nothing binds individuals and institutions together except self-interest, and if one starts with individual and separate atomic bits of this sort, there is no way to get to a true community. True unity can arise only in a form of action and thinking that does not attempt to fragment the whole of reality.[15]

Consistent with this view of individualism is the notion that rights inhere in individuals who are born with certain inalienable rights that are part and parcel of their being. These rights do not come from outside or in any sense belong to a community, but are inherent in individuals in some sense when they are born. Our declaration of independence is based on this notion of rights, as is the Bill of Rights spelled out in the first ten amendments to our Constitution. The former states that certain truths are held to be self-evident and that men are endowed by their Creator with certain unalienable Rights. This notion of rights is more or less universal as nations all over the world insist they have a right to do whatever they deem appropriate for their survival.

Rights have been used throughout history to overthrow systems of governance and establish new forms of social and economic power. In the Middle Ages, kings claimed a divine right to govern their subjects in order to throw off the shackles of the church, and then went on to claim ever more extensive powers over the subjects they came to dominate. Fledging democracies such as our own claimed a natural right to liberty in order to overthrow this order and establish a new system of government based on the sovereignty of the people. The notion of natural rights arises out of a need to check the sovereign power of kings, as was the case in the establishment of our country. Such rights can also be used to put a check on the sovereign power of the state, as in Locke's view of property rights.

John Locke developed an individualistic political theory that contained a strong defense of property rights among other things.[16] The key elements in this political theory are natural rights, social contract, government by consent, and the right of revolution. Locke derived his theory of property rights from natural law, which he believed provided the basis for a claim to innate, indefeasible rights inherent in each individual. According to Locke, the true end of government is to protect property, and the right of property provided an effective limitation upon the powers of the government.

Human life begins in a hypothetical state of nature, according to Locke, where each individual is perfectly equal with every other and all have the absolute liberty to act as they will without interference from any other. The earth and everything in it belonged to everyone in common and individuals had the same right to make use of whatever they could find and use for themselves, except that each individual has an exclusive right to his/her own body and its actions. Everyone has a right to draw subsistence from whatever is offered in nature, and when things are taken out of a state of nature for this purpose and individual actions are applied to natural objects, an individual's labor is mixed with natural objects.

This mixture of nature and labor provided a clear moral basis for appropriating nature as an extension of our own personal property. Everyone has a natural right to that with which he has "mixed" the labor of his body. By expending energy to make natural objects useful, people make them a part of themselves. Individuals who plow the land and take it out of a state of nature, for example, and improve its productivity by spending their own time and effort on its cultivation, acquire a property interest in the result. The plowed field is worth more than the virgin prairie because someone has invested labor in plowing it, so even if the prairie was originally held in common by all, the plowed field belongs to the person who expended the energy to make it productive.

Society does not create this right to property, according to Locke, it is a natural right that each person brings to society in his or her own person. This right can be regulated only to the extent necessary to make effective the equally valid claims of another individual to the same rights. The legitimacy of political power is derived from this individual right of each person to protect his or her property. The creation of government is justified because it is a better way of protecting this natural right to property than the self-help to which each individual is naturally entitled. The power of the government, however, cannot be exercised in an arbitrary manner and property cannot be taken from individuals without their consent. Government exists to protect the prior right to private property.

The Declaration of Independence refers to certain basic rights that are believed to be self-evident. This notion seems to be based on some kind of a natural-law concept and assumes that there is an ideal standard of justice fixed by nature that is binding on all persons. This standard takes precedence over the particular laws and standards created by social convention. The concept of natural rights provides absolute standards against which the laws and policies of particular states and institutions are to be measured. These rights are considered to be fundamental regardless of merit, due to be respected because they are rooted in a knowledge of certain universal regularities in nature. They refer to a proper ordering of the universe. Knowledge of this structure was believed to be accessible to all people by virtue of the reason they possessed.[17]

Thus a right is an individual's entitlement to something. A person has a right when that person is entitled to act in a certain way or have others act in a certain way toward him or her. This entitlement may derive from a legal system that permits or empowers the person to act in a specified way or that requires others to act in certain ways toward that person. Legal rights are derived from political constitutions, legislative enactments, case law, and executive orders of the highest state official. They can be eliminated by lawful amendments or other political actions and are limited to the particular jurisdiction within which the legal system is in force.

Entitlements can also be derived from a system of moral standards independently of any particular legal system and cannot be eroded or banished by political votes, powers, or amendments. They can be based on moral norms or principles that specify that all human beings are permitted or empowered to do something or are entitled to have something done for them. Moral rights provide individuals with autonomy and/or equality in the free pursuit of their interests. These rights identify activities or interests that people must be left free to pursue or not to pursue as they themselves choose, and whose pursuit must not be subordinated to the interests of others except for special and exceptionally weighty reasons. Moral rights provide a basis for justifying one's actions and for invoking the protection or aid of others. They express the requirements of morality from the point of view of the individual instead of society as a whole, and promote individual welfare and protect individual choices against encroachment by society.

Utilitarian considerations promote society's aggregate utility and are indifferent to individual welfare except insofar as it affects this social aggregate. Moral rights, however, limit the validity of appeals to social benefits. If a person has a right to do something, then it is wrong for anyone or any institution to interfere with this right, even though a large number of people might gain much more utility from such interference. If utilitarian benefits or losses imposed on society become great enough, they may be sufficient, in some cases, to breach the walls of rights set to protect a person's freedom to pursue his or her interests.

Negative rights can be considered to be duties others have not to interfere in certain activities of individuals. A negative right is a right to be free to hold and practice a belief, to pursue an action, or enjoy a state of affairs without outside interference. Negative rights protect an individual from interference from the state and from other people. The state is to protect this basic right to be left alone and is not to encroach on this right itself. Positive rights, on the other hand, mean some other agents have a positive duty of providing the holder of rights with whatever he or she needs to freely pursue his or her interests. Positive rights are rights to obtain goods and services, opportunities, or certain kinds of equal treatment.

Both kinds of rights entail some kinds of responsibilities on the part of certain persons and groups. Negative rights involve responsibilities that others have not to interfere in certain activities of a person and leave him or her alone. These rights are to be respected by other people as well as the institutions of society. Positive rights involve responsibilities some agents have to provide the rights holders with the things they have coming to them as a result of these rights. But these responsibilities are derived from rights in that they stem from the rights people hold to be left alone or to be provided with certain things. Rights are prior and responsibilities would not exist in the absence of rights.

Today we speak a good deal about human rights and attempt to promote such rights throughout the world. These rights are not derived from the operations of natural reason, but rather from ideas of what it means to be human. It is assumed that human beings have an essential nature that determines the fundamental obligations and rights that are to be respected by other people and social institutions. The rights that are asserted as fundamental to the development of human beings are believed to stem from knowledge of certain essential properties of human nature.

Thus people have a right to be treated equally in the workplace, to work and play in a smoke-free environment, to carry out their work-related activities in a safe workplace, and the right to a clean environment, among other things. These rights often clash with property rights, which still seem to be rooted in a system of natural liberty, that people have a natural right to use their property in their own interests. Affirmative-action programs, job-safety programs, pollution-control programs, and similar measures sometimes override property rights and limit the freedoms of property owners. At other times property rights take precedence. Rights clash because they are rooted in individualism and these clashes have to be sorted out by whatever political system is in place. As Richard Bronk writes:

> All democracies have championed the freedom to participate in government, and most have also sought to enshrine in law certain individual rights which seek to secure for individuals some inalienable areas of freedom of action and thought. Progress has, in part, been defined in the liberal tradition as the gradual extension of these individual freedoms and rights. The central problem for liberal democracy, however, is that one person's right to freedom of action may clash with another person's right not to be harmed . . . But in our increasingly interconnected and congested world, many people argue that surprisingly few actions by individuals are without important consequences for others. The crucial debate has centered around what role democratic government should have in trying to ensure greater harmony of interests between members of society, and what role government should have in forging the best social and environmental outcome for society as a whole.[18]

When rights are seen as stemming from an individualistic conception of the self, such clashes are inevitable. While the concept of public policy does contain some notion of community, it is undermined by an individualistic approach where public policy represents nothing more than the aggregation of citizen preferences for public goods and services as expressed through the political process. This is the same way a market system works as it aggregates individual preferences for private goods and services. This view is reinforced by the notion of rights that inhere in individuals and are part and parcel of their nature. Thus public policy reflects these ideas of individualism and rights that are part of the society at large and the political process ends up being in irreconcilable conflict over which rights take priority as individuals and groups battle each other in pursuing their interests.

FRAGMENTED GOVERNMENT

At the turn of the century, in 1908 to be exact, the University of Chicago Press published a book entitled *The Process of Government* written by Arthur Bentley, a newspaperman who worked mostly at the Chicago *Times-Herald*.[19] In this book, which received almost no attention at the time, Bentley maintains that all politics and all government are the result of group activities and any other attempt to explain how politics and government works is doomed to failure. In its time this was a wildly contrarian position, according to Nicholas Lemann, writing in *The New Yorker,* as many people believed in a more idealistic vision of government and saw interest groups as subverting good government. For Bentley, there was no such thing as the public interest; it was a useless concept, he said, because there was nothing that was best for the society as a whole. Politics involved deal making, and morality is not a force in politics because such talk is almost always a cover for somebody's interests. While we would like to think that procedural reforms will eventually lead to something we can call "good government," the truth is that the only way to defeat one set of interests is with another set of interests.

Bentley's view of government, many would argue, accurately describes the way government operates today, and is consistent with the scientific worldview where competitive interests clash in a political marketplace much like atoms bumping up against each other. The problem with such a view, which is often called interest-group pluralism, is that there is anything but fair and balanced competition in the political marketplace, as corporations and their representatives, such as the U.S. Chamber of Commerce, usually have an advantage when it comes to lobbying and other forms of political influence.[20] Corporations have vast sums of money to tap into for political influence that most other groups and interests in society do not have, and money seems to be what counts when it comes to political influence.

Many lobbyists, for example, have had previous experience in government and thus have access and expertise in a particular area that others in the political arena do not that gives the firms that hire them an unfair competitive advantage. Politicians gain experience in government and then, when they either lose an election or just quit government for other reasons, they can get lucrative positions as lobbyists for companies that value their expertise and access to the political system. They can sell their influence for big money as their salaries can go from $162,500 a year if they are in Congress or $95,000 if they are staff to $300,000 a year or more overnight.[21] There were approximately 2,000 lobbyists involved in the financial reform bill that Congress passed in 2010, and more than 1,400 of these had been in government working as congressional staffers or in some position in the Executive Branch itself. Some seventy-three of these lobbyists previously had been in Congress and moved into lucrative lobbying positions upon leaving government. These lobbyists were able to exercise a great deal of influence over the bill that finally emerged.[22]

The influence of corporations in the political process was extended in a 2010 Supreme Court ruling. In *Citizens United v. Federal Election Commission*, the court ruled that First Amendment rights of free speech applied to corporations and unions as well as individuals, and thus these collective entities could make unlimited expenditures supporting the election or defeat of specific federal candidates. Before this ruling, corporations and unions could runs ads as long as they did not explicitly endorse or oppose specific candidates. This ruling overruled two prior Supreme Court opinions and struck down part of the McCain-Feingold election law passed in 2002, which, among other things, banned the use of corporate treasury funds to back or oppose candidates in elections.[23]

This ruling contributed to the development of what are called "super PACs," which was one of the first effects that became apparent. These PACs were seen as a new potent political weapon because they spent more than $8 million on TV advertising and other expenditures mostly within one month alone during the 2010 elections and proved to be an easy way for corporations to spend unlimited funds on an election. They are free of most constraints that apply to other types of corporate PACs that must comply with strict limits on donations. The only thing they are not allowed to do is coordinate their ads directly with candidates or political parties. Corporations can donate unlimited funds to these PACs because of the ruling that overturned the ban on corporate expenditures for specific election campaigns.[24]

One thing missing in this controversy over corporate contributions is the issue of who speaks for the corporation. The corporation obviously cannot speak for itself, so the question of who controls where the corporation chooses to spend its money on political advertising and which candidates to support or oppose is critical. Most likely it is senior management that makes these decisions without any input from shareholders who in theory, at least, own the corporation, or employees who work for it on a daily basis. What this ruling has done is give more political power to a class of people who already have enormous power in society and are able to extract huge sums of money from the corporations for their services.[25]

So what we have is a government that is for sale to the highest bidder, which quite often are corporations or, more precisely, the managers of these organizations. This does not sound like a government of the people, by the people, and for the people.[26] It sounds more like a government that is beholden to corporate interests who have the money to wield undue influence in the political process and can shape public policy to enhance or protect those interests. Reforms to this process to open it up to more public participation are not going to work until we get a new philosophy of government, one that undercuts the notions of isolatable individuals with absolute rights in favor of inherently social persons that are an integral part of a larger community.

5 Culture

The scientific revolution enabled us to understand how nature worked, and based on the laws discovered by science, technologies were able to be developed and resources processed to make goods and services available to people on a scale never before imagined. Science spawned the industrial revolution and changed societies in the Western world beyond recognition. Cities grew as factories were built to produce products and motivated people to move from farms to cities to take jobs in these factories and become part of the new industrial order. The feudal system that had governed people's lives for years broke apart and new classes developed that reflected this new order. Both nature and workers were exploited in the interests of creating economic wealth and promoting economic growth as nation-states sought to gain power and influence in this emerging order.

What emerged in the Western world was a capitalistic culture where economic values came to dominate people's lives and provided the context in which many of their activities took place. Science was a major factor in the development of capitalism as it provided a new way of looking at the world that allowed for the invention of new technologies that gave people the ability to manipulate nature and shape it to serve their interests. Capitalism allowed these technologies to be exploited better than any other economic system and became linked to progress defined by continued economic growth. Science has served these interests in the Western world for centuries, but as socialistic systems have collapsed, capitalism or some variation of it has taken hold throughout the world as former socialistic countries have adopted some form of capitalistic economic organization.

THE PROTESTANT ETHIC

The social context for the emergence of capitalism was provided by the Protestant Reformation and the resultant social upheaval this produced in leading to the breakup of medieval society. The Reformation challenged the authority of the Catholic Church and focused on *individual* authority. Individuals had direct access to God through the notion of the priesthood of all believers and did not need the intervening authority of the church for this access. Individual rationality became a source of truth that challenged the authority of institutions including both religions and political institutions. The Reformation thus supported the atomization of society by focusing on the individual rather than a community of believers.

Feudalism proved to have inadequate answers to the social and economic problems created by the growth of towns, the expansion of trade, the development of technology, and the growth of banks and other large-scale enterprises. It no longer provided an institutional context in which the potentials of these emerging developments could be exploited. Economic forces had to be given their own course free from the domination of the church and the old feudal order. Eventually a new economic order emerged that we now call capitalism with new power centers and new sources of wealth. As Michael Lerner writes:

> Leading the rebellion were the merchants, traders, shopkeepers, bankers, and independent professionals of the social middle class (collectively referred to as "the bourgeoisie"), who felt most resentful of the older feudal order. These people resented the degree to which the church had set limits on their own economic activities. For example, the church often set a "fair price," a "fair profit," and a "fair wage," in ways that impeded the creation of a free market. The traders and shopkeepers did not want the larger society to limit the profits they could make or to demand that they be responsible for the well-being of their workers.[1]

A new moral context was provided by the Protestant ethic that informed the development of capitalistic systems and provided legitimacy for their existence. On the one hand, it created a moral incentive for people to be productive and increase economic wealth. On the other hand, it provided a moral limit to consumption in the interests of building up a capital base for production. Max Weber provided us with the first comprehensive study of the significance of the Protestant ethic.[2] In his book *The Protestant Ethic and the Spirit of Capitalism*, he sought to provide an explanatory model based upon religious beliefs for the growth of capitalistic activity in the sixteenth and seventeenth centuries.[3]

These religious beliefs, which Weber called the Protestant ethic, produced a certain type of personality with a high motivation to achieve success in worldly terms by accumulating wealth and working diligently to create more wealth. This ethic contained two major elements: (1) an emphasis on the importance of a person's calling, which involved a primary responsibility to do one's best at the worldly station to which one was assigned by God rather than to seek religious meaning in withdrawing from the world, and (2) the rationalization of all of life by Calvin's notion of predestination through which work became a means of dispersing religious doubt and anxiety by proving through worldly success that one was part of the sample of those elected for salvation.[4]

The self-discipline and moral sense of duty and calling which were at the heart of this ethic were vital, according to Weber, to the kind of rational economic behavior that capitalism demanded (calculation, punctuality, productivity). The Protestant ethic thus contributed to the spirit of capitalism, a spirit that was supportive of individual human enterprise and accumulation of wealth necessary for the development of capitalism. Within this climate, people were motivated to behave in a manner that proved conducive to rapid economic growth of the capitalistic variety and shared values that were consistent with this kind of development.[5]

Within this ethical system, work was understood to be something good in itself and was neither a curse nor something fit only for slaves. Rather, work itself, which in the period before the Reformation was by and large considered to be a morally neutral activity at best, was given a clear moral sanction. Every person's work was of equal value in the eyes of God and contributed to the creation of more and more economic wealth in society. This ethic thus motivated one to work hard to be productive and accumulate wealth, which was a sign that one was doing things right and proving that one was predestined for salvation.

But this wealth was not to be pursued for its own sake or enjoyed in lavish consumption. The world existed to serve the glorification of God and for that purpose alone. The more one had, the greater was the obligation to be an obedient steward and hold these possessions undiminished for the glory of God by increasing them through relentless effort. The accumulation of material wealth was as sure a way as was available to dispose of the fear of damnation. One was not to rest on one's laurels or enjoy the fruits of one's labor. Whatever wealth one was able to accumulate must be reinvested to accumulate more wealth in order to please God and as a further manifestation of one's own election.

> The upshot of it all, was that for the first time in history the two capital producing prescriptions, maximization of production and minimization of consumption became components of the same ethical matrix. As different from medieval or communist culture these norms were not reserved for or restricted to specific individuals or groups. Everyone hypothetically belonged to that universe from which the deity had drawn the salvation sample, without disclosing its size or composition. The sampling universe had no known restriction of biological or social background, aptitude, or occupational specialization. Nobody could opt out from the sampling process, indeed, everyone had to act as if indeed he had been selected. For the mortal sin was to mock the deity by contradicting through his behavior God's primeval sampling decision. Everybody not only could but had to presume potential sainthood and correspondingly

optimize his performance both as producer and consumer. The more his performance excelled relative to his reference group's, the higher the probability that indeed he had been selected. The ethic then pressured equally towards effective production and efficient consumption, which, while sustaining maximum productivity also maximizes savings and potential investment capital.[6]

Not only did the ethic thus stress physical work on the part of every person, but also whatever money one had was also to be put to work in making more money. A worldly asceticism was at the heart of this ethic, which gave a religious sanction for the acquisition and rational use of wealth to create more wealth. This new understanding of acquisitiveness and the pursuit of wealth became something of a moral imperative because what formerly had been regarded as a personal inclination and choice had now become something of a moral duty.

The Protestant ethic was an ingenious social and moral invention that offered a moral sanction to behavior that was of crucial importance in the early stages of capitalism. It emphasized both the human and capital sources of productivity and growth, by focusing on hard work and the aspect of the calling, but also advocating that the money people earned should also be put to work in earning more money. Inequality was thus morally justified if the money earned on capital was reinvested in further capital accumulation, which would benefit society as a whole by increasing production and creating more economic wealth.

The Protestant ethic proved to be consistent with the need for accumulation of capital that is necessary during the early stages of industrial development. Money was saved and reinvested to build up a capital base. Consumption was curtailed in the interests of creating capital wealth. People dedicated themselves to hard work at often disagreeable tasks and accepted the rationalization of life that capitalism required. Such attitudes and activities represented a major shift away from the behavior and attitudes that informed medieval agrarian society.

The Protestant ethic served to pattern behavior and for its adherents it helped to make sense of the new industrial order where people had to learn new roles and occupations. The pursuit of gain was legitimized and made something of a moral duty. People were to work diligently at their ordained tasks and accumulate wealth for the glory of God and as an indication of their own salvation. The Protestant ethic was something of a road map that provided a guide for behavior in the midst of a terribly confused and disorganized cultural system. It gave meaning to people's lives in the form of a religious and moral symbol system in a rapidly changing society and enabled its adherents to act purposely within the emerging economic order. It provided a moral foundation for productive activity and legitimized the pursuit of profit and accumulation of wealth on the part of those who worked hard and invested their money wisely.

While the Protestant ethic contained a moral limit on consumption in the interests of generating more economic wealth and building up a capital base to increase production for the entire society, it also made production of the wealth an end in itself and did not provide a moral purpose for production that was rooted in the fulfillment of human existence. It was tied to religious justifications that were abstractions from human existence and allowed for exploitation of both humans and nature in the interests of increasing production. Natural law in which the state confines itself to the protection of individual rights in the context of an emphatic respect for the free market became sanctioned along with a utilitarian ethics which imposed only one moral demand on the new industrialists, that is, to strive for the greatest possible quantity of utilities for themselves and, so it was thought, for their fellowmen.[7]

During the enlightenment, nature came to connote not divine ordinance but human appetites, and natural rights were invoked by the individualism of the time as a reason why self-interest should be given free play. The conception that the church possesses its own authority as an independent standard of social values which it could apply to the practical affairs of the economic world grew weaker.[8] Economic life came to be grounded in a naturalistic conception of society in which the world of human affairs is regarded as self-contained and in need of no supernaturalistic explanation.

> It was precisely in the spiritual climate provided by deism, which looked upon the social and economic life of man as a cosmos controlled by natural laws and completely accessible to human analysis, that the science of economics could gradually emerge. The character of this science of course presupposed a primarily mechanistic view of the world. The timepiece manufactured by the clockmaker could, so to speak, now be opened up by man, and the wheelwork inside could be analyzed as carefully as possible.[9]

This ethic was of particular importance in American society as capitalism developed and economic wealth was created. The country needed investment capital to expand industry and build railroads and canals to link the country together. People worked hard and saved their money to be invested in this expansion and share in the growth of the economy. The opportunities in this country seemed limitless and resources were considered to be infinite. One could become as wealthy as one wanted by taking advantage of these opportunities and pursuing the American dream. But this dream was never realized; it was always in the future and was thus something that continued to provide motivation and purpose.

The notion of the Protestant ethic eventually became secularized in American society and stripped of its religious trappings. Secularization refers to the process of deemphasizing the religious elements of any particular notion or concept and increasingly referring to worldly or temporal elements as distinguished from the spiritual or eternal realm. Thus a secular view of life or of any particular matter is based on the premise that religion or religious considerations should be ignored or purposely excluded. The Protestant ethic thus became known as simply the work ethic and is now almost exclusively discussed in secular terms with very little reference made to its religious origins except in certain scholarly and religious circles.

However, its basic assumptions about the importance of work and investment remained much the same and continued to inform American society. Embedded in the notion of the Protestant ethic is the moral imperative both for the maximization of production and for the minimization of consumption. This ethic thus pressured equally towards effective production and efficient consumption, which also maximized savings and potential investment capital. But of even deeper significance is the fact that while the Protestant ethic contained a moral limit on consumption in the interests of generating more economic wealth and building up a capital base to increase production, production of this wealth became an end in itself as the ethic became secularized. As stated by Christopher Lasch:

> Until recently, the Protestant work ethic stood as one of the most important underpinnings of American culture. According to the myth of capitalist enterprise, thrift and industry held the key to material success and spiritual fulfillment. America's reputation as a land of opportunity rested on its claim that the destruction of hereditary obstacles to advancement had created conditions in which social mobility depended on individual initiative alone. The self-made man, archetypical embodiment of the American dream, owed his advancement to habits of industry, sobriety, moderation, self-discipline, and avoidance of debt. He lived for the future, shunning self-indulgence in favor of patient, painstaking accumulation; and so long as the collective prospect looked on whole so bright, he found in the deferral of gratification not only its principal gratification, but an abundant source of profits. In an expanding economy, the value of investments could be expected to multiply with time, as the spokesman for self-help, for all their celebration of work as its own reward, seldom neglected to point out.[10]

However, production was no longer part and parcel of a social process; its purpose was no longer part of the ongoing enrichment of human existence. While it was initially tied to religious doctrine, it was an abstraction from human experience and allowed for exploitation of both humans and nature in the interests of increasing production. As these religious ties were loosened and as the Protestant ethic gave way to the more general work ethic, even its religious justification lost its moorings. Production became a self-justifying end in itself. And, intertwined with the notion of production as an end in itself, came the view of the "economic system" as having a life of its own guided by the single mindedness of the "profit motive." Thus a reductionistic approach to economic activity took hold as capitalism grew and became the dominant way to think about a new economic order.

CONSUMPTION

For many years, the Protestant ethic was one of the most forceful shapers of American culture, but in the 1970s people began to take note of a gradual conceptual shift in values. One topic of interest and concern that appeared frequently in both popular and professional literature during this time was the weakening or disappearance of the Protestant ethic from American culture. There was a good deal of evidence to suggest that the traditional values regarding work and the acquisition of wealth as expressed in the Protestant ethic were changing in some fashion. Many articles indicated that young adults in particular had little interest in the grinding routine of the assembly line or in automated clerical tasks. They were turning away, it was suggested, from their parents' dedication to work for the sake of success and became more concerned about finding meaningful work, something that was satisfying and personally rewarding in terms other than money. Young people were seeking to change existing industrial arrangements to allow these intangible goals to be pursued.[11]

They also began to discard the notion of deferred gratification, and the worldly asceticism that provided a limit to consumption began to be less effective in shaping behavior. There was more of a sense of immediacy in living life to the fullest rather than waiting for some future time period. Young people were motivated to spend money on immediate consumption rather than save it for something they could purchase in the future. This was again consistent with the developing economy as a capital base was created that became more productive. Somebody had to buy the things that were being produced in order to keep the economy growing.

Change in values was already noted as early as 1957 by Clyde Kluckhohn, who did an extensive survey of the then available professional literature to determine if there had been any discernible shifts in American values during the past generation. As a result of this survey, he discovered that one value change which could be supported by empirical data was a decline of the Protestant ethic as the core of the dominant middle-class value system.[12] Kluckhohn cited numerous studies to support this conclusion.

> The most generally agreed upon, the best documented, and the most pervasive value shift is what Whyte has called "the decline of the Protestant Ethic." This a central theme of Whyte's book. It is a clear-cut finding of the Schneider-Dornbusch study of inspirational religious literature. It is noted by essentially all the serious publications on recent value changes and on the values of the younger generation.[13]

Related to this fundamental shift are a number of others mentioned by Kluckhohn which have the Protestant ethic as their central point of reference. These shifts are interconnected and mutually reinforcing and are a result of the weakening of the Protestant ethic but may also, in turn, contribute to its weakening. There had been a rise in value upon "being" or "being and becoming" as opposed to "doing" according to many studies cited by Kluckhohn. Another such shift was the trend towards "present time" in contrast to "future time" value orientation, which meant that the notion of deferred gratification was changing.[14]

Lastly, there was a trend towards an increase of aesthetic and recreational values as good in themselves, a development of "values which the Puritan Ethic never placed upon recreation (except as a means to the end of more effective work), pleasure, leisure, and aesthetic and expressive activities. American enjoyed themselves more and with less guilt than ever before. Moreover, there had been a remarkable diversification and broadening of the base of leisure-time activities within the population."[15]

In 1976, Daniel Bell argued that the Protestant ethic has been replaced by hedonism in contemporary society: the idea of pleasure as a way of life. During the 1950s, according to Bell, the American culture had become primarily hedonistic, concerned with fun, play, display, and pleasure. The culture was no longer concerned with how to work and achieve but with how to spend and enjoy.[16]

> In the early development of capitalism, the unrestrained economic impulse was held in check by Puritan restraint and the Protestant Ethic. One worked because of one's calling, or to fulfill the covenant of the community. But the Protestant ethic was undermined not by modernism but by capitalism itself. The greatest single engine in the destruction of the Protestant Ethic was the invention of the installment plan, or instant credit. Previously one had to save in order to buy. But with credit cards one could indulge in instant gratification. The system was transformed by mass production and mass consumption, by the creation of new wants and new means of gratifying those wants.[17]

Thus the cultural if not moral justification of capitalism had become hedonism. This cultural transformation was brought about by (1) demographic change which resulted in the growth of urban centers and shift in political weight, (2) the emergence of a consumption society with its emphasis on spending and material possessions rather than thrift and frugality, and (3) a technological revolution which through the automobile, motion picture, and radio broke down rural isolation and fused the country into a common culture and a national society.[18]

Bell argued that this abandonment of the Protestant ethic left capitalism with no moral or transcendental ethic, and produced an extraordinary contradiction within the social structure of American society. The business corporation requires people who work hard, are dedicated to a career, and accept delayed gratification, all traditional Protestant ethic virtues. Yet in its products and advertisements, the corporation promotes pleasure, instant joy, relaxing, and letting go, all hedonistic virtues. In Bell's words, "One is to be straight by day and a swinger by night."[19] Capitalism thus continued to demand a Protestant ethic in the area of production but needed to stimulate a demand for pleasure and play in the area of consumption.[20]

Finally, Christopher Lasch argued that a new ethic of self-preservation had taken hold in American society. The work ethic had been gradually transformed into an ethic of personal survival.[21] The Puritans believed that a godly man worked diligently at his calling not so much in order to accumulate personal wealth as to add to the wealth of the community.[22] The pursuit of self-interest was changing from the accumulation of wealth to a search for pleasure and psychic survival. The cult of consumption, with its emphasis on immediate gratification, created the narcissistic man of modern society. Such a culture lives for the present and does not save for the future because it believes there may not be a future to worry about.[23]

This alleged weakening of the Protestant ethic with its inherent restriction on consumption is consistent with behavioral changes in American society. Prior to the Second World War, people by and large were savings oriented and lived by the ethic of deferred gratification. They would not buy houses with large mortgages and run up huge credit-card balances, as these options were not available to many people. Rather, they would save their money until they could buy things outright. Gratification of their desires was deferred until they could afford to satisfy them and then, and only then, was it appropriate to buy things to enjoy. In other words, people lived within their immediate means and did not borrow for purposes of increased consumption.

After the war this ethic changed into one of instant gratification as a consumer society was created where people were encouraged to satisfy their desires now rather than wait until they had the money in hand. Buying on credit was encouraged and long-term mortgages became the order of the day with respect to housing. Why defer gratification when one could buy things immediately and pay for them in the future. Companies helped to create this kind of society by making credit easy to obtain through the use of credit cards and by using more sophisticated forms of advertising to increase demand for their products.

These were the days when the throwaway society was created and obsolescence was built into products so that people would have to buy newer products more quickly than planned. Packaging was improved so that products looked more attractive and could be purchased more easily. This meant the amount of stuff to be disposed of increased dramatically as products that had outlived their usefulness had to be discarded along with all the packaging materials that were used to encase products. Eventually the country began to experience problems with waste disposal that resulted in regulations of one sort or another to assure this waste material was disposed of properly and safely.

The United States became a society where consumption was emphasized and money was made available so people could buy on credit and pay their debts sometime in the future. Television fed this change with sitcoms that portrayed the typical American family as one that lived in a nice house in the suburbs with two cars and all the latest kitchen appliances and electronic gear in the rest of the house. Advertising on television also became more sophisticated to stimulate demand for products. Companies fed this consumption binge with a proliferation of products that appealed to every taste that could be imagined, which encouraged people to go into debt to enjoy the pleasures these products could bring immediately rather than in some future time period.

Government contributed to the development of this culture with the notion of entitlements and the development of programs based on the idea that people in American society were entitled to certain amenities whether or not they earned them in the traditional sense. Social security was provided to assure that people could retire with a certain level of income. Welfare programs were established to provide a minimum level of goods and services to those who were not working. Medicare and Medicaid programs provided medical care to older people and those in poverty. All of these entitlement programs came at great cost and involved the government itself going into greater and greater debt to pay for them.

Perhaps the development of the atomic bomb also had an impact on generations growing up after the Second World War, because the future has never been as certain since that time because we have had to live with the knowledge that humans have the ability to destroy the planet. Thus one might as well live as well as one possibly can now rather than defer gratification for some future time that may not be there. Changes in religion and the increasing secularization of society at that time may also have weakened belief in an afterlife, and more people came to hold the belief that you only go around once in life and you might as well enjoy it to the fullest extent possible.

There were many factors behind this change in behavior and no one factor in particular was responsible for this change. They all helped to create a new approach to consumption where instant gratification became a cultural trait in contrast to earlier times when saving for the future was emphasized. The implications of this change were profound for lifestyles and habits of people as society became more wealthy and prosperous. Many people lived more interesting lives and had more diversity available to them as never before. They traveled more miles, wore more and different clothes, drove more expensive and sophisticated cars, and in general enjoyed rising standards of living that involved consumption of the latest products.

Thus the Protestant ethic failed to provide a moral framework for production and consumption activities as it apparently did during the early stages of industrial development. In the midst of affluence and advanced technology that made possible a high level of consumption, it has not enabled many people to act purposively in keeping the system going and in enjoying the benefits of technology. It has not provided the kind of information necessary to deal adequately with the present cultural and economic situation nor did it provide a means of effectively responding to environmental problems. It became more and more irrelevant to the economic system as it emerged and changed to deal with new concerns.

In a consumer society, the emphasis on production has remained strong as the secularized work ethic continued, but the restraints on consumption provided by the Protestant ethic have given way to an ever-increasing demand for products that could produce pleasure and self-gratification. In a consumer culture, consumption activities have become separated from whatever moral limits and justifications the Protestant ethic provided. The purposes and meanings provided by this moral matrix are no longer relevant to a consumer culture that emphasized instant gratification and increased consumption. Now not only production but also consumption has become an end in itself. Both production and consumption are now divorced from any broader or larger moral purpose beyond the production and consumption of more goods and services themselves. Moreover, the assumed external relation of business and the natural environment, which had remained somewhat innocuous until recent years, began to take on ominous dimensions as increased production and consumption resulted in more waste that needed to be disposed of, more pollution that harms human health and the environment, and uses more resources—all to support a growing consumer culture that has become worldwide.

The demise of the Protestant ethic left capitalism without a comprehensive ethical or moral system to provide legitimacy for the accumulation of wealth and root capitalism in a larger moral purpose beyond itself. The system became self-justifying and any ethical concerns had to adapt themselves to the requirements of the economic system. Perhaps this was inevitable because during the Reformation the authority of the medieval Catholic Church was broken and the unity of civilization it symbolized was destroyed, enabling secular forces to develop free from the church's overpowering domination. Economic forces in particular were set free to develop without being hampered by the notions of "just wage" or "just price" that were of concern to medieval religion. Wages and prices were set by the laws of supply and demand rather than some moral principles stemming from religion, and the capitalistic system came to operate according to its own "scientific" principles born out of an Enlightenment philosophy. While the Protestant ethic may have played a role in the development of capitalism, it had to shape itself to the capitalistic organization of production. According to Robert H. Tawney:

> As a result of the Reformation the relations previously existing between the Church and State had been almost exactly reversed. In

the Middle Ages the Church had been, at least in theory, the ultimate authority on questions of public and private morality, while the latter was the police officer which enforced its decrees. In the sixteenth century, the Church became the ecclesiastical department of the State, and religion was used to lend a moral sanction to secular social policy . . . Religion has been converted from the keystone which holds the edifice together into one department within it, and the idea of a rule of right is replaced by economic expediency as the arbiter of policy and the criterion of conduct.[24]

C. E. Ayres makes the same point: "As industry and thrift came to recognized as Christian virtues, inevitably the Christian conscience adjusted itself to the rewards of industry and thrift—to the accumulation of capital."[25] The fact of the matter is that people began to find capitalistic society much more exciting and full of promise that the status quo the Church was trying to maintain. The world for many people became a more interesting place in which to live and worldly activity came to be valued for its own sake and not merely as preparation for an afterlife of some kind. Production and consumption eventually became ends in themselves and religion could not dominate these activities or provide any meaningful moral purpose for the system.

IMPLICATIONS OF INSTANT GRATIFICATION

For the past fifty years, the overriding goal of people in advanced industrial societies has been one of buying more goods and acquiring more things in the interests of increasing their stock of material wealth. Corporations have profited from this consumer culture by catering to the consumer in making more goods available and bombarding them with advertising to encourage them to buy more things. They have promoted a consumer society by creating and perpetuating a certain materialistic conception of the good life. Science and technology have fueled this development with their promise of a never-ending supply of new goods and services that can satisfy our every want and desire.

Because of this trend, the world's people have consumed as many goods and services since 1950 as all previous generations put together. Since 1940, the United States alone has used up as large a share of the earth's mineral resources as did everyone before them combined. Nonetheless, we continue to think that more is better, reflecting a quantitative approach to life, and continue to emphasize economic growth as the way out of all our problems. We continue to develop and industrialize wilderness areas and crowd out wildlife by destroying their habitats in the process. We continue to cut down our old-growth forests and open up new areas for mining and oil and gas exploration. Sometimes it seems as if we won't be satisfied until we have cut down every last tree, paved over every remaining acre of wilderness, and destroyed every last animal that stands in the way of progress. The economic juggernaut continues unabated as science and technology promise us a better world through continued exploitation of nature. We are creating an artificial world by destroying the natural one in which we have lived for most of human history.

There have been many adverse implications to the rise of consumer culture as far as resource usage and environmental impacts are concerned. Environmental concerns began to emerge in the 1960s and a great deal of legislation was passed and regulations were issued related to these concerns. Most of this legislation focused on pollution control, as before the advent of this legislation and regulation, air, water, and land were considered to be freely available for disposing of waste material. This caused no problem when the population was sparse, factories small, and products few in number compared to today. The natural environment's dilutive capacity was not exceeded very often and was perceived as infinite in its ability to absorb waste material. Changes in society, however, began to cause serious pollution problems. The following factors were critical in this transformation.

Population Growth and Concentration

More people means more manufactured goods and services to provide for their needs, which, in turn, means more waste material to be discharged into the environment. The concentration of people in urban areas compounds the problem. Eventually the dilutive capacity of the air, water, and land in major industrial centers becomes greatly exceeded and a serious pollution problem arises.

Rising Affluence

As real income increases, people are able to buy and consume more goods and services, throw them away more quickly to buy something better, travel more miles per year using various forms of transportation, and expand their use of energy. In the process much more waste material is generated for the society as a whole.

Technological Change

Changes in technology have expanded the variety of products available for consumption, increased their quantity through increases in productivity, made products and packaging more complex, and raised the rate of obsolescence through rapid innovation. All of these activities have added to the waste-disposal problem. In addition, the toxicity of many materials was initially unknown or not given much concern, with the result that procedures for the abatement of these pollution problems have lagged far behind the technology of manufacture.

Increased Expectations and Awareness

As society becomes more affluent, expectations for a higher quality of life increase, and the physical environment is viewed as an important component of the overall quality of life. One cannot fully enjoy the goods and services that are available in a hostile or unsafe environment. In addition, people's awareness of the harmful effects of pollution increase due to mounting scientific evidence, journalistic exposés, and the attention given environmental problems by the media.

Environmental concerns not only involved pollution but also resource limitations as questions were raised about the wisdom of a continued emphasis on economic growth. In the 1970s there was intense debate about limits to economic growth in the world in general and advanced industrial nations in particular. The first Club of Rome's study emphasized resource shortages, pollution problems, and population pressures in the industrialized nations and the world. The study proceeded to show that, even under the best of assumptions, the limits to growth on this planet would be reached sometime within the next hundred years. The most probable result would be a rather sudden and uncontrollable decline in both population and industrial capacity. If this danger were recognized, it would be possible to alter these growth trends and establish a condition of ecological and economic stability that could be sustained far into the future.[26]

This study was followed by the second Club of Rome study, which made many of the same points and recommendations.[27] This report was followed by the Global 2000 Report, with equally pessimistic conclusions.[28] These predictions became all too real with the oil embargo in the mid-seventies that caused long lines for gasoline in the United States and brought home to every American our vulnerability regarding energy resources. This started an emphasis on the search for alternative sources of energy in the hopes of reducing our dependence on foreign sources of oil and gaining some degree of energy independence. However, over the next several decades our imports of foreign oil increased and we were not closer to energy independence in spite of all the rhetoric about it that has only increased in intensity.

These efforts to raise questions about the feasibility of continued economic growth came to naught during the 1980s when talk about limits to growth came to an end for all practical purposes except perhaps in some isolated corners of academia. Instead, the emphasis was on opportunity and the unlimited potential of technology and the human spirit. The debate about supply-side economics shifted concern about the redistribution of an existing set of resources in a zero-sum type of situation to expanding the size of the pie and lifting the boats of everyone, rich and poor alike, through uninterrupted economic growth. Investment, growth, creativity, and entrepreneurship were the hallmarks of the early part of the decade, which harbored an unbounded optimism in the future of America and the spirit of the American people.

It is no mystery that young people in particular warmed to this emphasis on growth and opportunity. People just starting their careers and families want to hear about opportunity and don't want to hear about limits to growth and shrinking opportunities, particularly from middle-aged people who have made their mark in life and accumulated their share of the world's goods. Limits to growth only appeal to those who already have enough wealth to live comfortably and such people can be accused of opposing further growth because it threatens their lifestyle. Thus the limits to growth movement came to be seen as something of an elitist concern and did a great deal of harm to the environmental movement in getting it labeled as antigrowth and obstructionist to those on the lower rungs of the economic ladder who wanted a better life for themselves and their families.

There was a need for a new concept to capture the concerns about resource usage raised in the limits-to-growth movement. These concerns were eventually encapsulated in the idea of *sustainable growth*, which became a much discussed concept in later decades. This concept is concerned with finding paths of social, economic, and political progress that meet the needs of the present without compromising the ability of future generations to meet their own needs and aspirations. It has an appeal to people at all levels of development as sustainability makes sense to even the most ardent advocate of continued economic growth. Such growth cannot continue if it erodes the foundations for future growth through unsustainable paths of development.

TOWARD A NEW MORAL MATRIX

Later stages of capitalistic development, which saw the secularization of the Protestant ethic as both production and consumption were taken out of a moral context and became ends in themselves, have led to questions about the sustainability of continued high levels of production and consumption as the world continues on its path of increasing economic wealth. However, any concerns about pollution and resource usage, even if couched in a more acceptable language, run headlong into cultural values related to increased consumption and immediate gratification. But questions are being raised about the feasibility and morality of a society hooked on an ever-increasing standard of living using up more and more of the world's resources and causing more and more pollution and emitting more and more greenhouse gases.

Are advanced industrial societies like the United States sustainable from an environmental point of view and are they just in relation to developing countries from a moral point of view? Do these societies need to cut back on consumption and share some of their largesse with developing nations? Do they have a moral obligation to save something for future generations? These are moral questions related to intragenerational and intergenerational equity and are critical questions that need to be raised as more and more nations around the world like China and India develop some form of market economy where economic growth is promoted. Does the earth have sufficient carrying capacity to sustain economic growth for the entire population of the world? Can everybody emulate the United States and adopt its lifestyle?

Alan Durning has written a book appropriately entitled *How Much Is Enough?* in which he argues for the creation of what he calls the culture of permanence—a society that lives within its means by drawing on the interest provided by the earth's resources rather than its principal, a society that seeks fulfillment in a web of friendship, family, and meaningful work. Yet he recognizes the difficulty of transforming consumption-oriented societies into sustainable ones and the problem that the material cravings of developing societies pose for resource usage.[29] These forces cause what he calls a conundrum that is described as follows:

> We may be, therefore, in a conundrum—a problem admitting of no satisfactory solution. Limiting the consumer life-style to those who have already attained it is not politically possible, morally defensible, or ecologically sufficient. And extending the life-style to all would simply hasten the ruin of the biosphere. The global environment cannot support the 1.1 billion of us living like American consumers, much less 5.5 billion people, or a future population of at least 8 billion. On the other hand, reducing the consumption levels of the consumer society, and tempering material aspirations elsewhere, though morally acceptable, is a quixotic proposal. It bucks the trend of centuries. Yet it may be the only option.[30]

Aside from the question as to whether all this consumption has really made people happier and more fulfilled, the environmental impacts have been severe as more and more resources have become depleted and it becomes more and more difficult to dispose of waste material. Consumer society is built on two critical assumptions: one, that the earth contains an inexhaustible supply of resources to satisfy our material needs and wants; and two, that there are bottomless sinks in which to dispose of waste material. Both of these assumptions are now in question, causing many to take a serious look at the sustainability of consumer culture into the future.

Is there, then, a need for a new kind of ethical approach that would provide a new moral matrix for production and consumption activities? While the Protestant ethic served an important function in limiting consumption to build up a productive capital base, once that base was established, people needed to consume more in order to keep the system going. Such increased consumption, however, has precipitated environmental problems related to pollution and resource usage. Perhaps there is a need for a new kind of ethic, an environmental ethic that would essentially function like the Protestant Ethic in terms of providing moral limits on consumption and production or would at least place these activities in some kind of moral framework that infuses them with a meaning beyond themselves. But any new ethic of this sort runs headlong into the ethic embedded in a materialistic conception of life wedded to the notion of progress that is part and parcel of the scientific worldview.

> The combination of independent and primary factors of progress with dependent and secondary socioethical norms prevents simultaneous and harmonious realization of norms—economic as well as ethical and legal. This combination has made it impossible for capitalism to do justice to noneconomic norms for human life. Norms or ethics and justice are allowed to play a role only after economic production has already occurred. They are permitted to make limited correction and modest alteration in the process of industrialization, but only after this process has autonomously and sovereignly chosen its path though society.[31]

Reduction of consumption in industrial societies, whether done for moral reasons or for more prudential reasons having to do with sustainable growth, can have severe repercussions. Since about two-thirds of gross national product or its equivalent in developed countries consists of consumer purchases, it seem obvious that any significant reduction of consumer expenditures will have serious impacts on employment, income, investment, and everything else tied into economic growth. Lowering consumption could be self-destructive to advanced industrial societies. The capitalistic economy is only in some kind of balance as long as economic growth persists, as long as a growing market for products exists. If economic growth declines only slightly, a threat to the internal stability of society emerges.[32] While companies talk about wanting satisfied consumers, the consumer who is satisfied is a threat to the system. According to Zygmunt Bauman, writing in *Does Ethics Have a Chance in a World of Consumers?*:

> The consuming life is not about acquiring and possessing. It is not even about getting rid of what had been acquired the day before yesterday and was proudly paraded a day later. It is, first and foremost, about *being on the move*. If Max Weber was right and the ethical principle of the producing life was (and is, whenever a life wishes to become a producing life) the delay of gratification, the ethical principle of the consuming life (if its ethics could be at all frankly articulated) would be about the *fallaciousness of resting satisfied*. The major threat to a society that announces "consumer satisfaction" to be its motive and

purpose is a satisfied consumer. To be sure, the "satisfied consumer" would be a catastrophe to herself or himself as grave and horrifying as it would be to the consumerist economy. Having nothing left to desire? Nothing to chase after? . . . those who go solely by what they need, and are activated only by the urge to satisfy those needs, are *flawed consumers* and so also *social outcasts*.[33]

While consumer society rests its case on the promise to gratify human desires like no other society in the past could do or dream of doing, the promise of satisfaction remains seductive only so long as the desire stays *ungratified*. More important, it tempts only so long as the client is not "completely satisfied"—so long as the desires that motivate the consumers to further consumerist experiments are not believed to have been truly and fully gratified . . . It is the *non*satisfaction of desires, and a firm and perpetual belief that each act of their satisfaction *leaves much to be desired and can be bettered*, that are the genuine flywheels of the consumer-targeted economy . . . If the search for fulfillment is to go on and if the new promises are to be alluring and catching, promises already made must be routinely broken and the hopes of fulfillment regularly frustrated . . . Without the repetitive frustration of desires, consumer demand could quickly run dry and the consumer-targeted economy would run out of steam.[34]

In the final analysis, the consumer culture in which we live may be unsustainable and people may have to find other sources of satisfaction and get off the endless treadmill of increased consumption. Economic values are dominant in our culture, values that can be quantified and provide the basis for decisions as to use and abuses of the environment. The economy takes precedent in our decisions and operates according to scientific economic principles devoid of any moral content. We do not have an ecological perspective that informs our decisions and guides our actions, leaving nature as something to be exploited and shaped for human purposes. The individual consumer is detached from the world and does not feel part of a larger ecological community. Nor do we have a moral perspective that places our production and consumption in a larger context that serves their natural function of enriching human existence that is consistent with the world in which we live that has both limits to economic growth and yet possibilities for human fulfillment and purpose beyond production and consumption.[35]

INSTRUMENTAL REASON

The primary roles that people play in Western culture have thus been reduced to production and consumption. These roles also involve the use of what has been called instrumental reason, which is a way of thinking that provides direction for the path that science and technology take in our society. Such an understanding of instrumental reason has to do with dominance over nature and other human beings that is the essence of management in a capitalistic society. Such reasoning is used for the purpose of increasing the profits of the organization and the economic wealth of the society. It is concerned with economic exploitation of nature and humans to attain certain materialistic ends that are believed to create a good society based on an ever-increasing supply of goods and services.

There are many different ways to think about the reasoning process humans employ, but instrumental reason, at least as defined in certain philosophical schools, is reason used for the particular end of dominating and exploiting nature and people in the interests of capitalist production and consumption.[36] People are seen as human resources that are necessary elements in the production process and are to be managed so as to contribute to the goal of profit making for capitalistic enterprises. Likewise, nature is seen as merely something that contains resources that are necessary to production so that things can be made for sale on the market. Instrumental reason is not concerned with any other meanings in life except those that are associated with production and consumption of commodities produced for sale on the market. It does not allow for self-reflection on deeper meanings of life that may come from philosophy or religion, but reduces things to matter, history to fact, and everything to a number. Commodity exchange is merely the historically developed form of instrumental rationality.

Social relations are reduced to administration and the role of a manager is to manipulate people to work towards the goals of the corporate organization. Organizations are thus totally administered and the freedom of individuals to pursue their own goals and interests is curtailed in the interests of the organization's objectives. Nature is raped for resources and used as a dumping ground for waste material. No thought is given to the ecological health of the environment or the long-term implications of this continued exploitation. The potentiality of humans and nature is thus utilized to pursue the goals of capitalism. All that matters is more and more production and consumption and the entire society is subject to the logic of the capitalistic system. Thought itself is thus turned into a thing, an instrument that is directed to the ends of capitalistic society; it is restricted to organization and administration. Reason becomes a mere instrument of an all-inclusive economic apparatus.

Manipulative intervention into natural processes replaces a passive defense against natural dangers with active control of nature. Under the imperative of self-preservation, humans place the natural environment under their conceptual and practical control. It is made into an objectified reality suited to the goals of manipulative intervention, and becomes more and more a product of human activity. We reshape nature to suit capitalistic interests, even to the extent of creating our own climate. This manipulation of nature results in the neutralization of its sensible qualities and its variety as nature becomes subject to standardization and uniformity by being developed to suit human interests. The cost is the exclusion of living nature as it is gradually despiritualized and cognitively deprived of its sensory richness and loses any sense of the sacred. Industrialization turns the natural environment into a lifeless and barren wasteland.

Labor requires a single-minded vigilance and directed energy to accomplish the goals of the organization. Only those instinctual impulses that can be channeled into instrumental performance are allowed. All the diverting, distracting, or superfluous instincts of workers must be sublimated or suppressed. In the corporation, labor is directed by a privileged class called management, which dominates the other employees and extracts a disproportionate remuneration for its services. Control is exercised through socially allocated work assignments as workers are made into objects subject to goal-oriented manipulations. This is analogous to the objectification of nature, making it subject to repeatable operations of exploitation. Money commands the obedience of the dominated subjects as submitting to corporate goals is the only way most employees can attain the resources they need to sustain themselves and their families.

This domination of a privileged class is a social extension of the human domination of nature, and the despiritualization of nature that results is analogous to the cultural impoverishment of employees, many of whom do boring and meaningless tasks in the corporation. The employee is a passive and intentionless victim of the same techniques of domination that are aimed at nature. Thus instrumental reason is used to both control and dominate the employees of the organization and to control and dominate nature, all in the interests of increasing production and consumption and growth in a capitalistic society. This use of reason has undermined moral considerations and has helped create a moral vacuum that is only too evident in the business community. It has led to an acceptance of the economic model of the firm as the ultimate justification for business activities. It also involves a certain view of government as well as culture and nature and determines the way business relates to these aspects of society.

6 Nature

The natural environment poses a profound challenge to a consumer culture which is hooked on economic growth and an ever-increasing material standard of living. The American dream is one of unlimited economic opportunity in a land of abundant resources: opportunity for people to better themselves economically limited only by their own lack of ambition or vision. It is a dream of unending economic prosperity, that every new generation should be better off than the next, that gross national or domestic product should ever increase, that we should be able to produce more cars, more houses, more consumer goods, more of everything. This is a dream that is now taking hold all over the world as countries like China and India are promoting economic growth as never before.

Environmental problems threaten to overwhelm our ability to deal with them. We seem unable to come to grips with global warming or climate change, for example, as Congress has stalled again and again in coming up with a cap-and-trade system or some other means of limiting carbon emissions. Meanwhile, the Arctic ice pack is disappearing faster than scientists had predicted and the Greenland ice sheet is melting at a faster rate than anyone expected. Weather patterns are changing all over the world as freak storms wreak their devastation on various regions and old weather related records are continually broken. Deforestation continues at an alarming rate as the rain forest is cut down or burned for various reasons that causes serious environmental problems. Fisheries are depleted in various parts of the world and are not able to recover. The list could go on and on as environmental problems continue to worsen and raise serious questions about survival of people in various parts of the world who face starvation and depletion of necessary resources.

Yet most countries around the world remain committed to economic growth as their main purpose and do everything they can to promote such growth. Countries such as China and India, with huge populations, are now trying to emulate the Western world and grow their economies as fast as possible. People in China who once used to ride bikes are now driving cars, making congestion a problem in many cities and helping China to become the world's major emitter of carbon dioxide into the atmosphere contributing to global warming. These countries cannot be blamed for improving the lot of their citizens, and yet this emphasis on economic growth puts added stress on the environment and uses up more and more natural resources. Developed countries continue to pursue economic growth as their major objective and adopt policies to promote growth, often at the expense of the environment.

Science contributes to these environmental problems as it *dehumanizes* nature by treating nature objectively in the interests of manipulating it to suit human interests. In doing so it abstracts nature from the relational context in which humans exist and flourish. It treats nature as something external to humans that can be exploited for self-interested purposes and views nature in instrumental terms as existing only to serve human needs and interests. The traditional view of humans and their relationship to nature has been dualistic: the idea that humans stand over against nature and are somehow seen apart from nature. The task of humans has been to conquer nature, to take dominion over the animals and the natural world as some religious doctrines have emphasized, to gain more and more power over nature and shape it according to our visions and our interests. This dualistic view leads to an objectification of nature and allows us to manipulate it to our advantage and exploit it for our own purposes. Such a dualism, which may go back all the way to Descartes, with his separation of mind and body, leads to a disconnect between humans and nature.

We are victimized by all the dichotomies we live with, such as mind and body and subjective and objective, which tend to separate us from the natural world on which we depend for our existence. This is a philosophical problem that is part of the scientific worldview which involves a certain way of thinking about nature that has hindered thinking of ourselves as being connected with nature. We do not think of ourselves as being embedded in nature, but tend to see nature in objective terms that is something apart from us and can be shaped to serve our interests. We are the subject that has dominion over nature and can use it for various self-interested purposes.

The idea that nature exists to serve human interests has been called an anthropomorphic view of nature. This term simply refers to the human-centered way we have traditionally approached nature. We manipulate it to serve our own visions of the good life and our own sense of progress. Nature must be "developed" to fit this vision and has no value in its natural state. It only has value as it is shaped to serve some human purpose. Resources in the ground have no utility until they are extracted and processed by some industrial system to make something useful that can be sold to consumers. Only then does nature have any use or value and become part of the system that measures economic wealth. This kind of exploitation has resulted in serious environmental problems that call for new approaches and strategies. One of these approaches is based on the idea of sustainable growth, which questions the way economic growth is being promoted around the world.

SUSTAINABLE GROWTH

Talk about limits to growth or more recently sustainable growth has raised concerns about resource availability and limits relative to the ability of the planet to provide everyone with a continually improving standard of living. There is good reason to believe that our present industrial and consumer societies are not sustainable in that they use too many virgin resources and degrade the environment in too many ways that will ultimately make the planet uninhabitable. How long can such practices continue? If people all over the world want to increase their standard of living on a par with advanced industrial societies like the United States, resources will be used even faster and environmental degradation will increase. The world simply cannot sustain such activities and aspirations of this sort because they exceed the earth's carrying capacity with respect to resources and the environment.

According to some estimates, since 1900, the number of people inhabiting the earth has multiplied more than three times, and the world economy has expanded more than twenty times during the same time period. The consumption of fossil fuels has grown by a factor of thirty, and industrial production has increased by a factor of fifty, with four-fifths of that increase occurring since 1950 alone.[1] And these figures do not even take into account the recent growth of China and India. While there have been great gains in human welfare because of these developments and the potential for future gains is even more promising, development at this pace has also produced environmental destruction on a scale never before imagined and is undermining prospects for future economic development as well as threatening the very survival of the earth's inhabitants.

Estimates made in 1990 indicated that by the year 2030, there will be approximately 10 billion people on this planet, all of whom would like to enjoy a living standard that is roughly equivalent to the advanced industrial economies. But if all these people were to consume critical natural resources such as copper, cobalt, petroleum, and nickel at current US rates, and if new resources are not discovered or substitutes developed, such living standards could be supported by existing resources for only a decade or less. On the other side of the ledger, as regards waste disposal, at current US rates 10 billion people would generate 400 billion tons of solid waste every year, which is enough to bury greater Los Angeles under 100 meters of such material.[2]

Changes are taking place in the world that have profound implications for resource usage and waste-disposal problems. The citizens of Eastern Europe that were freed from decades of communist rule have established some kind of market systems to provide more goods and services for their people. Economic growth in Russia is taking place at a faster rate than was ever possible under its former socialistic economic system, although this growth is mitigated to some extent by a declining population. Changes of a similar nature are taking place in China and India, which have enormous populations. As growth takes place in these countries and more cars are produced and power plants built, further stresses are placed on the environment. And there are many Third World nations in Africa and elsewhere who have aspirations for a better life for themselves.

More recent estimates show that consumption expenditures per person almost tripled between 1996 and 2010, resulting in increased use of fossil fuels, more mining of minerals and metals, increased deforestation, and more land used for agricultural purposes to feed an ever-growing population. An indicator called the Ecological Footprint Indicator, which shows the world's sustainable biological capacity, shows that in 2005 people were using the resources and services of 1.3 earths, meaning that we were using about a third more of the earth's capacity than was available on a sustainable basis. This kind of usage puts increasing pressure on the earth's ecosystems and disrupts these systems on which human beings and animal and plant species depend.[3]

A fivefold to tenfold increase in economic activity translates into a greatly increased burden on the ecosphere. Such an increase is not unrealistic as it represents annual growth rates of only between 3.2 and 4.7 percent, well within the aspiration levels of many countries of the world. Such growth has severe implications for investment in housing, transportation, agriculture, and industry. Energy use would have to increase by a factor of five just to bring developing countries, given their present populations, up to the levels of consumption now existing in the industrialized world. Similar increases could be projected for food, water, shelter, and other things that are essential to human existence.[4]

The question being asked ever more frequently by commissions and policymakers all over the world is whether growth on the scale projected over the next one to five decades can be managed on a basis that is sustainable both economically and ecologically. Continued growth in consumption of goods and services and the expansion and growth of a materialistic lifestyle may not be possible under conditions of sustainable growth.[5] The world is already over consuming many resources, as is evident in the depletion of fish stocks around the world, and cannot continue on the path of more and more production. Thus the challenge the environment poses to continued economic growth is an important one and whether overconsumption is a legitimate problem and changing patterns of consumption are necessary are questions that need consideration.

If we have not attained sustainability within the next forty years, say some experts, environmental deterioration and economic decline are likely to be feeding on each other, pulling us into a downward spiral of social and economic disintegration.[6] The foundations for further economic growth will be eroded and social upheaval will take place throughout the world on an unprecedented scale. But sustainable growth has implications for the distribution of economic wealth and income throughout the world and raises questions about intergenerational equity as well as equity among peoples of the world as developing nations strive to better themselves with shrinking resources.[7] Greater equity must be achieved between the industrialized world and developing countries, as the latter consume about 80 percent of the world's goods and have only one-quarter of the world's population. With three-quarters of the world's population, developing countries command less than one-quarter of the world's wealth. This imbalance is getting worse and cannot be continued if sustainable growth is to become a reality throughout the world.[8]

Many developing countries, as well as large parts of many developed countries, are resource based in the sense that their economic capital consists of stocks of environmental resources such as soil, forests, fisheries, and other such natural resources. Their continued development depends on maintaining and perhaps increasing these stocks of resources to support agriculture, fishing, and mining for local use and export purposes. But during the past several decades, the poorer countries of the developing world have experienced a massive depletion of this capital. Environmental and renewable resources are being used up faster than they can be restored or replaced, and some developing countries have depleted virtually all of their ecological capital and are on the brink of environmental bankruptcy.[9]

According to the World Commission of Environment and Development, sustainable growth is based on forms and processes of development that do not undermine the integrity of the environment on which they depend. But modern civilizations have been characterized by unsustainable development utilizing forms of decision making that do not take the future into account. They have ignored the long-term ecological costs of development and these costs are now coming due in economies all over the world. Yet many governments refuse to change their policies to correspond with an emerging reality and continue to act as if environmental conditions can be ignored and that nature will take care of itself.[10]

While governments may ignore the environmental implications of policymaking, the costs of environmental degradation cannot be wished away and are borne by the world community in the form of air, water, land, and noise pollution and resource depletion and climate change. Or these costs are transferred to future generations who are stuck with a degraded environment that will no longer support growth rates that have been attained in the past. Internalizing these costs requires some acceptable means of determining the costs of this degradation and then finding the political will to impose these costs on marketplace transactions so the cost of goods and services will reflect the environmental impacts of production and consumption activities. Environmental degradation should also be integrated into resource accounts in national economic systems so policymakers will have a more accurate picture of the way certain economic policies will affect ecological systems and stocks of resources.[11]

These concerns have profound implications for corporate activity that is based on the promotion of consumption and an ever-increasing gross national product. The corporation is the primary instrument of economic growth in industrialized societies, and one of its primary reasons for existing is producing goods and services to enhance people's material well-being. If this activity is to be curbed in the interests of conserving resources and reducing pollution, what will become of the corporation and the continued growth on which its legitimacy is predicated? What will happen to American culture, which is based on materialism and continued economic growth and development?

THE END OF NATURE

Science objectifies nature and considers it to be something apart from humans and their activities. Nature operates according to its own laws that govern its comings and goings and humans seek to understand and increase their knowledge of nature so they can manipulate it and exploit it to serve their interests. But nature is by and large left to take care of itself and humans pay minimal attention to what impacts their activities make on nature and its workings. They tend to think that nature will go its own way and continue to provide humans with a nurturing environment that will support their growth and development.

Several years ago a very thoughtful book written by Bill McKibben, entitled *The End of Nature*, provided a new way of viewing nature that has profound implications for the way we think about our relationship to the natural environment.[12] By the "end of nature" the author did not mean that nature does not matter but that nature as we have known it in the past no longer exists. Human beings have conquered nature as the entire natural world now bears the stamp of humanity and we have left our imprint on nature everywhere. We have made nature a creation of our own and have lost the "otherness" that once belonged to the natural world because it is so affected by human activities that it is more and more becoming one of our own creations. Nature is no longer the autonomous entity in which we sought refuge from human activities and where we could relate to something that was beyond our control and feel humble in its presence.

What this view suggests is that the world has crossed a threshold with respect to the environment where human activities can alter natural processes to a far greater extent than anyone could have imagined even a few decades ago. Nature has been subjugated and reconfigured according to human needs and desires as science and technology have given us the ability to alter the natural environment to suit our values and objectives. We can reshape the landscape to make it suitable for a housing development, tear apart whole mountains for the ore or coal they contain, alter the course of rivers and the amount of water that flows through them, build huge indoor malls with a controlled climate, create cities with millions of people in the middle of a desert where most everything to sustain life has to be imported, and are even altering the world's climate with our industrial activities.

This ability gives us a sense of power to manipulate the environment to serve human purposes better, but with it comes a sense of responsibility to deal with the environment in ways that do not destroy the very foundation of our existence. We simply cannot proceed as we have in the past to exploit nature and not worry about the environmental consequences of our activities. Nature can no longer take care of itself and we have to take responsibility for our activities and their impact on nature. Thus far we are not doing a very good job in this regard. Daily news reports give ample evidence of collapsing fisheries, eroding soils, deteriorating rangelands, expanding deserts, disappearing wetlands, falling water tables, more destructive storms, melting glaciers, rising sea levels, and dying coral reefs. The world is said to be losing its biological diversity as plant and animal species are being destroyed by human encroachment on their habitats. Deforestation continues and shows no sign of slowing as demand mounts for wood and wood products. The earth continues to get hotter and more and more wildfires are one result. And the population keeps on growing and now stands at six billion and counting.

Taking responsibility for nature involves making conscious and responsible value judgments regarding the kind of planet we want. These value judgments include the answer to such questions as how much species diversity should be maintained. How much of nature should be preserved and placed off limits to industrial development? What natural resources do we wish to leave for our children? How much climate change is acceptable? Does population growth need to be limited in some fashion? Science can tell us something about the broad patterns of global transformation taking place, but value questions about the pace and directions of those patterns have to be answered through political and economic systems.

It is not a matter of saving planet earth, as it is often put in the literature. The planet will be here for millions if not billions of years and will have some kind of a natural environment. The real question is whether that environment is such that it can continue to sustain human life and provide an enriching experience for human existence. Creating such an environment involves a new approach that emphasizes responsibility and community; taking responsibility for enhancing the environment to promote a human community that can thrive and experience continued enrichment of its existence. A continued emphasis on the right to use one's property in one's own individual interests will not get us where we need to go and will only continue down the path of self-destructiveness.

It seems that the consumer culture that has emerged over the past several decades cannot continue on its current path. Yet other countries are tying to emulate the United States and develop consumer cultures of their own, counties like China and India, which have huge populations. The implications that economic growth in these countries has for continued pollution and resource usage is profound, making the need for some kind of ethic to direct these activities along sustainable pathways critical.. Consumer culture is built on two assumptions: (1) that the world contains an inexhaustible supply of raw materials and (2) that there bottomless sinks in which to continue to dispose of waste material. Both of these assumptions have been questioned in the past several decades, causing many to take a look at the sustainability of consumer culture into the future. These concerns have profound implications for corporate activity that is based on the never-ending quest for profits through the promotion of consumption and an ever-increasing material standard of living throughout the world.

Concerns for the environment as embodied in sustainable growth and other such concepts provide ample evidence for the emergence of an environmental ethic. Many are beginning to recognize that nature provides an enriching experience in itself and that harming nature is ultimately destructive of the search for meaningfulness and self-fulfillment. Environmental concerns about pollution, climate change, resource usage, and the enjoyment of nature obviously run headlong into cultural values related to increased production and consumption and immediate gratification. Production, consumption, and continued economic growth, with their own self-justifying ends, seem on a collision path with a concern for the environment and the self-fulfillment it provides.

Questions are being asked as to whether advanced industrial societies like the United States are sustainable from an environmental point of view and whether they are just in relation to the rest of the world from a moral point of view. Questions are also being raised about the feasibility and morality of a society hooked on an ever-increasing standard of living which uses up more and more of the world's resources and causes more and more pollution of the environment. Do the United States and other advanced industrial societies need to cut back on consumption and share some of their largesse with developing nations? Do developed societies need to save something for future generations if they take the concept of sustainability seriously?

These are moral questions related to intragenerational and intergenerational equity. These are critical questions that need to be raised as more and more nations around the world develop some form of market economies and promote economic growth as the way to modernize their societies. Does the earth have sufficient carrying capacity to sustain such economic growth for the entire population of the world, which is also increasing? Is there a need for some new kind of ethic that would essentially function as the work ethic by providing moral limits on consumption and directing production into less environmentally harmful paths?

ENVIRONMENTAL ETHICS

What some see as necessary to adequately account for the natural environment in our decision making is the development of an environmental ethic as a comprehensive ethic that can place production and consumption activities in a moral context. An environmental ethic of some kind is the best candidate for a comprehensive ethic, it is believed, because of the persistence and pervasiveness of environmental problems. Such an ethic is necessary to guide the direction of production and consumption in a manner which nourishes the desire of humans for opportunities to live a meaningful life and for self-development that enriches their existence. This entails the growth and flourishing of the multiple environments in which they are embedded and that contribute to the fullness of human existence in all its richness and complexity. An answer to environmental problems is not to be found in a forced choice between artificially created alternatives such as the conflict between economics and the environment. These alternatives distort the nature of the reality they must ultimately serve, that of enriching the life of humans in all the multiple dimensions in which they work out a meaningful and fulfilling life for themselves.

The theories that are part of business ethics such as utilitarianism and the like are not congenial to the needs of an environmental ethic because they have no philosophical structure to provide an inherent relatedness of the individual and the broader natural environment. For all of these positions, the source of ethical action lies either in the application of abstract rules to cases or in the inculcation of tradition. Neither approach incorporates the type of attunement to nature that is required for an environmental consciousness. They are by and large anthropocentric in nature and view the environment as something separate or external to humans. They reflect the individualism and dualism of the modern worldview where the environment has merely instrumental value. Thus in the environmental literature one finds little application of these theories to the natural environment.

This problem has given rise to a separate area of ethics called environmental ethics, which has developed its own approaches and theories. One such approach is called *moral extensionism and eligibility*, which has to do with the extension of rights to the natural world. Rights have been extended to blacks and other minorities in civil rights legislation, rights given to women under equal rights legislation, rights extended to workers regarding safety and health in the workplace, and rights provided to consumers for safe products and other aspects of the marketplace. The question is whether rights can also be extended to the natural world or at least some aspects of it and whether this approach can help deal with environmental problems in an effective manner. Where does the ethical cutoff fall with regard to moral eligibility? What aspects of nature can be justifiably brought into the moral realm in this manner?

Many philosophers extend such rights only to animals on the grounds that animals are sentient beings in that they are able to suffer and feel pain. But more radical thinkers widen the circle to include all natural organisms, including plants. Still others see no reason to draw a moral boundary at the edge of organic life and argue for ethical consideration for rocks, soil, water, air, and biophysical processes that constitute ecosystems. Some are even led to the conclusion that even the universe has rights superior to those of its most precocious life-form.[13]

Peter Singer thinks that believing the effects of our actions on nonhuman animals have no moral significance is arbitrary and morally indefensible. He makes an analogy between the way we treat animals with the way we used to treat black slaves. The white slave owners limited their moral concern to the white race and did not regard the suffering of a black slave as having the same moral significance as the suffering of a white person. Thus the black could be treated inhumanly with no moral compulsion. This way of thinking is called racism but we could just as well substitute the word *speciesism* with regard to the manner in which animals are treated. The logic of racism and the logic of speciesism are the same according to Singer.[14]

Just as our concern about equal treatment of blacks through legislation and regulation moved us to a different level of moral consciousness, so will treating animals as beings who have interests and can suffer and therefore deserve moral consideration move us to a different level of moral consciousness. Moving to this level with regard to animals may involve stopping certain practices such as using animals for testing purposes and subjecting them to slow and agonizing deaths. It may also involve stopping the practice of raising animals in crowded conditions solely for the purpose of human consumption. The decisions to avoid speciesism of this kind will be difficult, but no more difficult, thinks Singer, than it would have been for a white Southerner to go against the traditions of society and free his slaves.[15]

The creatures in Singer's moral community have to possess nervous systems of sufficient sophistication to feel pain, that is, they have to be sentient beings. Ethics ends at the boundary of sentience for Singer. A tree or a mountain of a rock being kicked does not feel anything and therefore does not possess any interests or rights. Since they cannot be harmed by human action, they have no place in ethical discourse. There is nothing we can do that matters to them and thus they are not deserving of moral consideration.[16]

Other philosophers, such as Joel Feinberg, also limit their moral concerns to animals. Feinberg excluded plants from the rights community on the grounds that they had insufficient "cognitive equipment" to be aware of their wants, needs, and interests. He also denied rights to incurable "human vegetables," and using the same logic disqualified certain species from moral consideration. Protection of rare and endangered species became protection of humans to enjoy and benefit from them. Even less deserving of rights were mere things.[17] While many philosophers found these requirements too limiting, Singer and Feinberg did help to liberate moral philosophy from its fixation on human beings.

Scholars such as Christopher Stone pushed the boundaries of moral eligibility further to include other aspects of the natural world. Stone saw no logical or legal reason to draw any ethical boundaries whatsoever. Why should the moral community end with humans or even animals? While this idea may sound absurd to many people, so did the extension of certain rights to women and blacks at one point in our history. The extension of rights in this manner, according to Stone, would help environmentalists better protect the environment and also reflects the view that nature needs to be preserved for its own sake and not just for the interests of human beings.[18]

Stone's experience with the Mineral King case in the late 1960s stimulated him to write his landmark essay which made a case for the extension of moral concern to the plant community. Mineral King was a beautiful valley in the Southern Sierras that was the subject of a proposal by Walt Disney Enterprises for the development of a massive ski resort. The Sierra Club saw itself as a long-time guardian of this region and tried to stop the development. But the U.S. Court of Appeals of California ruled that the club was not itself injured and thus had no standing or legal reason to sue against the development. But something was going to be injured, Stone reasoned, and the courts should be receptive to its need for protection. Thus he argued in his essay that society should give legal rights to forests, oceans, rivers, and other natural objects in the environment, and indeed, to the natural environment as a whole.[19]

The attempt to extend rights in this manner represents an effort to build a wider moral community that includes all or parts of the natural world and to overcome the anthropocentrism which separate humans from nature. But while moral extensionism and eligibility in environmental ethics attempts to bring animals and even other aspects of nature into the moral community by extending rights to them, these arguments are subject to strong theoretical attack. Rights are bestowed on animals and other aspects of nature by humans, thereby making the moral standing of nonhuman aspects of nature dependent on humans. Animals cannot pursue their own interests through the courts but need someone to take up their cause for them. While rights theory in environmental ethics thus tries to overcome traditional limitations on rights by extending them to animals and other aspects of nature, it is caught up in the theoretical web of anthropocentrism and atomic individualism, which is found in the tradition of rights theory.

Partly as a result of the problems with moral extensionism and eligibility, a *biocentric ethics* or *deep ecology* developed as an alternative approach to the environment. Kenneth Goodpaster argued that the extension of rights beyond certain limits is not necessarily the best way to deal with moral growth and social change with respect to the environment. The last thing we need, he states, is a liberation movement with respect to trees, animals, rivers, and other objects in nature. The mere enlargement of the class of morally considerable beings is an inadequate substitute for a genuine environmental ethic. The extension of rights to natural objects does not deal with deeper philosophical questions about human interests and environmental concerns. Moral consideration should be extended to systems as well as individuals. Societies need to be understood in an ecological context and it is this larger whole which is the bearer of value. An environmental ethic, while paying its respects to individualism and humanism, must break free of them and deal with the way the universe is operating.[20]

John Rodman protests the whole notion of extending human-type rights to nonhumans because this action categorizes them as "inferior human beings" and "legal incompetents" who need human guardianship. This was the same kind of mistake that some white liberals made in the 1960s with regard to blacks. Instead, we should respect animals and everything else in nature "for having their own existence, their own character and potentialities, their own forms of excellence, their own integrity, their own grandeur." Instead of giving nature rights or legal standing within the present political and economic order, Rodman urged environmentalists to become more radical and change the order. All forms of domestication must end along with the entire institutional framework associated with owning land and using it in one's own interests.[21]

J. Baird Callicott, an admirer of Aldo Leopold's land ethic, declared that the animal liberation movement was not even allied with environmental ethics because it emphasized the rights of individual organisms. The land ethic, on the other hand, was holistic and has as its highest objective the good of the community as a whole. The animal-rights advocates simply added individual animals to the category of rights holders, whereas "ethical holism" calculated right and wrong in reference not to individuals but to the whole biotic community. The whole, in other words, carried more ethical weight than any of its component parts. Oceans and lakes, mountains, forests, and wetlands are assigned a greater value than individual animals that might happen to reside there.[22]

Thus deep ecology leads to a devaluation of individual life relative to the integrity, diversity, and continuation of the ecosystem as a whole. This perspective on environmental ethics created entirely new definitions of what liberty and justice mean on planet earth and involved an evolution of ethics to be ever more inclusive. This approach recognized that there can be no individual welfare or liberty apart from the ecological matrix in which individual life exists. "A biocentric ethical philosophy could be interpreted as extending the esteem in which individual lives were traditionally held to the biophysical matrix that created and sustained those lives."[23]

This approach holds that some natural objects and ecosystems have intrinsic value and are morally considered in their own right apart from human interests. Nature has value in and of itself apart from human concerns. This ethic respects each life-form and sees it as part of a larger whole. All life is sacred and we must not be careless about species that are irreplaceable. Particular individuals come and go but nature continues indefinitely, and humans must come to understand their place in nature. Each life-form is constrained to flourish in a larger community according to this view, and moral concern for the whole biological community is the only kind of an environmental ethics that makes sense and preserves the integrity of the entire ecosystem.[24]

Nature itself is a source of values, it is argued, including the value we have as humans, since we are a part of nature. The concept of value, according to this position, includes far more than a simplistic human-interest satisfaction. Value is a multifaceted idea with structures that are rooted in natural sources.[25] Value is not just a human product. When humans recognize values outside of themselves, this does not result in a dehumanizing of the self or a reversion to beastly levels of existence. On the contrary, it is argued, human consciousness is increased when we praise and respect the values found in the natural world and this recognition results in a further spiritualizing of humans.[26] Thus this school of thought holds that there are natural values that are intrinsic to the natural object itself apart from humans and their particular valuing activities. Values are found in nature as well as humans. Humans do not simply bestow value on nature; nature also conveys value to humans.[27]

The world of nature is not to be defined in terms of commodities that are capable of producing wealth for humans who manage them in their own interests. All things in the biosphere are believed to have an equal right to live and reach their own individual forms of self-realization. Instead of a hierarchical ordering of entities in descending order from God through humans to animals, plants, and rocks, where the lower creatures are under the higher ones and are ruled by them, nature is seen as a web of interactive and interdependent life that is ruled by its own natural processes. These processes must be understood if are to work in harmony with nature and preserve the conditions for our own continued existence.[28]

Deep ecology thus accords nature ethical status that is at least equal to that of human beings. From the perspective of the ecosystem, the difference is between thinking that people have a right to a healthy ecosystem and thinking that the ecosystem itself possesses intrinsic or inherent value.[29] Deep ecologists argue for a biocentric perspective and a holistic environmental ethic regarding nature. Human beings are to step back into the natural community as a member and not the master. The philosophy of conservation for Holmes Ralston was comparable to arguing for better care for slaves on plantations. The whole system was unethical, not just how people operated within the system. In Ralston's view, nothing matters except the liberation of nature from the system of human dominance and exploitation. This process involves a reconstruction of the entire human relationship with the natural world.[30]

Both of these approaches are useful in understanding the relationship between humans and nature, but these approaches treat the environment differently and make different assumptions about the locus of moral consideration. Moral extensionism and eligibility use the vehicle of rights to extent moral concern to various aspects of nature, but these rights are bestowed by humans and are not intrinsic to nature itself. Deep ecology assumes nature already has intrinsic value that needs to be recognized by liberating nature from the system in which it is currently trapped. By recognizing this intrinsic value of nature, the last remnants of anthropocentrism, still operative in moral extensionism and eligibility, are supposedly excised. Further, while moral extensionism and eligibility stress the individual to the exclusion of the whole, deep ecology subordinates the individual to the good of the whole.

The biological egalitarianism of deep ecology provides no means to make distinctions between which parts of nature to preserve and which to use for the promotion of human welfare. The debate over systems versus individuals is still rooted in atomic individualism and deep ecology and does not provide an adequate framework for understanding the relation of humans and nature in all its richness. Each of these alternatives may provide a sense of moral concern for nature but neither offers a useful framework for understanding the moral dimensions of economic activity in relation to the natural environment. They do not provide an adequate reconceptualizing of the relationship of humans and nature that can challenge the scientific worldview, which objectifies nature and seeks to manipulate it to serve human interests.

Part II

Toward a New
Understanding of Science

7 The Pragmatic View of Science and Its Characteristics

There is no doubt that science has had an enormous impact on modern societies and that the technological applications of scientific discoveries have made our lives better. Science has enabled us to understand more and more aspects of our world and given us the ability to manipulate the world to deal with problems with which we are faced. We by and large turn to science for answers to questions about our natural world and increasingly for answers to questions about human behavior. While there are still elements of mythology operative in many cultures, including our own, science has largely replaced the mythological worldview and influences how we think about all aspects of our world, as the previous chapters attempted to illustrate. Science is by and large accepted as the way to get at the truth about our world through its rigorous methodologies and self-correcting process of inquiry.

PROBLEMS WITH MODERN SCIENCE

The major problem of science in our contemporary world is when science becomes a metaphysical dogmatism that makes claims about absolute and complete knowledge and is considered to be the only source of true knowledge of the world in which we live and the only way to get in touch with the most basic reality about this world. Such dogmatism holds that our lived experience in the world is of little or no value because what we observe in the world during the course of our daily lives is mere appearance. While we may observe color and smell something and sense how something feels to the touch, these are only appearances. The true reality behind these appearances is the waves and particles that make up these sensory illusions. While we may observe human behavior with its moods and emotions, these are only appearances and the realities behind these observations are the chemicals and neurons that go to make up our bodies and determine our behavior. It is when science becomes dogmatic and makes such metaphysical claims that it becomes a problem in contemporary society and is subject to philosophical inquiry as to whether such claims are valid. As stated by Maurice Merleau-Ponty in *The World of Perception*:

> The question which modern philosophy asks in relation to science is not intended to contest its right to exist or to close off any particular avenue to its inquires. Rather, the question is whether science does, or ever could, present us with a picture of the world which is complete, self-sufficient and somehow closed in upon itself, such that there could be no longer any meaningful questions outside this picture. It is not a matter of denying or limiting the extent of scientific knowledge, but rather of establishing whether it is entitled to deny or rule out as illusory all forms of inquiry that do not start out from measurements and comparisons and, by connecting particular causes with particular consequences, end up with laws such as those of classical physics.[1]

In the classical scientific worldview, our ordinary lived experience becomes disconnected from knowledge and is considered to be purely subjective in nature. Real knowledge is the building up of a storehouse of so-called objective facts gleaned from scientific studies and the only accepted approach to reality is a scientific one based upon a spectator theory of knowledge where the researcher is only an observer of nature. We can't learn anything from our lived experience because it cannot be quantified and studied scientifically and is, therefore, useless for making predictions about future behavior or for learning anything significant about the world in which we live and move and have our being.

Science relegates ordinary experience to the subjective realm where it can be ignored as having no relevance to our knowledge of the world. Yet the knowledge that most people have about the world comes through this lived experience. This experience teaches us things about the world in which we live and this knowledge helps us navigate our way through life's trials and tribulations. For most people, this knowledge is just as important as scientific knowledge is to the scientist. Science can be considered to be one type of experience that gives us a certain kind of knowledge. Indeed, experience is the foundation for all scientific activity. But science is by no means the whole story about nature and human behavior even though it may have a privileged position with respect to knowledge. It all depends, as stated by John Dewey, on what kind of knowledge is relevant to the task at hand.

> Thus "science," meaning physical knowledge, became a kind of sanctuary. A religious atmosphere, not to say an idolatrous one, was created. "Science" was set apart; its findings were supposed to have a privileged relation to the real. In fact, the painter may know colors as well as the physicist; the poet may know stars, rain and clouds as well as the meteorologist; the statesman, educator and dramatist may know human nature as truly as the professional psychologist; the farmer may

know soils and plants as truly as the botanist and mineralogist. For the criterion of knowledge lies in the method used to secure consequences and not in metaphysical conceptions of the nature of the real.[2]

Thus it is not going to help the painter do a better job if he knows something about physics and how it breaks down color into its component parts. This knowledge is not relevant to the job he or she is trying to accomplish and the consequences that are trying to be attained, such as creating a pleasing effect in a particular room by choosing certain colors that will create this outcome. The same is true for the poet, the educator, or the farmer. What knowledge is important to them depends on the consequences they are trying to bring about. They are not interested in metaphysical claims about what is really real; what is real to them is what works to bring about the consequences they desire. They are interested in certain qualities of the things that they are dealing with that will help them to attain their goals and objectives. These qualities are as real to them as the qualities that are of interest to scientists even though scientists might consider them to be secondary qualities that are subjective in nature.

One of the most persistent problems created by modern science is what to do with qualities like color, sound, smell, taste, and the like, qualities that we encounter every day in ordinary experience. Scientific definitions and descriptions left no room for qualities because it was believed that the business of knowledge is to penetrate into the inner being of objects. Qualities were thus held to be subjective, existing only in the consciousness of individuals, and had no objective reality. However, the discovery that absolute space and time do not exist but are relative and relational showed that the primary qualities of solidity, mass, size, etc., are no more inherent properties of scientific objects than the secondary qualities of odors, sounds, and colors. Both are relational and changing.[3] As Steven Shapin writes:

> Primary qualities were those that really belonged to the object in itself: its parts' shape, size, and motion. They were called primary (or sometimes "absolute") because no object, or its constituents, could be described without them. Secondary qualities—redness, sweetness, warmth, and so on—were derived from the state of an object's primary qualities. The primary caused (and was held to explain) the secondary . . . Only some of the ideas of our bodies might now be treated as objective—that is, corresponding to the nature of things themselves— and these would include our ideas of bodies as having certain shapes, sizes, and motions. However, other experiences and ideas would now have to be regarded as subjective—the result of how our sensory apparatus actively processes impressions deriving from the real, primary realm. Yet the rose of common experience is experienced not as an ordered aggregate of qualities but as itself: red, roughly circular, sweet smelling, three inches across, etc. The distinction between primary and

secondary qualities, just like the Copernican view of the world, drove a wedge between the domain of philosophical legitimacy and that of common sense. Micromechanical reality took precedence over common experience, and subjective experience was severed from accounts of what objectively existed. Our actual sensory experience, we were instructed, offered no reliable guide to how the world really was.[4]

This distinction took human experience of secondary qualities out of the realm of the real, and primary and ordinary human experience was not seen as a valid approach to reality. What was really real was what science discovered through its methods of inquiry, which were believed to be free of any human or subjective influence and only thus could objective truth be ascertained. Ordinary human experience was thus considered to be a lower form of knowledge, or not knowledge at all, but merely subjective impressions that had no validity as far as real knowledge of the world was concerned. The split between primary and secondary qualities mirrors the split between the objective and subjective world, with the former treated as having an independent existence that could only be discovered through the methods of science and the latter considered to be conditional and dependent on the observer.

The difference between a scientific approach to reality and that of ordinary experience is to some extent a difference between theories of knowledge. Experiential knowledge is connected to the everyday affairs of humans and serves the purposes of the ordinary individual who is not interested in a specialized intellectual pursuit, but instead wants some kind of working connection with his or her immediate environment. This kind of knowledge is depreciated, if not despised, according to Dewey, and is considered to be purely utilitarian, lacking in any scientific significance. Rational knowledge, on the other hand, is considered to be something that touches reality in an ultimate and intellectual fashion to terminate in theoretical insight into the workings of nature and not debased by application in behavior. Reason used in this manner is concerned with general principles and universals which are above the welter of the concrete details involved with living in the world.[5]

Science gets hold of nature through a certain kind of method that involves reductionism and quantification along with the other characteristics mentioned in an earlier chapter. But other experiences with nature may be equally important in certain circumstances to understand what the world is about and dealing with it in an appropriate manner. Despite its enormous success in the contemporary world, science does have limits in its ability to grasp and understand nature. It only understands that part of nature that can be fit into a scientific framework. What does not fit is left out of consideration as far as real knowledge is concerned. But in doing so science leaves behind a great deal of the richness that exists in nature and our experience with it and does not deal with any moral considerations regarding our responsibility to each other and for the world in which we live.

The scientific approach to nature splits it apart with its reductionistic method and its need to create discretes that can be measured and quantified so that nature can be manipulated. The problems that such a worldview poses for our understanding of the world in which we live can only be dealt with by a new philosophy that undercuts the dichotomies that science creates and presents alternative characteristics of science that lead to a different understanding of what science is doing. These problems cannot be addressed by the sciences themselves because every science is hopelessly trapped in its own worldview. They cannot be dealt with by a theory of everything that attempts to put the parts that science has created back together in some kind of overarching view that unifies the parts because the whole is more than the sum of the parts.[6] They cannot be solved by trying to find the basic building blocks of the universe because such a search assumes that reality is linear the same as did the medieval theologians who argued for the existence of God as first cause of everything.

What seems to be needed is some kind of a philosophy that is not based on the traditional reductionistic and atomistic assumptions of science but instead is a holistic philosophy that is relational in nature so as to capture relations between things in a nonmechanistic manner. This philosophy must have a language structure that can get at a holistic relational view of nature and express it in a way that can be grasped by people rooted in atomic individualism. It must present a new way of looking at the world that is different from the scientific worldview and yet does not reject the knowledge that has been discovered by the scientific approach. It must treat ordinary experience as a form of knowledge that is useful for certain purposes. It must also bring the moral dimension into focus and show how morality is an essential part of all human experience and cannot be compartmentalized into mere subjective experience that has no objective reality and therefore no validity.

PRAGMATISM AND SCIENCE

Classical American pragmatism is a uniquely American philosophy that attempts to do these things. It is not claimed that this philosophy is *the* answer to the problems of science but only that it offers a unique and different way of looking at science and what it is doing. It overcomes many of the self-defeating dichotomies that science has created and tries to preserve the unity that exists prior to any attempt by science to reduce the world to manageable categories that can be investigated by the scientific method. While it has some similarities to other philosophical movements such as existentialism and phenomenology, it is a more robust and comprehensive philosophy that encompasses the essential ideas of these philosophies and 'goes beyond them to open up new avenues of thinking.[7]

Pragmatism as a philosophical movement must not be confused with the popular use of the term to refer to the sort of practical approach to life's problems that is seen to be a critical part of the American character. Pragmatism as used here has nothing to do with this "pragmatic" approach that one often encounters in this country. The development of pragmatism as a distinctive philosophy represents a historical period in American philosophy that spans the writings of pragmatism's five major contributors: Charles Peirce, William James, John Dewey, C. I. Lewis, and George Herbert Mead. It is these philosophers who created what is called classical American pragmatism.

At the heart of American pragmatism is a philosophic spirit, a philosophic pulse, enlivening a unique philosophic vision which, though brought to life in a particular period through diverse specific doctrines, is yet not confined within the limits of that period or those specific doctrines. Statements made about American pragmatism in these pages may not always be found in the writings of the classical American pragmatists in the precise form in which they are stated, though they are inspired by what is in these writings and are intended to capture and further the spirit of the pragmatic approach. For this approach is more than just an interesting intellectual exercise, but has vital importance for understanding ourselves and the world in which we live and offers guidance in our choices for the future we are creating.[8]

Classical American pragmatism offers a way of understanding science and the scientific worldview that undercuts the fact-value distinction that poses a problem for ethics and the traditional dichotomies between subjective and objective and absolute and relative, dichotomies that reappear again and again in discussions of science and philosophy and appear to be unresolvable. It involves a different approach to understanding what science is doing and what it means to "think scientifically." While pragmatism embraces science and focuses on the scientific method, it rejects scientific dogmatism and the claim that science provides the only way to get at the truth or what is real about our world.

The philosophy of pragmatism arose in part as a reaction to the modern worldview regarding the nature of science and the scientific object. Such an approach, based largely on the presuppositions of a spectator theory of knowledge, led to the view that scientific knowledge provided the literal description of objective fact and excluded our lived qualitative experience as providing access to the natural universe. This worldview resulted in a quantitatively characterized universe and the atomicity of discrete individual units which are related to each other through mechanistic laws or some mechanistic process. This, in turn, led to the alienation of humans from nature and a radical dehumanizing of nature. Nature as objectified justified nature as an object of value-free human manipulation.[9]

The human being was saved from being reduced to an atomistic object by being truncated into a dualism of mind and matter. The human body was a part of this atomistic and mechanistic nature but mind was considered to be "outside" of nature and beyond the realm of scientific study. Such a view, however, was not amenable to the emerging sciences of human behavior, and eventually the human being as a whole, including mind, became understood as part of this view of nature. As a result, humans, like atoms, were understood in terms of isolated, discrete entities which interact with each other through mechanistic relationships. Humans and their behavior were "reduced" to the mechanistic atomism of nature as characterized by Newtonian physics. The social and behavioral sciences as they developed thus became reductionistic in nature and shared these features of the physical sciences.[10]

A deep-seated philosophical tendency that is completely rejected by pragmatism is the acceptance of this framework of Cartesian dualism. Humans are within nature, not outside of it, and inexplicably linked to nature. However, they are not reducible to nature and their behavior cannot be solely understood in a quantitative and atomistic manner that is no longer human but mechanistic and deterministic. The pragmatic approach is naturalistic in that humans are within nature, but nature is not the atomistic and mechanistic universe of the traditional scientific worldview. What is involved is a more holistic understanding of nature where humans are an essential part of the naturalistic process and cannot be separated or abstracted out of this process. As Larry Hickman, a Dewey scholar writes:

> For the bulk of philosophy in its modern period, nature was thought to be a vast machine. Living in the shadow of Darwin as he did, Dewey rejected the metaphor of the machine and replaced it with the organism. But even to those who have transcended the metaphor of world-as-machine there is still the fact of machine and the problem of how to relate to them. A machine can be contemplated as something finished and its workings discovered and admired. Further, it can be examined as something complete but in need of occasional repair. Or it can be treated as something ongoing, unstable, and provisional—as a tool to be used for enlarging transactions of self and society with environing conditions. It was Dewey's contention that the discussions of the nature of the world-as-machine in the seventeenth and eighteenth centuries were primarily focused on the first two of these attitudes. Of course each of these three possibilities involves some level of interaction with nature. But it is only with the third that there comes to be a genuine transaction with nature, awareness of such transaction, and inclusion of that awareness with the metatheories of science.[11]

Pragmatism is concerned with a philosophy of experience in attempting to broaden our conception of knowledge to include ordinary lived experience.

Such experiential knowledge is practical rather than abstract; it does not deal with universal abstract laws and theories even though these may underlie such experience. These laws and theories are implicit rather than explicit and they are not necessarily available or relevant to practitioners. Ordinary experience is specialized and related to a particular time and place. It is contextual and exists for a particular purpose. It cannot be universalized to all time and places or generalized beyond the particular context in which the experience takes place.[12]

Abstractions, according to pragmatism, do not belong to a metaphysical or ontological order that is superior to concrete experience. This view of experience goes against a long tradition of Western philosophy that began with Plato, who treated abstractions as metaphysical entities. For Dewey, abstractions are not an end in themselves but instead are tools for developing new meanings that can then be related to concrete experience. Abstraction is always involved in inquiry, as hypotheses are developed to guide inquiry. Experimentation maintains the relationship between the abstract and concrete, as it is through experimentation that the abstract is determined to have succeeded or failed and proves to be useful or not in the course of ongoing concrete human experience.[13]

Experience must be free from constraints such as norms, ideals, theologies, prejudices, and other constraints that are used to regulate experience from "outside" of the experience itself, and must be allowed to develop on its own account. Experience, then, in the pragmatic sense, does not have to conform to supernatural, ideological, or transcendental ideals or norms. Experience itself is capable of generating the norms and ideals that allow that experience to grow and develop.[14] Experience is not to be shaped and interpreted by anything outside experience itself, as experience must be allowed to develop as it will and allowed to follow its own internal norms and ideals.

Pragmatism questions virtually all the assumptions governing what might be called the "mainstream" philosophical tradition and the kinds of alternatives to which they give rise. It offers novel solutions to the assumptions, alternatives, dilemmas, and impasses this tradition has reached. These solutions cannot be understood as an eclectic synthesizing of traditional alternatives, but must be seen as an entirely new approach to philosophical problems. As Mead well warns in a statement which is echoed in various ways throughout the writings of the classical American pragmatists, "There is an old quarrel between rationalism and empiricism which can never be healed as long as either sets out to tell the whole story of reality. Nor is it possible to divide the narrative between them."[15] What is needed is an entirely new approach that avoids these impasses.

The remainder of this book will utilize the vision offered by classical American pragmatism as a conceptual framework for rethinking science and the issues raised by the scientific worldview in relation to the areas of American life discussed in the first section of the book. These chapters will trace the way the paradigmatic novelty of pragmatism weaves it way through fundamental issues facing American society, undercutting old alternatives and offering constructive new ways of thinking about these issues and advancing beyond traditional alternatives. Such a vision can best be brought to light not through the doctrines of any one of the pragmatists but through the collective corpus of their writings. In what follows, then, the text will roam freely through this collective corpus to clarify and make use of its common conceptual framework.[16]

PRAGMATISM AND THE SCIENTIFIC METHOD

The language of science is quantitative as even the social sciences such as economics and political science have become more quantitative in recent decades. However, what unifies the sciences is not a reduction of their content to a quantitative calculative language and mathematical laws which underlie the subject area they are trying to understand. From the perspective of pragmatism, what unifies the sciences is the method by which they gain an understanding of the subject matter with which each science is concerned. The scientific method is practiced by the scientist no matter what his or her field of endeavor. It is what the scientist does that is the focus of attention in pragmatism, not what the scientist finds as a result of his or her activities.

While there is a great deal of debate about what exactly constitutes scientific method and most would probably agree that there is no one method that can be identified as "the" scientific method, pragmatism nevertheless holds that it is possible to identify a general method of inquiry that can be termed "scientific." This method involves repeatability, falsifiability, transparency, and objectivity. This general method is different from methods of authority or a priori reasoning and is a self-correcting process. This method of inquiry rejects the notion of "absolute" and "timeless" truths, and treats ideals and hypotheses as tools that may be altered when confronted with concrete experience.[17] Thinking and beliefs should be experimental, not absolutistic.

A proper understanding of scientific method shows that the nature into which the human organism is placed contains the qualitative fullness revealed in lived experience and that a full grasp of nature is not a mere passive assimilation of data to fit a preconceived theory but is rather a creative activity within nature. The human being is embedded within nature and neither human activity nor human knowledge can be separated from the fact that human beings are natural organisms dependent upon a natural environment. The human organism and the nature within which it is located are both rich with the qualities, values, and meanings of our everyday experience.[18]

While pragmatism is concerned with scientific method as a particular kind of human activity, this does not mean that it ignores the findings of science and their import for human existence. Pragmatism pays careful attention to these findings and is influenced in its philosophical claims by the findings of the various sciences. However, pragmatism's concern with scientific method is one thing and its attention to the findings of the various sciences achieved by the general method of science is something quite different. These two realms should not be confused as it is the method of science which provides the key to pragmatism. What, then, does a pragmatist find when examining scientific methodology and focusing on the lived experience of scientists rather than on the objectivities they present as their findings?

Looking at the very first stage of scientific inquiry, pragmatism holds that such inquiry requires human creativity.[19] Scientists are not mere passive spectators gathering brute data about the world but rather bring creative theories to the data which enter into the character and organization of the data which are gathered. The creation of theories goes beyond what is directly observed and without such meaning structures there is no scientific world and there are no scientific objects. This creativity implies a radical rejection of the passive spectator view of knowledge and involves the introduction of an active agent who through meanings helps structure the objects of knowledge and thus cannot be separated from the world the agent is trying to understand. Both scientific perception and the context within which it occurs are shot through with an interactional unity between knower and that which he or she is attempting to know though scientific research.[20]

Dewey illustrates this creativity by discussing the significance of Heisenberg's principle of indeterminacy. As he states, "What is known is seen to be a product in which the act of observation plays a necessary role. Knowing is seen to be a participant in what is finally known."[21] Neither the position nor the velocity of the electron may be fixed and depends on the context in which research is conducted. Both perception of what is there and the meaningful context within which it occurs are shot through with the interactional unity between knower and known, and how the electron or any other particle is seen depends upon the goal-driven activity of the scientist who utilizes one frame of reference rather than another.

Scientific creativity arises out of ordinary experience and refers back to this everyday ordinary "lived" experience. The objects of scientific creativity gain their meaning from and fuse their own meaning into ordinary experience. Though the contents of an abstract scientific theory may be far removed from the qualitative aspects of primary experience, such contents are not some "ultimate reality" that has been discovered, but are rather creative abstractions the very possibility of which require and are founded upon the lived qualitative experience of the scientist.[22] The return to everyday primary experience is approached through the

systematic categories of scientific thought by which the richness of experience is infused with new meaning.

This creativity implies a radical rejection of the passive spectator view of
knowledge and an introduction of the active, creative agent who through
meanings helps structure the objects of knowledge. The creation of scientific meanings requires a free creative interplay that goes beyond that which
is directly observed. Without such creativity there is no scientific world and
there are no scientific objects. As William James notes in regard to scientific
method, there is a big difference between verification as the cause of the
preservation of scientific conceptions and the creativity which is the cause
of their production.[23]

For James, science itself was grounded in faith: that one method of
verification, involving repeated testing and gathering of large amounts of
empirical data, would lead inevitably to a discovery of truth. The scientific
investigator, he said, "has fallen so deeply in love with the method" that
"truth as technically verified" has become the only goal of science. James
was skeptical, though, about science's claim of objectivity. Science should
imply, he said, a "certain dispassionate method. To suppose that it means
a certain set of results that one should pin one's faith upon and hug forever
is sadly to mistake its genius, and degrades the scientific body to the status
of a sect." As James saw it, the sect held a "certain fixed belief,—the belief
that the hidden order of nature is mechanical exclusively, that non-mechan-
ical categories are irrational ways of conceiving and explaining such things
as human life." Other ways of thinking—religious, poetical, emotional—
were based on "the personal view of life" rather than the mechanical, the
"romantic view" rather than the rationalistic.[24]

In the second stage of scientific inquiry there is directed or goal-oriented
activity dictated by theory. Theory requires that certain activities be carried out and certain changes brought about in the data to see if anticipated
results occur. These activities are guided by the possibilities that are contained within the meaning structures that have been created. The system
of meanings sets both the context for certain activities and limits the directions which such activity takes. Thus James remarks that scientific conceptions are "teleological weapons of the mind,"[25] or instruments developed
for goal-oriented ends, while Peirce claims that a concept is the mark of a
habit of response or general purpose.[26]

As a third general characteristic of scientific method, the adequacy of
such meaning structures in grasping what is there or in allowing what is
there to reveal itself in a significant way must be tested by consequences
in experience. Only if the anticipated consequences occur can truth be
claimed for the assertions than have been made in theory. The test for truth
is in terms of consequences. Does the theory work in guiding us to a better
understanding of that part of our world anticipated by its claims? Does it
resolve a problematic situation in a meaningful manner and can the claims
that have been made be appropriately defended in a scientific context?

Initial feelings of assurance, insights, and common assent or any other origins of a hypothesis do not determine its truth. To be counted as true a claim must stand the test of consequences in experience. Thus Peirce stresses that scientific method is the only method of fixing belief, for it is the only method by which beliefs must be tested and corrected by what experience presents.[27] In brief, scientific method as representing a self-corrective rather than a building-block model of knowledge is the only way of determining the truth of a belief. Our creative meaning organizations developed through our value-driven goals and purposes must be judged by the consequences they produce.[28]

Truth is thus not something passively attained either by the contemplation of absolutes or by the passive accumulation of data, but by activity shot through with the theory that guides activity. The theory itself is constituted by looking at many possible ways of acting toward the data and the anticipated consequences of these different theoretical possibilities. This role of purposive activity in the development of theory, which must ultimately be justified by workability, is a key feature of the scientific method. When a theory does not work well, when it cannot integrate the data in meaningful ways which lead to anticipated consequences, when some data just do not seem to fit with the theory, then new theories must be developed that provide a broadened context that can encompass the problem being investigated in a newly integrated whole. Thus the process continues and in this way scientific method is self-corrective.

Humans know the world through the structures of meanings they have created by their responses to the environment. Pragmatism's concern with the method of science is not just with the application of knowledge but with the way knowledge is obtained. Theory and practical activity are interrelated and knowledge is not contemplative or otherworldly as opposed to a lesser realm of practice. Knowledge incorporates an awareness of human activity and its consequences. Humans are active agents in the production of knowledge and human activity is built into the very structure of meaningful awareness of the world and its workings. The gaining of knowledge is structured by possible purposive activity.

The method by which science inquires into the nature of the world in which we live is experimental in nature and this experimental method is embedded in the very nature of experience in general. All experience involves an interpretive perspective which directs our activity and in turn is tested by its workability relative to the consequences it brings about, and is revised when it does not work properly.[29] By focusing on the method of science rather than its contents, the proper understanding of human experience is not one that reduces it to mechanistic laws or attempts in any way to substitute a quantitative calculative focus for the full richness of that experience.

While scientific objects are highly sophisticated and intellectualized tools for dealing with experience at an abstract level, they are not the product of any isolated intellect. Rather, the total biological organism in its response to the world is involved in the ordering of any level of awareness of this world and scientific knowledge involves even the most rudimentary aspect of organism-environment interaction. While the purpose of science is to understand and manipulate the environment and the use of scientific concepts is an instrument of such manipulative control, all human activity, even at its most rudimentary level, is guided by values and potentially transformative of its environment. Human activity and the concepts which guide such activity are permeated by a value-laden and value-driven dimension, and this dimension pervades the activity of the scientist just as it pervades all human activity. As such it is instrumental and the abstractly manipulative and instrumental purposes attributed to science have their roots in human experience.[30]

Dewey recommends giving up the word *object* to refer to the distinctive material of the physical and adopt the more neutral term *scientific subject-matter*, and that this would greatly clarify the subjective-objective problem that modern science introduced into the nature of reality.[31] In other words, rather than trying to relate both subject and object in a way that does justice to both the nature of an independent reality and a consciousness that is attempting to know and understand this reality, Dewey would change the terms of the endeavor and thus do away with the problem. The reality that science thus pursues would be called the subject matter of science as opposed to the subject matter of ordinary experience, both of which require a human consciousness to know and understand.

All experience is experimental, not in the sense that it is guided by sophisticated levels of thought as in scientific endeavors, but in the sense that the very structure of human activities both as a way of knowing and as a way of being, embodies the features revealed in the examination of scientific method. It is not that human experience in any of its facets is a lower or inferior form of scientific endeavor, but rather that scientific endeavor as experimental inquiry is a more explicit embodiment of the dynamics operative at all levels of experience and hence the ingredients are more easily distinguished.[32]

In focusing on scientific method, pragmatism is providing an experientially based description of the lived activity of scientists which results in the emergence of scientific objects. In doing so, pragmatism is focusing on the ways in which any object of awareness can emerge within experience from the most rudimentary contents of awareness within lived experience to the most sophisticated objects of scientific knowledge. In providing a description of the lived experience within which the objects of science emerge, pragmatism is uncovering the essential aspects of the emergence of any object of awareness. In brief, an examination of scientific method provides the features for understanding the very possibility of its existence as emerging from rudimentary experience.

The commonsense world and the scientific world result from two diverse ways in which the richness of the natural universe is approached by us in our interpretive activity. They do not get hold of different realities, nor does one approach get hold of what is "really real" to the exclusion of the other. Rather, they arise as different ways of understanding the natural universe in which we live as different areas of interest serving different purposes. The nature onto which our everyday experience opens is not captured by the contents of science, for its richness overflows such abstractions. The perceived world of everyday experience grounds the abstract inferences and experimental developments of the physical sciences which leave behind through the use of mathematics the sense of ordinary experience which grounds its endeavors. The things and events within nature as they arise within the world of science cannot be confounded with the natural universe in its fullness. If the explanatory net of science is substituted for the temporally grounded features of an indefinitely rich universe or becomes in any way the absolute model for understanding that universe, science has overstepped its boundaries.

Nature can be understood in three senses. First, there is nature as a "thick" and dense independent reality which is the foundation of all that is and for all the ways of being, including meaningful human activity. Second, there is nature as our worldly environment as it emerges as a network of relations of things used in everyday purposive activity. Finally, there is nature as an object of science which we theoretically abstract from our everyday natural environment as a higher level reflection on the world. Neither the richness of nature as that from which all life springs nor the richness of nature as the human everyday worldly environment can be confounded with or reduced to the abstract character of the events and objects in the world of science.

The abstract worlds of the various scientific disciplines, each utilizing their specialized tolls of abstraction, are diverse and limited approaches to the rich intertwined relational webs within which humans function. Each area of interest is highlighting a dimension of a unified and rich complexity from which each area draws it ultimate intelligibility and vitality. The problem is not how to unite ultimately discrete facts that are studied by the different disciplines but to distinguish the various dimensions of the concrete relational webs in which human experience is enmeshed.

Distinguishing these dimensions is necessary for purposes of intellectual clarity and advancement of understanding and is accomplished through the dynamics of experimental method. If the problem being investigated and its solution are viewed in this manner, then there will be no temptation to view the resultant "products" in ways which distort both the infinitely rich natural universe they are intended to clarify and the creative process by which these products are obtained. If such distortion is allowed to happen, then these products can too easily be seen as either self-enclosed relativistic environments immune from criticism from "outside" or as a direct grasp of "what is" in its pristine purity.

This is especially the case when one operates within the universe of mathematical quantification and the "rigor" this allows. One tends to forget that this tool, in the very process of quantifying the world, leaves behind all of the richness of nature which cannot be caught by a quantitative net. The use of quantification predetermines the type of content which is apprehended as being inherently mathematizable, while the exclusively mathematizable type of content apprehended in turn reinforces the belief that it alone provides the truth about nature.

Nature as described by science is the creative product of an abstract, reflective restructuring of the nature revealed in everyday experience. It is not a substitute for this experience. As Mead stresses in rejecting such a realistic interpretation of science and the reductionism to which it gives rise, "The ultimate touchstone of reality is a piece of experience found in an unanalyzed world . . . We can never retreat behind immediate experience to analyze elements that constitute the ultimate reality of all immediate experience, for whatever breath of reality these elements possess has been breathed into them by unanalyzed experience."[33] In Dewey's terms, the refined products of scientific inquiry "inherit their full content of meaning" within the context of everyday experience.[34] Lewis's agreement with such a position is shown in his claim that any "truth about nature" must refer back to "what is presented in sense." This position is most succinctly expressed in Peirce's claim that the foundationally "real world is the world of sensible experience."[35]

The notion that if our concepts are to relate to reality they must be able to capture a series of independently existing fully structured facts, and if they cannot do so they bear no relation to reality at all, is itself a remnant of the alternatives offered by the spectator theory of knowledge and the atomism of classical science. For the pragmatist, the world enters experience within the interpretative net we have cast upon it for delineating facts, for breaking its continuities, and for rendering precise its vagueness. Pragmatism does not reject the linkage of concepts and the world but rather looks at the nature of this linkage in a different manner than classical science. It does not reject the idea of reality's constraints on our language structure but rather rethinks the nature of these constraints in a way that rejects correspondence.

Our creative meanings do not deny the presence of reality within experience nor do they mirror this reality, but rather they open us onto reality's presence as mediated by meanings, for meanings are emergent from and intertwined with ongoing interaction in a "dense" universe. We do not think our way to a reality to which language or conceptual structures correspond, but rather we live through a reality with which we are intertwined. Our primal interactive embeddedness in a complex and rich world is something which can never be adequately objectified. All knowledge claims are fallibilistic, perspectival, and temporal, but nonetheless grounded in the richness of the natural universe.

The purpose of knowledge is to allow us to engage this reality which is not beyond the reach of experience but is eminently knowable through a perspectival net by which we render intelligible its indeterminate richness. Within such a context, Lewis compares facts to a landscape. "A landscape is a terrain, but a terrain as seeable by an eye. And a fact is a state of affairs, but a state of affairs as knowable by a mind."[36] Peirce notes that instead of being "a slice of nature," facts are abstracted from it, for "Any fact is inseparably combined with an infinite swarm of circumstances, which make up no part of the fact itself."[37]

We do not know the natural universe in its pristine purity independently of the interpretations we bring to it, but the natural universe is always that which we experience providing the given dimension within experience. Our lived perceptual world and the independently real natural universe are not two spatially, temporally, or experientially different realities. Our everyday worldly environment is the result of the way the natural universe enters into our interpretive experience and into our everyday active engagement with that environment. Various abstract levels of reflection arise from within this concrete everyday world of lived perceptual experience as various explanatory nets are cast upon it in an attempt to understand and live within this world.

The scientific method works well in investigating certain types of problems, but it is applicable far beyond these problems and has implications for human experience in general. Pragmatism extends the relevance of scientific method and its mode of inquiry to all of human experience. Inquiry begins with a feeling of unease about something or dissatisfaction with some aspect of experience. The one who is inquiring then uses whatever tools of inquiry are at his or her disposal and are relevant to the nature of the thing being examined. These tools can include laboratory equipment, mathematics, formal logic, interviews, review of literature, therapy, or whatever is useful to the inquiry and can bring it to a fruitful conclusion. The outcome desired is a feeling of satisfaction with the results of the inquiry. If this result is not obtained, either the inquiry needs to be continued until satisfaction is reached or abandoned if the inquiry cannot be continued or is considered to be fruitless.[38] As Hickman again writes:

> Inquiry is thus a technological enterprise because it involves techniques: the invention, development, and cognitive deployment of tools or other artifacts (such as rules of inference), brought to bear on raw materials (such as data) and intermediate stock parts (such as the results of previous inquiries), to resolve and reconstruct situations which are perceived as problematic.[39]

From this understanding of a nonpassive or nonspectator view of scientific method, humans and their environment, organic and inorganic, take on an inherently relational aspect. To speak of organism and environment in isolation from each other is never true to the situation, for no organism can exist in isolation from an environment, and an environment is what it is in relation to an organism. The properties attributed to the environment belong to it in the context of that interaction. What exists is interaction as an indivisible whole, and it is only within such an interactional context that experience and its qualities function.

Pragmatism thus emphasizes the relational nature of things in the world, even space and time itself, a position that is consistent with what some scientists themselves are saying. Classical Newtonian physics believed that everything in the world existed against an absolute preexisting framework of space that is eternal and goes on forever. Particles move around in this space and their properties are defined with respect to this space. Time was also believed to be absolute and flowed whether anything happened or not in the same manner. This view changed with Einstein, who discovered that there is no fixed background and space and time are dynamic and no more than relations between events that evolve within time itself. "So space has no meaning apart from a network of relationships, and time is nothing but change in that network of relationships."[40]

Such a relational view of humans and their environment has pluralistic dimensions, for environments are contextually located and significant solutions to problematic situations emerge within such contextually situated environments. Diverse perspectives grasp the richness of reality in different ways and must be judged in terms of workability. And workability requires growth: resolution of conflicts by an enlargement of context in which adjustments or adjudicating of conflicting perspectival claims can take place. Growth cannot be reduced to material growth or mere accumulation of knowledge, but rather is best understood as an increase in the moral richness of experience.

Extending scientific inquiry to all of human affairs would allow the benefit of such inquiry to be realized by the entire society. Science would then contribute to making a better society as a whole and bringing about better consequences and not be limited to certain industrial endeavors. Science would thus become humanistic, not just physical and technical, and would be used to contribute to bettering the material conditions of life rather that making a profit for private business organizations. Science can be, according to Dewey, a tool for creating a "liberating spiritualization" in being used to control the social effects that new technologies produce and directing these technologies to produce better consequences for the society as a whole.[41]

CHARACTERISTICS OF THE PRAGMATIC APPROACH TO SCIENCE

Instead of the characteristics of reductionism, atomism, discreteness, quantitativeness, and determinism, pragmatism deals with emergence, holism, continuity, the qualitative, and indeterminism. Thus pragmatism involves a different view of the characteristics that go to make up the traditional or classical view of science and the scientific worldview. This view involves a reinterpretation of science, a different way to understand science and what it is doing. Pragmatism does not reject science or its approach to knowledge, but looks at the scientific enterprise from a different perspective which in some sense constitutes a different worldview.

Instead of reductionism, the pragmatic view of science emphasizes *emergence*. While reductionism thinks of parts in isolation, emergence focuses on the relationship between the parts of a system and emergent properties that stem from this relationship. For example, scientific reductionism would think of water as composed of its constituent elements hydrogen and oxygen, that these are the fundamental parts that go to make up what we call water. Emergence, however, would focus on the property of wetness that arises from the relationship of hydrogen and oxygen, a property that emerges out of the relationship between the parts. It is the wetness that is of concern to us in our everyday lived experience while the constituent elements are of concern to scientists.

This is a much different way of looking at nature and leads to different conclusions. In particle physics, scientists are looking for the fundamental building blocks of matter. This is a reductionist approach that is linear in nature in going back to the most fundamental particle that is the unmoved mover, so to speak. From the standpoint of emergence, however, what results from experiments using supercolliders are new and different particles, no one of which can necessarily be taken as the most fundamental. Thus emergence is related to nonlinearity, in that what particle physics is doing is discovering more and more complexity in the structure of atoms and is not necessarily going to find the most fundamental particle from which all other matter stems. How these particles relate to each other is more important than the search for some ultimate particle.

The limits of reductionism are evident at levels of organization with higher amounts of complexity such as culture, ecosystems, and other systems that are formed from large numbers of interacting components. Given this complexity, it is impossible to reduce a system to one or even a few fundamental components. The important thing to deal with in these cases is the relationship between the components of a system and the emergent properties that arise from these relationships. Some scientists themselves, including a Nobel Prize winner by the name of Robert Laughlin, believe that we have moved into an age of emergence which has important implications for our understanding of what science is doing.

> Much as I dislike the idea of ages, I think a good case can be made that science has now moved from an Age of Reductionism to an Age of Emergence, a time when the search for the ultimate cause of things shifts from the behavior of parts to the behavior of the collective. It is difficult to identify a specific moment when this transition occurred

because it was gradual and somewhat obscured by the persistence of myths, but there can be no doubt that the dominant paradigm now is organizational . . . Ironically the very success of reductionism has helped pave the way for its eclipse. Over time, careful quantitative study of microscopic parts has revealed that at the primitive level, at least, collective principles of organization are not just a quaint side show but *everything*—the true source of physical law, including perhaps the most fundamental laws we know. The precision of our measurements enables us to confidently declare the search for a single ultimate truth to have ended—but at the same time we have failed, since nature is now revealed to be an enormous tower of truths, each descending from it parent, and then transcending that parent, as the scale of measurement increases . . . The transition to the Age of Emergence brings an end to the myth of the absolute power of mathematics. This myth is still entrenched in our culture, unfortunately, a fact revealed routinely in the press and popular publications promoting the search for ultimate laws as the only scientific activity worth pursuing, not withstanding massive and overwhelming experimental evidence that exactly the opposite is the case . . . The myth of collective behavior following from the law is, as a practical matter, exactly backward. Law instead follows from collective behavior, as do things that flow from it, such as logic and mathematics.[42]

Thus Newton's laws of motion are not fundamental, according to Laughlin, but rather they emerge from a collective organizational phenomenon. With the rise of quantum theory, the behavior of atoms, molecules, and subatomic particles has been described by the laws of quantum mechanics, and laws emerge from the aggregation of quantum matter.[43] Emergence is thus introduced in the heart of physics. It is also evident at the level of the universe itself as with the rise of big bang theory it is now believed that everything we see in the universe today emerged from a singularity as small as the tip of a pencil. And in biology with evolutionary theory it is believed that more complex life forms emerged from simpler ones rather than being created directly by some supernatural entity. And new life-forms are emerging all the time as viruses develop new strains, for example, to counter the effects of human efforts to eradicate them.

Emergence is also operative in the different sciences that have developed. To a strict reductionist, science is a straightforward hierarchy; biology is founded upon chemistry, for example, and chemistry is founded on physics, and physics leads to the most elementary particles of matter. When these are found, then we have completed the linear chain back to the first cause that can explain everything else.[44] But in an emergent view, one science is not just an applied version of the science that precedes it. Each of these sciences is a different approach to its own part of the world; it deals with different theories and entirely new laws and concepts are necessary to explain the phenomena it is interested in understanding. No one of these sciences is necessarily more fundamental than the other. They are all necessary and equally valid in understanding the complexity of our world.

A second characteristic of the pragmatic view of science is it's *holistic* approach to nature. What science does is to break the whole apart through reductionism, which allows us to manipulate more and more aspects of our world. However, what science separates science cannot put back together. The whole cannot be created by putting the parts back together. The whole has to be grasped with a new kind of consciousness that does not start with reductionistic parts, but that has a different starting point that can grasp the whole more immediately. Only then can we get a realistic understanding of what nature is worth and what qualities of nature are worth preserving.

Rather than assuming that nature is atomistic and thus focusing on the parts in isolation from each other, pragmatism considers the whole phenomenon and the interactions of the parts within this whole. These relationships are considered to be nondirectional or nonlinear in nature; they do not lead back to some fundamental atomistic something.[45] While an atomistic view of nature has proved useful in the physical sciences, such a view is more problematic in the social sciences because it seems impossible to isolate a single cause for any social process that is the primary determinant of something in society. It is more realistic to look at the whole society and study how the various parts of interest interact with each other within a holistic perspective.

This perspective thus asserts that the whole is more than the sum of its parts and that the parts do not give the entire meaning to the whole.[46] All the properties of a given system cannot be explained by its component parts alone. The wetness of water cannot be explained by breaking water into its component elements of hydrogen and oxygen. Nor can the behavior of the system be determined from an examination of how the parts of the system behave. Instead, the system as a whole and the way the parts are organized and relate to each other within the system determine the way the parts behave. The emergence of quantum mechanics introduces holism into particle physics itself.

> The emergence of a quantum entity's previously indeterminate properties in the context of a given experimental situation is another example of relational holism. We cannot say that a photon is a wave or a particle until it is measured, and how we measure it determines what we will see. The quantum entity acquires a certain new property—position, momentum, polarization—only in relation to its measuring apparatus. The property did not exist prior to this relationship. It was indeterminate.[47]

When we look at anything in our world, we experience it as a totality, not as an individual, atomistic, isolated part. We may intend to focus on a part, but all the background related to that part comes into play, even if it is on the periphery. For example, I may want to focus on the capitol building when I look out my window, but it is impossible to ignore all the other buildings, the sky, the trees, and everything else that is taken in by my vision. All these other things place the capitol building in a certain context and how I see that building is affected by all these other things in a holistic perspective. It is not possible for me to focus solely on a certain part of that totality.

We live in the world as a whole and derive meaning from this relationship. The parts have no particular meaning in and of themselves, so that adding up these parts will give meaning to the whole. For example, any one part of an automobile engine is meaningless, and for that matter useless, in and of itself. However, when all these parts are combined into an engine that can power our car, the parts become useful to us and are meaningful in enabling us to go places and do things we could not experience before the invention of the automobile. The combination of these parts has enhanced our lives and made life easier and more meaningful than it was before this technology was employed.

The pragmatic view of science also views reality as *continuous* rather than discrete. While science has to divide reality into discrete entities for purposes of analysis and measurement so that nature can be better understood and manipulated, we actually experience nature as continuous. When we walk to the door we actually get there despite Zeno's paradox. While time is broken up into hours, minutes, and seconds and we are conscious of these divisions under certain circumstances, like when we have to get to a certain place on time, for example, for our ordinary experience time is a continuous flow and is not discrete. The table we eat off is experienced as a continuous whole; it is not experienced as a bunch of atomic particles that are held together by an unseen force. These continuums are as real to us in our everyday experience as are the discretes to the scientist who is studying a certain part of nature. According to Charis Anastopoulos, writing in *Particle or Wave*:

> But even if we rested at the present level of knowledge and assumed that quarks and leptons are themselves the ultimate building blocks of matter, it would still be difficult to make the case that matter consists of discrete objects. The fundamental theory for the micro world, quantum field theory, relies on a rather physical principle; the duality between particles and fields. Particles are genuinely discrete objects, but fields are supposed to be continuous up to the tiniest of scales, and both descriptions seem to hold simultaneously.[48]

Dewey speaks about a continuity of the life process, that life is a self-renewing process that interacts with the environment in which it exists. This process, however, is not dependent upon the continued existence of any one single individual. While individual lives come and go, reproduction of life in all its forms goes on in a continuous sequence. Some species may even become extinct, but the life process continues to evolve ever more complex forms of life that are better adapted to their environment. Life goes on in a continuous fashion and new forms of life evolve in relation to environmental conditions. As Dewey says: "Continuity of life means continual readaptation of the environment to the needs of living organisms."[49]

Humans are continuous with nature; they do not exist apart from nature and are not outside of nature. Nature cannot be dehumanized nor can humans be denaturalized. Science treats nature as an objective reality that can be manipulated to serve human interests. Nature becomes dehumanized and human impacts on nature are ignored. Some religions hold that humans, or at least the human soul, can exist apart from nature in some supernatural realm. Neither approach does justice to the interactions between humans and nature and the fact that there is a continuous relationship between humans and nature where nature shapes humans and humans shape nature in an ever-evolving universe.

Continuities exist in all of our life experiences. We do not experience life as a series of discrete events or objects that we then have to put together somehow. We do not think of ourselves as subjects that exist in an objective world. We experience ourselves as continuous with that world, not as something standing over against a world that is seen as something alien and foreign to our existence. We exist in the world and live our lives in interaction with all parts of that world. Our lives are social in that we grow up in a certain social context that shapes who we are and gives meaning and purpose to our lives. We are not individuals that grow up in isolation from other selves and the natural environment. While science has to break the world into discretes for its purposes, this is not what we experience in our everyday lives.

Instead of a quantitatively characterized universe, pragmatism emphasizes the *qualitative* aspects of our experience. While a quantitative approach tells us something about how much of something we have, it does not say anything about the quality of that something. Quality in this sense does not refer to the qualities that a particular object may have, like color, texture, and the like.[50] Quality is really a judgment we make about something as to what it does to enhance our life experience. When we are considering whether to buy a work of art, for example, we do not make the decision solely on the price of the work. We make the decision on the basis of whether the artwork pleases us and will enhance our life as it hangs on the wall, and then take into consideration the price and whether it is worth the quantity of money we will have to part with in order to buy it. The same holds true for clothes, furniture, and all of life's choices relative to particular objects. They all come with a price, but the qualitative value of these objects is at least as important as the quantitative aspects.

Quality is a unitary concept unlike quantity where an object can be measured and expressed in units of something. We experience quality as a whole; the whole artwork enters into our judgment as does the whole house and its environment when we are making a decision about purchasing a home. The experience of quality is continuous; it is not broken up into discretes. While we may like certain aspects of a house more than others, like a kitchen, for example, or a family room, the final judgment has to take the whole house into consideration. And its environment is equally important, whether it is in a safe neighborhood, the quality of the schools if we have children, and other such factors. All of these aspects are important and they all blend together in a final judgment about the quality of the experience. Everything depends on the quality of this experience and the expectations about the ability of the house to continue to provide this quality in the future.

Attempts to quantify nature are problematical at best and bound to fail at worst. Where there is no discrete owner and nothing to exchange, it is difficult if not impossible to put a quantitative value on nature. What is the value of preserving wilderness so people can enjoy hiking and camping in it and get away from the hustle and bustle of city living? These are qualitative experiences and it is difficult to put a price on them. They are worth everything and nothing. Perhaps people can be forced to quantify these experiences by making them pay for it, but the quality of the experience is the determining factor that then has to be translated into some quantitative measure so decisions can be made about how much wilderness to preserve.

Modern science changed our understanding and approach to nature. In ancient Greece and the Middle Ages, science understood the world as impregnated with aesthetic and moral values; it was not considered to be value neutral. According to John Dewey, nothing was less important in ancient science than quantity. With the rise of modern science, however, matter and motion were transformed and the quantitative measurement of change in space and time became the foundations of natural science.[51] Thus there was a change from a qualitative approach to a quantitative approach where nature was devoid of value and was measured and manipulated in human interests. Nature only had an instrumental value as it proved useful for human purposes; it had no value in and of itself.

Qualitative thinking is involved in appraising a work of art, as it is the underlying quality of the art that defines the work, "that circumscribes it externally and integrates it internally," and also controls the work of the artist as he or she creates the work. The nature of good art is a genuine intellectual and logical whole where the parts "hang" together and reinforce and expand the quality of each other. Such a work cannot be understood by a quantitative approach that measures its size and amount of time involved or its price. Properties such as symmetry, harmony, rhythm, and proportion are what matter in judging a work of art to be valuable and form the basis of any quantitative measurement.[52]

Finally, rather than holding to a deterministic universe, pragmatism involves *indeterminism*. Recall that in a deterministic universe, all the information about its structure is contained in the initial conditions. Everything that is going to happen in the future is implicit in the starting state, which contains all the information necessary to reconstruct the past and predict the future. But the quantum aspects of reality make perfect knowledge of the initial conditions impossible, not only in practice but in principle. This means that we cannot make accurate predictions of the future based on present conditions and the assumption of a deterministic universe has to be abandoned in favor of a more complex and indeterminate universe.[53] As John D. Barrow states in *New Theories of Everything*:

> Even if we can overcome the problem of initial conditions to determine the most natural or uniquely consistent starting state, we may have to face the reality that there is inevitable uncertainty surrounding the prescription of the initial state which makes the prediction of the exact future state of the Universe impossible. Only statistical statements will be possible.[54]

Indeterminism is thus built into the structure of the universe. It is intrinsic and we will never be able to predict future events with absolute certainty. The issue is not one of needing more information about the initial conditions, as these conditions are themselves indeterminate. We live in an indeterminate universe and uncertainty is part and parcel of our experience. It cannot be avoided by developing better techniques of scientific analysis or better ways of processing information. There are too many complexities and too many unknowns for us to deal with making the universe unpredictable and full of surprises.

Every situation with which we are faced is unique; it is indivisible and cannot be duplicated.[55] A fully deterministic universe has no place for such uniqueness and novelty, no place for growth and genuine change.[56] It is a fixed and closed world that is mechanistic in nature. An indeterministic universe, on the other hand, is open to change and novelty, the unexpected becomes the expected, and there is disorder as well as order. Rather than being a detached observer that is outside of nature, humans are a participant in changing nature through their interactions. The intelligibility of the universe, according to John Dewey, is not based upon the notion of fixed laws that make possible exact predictions but incorporates probabilities and uncertainty.[57]

> In technical statements, laws on the new basis are *formulae for the prediction of the probability of an observable occurrence.* They are designations of relations sufficiently stable to allow the occurrence of forecasts of individualized situations—for every observed phenomenon is individual—within limits of specified probability, not a probability of error, but of probability of actual occurrence. Laws are inherently conceptual in character, as is shown in the fact that either position or velocity may be fixed at will. To call them conceptual is not to say that they are merely "mental

and arbitrary." It is to say that they are *relations* which are thought not observed. The subject matter of the conceptions which constitute laws is not arbitrary, for it is determined by the interactions of what exists. But determination of them is very different from that denoted by conformity to fixed properties of unchanging substances.[58]

Laws are thus means of calculating the probabilities related to observing an event in nature. They are not based on properties immutably inhering in things and of such a nature as to be capable of exact mathematical statement.[59] Nature is not irrational, however, as there are regularities and uniformities that make nature intelligible and understandable and subject to being manipulated for human purposes.[60] Our knowledge of nature may be indeterminate, but that does not mean nature is arbitrary and completely unpredictable. We can predict what effects global warming will have on the earth's climate and on the polar ice caps with some degree of confidence, but that does mean that nature won't surprise us—as it has with faster melting of polar ice caps than was predicted. We cannot know with certainty what will happen in the future, but we can make intelligent predictions based on what we do know about climate change and need not wait, in some cases, for greater certainty before taking action.

Observation of any natural system also involves acting on it in some fashion. When dealing with large systems such as the universe as a whole, our actions can be ignored because they do not have a measurable effect on the bodies we are observing. Particle physics, however, is another matter. The uncertainty principle, which could perhaps more accurately be called the indeterminacy principle, holds that it is impossible to get an accurate measurement of the velocity and position of any body because of the interaction between the observer and the body being measured. The position and velocity of a particle is not fixed but is changing all the time because of this interaction with the act of observing, or, as Dewey puts it, "with the conditions under which observation is possible." This principle is the final blow to the old spectator theory of knowledge.[61]

> The change for the underlying philosophy and logic of science is, however, very great. In relation to the metaphysics of the Newtonian system it is hardly less than revolutionary. What is known is seen to be a product in which the act of observation plays a necessary role. Knowing is seen to be a participant in what is finally known. Moreover the metaphysics of existence as something fixed and therefore capable of literally exact mathematical description and prediction is undermined. Knowing is, for philosophical theory, a case of specially directed activity instead of something isolated from practice. The quest for certainty by means of exact possession in mind of immutable reality is exchanged for search for security by means of active control or the changing course of events.[62]

CONCLUSION

Pragmatism is an antifoundational philosophy. It rejects attempts to provide ultimate foundations for knowledge claims and is in this sense a postmodern philosophy. Likewise, classical pragmatism rejects a spectator theory of knowledge where true knowledge is constituted by an accurate internal representation of external facts that we can know objectively. Instead, pragmatism is perspectival with regards to knowledge, holding that we approach the world from a certain perspective that influences how we go about inquiring into something. Pragmatism also holds that knowledge is gained from experience and rejects sources of knowledge located outside of experience such as religious supernaturalism and other transcendental accounts of knowledge. Finally, it rejects the view that humans can achieve absolute certainty, "opting instead for versions of fallibilism according to which working hypotheses, rules of thumb, and even well-proven instruments are open to revision under appropriate circumstances."[63]

For pragmatism, there is no objective nature that provides a firm foundation for knowledge. Nature is not a "thing" but is instead a complex matrix of objects and events that are constructed within the history of human inquiry. Pragmatism rejects the epistemological foundations of classical science—a faith in quantification, a vision of linear and inevitable progress, an acceptance of the physical sciences as paradigmatic of all rationality, and a conception of nature as a machine to be dominated and exploited. Pragmatism emphasizes that humans are situated within nature and holds that science is only one of the many productive areas of human experience. It views progress as fragile and attainable only in piecemeal fashion. Knowledge is perspectival and fallible, but some forms of knowledge are better than others for certain purposes. What works best is judged in terms of the consequences it produces. Finally, pragmatism denies any absolute or final split between fact and value or between culture and nature.[64]

The rest of the book will examine the same aspects of our lived experience that were discussed in the first section from the standpoint of this pragmatic philosophy. Economics, politics, culture, and nature will be looked at from this perspective and different understandings of these aspects of our lives will emerge than was the case when these aspects were interpreted for the standpoint of classical science. But first the ethical and value dimension of our lives must be reexamined because pragmatism has a different view of the relation between facts and values and the importance of the value dimension in our everyday lives. Values enter into every aspect of our decisions, even those that are scientific in nature.

8   Pragmatism and Values

There are several problems that science poses for the ethical enterprise in business-school education and business organizations that were mentioned in an earlier section on science. Pragmatism as a philosophy has an approach to these problems that is unique and offers the possibility of embedding ethics and moral considerations into the heart of what a business organization is all about. It does not allow ethics to be compartmentalized into the realm of mere opinion where it can be easily dismissed as having no particular relevance to business problems because it cannot provide firm answers to the moral considerations business faces. It provides a way of dealing with moral pluralism by incorporating different ethical theories into a comprehensive framework that utilizes the strengths of these various approaches. And finally, it provides a sense of community to overcome the individualism that pervades much of ethical thinking.

FACTS VERSUS VALUES

The separation of facts and values as described in an earlier chapter constitutes a problem that Dewey thinks is a serious one for contemporary society. According to Dewey, "The problem of restoring integration and cooperation between a man's beliefs about the world in which he lives and his beliefs about the values and purposes that should direct his conduct is the deepest problem of modern life."[1] This problem is particularly relevant for ethical and moral considerations in an educational program that is scientifically and technologically oriented. Since most of the top business schools consider themselves to be scientifically oriented rather than professional schools, ethics is a difficult subject to integrate into the curriculum in a manner than has a significant impact.

The problem as traditionally posed comes about because to be scientifically oriented means to collect "brute facts" that are empirically "there" in some sense and value free in that they can be observed objectively free from any subjective considerations. Facts provide value-free descriptions and causal explanations of human and organizational behavior and are independent of human observation at least as seen through the lenses of classical science. The observer is merely a spectator operating in a disinterested fashion to discover natural phenomena that will tell us how the world works in a kind of mechanical fashion. The problem has been described by Steven Shapin in the following manner:

> The very idea of the modern natural sciences is bound up with an appreciation that they are objective rather than subjective accounts. They represent *what is* in the natural world, not *what ought to be*, while the possibility of such a radical distinction between scientific "is-knowledge" and moral "ought knowledge" itself depends on separating the objects of natural knowledge from the objects of moral discourse. The objective character of the natural sciences is supposed to be further secured by a method that disciplines practitioners to set aside their passions and interests in the making of scientific knowledge. Science, in this account, fails to report objectively on the world—it fails to *be* science—if it allows considerations of value, morality, or politics to intrude into the processes of making and validating knowledge.[2]

Pragmatism rejects this spectator theory of knowledge and its assumptions that our observations of nature are value-free and that knowledge is a collection of brute facts by a disinterested observer. Pragmatism holds first and foremost that the study of values cannot be separated from "factual" matters. This argument has several dimensions. First, nature is rich with contextually emergent qualities and value is considered to be an emergent property in the interaction of organisms with nature. Value need not be, nor can it be, reduced to some experienced quality other than itself, for it is among the qualities which pervade our experience within nature. Our immediate experience with nature is characterized by value as a qualitative dimension of nature that is on an equal footing with the experiencing of other qualitative aspects of nature. Values are as real as all other qualities within nature, as indeed the experience of value is itself a discriminable fact within nature.

The pragmatic focus on scientific method as revealed through the experimental activity of scientists, drawing on such developments as evolutionary theory and Heisenberg's principle of indeterminacy and serving as a prelude to the Kuhnsian analysis of the history of science and scientific revolutions, casts a very different light on the fact-value issue and questions whether it is an issue at all or only the creation of a distinction to separate science and technology from its moral context. For the pragmatist, all human experience is inherently experimental in nature and the key features of scientific method reflect the key features of human experience in general. And human experience involves a value dimension that enters into the choices people make and their experience in general.

The problem is one of grounding values in the natural world, in our experience with the world. If the natural world is given over to science to describe and investigate, then ethics and values become subjective and have to be grounded either in religion or in the realm of pure reason.[3] They become divorced from the interests and biases that are operative in the world of experience. To counter this separation, values must be naturalized and arise from experience the same as facts about our world. They emerge from the rich world in which we live and are part of the same complex matrix in which we are embedded. Science gets at only a part of this reality, the part that can be quantified and mathematized, which leaves values behind, while idealism locates values in a realm beyond experience. According to Larry Hickman regarding Dewey's thinking on this subject:

> He [Dewey] was keen to reject what he regarded as two extreme positions, both of which involve an element of truth, but both of which are incomplete in the form in which they are usually advanced. The first was scientific realism, with its emphasis on representationally given facts, its reliance on a correspondence theory of truth, and its assumption of a split between facts and values that favors facts. The second was idealism, which included the so-called "humanistic" or "spiritual" critique of scientific technology, with its emphasis on values grounded elsewhere than an experienced world, its reliance on a coherence theory of truth, and its assumption of a split between facts and values that favors values.[4]

Second, when value issues arise in our experience we are confronted with determining what is actually valuable through the operation of scientific or experimental method. Normative claims about the valuable, about what ought to be, are experimental hypotheses about the enrichment of life, about creative ways of organizing values which will direct activity toward that which actually enhances the life experiences of those involved. What is ultimately considered to be valuable emerges out of the experience of humans as they critically examine their perceptions of value and determine whether a particular value actually contributes to moral growth and works to enhance life experiences for all those involved.

The resolution of conflicting moral perceptions cannot be resolved by appeal to abstract principles or to a moral absolutism, but neither are such resolutions to be evaded because such conflicts are merely expressions of different feelings or opinions or because dialogue is closed off by the self-enclosed relativism of each position. While different values arise from specific contexts shaped by particular traditions, this is neither a relativism nor a subjectivism, for an openness to other perspectives provides a way of breaking through these barriers to grasp different contexts, to take the perspective of "the other," to participate in dialogue with "the other," and to critically evaluate the contexts which give rise to one's own beliefs about what is valuable and ought to be pursued.

Our moral rules are about ways of organizing and enriching our values as contextual emergent properties within concrete situations, and if one is not attuned to experience a value dimension, then there is nothing for one's moral rules to be about. One cannot debate conflicting moral directives without attunement to values anymore than one can debate conflicting aesthetic principles of utilizing color in creating works of art if one has never experienced color. Debate about conflicting moral directives also cannot take place if one does not have knowledge of the relational context of, the reason for, and the consequences of particular types of valuing experiences.

This move from immediately experienced value that involves data to be organized to claims concerning what is valuable as established experimentally that can harmonize the diversity of values is not an attempt to derive an ought from an is, a value from a fact. There is no fact-value distinction and the entire fact-value problem as it has emerged from the past tradition of science and moral philosophy is a false dichotomy. [5] Any attempt to separate fact and value results in normative claims which are sterile and empty of any empirical content and empirical claims that have no meaning and purpose. When science relegates values and ethics to the noncognitive realm where they become mere opinion or subjective feelings, then any value that arises in the course of our experience is not considered to be knowledge of any sort that deserves further examination or dialogue about values or valuing activities.

Our factual beliefs are indeed beliefs because we have to give assent to them for them to be facts. They are not about something brutely given and value free. This view that they are value-free stems directly from the atomistic and mechanistic view of nature discussed in an earlier chapter, where experience need only be broken down to smaller and smaller units until the real essence is known. In this way, so-called organic systems are actually mechanistic systems obeying universal laws all of which are separate from the knower and can be grasped in their brute thereness. [6]

Such a view gives rise to the widespread understanding of economic systems as separate from the rest of society and knowable without entanglement with our knowledge of the larger context in which an economy functions. A disinterested observer can then collect the facts of this deterministic, mechanistic system. These facts are considered to be brutely there and value free. Thus economics can be a science in which one discovers the facts and determines the mechanistic laws governing them, avoiding the "fuzzy" and unscientific realm of values.

What the pragmatic position has to say about the study of "facts" is also twofold. First, scientific method in its most general sense as actually practiced by scientists itself rules out facts as brutely given and passively received. Science operates from a creative perspective which sets the questions one asks, and this, in turn, affects the operations one performs and the answers one gets. What we believe is valuable enters into the way experiments are structured. At the deepest level, the structuring of a theory determines what is acceptable as factual evidence as well as what kind of facts there can possibly be. As Kuhn has so well illustrated, revolutionary theories create different facts, for facts are always theory dependent; facts do not come to us ready made.[7] Indeed, the very determination to ignore what cannot be reduced to quantification is motivated by the kind of results one thinks are valuable.

Second, our values enter into the way we interpret the same kinds of facts. Diverse values can lead to radically diverse interpretation of the significance of the facts obtained through a particular experimental inquiry. The biases of those interpreting the results one gets from the complexities of human interactions are inseparably intertwined with the interpretation of the results. Sometimes there are no value disagreements which would undermine a consensus concerning the data, sometimes the value dimension which enters into the differing interpretations is so subtle as to be difficult to discern, and sometimes it manifests itself with stark clarity.

Facts, then, do not just come to us as ready-made, announcing their brute givenness. Eventually human beings have to decide what they accept as "facts" and what they believe to be true about the nature of their experience. They have to decide what constitutes adequate evidence and what are valid methodologies so that they will be persuaded that a descriptive claim deserves to be accepted as true and thus labeled as a fact about the world. Facts are not merely givens that we passively absorb, but they are defined by humans as they progress in knowledge and understanding of the world. This progression is influenced by values as humans make judgments about the facts in building a storehouse of knowledge.

There is a difference between normative and descriptive claims, but the difference is based on contextual and functional considerations, not on ontologically distinct types of entities. Whether a statement is descriptive or normative depends on its function in a problematic situation. Moreover, normative judgments involve the facts relevant to the potential production of values arising from our experience with nature. The issue is not facts versus values, but facts about values and their potential enhancement, about discriminating between them and constructing them in ongoing experience. Unless one has some awareness of how human and environmental factors interrelate in concrete situations that give rise to value qualities within experience, then normative claims are not possible.

The diversity of values as original qualitative emergents within the context of our natural interactions with the environment are real emergent facts within nature. The move to ought statements is not a move from fact to value, an attempt to pull an ought from an is, to fall into the trap of a naturalistic fallacy. Rather, this move is a claim about how to integrate originally conflicting data of problematic situations in ways which will enhance further value-relevant experiences within nature.

The pragmatic understanding of value qualities as naturally occurring irreducible contextual emergents and of normative claims as experimental hypotheses about ways of enriching and expanding the value-relevant dimension of human existence undercuts the entire problematics of the fact-value distinction. The problem of how values can exist in a world composed of facts, or of how one can get normative claims about what ought to be from descriptive statements of what is, is based on philosophical starting points which, according to Hickman, are alien to pragmatic thinking.

> Dewey's position avoids the traditional split between facts and values by means of his contention that: a) values and relations are experienced (his radical empiricism); b) facts are always not just given but always selected from a busy and complex environment as facts-of-a-case, that is, always and only in the context of a particular inquiry (his Instrumentalism and his anti-transcendentalism; and c) what is valuable is so only as a result of tests that have proven it to be a reliable basis for further action (his constructivism and his fallibilism).[8]

Modern empiricism is a narrow empiricism founded on the implicit acceptance of a scientific description of nature, and results in the view that empirical experience cannot include the experience of value, just as value cannot be a real irreducible quality unless it is nonnatural to be experienced in a nonnatural manner. For pragmatism, both facts and values emerge as wedded dimensions of complex contexts which cannot be dissected into atomic bits separated from each other. The entire fact-value problem as it has emerged from the past tradition of moral philosophy and as it appears in applied ethics today is a wrong way to look at the situation.

One cannot adequately evaluate moral behavior apart from the contextual situation in which it arises. These contextual situations involve interrelational networks of felt values, and evaluations which are contoured both by evolving human experience and evolving historical and cultural conditions that are the cause or source of the value experiences and moral beliefs of the participants. These beliefs lead to particular types of consequences because of causal relations holding between our belief-guided actions and the consequences they bring about. All of these factors must be examined in coming to grips with moral assessment of human activity in concrete situations.

Such an examination not only requires knowledge of cause-and-effect relations operative in the nonhuman environment, but the probable type of effect particular actions will have on other participants given the factors which shape their ongoing activity. Thus normative conclusions, though not reducible to factual dimensions, cannot be understood even abstractly in separation from more factual dimensions. The development of normative principles is guided by experience just as empirical studies are guided by values. And they both proceed via one general method, the method of experience as experimental, the method of experimental inquiry.

This recognition that one methodology, the methodology of experimental inquiry, guides the development of normative principles and empirical research alike need not result in collapsing the two endeavors into a single entity, for they each use experimental methods to abstract different dimensions of concrete situations because of their different focus, their different goals, and their different contextual interests. Each endeavor can maintain its own integrity, recognizing that this integrity does not separate it from or mark it out as superior to the other. The recognition of the common context within which their respective frames of reference take shape and which binds each to the other, along with a recognition of the common experimental method which unites their respective endeavors, allows for ongoing dialogue which strengthens the recognition of this intertwining.

As Patricia Werhane succinctly asserts, there is no purely empirical or purely normative methodology; social science cannot be purely objective and ethics cannot be purely nonempirical.[9] Each approach is highlighting a dimension of the unified rich complexity from which each draws its ultimate intelligibility and vitality. The problem is not to figure out how to unite two ontological discretes, but rather to figure out how to distinguish the two dimensions for purposes of intellectual clarity and advancement of understanding through experimental method without viewing the resultant "products" in ways which distort the concrete reality they are intended to clarify and process by which these products are obtained.

Normative claims are rooted in human existence and the value qualities included therein do not come from on high in the realm of pure thought or from some revealed truth of a religious system. Nor can normative claims come from science. When one operates within the realm of mathematical quantification and the "rigor" this allows, one tends to forget that this tool in the very process of quantifying leaves behind all the richness of reality which cannot be caught by a quantitative framework. The use of quantitative tools predetermines the type of content which is apprehended as being inherently mathematizable, and the exclusively mathematizable type of content apprehended, in turn, reinforces the belief that quantification is the tool of observational truth, and thus the separation of fact and value becomes complete because value cannot be mathematized.

Facts and values are two dimensions of one existential situation which can be relatively isolated and abstracted for purposes of conceptual focus. Often abstract discussions can tend to indicate fundamental disagreement when none exists; however, such acknowledgments frequently house and hide radically different fundamental intuitions about the fact-value problematic. As William C. Frederick states, there is no fact-value divide, but there is often a great divide between the two opposing sides of the fact-value controversy which is so fundamental, pervasive, and yet often so illusive that it is at times difficult to coax out of hiding.[10]

Numerous scholars interested in this problem acknowledge that of course scientific method has some value orientation and of course ethical claims cannot be made in a factual void. Yet, as these scholars attempt to reconcile the two realms and as they pose questions both in general and of other specific positions, it becomes evident that their basic intuition of the entire problematic is that of the need to bring together that which is ulti-mately disparate. It is this fundamental intuition which guides the kinds of questions they ask, the kinds of problems they envision, and the kinds of answers they see as allowable.

Our value-laden choices result in bringing about new interpretations of facts and these interpretations give rise to choices among possible values to pursue. What we believe about the world and the way it works and what we value are intertwined in manifold ways. So-called facts about the world cannot be reduced to values any more than values can be reduced to facts. But neither can they be as neatly separated as some philosophers and scientists would have us believe. They are not separate so that facts are objective and absolute and values are subjective and relative. Both facts and values emerge as wedded dimensions of complex contexts which cannot be dissected into atomic bits or reduced to mechanistic laws and deterministic relationships.

Moral disagreement can be resolved only by engaging in open and hon-est dialogue about what kind of world we want to live in and what we believe constitutes human fulfillment. Hiding behind either a bogus sci-entific or moral authority does noting to promote this dialogue. No one knows absolute truth, but we can search for better versions of the truth if we engage in human discourse with our fellow human beings. We should not let scientific or technical people resolve questions of value under the guise of dealing with "factual" information. Nor should a moral authority be imposed on a situation by applying principles that are supposedly devel-oped in the realm of pure thought separated from experience.

We must deal with value and ethical questions explicitly and debate them on both philosophical and empirical grounds. The pragmatic approach to moral and scientific thinking will hopefully take the dialogue and debate about normative versus empirical business ethics beyond the dead ends too often offered by traditional approaches. Pragmatism does not accept the traditional alternatives, nor does it bounce between them, but presents a different way of looking at humans and the moral situations in which they are enmeshed in a way which undercuts or renders irrelevant many of the traditional dichotomies. Facts and values both emerge out of human expe-rience as we constantly make decisions and critically examine the conse-quences of our actions. They are part and parcel of one ontological unity and are continually changing as we learn new things about our world.

For the pragmatist and others of a similar bent on the issue, the fact-value interrelation ultimately involves not the basic intuition of trying to bring together that which is ultimately disparate but rather the basic intu-ition of the emergence of that which is ultimately a relational whole where it may be useful to discriminate facts and values for more practical purposes. Pragmatism provides a framework which rejects the logic of the original questioning in terms of which both the problem and all its possible alterna-tives have arisen. As William James astutely notes, the solution will not be found by a choice among alternatives offered by the original questioning, but rather the solution to the fact-value problem "consists in simply closing one's ears to the question."[11]

THE NATURE OF VALUE

The belief in absolute or transcendental values and the desire for certitude in knowledge are deeply entrenched and intertwined with each other.[12] Pragmatism, however, treats all knowledge as fallible to be tested by its consequences in experience. And knowledge emerges through intelligent reflection on experience within nature. Our experience with nature undergoes continual change, and while some aspects of this experience are relatively stable, other aspects are unstable. The desire for some value to hold on to as a permanent basis of security in an uncertain world is strong, and hence it is all too easy to focus on certain value aspects of experience and then falsely project them into an absolute unchanging reality.

With the rise of modern science this means of attaining a feeling of security began to dissolve given the inherent uncertainty within science itself. Those who wanted to hold on to a view of absolute value had to make a sharp distinction between the experimental method of science and the methods of pure reason by which values could be grasped. It came to be believed that there are absolute unchanging values for all to know if they are reasoning correctly. These values were universal in that they applied to all situations in all times and places. If people were using pure reason they could transcend interests and biases and arrive at these values which were unchanging and unconditional in their application.[13]

Others, while accepting the dichotomy between the method of science and the way we come to hold certain values, rejected pure reason as an approach to value and instead claimed that values are whatever an individual thinks or feels is valuable and therefore value is merely subjective. Value was understood as a highly individualistic affair with no objectivity that would give value the status of knowledge within a scientific worldview. Experimental method was not needed because value was no more than a subjective feeling. That this view leads to a highly relativistic approach to value should be no mystery.

Within pragmatism, "value is not something subjective housed either as a content of mind or in any other sense within the organism, but neither is it something 'there' in an independently ordered universe." Values emerge out of human experience in interaction with the environment in which humans exist. The things that humans confront in their experience possess qualities such as fulfilling or stultifying, appealing or unappealing, that are just as real as more "objective" qualities such as color, size, hardness, and the like that are scientifically determinable. The former types of qualities, like all qualities, are real emergents in the context of our interactions with our cultural and natural environments. They are immediately experienced and are not reducible to other qualities, although they emerge in conjunction with other qualities.[14]

A scientist, for example, would reduce water to its components of hydrogen and oxygen in certain proportions. Water is reducible to and is nothing but a combination of these two elements as far as the scientist is concerned. From the standpoint of emergence, however, reducing water to its components in this manner loses hold of the qualities of water that make it an important factor in human experience. These qualities include wetness, buoyancy, thirst quenching, etc., all of which are dependent on the context of interaction between hydrogen and oxygen, but are as real in their emergence as the elements themselves. To ask where the wetness is located, in the hydrogen or oxygen, is a wrong question. It is in neither but emerges in the context of their interaction.

Similarly, to ask where value is located, in me or in nature independently of me, is a false question. Value emerges in the context of the interactions of humans in nature and is there in that context. Valuing experiences are not the experience of evaluating experience from the outside, so to speak, but arise from the immediate "having" of experience in its value-laden dimensions. Perhaps the word *felt* can also capture this immediacy of a value experience, but it must not be understood psychologically. What we come to hold as valuable is dependent on this more primary level of the immediate having of experience. For what we come to hold as valuable gains this status because of its ability to promote human experience in its entirety. The authority of moral claims lies in their experiential consequences, and in moral situations these experiential consequences are valuing experiences.

Our valuing experiences require a normative context to gain normative weight, and what we eventually claim or believe to be valuable eventually emerges from these experiences. Yet these claims or beliefs themselves must at other times be further evaluated as they are not immune from further inquiry and can become problematic in certain contexts and situations. Values which conflict with each other in a specific context are problematic. Even those values which have stood the test of time, and in this sense could be considered as secured values, are context dependent and are never immune from becoming problematic. What is a secured value in one context, according to Hickman, may become problematic in another context.

> In short, we human beings experience inherent value only in the highly attenuated sense that certain things are unreflectively *valued*. But since nature retracts what is valued as quickly and as unpredictably as it proffers it, it is the job of intelligence, or technology, to ascertain whether what is valued is also *valuable*; and if it be found to be such, to work to secure it.[15]

Value situations, like all situations, are open to experimental inquiry. Such inquiry requires creatively organizing or reinterpreting the problematic situation, directing one's activity in light of that creative reorganization, and testing for its truth in terms of consequences: does it work in bringing about the intended result? With respect to value, the intended result is the valuable result, one that can harmonize and integrate the diversity of conflicting values operative within the situation. When habitual modes of organizing behavior do not work in resolving problematic situations where conflict is involved, new evaluations take place and new moral claims emerge through the dynamics of experimental method. Moral action is planned rational action rooted in and awareness of potentialities for enriching the value experience for all involved. Experimental method is the way to increase the value ladenness of a situation through a creative growth of perspective which can incorporate and harmonize conflicting or potentially conflicting values.[16] According to Hickman again:

> He [Dewey] thought that what is experienced merely as *valued* . . . usually involves a quality of an experience that is just unreflectively enjoyed, of else just posited as an end-in-view to be tested . . . But what is determined to be *valuable* . . . is a deliberately (technologically) mediated and enriched relation between an inquirer and the subject matter of his or her inquiry . . . It is in fact one of the functions of enquiry to fix more precisely the locus of something that is just haphazardly experienced as valued, so that it can be more securely placed within the historical-cultural context of a person's life-world and thereby be made more secure qua valuable.[17]

The distinction between the valuing and the valuable, between what is satisfying in the immediate situation and what is satisfactory in a more universal sense, is not an attempt to derive an ought from an is, a value from a fact based on experience. Any experienced fact within the world can have a value dimension, and the value dimension emerges as an aspect of the context within which the fact functions as value relevant.[18] The functional relation between valuing experiences and objective value claims must work as an organic unity in the ongoing course of experience to increase the value dimension of experience. Such a relationship requires a constant openness to change through reconstruction of the valuable incorporating the dynamics of experimental inquiry.

Moreover, it must be remembered that experience is not something subjective which cuts us off from an objective nature, but rather experience occurs within nature and is the experience of nature. Qualitative experience is experience of that which emerges within our natural interaction with our environment.[19] Valuings are turned into the valuable by the organizing activity of the mind in the ongoing course of experience as experimental. Normative claims are claims concerning consequences of conduct as yielding that which is valuable, and that which is valuable is so because of its production of enriching valuing experiences. Our normative claims are thus naturally rooted in our contextual embeddedness within nature. As Hickman states:

> Put another way, one of the significant consequences of the Pragmatists' claim that ideas have consequences (that are operationally related to the situation or context from which they have come) is that not all ideas, not all standpoints, are equally valuable. This is not to deny that what is valued varies across cultures or even that conflicting statements may be equally valued. It is rather to hold that in many cases in which there are conflicts regarding what is to be valued, the Pragmatic method provides the tools by means of which we can determine which of the conflicting values can be demonstrated to be valuable.[20]

Value is not something which the individual experiences in isolation from a community nor are individual values something to be put in conflict with community values. Yet, community values are not merely the sum of individual values nor are individual values merely a reflection of community values. Rather, values in their emergence within everyday experience are dimensions of social experience. The experience of value emerges as both shared and unique as all experience is both shared and unique. It is the adjustment between these two aspects, the shared and unique, which gives rise to novel and creative aspects within moral community.[21] The emergence of moral norms and practices does not occur apart from the social interaction of concrete organisms, yet the creativity of the individual helps to bring about changes of moral perceptions and restructures moral behavior and practices and institutional ways of behaving.

Thus Dewey claims that though moral deliberation involves "social intelligence," the reaction of the individual against an existing scheme becomes the means of the transformation and restructuring of habits and institutional practices.[22] Each individual is under an obligation to develop advanced moral standards and to conscientiously use those which he or she already possesses.[23] As new standards and ideals emerge, the rational order which underlies a moral community and which provides the adjudication process for conflicts is re-created. Though the slow evolution of such a re-creation may at times be difficult to discern, it may at times seem to manifest itself with startling energy and immediacy.

The resolution of conflicting moral perceptions which provide the context for new ideals cannot be resolved by appeal to abstract principles, but through a deepening sensitivity to the demands of human valuing in their commonness and diversity. Such a deepening does not negate the use of intelligent inquiry, but frees it up from past rigidities and abstractions and focuses it on the immediate experience of value as it emerges in concrete human existence. This allows us to grasp different moral contexts, to take the perspective of "the other," to participate in dialogue with "the other" to determine what is valuable.[24]

Our moral claims can change the very quality of experience. And our moral claims are themselves always subject to evaluation and revision in terms of their ability to provide for the ongoing value dimension of existence. There is nothing immune from potential revision. In this ongoing process not all value-related experience can be accepted, for some, if pursued, would lead to conflict and disintegration. Thus while moral claims are about the production of value, the production of harmonious situations which allow for the unimpeded experience of value require that we at times attempt to alter the quality of our value-related experience because of new "oughts" which have emerged as a result of experimental inquiry.

MORAL PLURALISM AND COMMUNITY

In addition to the fact-value problem, business ethics is also faced with the problem of moral pluralism given the existence of many different ethical theories about what is right and wrong and good or bad, and this poses problems for ethical decision making. Moral pluralism is the view that no single moral principle or overarching theory of what is right or good can be appropriately applied in all ethical problematic situations. There is no one unifying monistic principle from which lesser principles can be derived. Different moral theories are possible depending upon which values or principles are included. The end result of moral pluralism is moral confusion regarding which theory or principles to apply in a given situation. This problem leads Derry and Green to conclude that there is "a persistent unwillingness to grapple with tensions between theories of ethical reasoning," which in turn hampers an understanding of ethical decision making.[25]

To deal with this problem of moral pluralism requires reaching a deeper unifying level of moral reasoning that explains why and how we choose among various theories and principles in an ongoing process of dealing with change and novelty. What is required is a philosophical grounding for moral reasoning that is itself inherently pluralistic in its approach to moral reasoning. Pragmatism offers such a philosophical foundation for dealing with moral pluralism that involves the deepening of moral reasoning to get beneath formalized abstract rules and procedures and stresses the central importance of attunement or sensitivity to individuals and the unique concrete situations in which they are enmeshed and within which moral problems emerge.

Within the pragmatic view of ethical reasoning, traditional ethical theories are taken as moral hypotheses that may shed light on a given situation, but are by no means to be taken as absolute. The belief in absolute or transcendental values and the desire for certitude are deeply entrenched in Western societies and particularly in business schools because of their scientific orientation. Pragmatism, however, threats all knowledge as fallible to be tested by its consequences in experience. Knowledge emerges through intelligent reflection on experience within nature and this experience undergoes continual change and gives rise to different situations that involve ethical dimensions. The desire for some value to hold on to as a permanent basis of security in an uncertain world is strong and hence it is all too easy to focus on certain value aspects of experience and then falsely project them into an absolute and unchanging reality. Dewey states:

> A moral law, like a law in physics, is not something to swear by and stick to at all hazards; it is a formula of the way to respond when specified conditions present themselves. Its soundness and pertinence are tested by what happens when it is acted upon. It claim or authority rests finally upon the imperativeness of the situation that has to be dealt with, not upon its own intrinsic nature—as any tool achieves dignity in the measure of needs served by it.[26]

Thus a moral law is not fixed and absolute; it is not something that is to be applied without evaluation as to its relevance to the immediate situation. And it is to be judged in terms of its consequences, does it produce good consequences for all involved? Does it promote the enrichment of human existence? One cannot say that adherence to a moral law or principle absolves one of further responsibility to evaluate the outcome of that application. One cannot rest on a conviction that at least the right thing was done regardless of the consequences. The consequences are essential in an evaluation as to whether the right thing was indeed done.

From the pragmatic perspective, moral action and decision making are not understood as the application of an absolute rule to specific situations since moral principles are considered to be hypotheses which require ongoing testing and interpretation in specific contexts. Nor can moral action be understood as the development of certain character traits or virtues through the inculcation of traditional ways of acting within the culture. The acceptance of inculcated habits and the formalized rigidities to which they lead hampers a deepened sensitivity to the moral dimensions of concrete situations. For pragmatism, moral character involves the ability to deal with changing and novel situations in ways which work to increase the moral richness of experience, which leads to moral growth for the individual and the community.

In place of the traditional understanding of moral reasoning as abstract and discursive, pragmatism understands moral reasoning to be concrete and imaginative. Moral reasoning as concrete does not work downward from moral rules to their application to concrete situations bur rather works upward from concrete moral experience toward guiding moral hypotheses. For pragmatism, rationality itself is imaginative, for imagination provides the capability of understanding what is actual in light of what is possible to create, of seeing conflicts between moral rules in light of a projected creative synthesis. It reinterprets and reappropriates the past in light of the possibilities operative in the present and the consequences for the future.

The past with its traditions and moral rules is not to be ignored. Many of our most ingrained rules and traditions have become such because they have worked remarkably well and need to be given attention. We evaluate and make moral decisions within the context of a traditional heritage that gives us a somewhat general consensus about moral behavior from which to begin our actions and decisions. For example, in our society we tend to agree in a general fashion that lying, cruelty, stealing, killing, etc., are to be avoided in favor of fairness, kindness, concern for others, and similar measures. Thus we have a general common moral orientation. Guidelines such as these are working hypotheses that have emerged from past concrete situations and are held so strongly because they continue to work well in creating and maintaining what we believe constitutes a moral society. But these can serve only as guides whose contours are shaped and reshaped in ongoing novel concrete situations.

Traditional moral theories attempt to explain our deeply ingrained moral orientation and concrete decision making in terms of one unifying principle or set of principles. It is not that traditional moral theories do not get hold of important dimensions operative in our moral decisions, but that in lifting out one aspect or one dimension they ignore the many others reducing moral action to some fixed scheme. Utilitarian theories, deontological theories, and the various social contract or libertarian theories of justice all get at something important in moral decision making, but they each leave out important considerations highlighted by the other theories.

Taken together, they are often contradictory because they each are attempting to substitute for a concrete, rich moral sense operative in decision making, some one consideration to which this moral sense gives rise which is interwoven with other considerations that function at various times and in various situations. The single consideration of each theory is then turned into a moral absolute which overrides all other considerations and rejects the very concrete moral sense which underlies it and mediates its role relative to specific moral situations. Any rule or principle, any schema, is an attempt to make precise and abstract some consideration which seems to be operative in concrete moral experience, but this experience is ultimately too rich and complex to be adequately captured in this manner.

The pragmatic approach thus denies the understanding of moral reasoning as rule application to specific situations. It may seem that what results is a turn to a more broadly based virtue ethics involving a concern with character development. However, the turn to an exclusive concern with being a virtuous person again oversimplifies, in its own way, the richness of moral decision making. In moral decision making we are, and should be, concerned with the kind of character we are developing. But moral decision making cannot be reduced to what kind of character one should develop.

This can be a very important concern, but some moral decisions are less relevant than others as regards their role in forming good habits, but they are of intense moral concern nonetheless. Moreover, the demands of concrete moral situations may lead to morally responsible decisions which go against character traits we have traditionally regarded as important.

What is necessary is not rigid adherence to what we consider good character traits but the intelligence, sensitivity, and flexibility to deal with moral situations in an ongoing context of moral growth. The exclusive focus on character is an abstraction from the contextual richness of moral decision making and the evaluation of consequences. As Dewey so well states: "Consequences include effects upon character, upon confirming and weakening habits, as well as tangibly obvious results. To keep an eye open to these effects upon character may signify the most reasonable of precautions or one of the most nauseating of practices. It may mean concentration of attention upon personal rectitude in neglect of objective consequences . . . But it may mean that the survey of objective consequences is duly extended in time."[27]

Understanding moral action as adherence to preestablished rules encourages rigidity and lack of moral sensitivity. Understanding moral action as the development of a good character of a good will encourages the self-engrossed concern with meaning well or of having good intentions. Each of these provides a comfortable substitute for the difficult task of bringing about good consequences in concrete situations. Morality is more than following rules and more that manifesting a set of inculcated virtues. The most important habits we can develop are habits of intelligence and sensitivity, for neither following rules nor meaning well can suffice. Morality is not postulated in abstract rules to be followed nor in virtues to be inculcated, but rather is discovered in concrete moral experience with all the richness and complexity this involves. It is here that the "foundations" of morality are to be discovered.

In this view, moral reasoning involves an enlargement of the capacity to perceive the complex moral aspects of situations rather than looking for a way to simplify dealing with that which is perceived. It involves sensitivity to the complexity of values involved in a situation and to the interwoven and conflicting moral dimensions. It involves the utilization of creative intelligence directed at the concrete situation rather than abstractions, and an ongoing evaluation of the eventual resolution. This kind of moral reasoning involves being responsive to the possibilities that experience presents to us and taking responsibility for the decisions we make. And these decisions change the situation, which will give rise to new problems requiring new solutions. One cannot just put the problem to bed and forget about it for all intents and purposes. The goal of moral reasoning is not to make the most unequivocal decision but to provide the richest existence for those involved.

This pragmatic pluralism rules out absolutism in ethics as well as subjectivism and relativism, for it is rooted in the conditions and demands of human living and the desire for meaningful and enriching lives. This deepening process gets beneath rules and principles and breaks through inculcated tradition to offer the possibility for operating in a truly open rather than closed perspective. In moral absolutism one claims to have a grasp of absolute truth which most often results in the dogmatic imposition of one's own principles or moral framework on others. In moral relativism one operates from a personal perspective that is closed to others and objective evaluation and results in irresponsible tolerance of any moral position because one is as good as another. Neither position is open to other possibilities for moral evaluation.

The pragmatic view attempts to combine the commonness of human beings exemplified in the accepted norms and practices of tradition and the uniqueness of each human being exemplified in novel approaches to moral situations in an intelligent grounded diversity accompanied by an ongoing reevaluation and continual testing of operative moral hypotheses. This approach to diversity leads neither to a relativism of arbitrary choice nor to an absolutism of no choice with regard to moral practices. It involves neither nihilistic despair nor utopian optimism. Rather it is a meliorism in which, to use Dewey's words, "the specific conditions which exist at one moment, be they comparatively bad or comparatively good, in any event may be bettered . . . it arouses confidence and reasonable hopefulness as (wholesale) optimism does not."[28]

Diversity can lead to irreconcilable conflict, in which case new ways of dealing with conflicting demands must be developed if factionalism is to be prevented and community is to be maintained. Such a development involves growth of the individual and the community, as growth cannot be understood only in terms of one's own interests alone. The growth of the self is a process by which one achieves fuller and richer more inclusive and more complex interactions with one's environment. Workable solutions to moral conflicts cannot be understood just in terms of the artificiality of oneself in isolation, but rather they must be workable for all those whose interests are there to be adjudicated. Mead holds that the process of recognizing the interests of others does not require that one become a sacrificed self but rather than one becomes a larger self.[29]

The pragmatic understanding of growth involves reintegration of problematic situations in ways which lead to expansion of the self and community. The materials for this growth are diversity and conflict. Thus Dewey can hold that growth itself is the only moral "end," that the moral meaning of democracy lies in its contribution to the growth of every member of society,[30] and that growth involves the rational resolution of conflict: conflict between duty and desire, between what is already accomplished and what is possible.[31] Though Dewey refers to growth as an "end," he does not intend this in a technical sense of "end," and indeed growth can best be understood not as an end to be attained, but as a dynamic embedded in the ongoing process of life, just as experimental method is a dynamic embedded in the ongoing course of experience. Experimental method is in fact an attempt to increase the richness of a situation through a creative growth of perspective which can incorporate and harmonize conflicting or potentially conflicting moral positions.[32]

Moral decisions must be judged in terms of their workability to produce good consequences. But workability cannot be taken in the sense of workable for only oneself, for individual selves are inextricably tied to the community of which the self is a part. Nor can workability be taken in terms of short-run expediency, for actions and their consequences extend into an indefinite future and determine the possibilities that become available in that future. Finally, workability cannot be taken in terms of some single aspect of life such as economic workability. Workability in the moral situation must concern the ongoing development of the concrete richness of human experience in its entirety. Workability cannot be understood in terms of one fixed end, for workability involves the enrichment of experience in its entirety. The full significance of workable consequences involved in a moral choice is found in the following quote from Dewey:

> The choice at stake in a moral deliberation or valuation is the worth of this and that kind of character and disposition . . . In committing oneself to a particular course, a person gives a lasting set to his own being. Consequently, it is proper to say that in choosing this object rather than that, one is in reality choosing what kind of person or self one is going to be. Superficially, the deliberation which terminates in choice is concerned with weighing the values of particular ends. Below the surface, it is a process of discovering what sort of being a person most wants to become.[33] [T]he thing actually at stake in any serious deliberation is not a difference of quantity, but what kind of person one is to become, what sort of self is in the making, what kind of a world is making.[34]

Thinking morally is not merely applying rules of community interest, self-interest, universalizability or whatever to some specific act, nor is it acting according to some ultimate value or to some set of ultimate values within which others can be seen as subsets. Nor are virtuous persons those who act merely from good intentions or through the inculcation of some tradition. What is needed for moral reasoning is the development of the reorganizing and ordering capabilities of creative intelligence, the imaginative grasp of authentic possibilities, the vitality of motivation, and a deepened sensitivity to the sense of concrete human existence in its richness, diversity, and complexity. As Dewey holds, a problem must be felt before it can be stated. It is this "felt" dimension that regulates the way one selects, weighs, and conceptually orders what one observes.[35]

Morality is discovered in concrete moral experience, and a vital sense of moral rightness comes not from the application of abstract principles but from attunement to the way in which moral beliefs and practices must be rooted naturally in the very conditions of human existence.[36] It is this kind of attunement which gives vitality of diverse and changing principles as working hypotheses embodied in concrete moral activity. And it provides the ongoing direction for well-intentioned individuals to continually evaluate and at times reconstruct their own habits and traditions as they utilize various human dimensions needed to bring about ongoing enrichment of experience in a changing world. Humans must live with the consequences of their actions within concrete situations in a process of change.

9   Pragmatism and Economics

The social sciences that have to deal with human behavior pose a particular problem for the scientific approach. In economics, for example, the goal of research is to discover those unchanging laws that shape human behavior relative to economic concerns on the assumption that these laws are observable and discoverable just like the natural laws of the physical world. Such research attempts to discover how society works with respect to its economic life and is not concerned with social change or social betterment. Such research claims to be objective in merely describing how things work with respect to economic matters and is not concerned with normative judgments. Scientific research of this nature is not concerned with changing the economic structures people live in to make life better or to promote certain values such as freedom or equality.

Behind every argument for the virtues of the free market is this view of scientific laws that operate best when left to their own devices. Government regulation only interferes with these laws and results in an inefficient allocation of resources. The economy works best when left alone and things are allowed to work according to natural laws that are embedded in the free market. Every argument that is made against government regulation or interference of any sort in the workings of the free market is predicated on this assumption. The scientific approach to the economy where there are laws of supply and demand that allocate resources to their most efficient uses in society is believed to be like that of the physical sciences where there are laws that govern the behavior of physical phenomena. As Dewey says:

> Economic "laws," that of labor springing from natural wants and leading to the creation of wealth, of present abstinence in behalf of future enjoyment leading to the creation of capital effective in piling up still more wealth, the free play of competitive exchange, designated the law of supply and demand, were "natural" laws. They were set in opposition to political laws as artificial, man-made affairs. The inherited tradition which remained least questioned was a conception of Nature which made Nature something to conjure with. The older metaphysical conception of Natural Law was, however, changed into an economic

conception; laws of nature, implanted in human nature, regulated the production and exchange of goods and services, and in such a way that when they were kept free from artificial, that is political, meddling, they resulted in the maximum possible social prosperity and progress.[1]

This view of economic laws is prevalent in the writings of Adam Smith, who saw the economy as some kind of machine that operated best when left alone. The doctrine of laissez-faire is based upon belief in beneficent natural laws that will bring about harmony of personal profit and social benefit. People are to be left free to pursue their self-interest and the invisible hand will assure that resources are allocated to their most productive uses in increasing the wealth of the nations through the production of more and more goods and services. Any interference with this system of natural laws will result in an inefficient allocation of resources and hence a reduction in the wealth of the nation. According to Bob Goudzwaard, writing in *Capitalism and Progress*:

> Adam Smith developed his economic system on the basis of this revised natural law concept. In his view also the correct natural price results from the operation of free competition on the market. Natural law becomes the law of free, unhampered competition. It is precisely this natural order which the government is called upon to guard and conserve. Its task lies first of all in the protection of the civil rights of property, contract, and free enterprise, for these rights constitute the natural order, the indispensable condition for a truly flourishing and prosperous society. If the government would go beyond that by interfering directly in the operation of the free market, it would place itself between man and his potential for self-realization according to the providential plan for this world . . . In short, for Adam Smith the concept of natural law became a suitable servant of the economy.[2]

Such a view of the workings of the economy has its problems, not the least of which is that if there are indeed economic laws that govern the allocation of resources, they will operate regardless of what government or anyone else does or does not do with respect to regulation. Physical laws operate regardless of what humans do and cannot be interfered with or canceled. The law of gravity cannot be repealed and will be operative as far as we know into the indefinite future. Economic laws are not of this nature. The so-called law of supply and demand can be modified to suit other goals and values such as a more equitable distribution of wealth than would be dictated by a free-market approach. Supply of something like drugs can be restricted in the interests of the public good and demand for some things can be made illegal. Government regulations can be adopted that will reallocate resources differently than would be the case if a strictly free-market approach were taken.

Behind the so-called laws of economics are human choices, choices of one good or service over another, one job over other alternatives, and one type of investment over all the choices available. There is nothing automatic or deterministic about these choices. Granted human behavior does fall into patterns or habits that sometimes can be predicted with a high degree of probability, however, there is always the chance of an unpredictable response to a situation. Humans are free to differing degrees to digress from predictable patterns and do something that is completely out of character and unexpected. These choices shape the nature of the facts that we observe which are not free from human interests and concerns. These choices are hidden in the mathematical formulas that are prevalent in economics and make it appear to be an objective science. Dewey states the problem as follows:

> The prestige of the mathematical and physical sciences is great, and properly so. But the difference between facts which are what they are independent of human desire and endeavor and facts which are to some extent what they are because of human interests and purpose, and which alter with alteration in the latter, cannot be gotten rid of by any methodology. The more sincerely we appeal to facts, the greater is the importance of the distinction between facts which condition human activity and facts which are conditioned by human activity. In the degree which we ignore this difference, social science becomes pseudo-science.[3]

The law of supply and demand says that if a good becomes scarce its price will increase to make it more costly; thus more producers will be motivated to supply the good and make a profit, thus increasing the supply and eventually bringing the price down and creating an equilibrium between supply and demand. This so-called law depends on people acting in a certain manner on the basis of certain materialistic values that are captured in the price mechanism. Economic theory assumes people to be rational self-interested creatures that are in competition with each other for the resources that are available in a given society and are expected to act in accordance with this value system. But these laws are only probabilities and are not written into the structure of the universe as are the laws of gravity or thermodynamics. Dewey says that:

> We live as if economic forces determined the growth and decay of institutions and settled the fate of individuals. Liberty becomes a well-nigh obsolete term; we start, go, and stop at the signal of a vast industrial machine. Again, the actual system would seem to imply a pretty definitely materialistic scheme of value. Worth is measured by the ability to hold one's own or to get ahead in a competitive pecuniary race.[4]

These economic forces are believed to be beyond the control of individuals and take on a life of their own that cannot be altered. At least this is what the conventional wisdom regarding markets would have us believe. Thus a depression has to run its course but the system will eventually right itself and economic growth will return. The economy is like a machine that needs to be kept oiled in order to run well, but any interference in its internal mechanism will only create problems. Government's role is only to protect property rights and justice is understood in this sense as it relates to property. Any attempt by government to redistribute resources on a more equitable basis is not to be condoned.

The argument about a free-market approach as opposed to government regulation, however, is not really about efficiency or innovation or any of the other reasons usually given in support of free markets. It is really about who is going to control the system and make the important decisions and about who is going to gain the benefits the system produces. Is it going to be corporate bureaucrats who supposedly make the major decisions about resource allocation and can then allocate themselves a disproportionate share of the resources the system produces as payment for their services, or is it going to be elected politicians whose pay is much less than corporate executives and government bureaucrats who are paid on the basis of civil service pay scales? Is it going to be corporate executives who are really accountable to no one or government politicians and other employees who are at least in some sense accountable to the citizens of the country?

There are no scientific laws that operate with respect to the economy apart from human activity. It is human choices based upon values that drive the economy and make it function in a certain manner. These choices can be made in the market or in the political arena depending on the nature of the problem to be addressed and the power that the actors in the public and private sectors possess. As this book was being written, health care was being debated and a new law passed that many people were unhappy about. The underlying issue about health care, however, is whether it should be considered a public good such that decisions about resource allocation are made primarily in the public sector, or whether it should be considered a private good to be supplied by private institutions interested in making a profit. Which way can provide the best health care for the most people in society? It is society that has to make these choices through individual participation in the market and in the political system.

CAPITALISM

Capitalism as an economic system seems to have won the day as far as organization of economic activity is concerned. It has proven to be more productive in providing goods and services to consumers and providing a way for people to pursue economic goals with greater freedom than alternatives such as socialism. Given its success, capitalism or some variation thereof has come to be the primary way people in countries around the world organize themselves to provide for their material needs and comfort. This development along with the growth of democracies around the world led some scholars to declare an end to history as free markets and democratic liberalism were considered to be the highest and final development of humankind as far as economic and political institutions are concerned.[5]

The defining characteristics of a pure capitalistic system are (1) private ownership of the means of production, (2) the existence of free or wage labor, (3) the existence of the profit motive, and (4) the drive to amass capital.[6] Many people think of socialism as any government program that restricts their freedom, but as long as the means of production remains in private hands pure socialism doesn't exist. The existence of unions is also not socialism but merely a means for workers to bargain collectively for the things they want, like higher wages and better working conditions. The profit motive is what supposedly drives people to do the things necessary for economic growth. And amassing both physical and financial capital is necessary to provide the means for production to take place on an ever-increasing scale.

The capitalistic system is rooted in science since economics as a scientific discipline provides a scientific explanation of how the system works to produce goods and services to meet consumer preferences and provide employment and income to workers. Macroeconomics describes the working of the economy as a whole and is concerned with the growth and stability of the overall economy, while microeconomics is concerned with the behavior of the firm in a competitive environment. While individual firms are concerned with their survival in a competitive environment, the government is primarily concerned with the macro aspects of the economy in managing fiscal and monetary policy keep the economy growing. In recent decades economics has become a highly mathematized discipline and has no need for any moral considerations related to the distribution of wealth in our society or to the adverse effects of economic growth.[7]

Science allows for the objectification of people so that they are seen as nothing more than cogs in a machine whose purpose is production of more and more goods and services so private companies can make a profit. The split between mind and matter that has characterized science for centuries contributed to this objectification. People are treated as objects in economic theory rather than living human beings with hopes and fears, dreams and disappointments. They are made to serve the capitalistic system, which is interested in profit and economic growth for its own sake. They have no responsibilities to each other or to themselves other than to make as much money as possible and keep on participating in the system so it can continue to grow and create economic wealth. Economics treats the self as a rational economic entity that is solely concerned with its economic well-being and thinks of society as solely concerned with the growth of economic wealth. Other aspects of the self and society are not considered to be part of the system and are abstracted out of consideration. Again, according to Goudzwaard:

Objectification of people can occur with reference to employees (who are accordingly plugged into the production process as mere suppliers of almost infinitely divisible units of labor), as well as with reference to consumers. Consumers are made into objects when they are manipulated by marketing techniques as just so may bundles of psychic impression and motivations. The mark of objectification is that people are no longer treated as bearers of responsibilities. A business enterprise, for example, treats a consumer as an object when it no longer appeals to his sense of responsibility, but instead attempts to overrule or manipulate his choice. Employees, similarly, can be reduced to objects by the minimization or destruction of the possibility of making responsible choices of their own. Morality is always a matter of the recognition of other people's responsibilities.[8]

Economics as a scientific discipline prescribes the role of business in a capitalistic society and provides a justification for its existence. Business is solely an economic institution whose purpose is to create more and more economic wealth. This purpose is able to be quantified and measured by the ability of a business organization to generate profits and increase the price of its shares traded on the stock exchanges. The success of society as a whole is measured by an increase or decrease in gross national product, or gross domestic product as it is often called. Our fascination with and belief in quantification is reflected in these measures of success. When things go wrong as indicated by these measures, we have confidence that we can manipulate things in the economy such as interest rates or change certain aspects of corporate behavior to make things right.

The economy, however, cannot be so neatly separated from or absorb the rest of society. The economic system is fully woven into the fabric of society as only one dimension, inseparable from other dimensions of the sociocultural matrix in which we act out our day-to-day existence. The economic dimension is but one aspect of our existence, and the economic system, far from being a reality engulfing the social aspect, is the result of giving a supposedly independent status to a discriminable dimension of our total existence, an existence which is inherently social in nature. The economic system ultimately cannot even stand on its own conceptually and to isolate it for purposes of analysis and manipulation severs it from the very context which makes it intelligible as a discriminable and moral force in society.

WEALTH

The capitalistic system has proven to be better at creating economic wealth than other systems, but what this wealth consists of is usually taken for granted. Economic wealth is created when resources that have no economic value in themselves are combined in such a way that goods and services are produced that are of value to the society. Most natural resources, for example, have no utility or economic value in their natural state. They have to be mined and processed through several stages in order to be made into something useful that can be sold in the marketplace. Similarly, land in its natural state usually has no economic value in and of itself, but must be plowed so that crops can be planted and eventually harvested to be processed into food products. Or the land can be reshaped so that it can be used for a housing development or for some commercial project. Humans have no value in and of themselves. It is only when they learn certain skills that they can get a job that is of value to employers or provide a service such as lawn care or household cleaning that can be sold on the marketplace.

When these resources are then made into useful products that can be sold on the marketplace, the economic wealth of the nation is increased. If companies have done things right in the sense of producing something people want to buy because it is useful to them, and have done so efficiently so that people can afford to buy the things that are produced, they are rewarded with profits that represent companies' share of the wealth that has been created. These profits are used to support the operations of the corporation and are paid out as dividends to shareholders who have risked their money by investing in the stock of the corporation.

Wealth is generally considered to be a neutral entity as far as morality is concerned. It is thought of as an economic concept that has no moral implications. However, wealth does not exist in a vacuum but exists in a particular social context. How that wealth was created and how it is distributed has all sorts of moral implications. Was it created by an honest effort where employees were paid reasonable wages and salaries and consumers were provided with product that was safe to use as directed? Or was it produced by exploiting employees and producing a product that harmed people? Did managers take an unreasonable share of that wealth to put in their own pockets, or was it shared fairly with employees and shareholders? Were the resources extracted from nature in a way that preserved the environment or was the natural environment seriously degraded in the process? These are all moral questions that can have serious consequences for the society at large.

Economic wealth is an elusive concept and something of a fiction. Several trillions of dollars disappeared from the American economy during the bursting of the high-tech bubble in the early years of the twenty-first century. All the major stock exchanges plummeted from their highs reached only a year or so earlier. Nasdaq was once over the 5,000 level but plunged below the 2,000 level as high-tech and dot.com stocks took a beating. The Dow went below the 12,000 level and stayed there for many months. Companies such as Cisco Systems, which in March 2000 had the largest market capitalization of any company in the country, larger even that General Electric or Microsoft, saw its stock, which at one time had been close to $90 a share, plunge to less than $20 a share. What happened to all this wealth? Where did it go? Can such wealth ever be created again?

A major reason for this loss was the end of the high-tech revolution, in particular the dot.com companies that had been created to revolutionize retailing. Many of these companies, such as E-Toys, which had one of the best Web sites in the business, did not make it and went out of business. Others, such as Amazon.com, struggled through this period but continued as viable companies. There was talk during the dot.com frenzy that economic realities such as profits were no longer relevant as many of these companies continued to increase in wealth as measured by their stock prices whether or not they made any profits. But economic realities eventually set in and profits again became relevant.

Apparently many of the assumptions behind the dot.com revolution failed to materialize, and many of these companies, despite the initial euphoria, did not produce something that was useful to enough people in society to make them a viable entity. People were not going to sit at home at their computers and do all their shopping. What may have been forgotten is the social nature of shopping, that people like to go to malls, even though it may be inconvenient, and do their shopping in a social context. Thus the large retailers like Walmart and Sears were not put out of business by the dot.com companies. The economic wealth that the latter companies generated through an increase in stock price was fictional and based on speculation that these companies were eventually going to be profitable entities that would continue in existence. But this did not prove to be true and the wealth they generated disappeared as fast as it was created.

Even more so-called wealth disappeared during the financial crisis later in the decade. Large investment banks like Lehman Brothers went bankrupt and others were saved only by merging with other companies. The Dow plunged below 8,000 and the S&P 500 went below 800 at one point. All told, some 8 trillion dollars disappeared as the housing bubble burst, which was based on the assumption that housing prices would continue to increase. Where did this money go? What happened to all the economic wealth this money supposedly represented? Was it all just fictional based on an assumption that proved to be false? Was there anything real and objective behind all this wealth?

Were the routers and other equipment Cisco Systems produced any less important to the future development of the Internet than they were before its stock price plunged and it became worth a great deal less in economic terms? Were the houses that people had to get out of because of foreclosure of any less value as far as providing living space to people? What is the real worth of a company like General Motors or General Electric? Was Citigroup worth the high stock price it once had or was it worth the near zero it plunged to in the financial crisis? Were the services it provided to the economy any less valuable? Thus economic wealth has a fictional quality;

it is an abstraction that represents something, but that something is elusive and certainly much less than an objective entity.

Who gets to decide what any company listed on the stock exchange is worth? The real worth of these companies, one could argue, lies in the goods and services they produce and whether these goods and services enhance the lives of people such that they are willing to buy them on the marketplace. But people change their minds about what is of value to them and sometimes this change can take place quite rapidly. The point is that wealth is more or less whatever the community says it is; wealth is not objective in nature. What something is worth does not reside in the product itself, nor does it lie in an individual consumer or investor, but emerges from the interaction of millions of people who participate in the marketplace. Value is an emergent property that represents the judgments of millions of people who express their preferences through marketplace transactions. It is a community or common product rather than being an individualistic and objective quality.

Value, then, is not something subjective housed either as a content of mind or in any other sense within the organism, but neither is it something "there" in an independently ordered universe. When we interact with objects in our natural or cultural environment, this interaction gives rise to qualities such as alluring or repugnant, fulfilling or stultifying, appealing or unappealing, and so forth. These qualities are real emergent properties that arise in the context of our interactions with our natural and cultural environments. These qualities are immediately experienced and are not reducible to other qualities and are as real in their emergence as the processes within which they emerge. Our value judgments make claims about the importance of promoting or not promoting the production of these qualities.

Values change, however, as our experience within nature and culture undergoes continual change. Some aspects of this experience are relatively stable; other aspects are unstable. Values can become problematic in certain situations. Humans have a strong desire to hold onto some values as a permanent basis of security in an uncertain world, and it is all too easy to focus on certain value aspects of experience and then falsely project them into an absolute, unchanging reality. Modern science challenges this view of values as absolute and claims that value is merely subjective and relative and a highly individualistic affair; no more than a subjective feeling or matter of opinion.

However, as emergent properties values are neither subjective nor objective, neither absolute nor relative, they are emergent in the ongoing course of experience. The experience of value is both shared and unique. Values are not experienced by the individual in isolation from a community nor are they to be put in conflict with or in opposition to community values. Yet community values are not merely the sum of individual values nor are individual values merely a reflection of community values. Instead, value in its emergence with everyday experience is a dimension of social experience. The adjustment between the shared and unique features of value gives rise to new dimensions of social change, brings creative solutions to the resolution of conflicting and changing value claims, and restructures the behavior and practices of individuals and institutionalized ways of behaving.

Thus the price of a stock represents the judgments of all the people who participate in the stock market as to the continued viability of a particular company. The price of a product represents the values of all the people who make a judgment about the usefulness of that product to themselves. This is the genius of market systems, as they allow for much more information to be exchanged and thus can come up with some level of economic value that represents the judgment of the community as a whole. Socialistic systems that did not allow this kind of information to be processed had trouble coming up with values that were workable such that the system could perform efficiently. This inefficiency eventually led to their downfall.

The invisible hand of Adam Smith, then, is not all that invisible. The interactions of millions of people on the marketplace give rise to values as to how much a company is worth or how much a given product is worth to consumers as a whole. These values represent wealth, economic wealth that we are able to quantify and count, which gives it a certain objective status. But this status is illusory; wealth is constantly changing as people's values change relative to what is important in their lives. This value dimension of human experience is what is most important and it is what companies try to tap into with their products and marketing programs that try to create new values and new experiences that are valuable to consumers.

Economics is about value and how this value is determined. It is not about quantitative measures that give the illusion of something objective and scientifically determinable. The goods and services that are exchanged are discrete units or they could not be traded on the market. The value that emerges from these transactions is an exchange value; it is not a value that resides in the thing itself or in the holder of the thing. Value emerges out of the interactions of thousands of people in the market and that value is expressed in economic terms as a price. No one person can dictate what that price is finally going to be based on their values nor can anyone ascertain on a scientific of any other basis the intrinsic value of the things traded on the market.

Economic wealth, then, is a community product. But communities are interested in much more than just economic wealth, as the people in those communities live out their lives in multiple contexts with the economic system being but one of their concerns. The community is also concerned about the state of its human resources, the health and educational level of its population, among other things. It is also concerned about the state of its culture and whether there are enough cultural activities for its people to enjoy. Society is also concerned about the state of the environment, its natural capital, if you will, and whether this is being depleted or degraded significantly so that the long-term prospects of the community will be seriously affected. These are all aspects of a community's wealth, if you will, and notions about wealth need to be expanded beyond just economic wealth to take in more contexts and embrace the fullness and richness of human existence in its entirety.

GROWTH

Consistent with viewing capitalism as solely an economic system is the focus on economic growth or wealth creation as the be-all and end-all of society. Economic growth, measured in terms of production and consumption, is a moral end in itself, a self-justifying process which has a life of its own. Capitalistic societies have to keep growing economically; they have to keep producing more and more goods and services to keep going. People have to be encouraged to keep working at producing things and persuaded to keep buying the things they are producing. Capitalism is a never-ending cycle of production and consumption that has no end and keeps using up natural and human resources in a quest for continued economic growth. In a sense, capitalism has no reason for existing other than to continue the production of goods and services for consumption. As Adam Smith said, the wealth of nations consists of the goods and services they can produce for their citizens.

But if we view the economy as being embedded in a larger social system of which economics is only a part, it is legitimate to ask what larger purpose all this production and consumption serves. Supposedly it is to make people's lives better in some sense, but in many cases the focus on economic growth seems to be an intrusion into the search for meaningfulness and enrichment of life which consists of multiple dimensions and is embedded in multiple environments. Yet people in capitalistic societies spend the majority of their lives in just the economic dimension playing out their roles as producers with jobs in capitalistic institutions and as consumers in the marketplace that is filled with ever more goods and services that promise an elusive fulfillment.

Viewing capitalism as a social system involves an understanding of growth that can provide direction for our productive and consumption activities in a manner that nourishes the desire of humans for a full and rich existence, the infusion of experience with meaningfulness and self-development and for the flourishing of the multiple environments in which they are embedded. This entails a radical rethinking which roots economic growth in a moral vision of human existence that provides production and consumption activities with moral direction rooted in the goal of the enhancement of human existence in all its richness and complexity. Economic growth is not an end in itself nor is it an unmitigated good in itself, but must be seen and evaluated in the total social context in which humans exist and how it enhances the life of the community.

With the pragmatic understanding of self and community, growth cannot be understood in terms of mere accumulation or mere increase of anything that can be quantified. Rather, growth involves the ongoing enhancement of experience to bring about the integration and expansion of the social contexts with which selfhood is intertwined. Growth is a process by which humans achieve fuller, richer, more inclusive, and more complex interactions with the multiple environments in which they are relationally embedded. To speak of economic development as enhancing the quality of life, while destroying the environments within which humans achieve ongoing growth, shows the abstract and nonrelational understanding of the self incorporated in the concept of economic development.

From the pragmatic perspective, economic growth is an abstraction from the complexity of a situation, and when economic growth stifles rather than furthers growth of the self and community this indicates that economic growth is an abstraction which has become distortive of the fullness of the reality in which it is embedded. It is a fallacy to think that an abstract and quantified view of economics has an ontological independence from the qualitatively rich, value-laden reality from which the abstraction of a quantified economic system developed. This abstraction removes the economy from its moral purpose and makes it into a mechanistic reality that operates according to its own laws without any larger moral purpose. However, the moral purpose of the economic system is embedded in nature as a dimension of ongoing growth of the self and community.

Questions have been posed asking, "How good are goods?" implying that economic goods are not an unmitigated blessing.[9] These questions can only be answered in specific contexts, however, because goods and services are only as good as their contributions to the enrichment of human existence, and this always occurs in specific situations. Economic wealth can enslave people as they spend more and more time worrying about their investments and have more and more goods to worry about, or wealth can offer further opportunities for ongoing growth. Too often increased consumption serves as a desperate substitute for meaning and purpose, but such consumption can also offer possibilities for enhanced attunement to the esthetic-moral richness of human existence.

Too often in the contemporary world the economy is pitted against the environment; that we have to choose between continued economic growth at the expense of the environment or that we have to choose to enhance and preserve the environment at the expense of economic growth. This choice is an artificially created alternative, however, that distorts the very nature of the richness of the reality that both the environment and the economy ultimately serve. The protection of the environment and economic growth are inextricably joined through their dependency on the esthetic-moral nature of growth as involving the ongoing integration and expansion of multiple contexts in their full qualitative richness. Human development is connected with its ecological as well as its economic context. The deepening and expansion of perspective to include ever-widening horizons must extend beyond the economic to the natural world with which we are inseparably intertwined.

Reduction of consumption in industrial societies can have severe repercussions. Since about two-thirds of gross national product or its equivalent in developed countries consists of consumer purchases, any severe reduction of consumer expenditures would have serious implications for employment, income, investment, and everything else tied to economic growth. Lower consumption could be destructive to advanced industrial societies. Yet if consumption is not reduced, ecological forces may eventually dismantle advanced societies in ways we can't control and that would be even more destructive.[10] If a holistic approach to growth is taken, the collision course between the economy and the environment could be undercut.

Dealing with this problem involves a new moral consciousness that can guide production and consumption in ways that allow for the ongoing development of human existence in its entirety. Economic and environmental policies must constantly be evaluated in terms of their contribution to this goal. If this change in moral consciousness can be brought about, consumers in industrial societies may begin to curtail the use of those things that are ecologically destructive and instead cultivate the deeper nonmaterial sources of fulfillment that writers like Durning claim are the main psychological determinants of happiness, such as family, social relationships, meaningful work, and leisure. In this way economic growth could be directed toward furthering the development of pathways that accommodate the ongoing enrichment of these human needs.

To accomplish this goal, there must be a reversal of the long, gradual evolution of the severing of the economy from its moral foundation which led to the establishment of production and consumption as ends in themselves and to an acquisitive society that sees growth as the accumulation of more and more economic wealth. These destructive abstractions must be returned to the moral ground of growth of the self and community which ultimately gives them meaning and vitality. What is needed is a new moral milieu, a new moral/cultural consciousness that undercuts the chasm between the economy and the environment as well as other contexts in which humans live and work out a meaningful existence.

Thus wealth and growth are reinterpreted from a pragmatic perspective to correspond with a social view of the self and community where capitalism is seen as a social system to enhance the multiple dimensions of human existence. It is not just an economic system that focuses on the creation of economic wealth, the enhancement of economic growth, and the promotion of the individual's right to use property in his or her own interests with no obligation to the community. Capitalism is much more than this and can be viewed as a system that enhances the efficient use of resources available to the community to enrich the total existence of the community in which individuals are embedded. In doing this the multiple environments in which humans exist must be enhanced rather that exploited in the interests of promoting a narrow focus only on economic growth and wealth creation.

10 Pragmatism and Politics

The United States has a problem with government that is related to its excessive individualism that a scientific worldview promotes. Government is seen as a necessary evil and not as something positive, something the populace must put up with while resenting the seeming necessity of government. The best government is the government that governs least and lets the market function with minimum interference. Many believe that our liberty itself depends on a distrust of government and that any acceptance of government as something positive in the life of our country will lead to extension of its powers that eventually will enslave its citizens. Many years ago Henry David Thoreau stated this credo in the following manner:

> I heartily accept the motto, "That government is best which governs least"; and I should like to see it acted up to more rapidly and systematically. Carried out, it finally amount to this, which I also believe, "That government is best which governs not at all."[1]

Our Constitution, with its separation of powers, was designed to prevent the government from the exercise of arbitrary power and is not concerned about promoting the efficiency of government. The system of checks and balances contained in the Constitution prevents any one branch of government from taking control and makes it necessary to get agreement from all three branches before any legislation can be passed and upheld. This makes government slow and deliberative but prevents, so it is hoped, any one branch of government from gaining power over the others and acting arbitrarily in the use of this power to dominate society and exercise its will over its citizens.

Liberty is considered to be a zero-sum game; that any power given to the government is by necessity subtracted from the liberty of the governed. Thus any attempt to pass a health-care bill is seen as taking away the freedom of individuals to choose their own way of fulfilling their health-care needs, which may mean no insurance coverage and visits to the emergency room when health problems arise. Nonetheless, it is better to go without health insurance than be enslaved by big government. Government is always under suspicion that it will take away more freedom from its citizens than its services are worth.[2] According to Garry Wills, it is seen as something that exists apart from the citizens that can take away their liberty.

> Upon its face, the struggle for individual liberty was a struggle against the overbearing menace of despotic rulers. This fact has survived in an attitude towards government which cripples its usefulness as an agency of the general will. Government, even in the most democratic countries, is still thought of as an external "ruler," operating from above, rather than as an organ by which people associated in pursuit of common ends can most effectively cooperate for the realization of their own aims. Distrust of government was one of the chief traits of the situation in which the American nation was born. It is embodied not only in popular tradition, and party creeds, but in our organic laws, which contain many provisions expressly calculated to prevent the corporate social body from affecting its ends freely and easily through government agencies.[3]

Ever since Ronald Reagan declared government to be the problem and not the solution to our problems, this negative view of government has increasingly informed our political environment and made governing more and more difficult. We have been asked to love our country by hating our government, as if the two were totally separable entities. Reagan denigrated a government career so that we are obliged to despise the people we vote into office.[4] Rather than attracting the best and brightest people in society to go into public service, what we have seen is more people in government who do not believe in governing or in serving the public.

No other organization would hire people who do not believe in what the organization is doing and have some commitment to its mission in society. Yet these days we have so many politicians who do not believe in government and who run against government in their campaigns. They like the power and perks that go with government service but do not seem much interested in actual governing and want to reduce the size and scope of the government and let the market function without government regulation. Many have a libertarian streak and want to reduce government to the absolute minimum of providing for national defense and a means to adjudicate disputes over property.[5] These kinds of politicians will often serve in Congress long enough to make themselves valuable as lobbyists to the private sector, where they are then paid large sums of money for their services.

Government is broken and while there are many reasons for this condition, this development is certainly a major reason. For people to function effectively in any organization they have to believe in what they are doing and do their best to fulfill the mission of the organization for which they are working. But it is not only politicians who have a negative view of government; it exists in the society at large or they wouldn't get elected. To some extent, the government we have is a self-fulfilling prophecy. We get the government we want by electing politicians that share our values with respect to government service, and if the society at large does not believe in government they will elect politicians that reflect this belief and will act accordingly in making government dysfunctional.

To a large extent this view of government is the result of the excessive individualism that exists in American society where the individual is taken as the basic building block of society and there is little or no sense of community. Science informs this view of individuals as atoms bumping up against each other in competition for the resources of society. This view is consistent with a free-market orientation. A scientific approach to reality undermines any sense of community that is based on something other than individuals and has a life of its own that goes beyond individual interests; where something like the public good is a reality that can be pursued by government in the interests of the society as a whole. What we have is a fragmented government that has no vision of the public good or the public interest but only appeals to individual interests as they compete for the goods and services government has to offer.

We like to think we are a procedural republic where the only agreed-upon value is that every individual should be free to pursue his or her own conception of the good without undue government interference. Government's only role is to assure that everyone has an equal opportunity to pursue their own goals and objectives in the context of a competitive marketplace. Critics of this notion, such as Michael Sandel, think the procedural republic is a figment of the imagination rather than a basis for any kind of social reality.[6] For any kind of social cohesion to exist there must be some consensus beyond the virtue of pursuing one's own conception of the good. Otherwise there is no possibility of community or of ever reaching an agreement about things that individuals cannot provide for themselves.[7]

The pragmatic view of government builds on this notion of community. John Dewey thinks of government not so much as an institution but as a way of life that is "controlled by a working faith in the possibilities of human nature" that are exhibited by every human being irrespective of color, sex, race, birth and family, and material or cultural wealth. Democracy involves the belief that in spite of individual differences regarding ends and means, people can cooperate on common courses of action by giving the other a chance to express itself instead of having one party forcefully suppress the other. People can learn from each other if differences are given a chance to show themselves. This freedom of expression is not only a right but a means of enriching one's own life experience in the context of community.[8]

Reaching a true community requires a view of the self which is inherently communal rather than individualistic. This social view of the self, which is essential to pragmatism, is embedded in a moral bond that allows for progression toward a common good. This notion of inherently communal selves enmeshed in a common "telos" is supported by a substantive political theory which envisions deliberation among citizens that leads to legislation which promotes the common good or a common conception of the good. This is in contrast to the notion of independent selves that are free of encumbrance by any social or moral bonds that are not self-chosen and is supported by a political theory which advocates a procedural political theory that is devoid of any social or moral content.[9]

PUBLIC GOODS AND SERVICES

A more pragmatic view of government would focus on the idea that government exists to provide those goods and services that cannot be made available through the market. These goods and services can appropriately be referred to as public goods and services as distinguished from the private goods and services exchanged in the market system. Public goods and services are provided to meet the needs of people as expressed through a political system which deals with things that are held in common such as clean air and water and national defense.[10] These goods and services are something tangible provided by the government for all its citizens that cannot be provided by the citizens themselves through market activities.

Most of these things held in common are indivisible in the sense that they cannot be divided into discrete individual units to be purchased by people according to their individual preferences. For all practical purposes, for example, one cannot buy a piece of clean air to carry around and breathe wherever one goes. Nor can one buy a share of national defense over which one would have control. This indivisibility gives these goods and services their public character because if people are to have public goods and services at all, they must enjoy roughly the same amount.[11] No one owns these goods and services individually; they are collectively owned in a sense or held in common and private property rights do not apply. Thus there is nothing to be exchanged on the market and the values people have in regard to these goods and services and decisions about them cannot emerge through a market exchange process.[12]

Those committed to the free market might want to argue that even though public goods and services have these characteristics, they could still be provided through the market system. Suppose, for example, the market offered a consumer the following choice: two automobiles in a car dealer's showroom are identical in all respects even with regard to gas mileage. The only difference is that one car has pollution-control equipment to reduce emissions of pollutants from the car's exhaust system while the other car has no such equipment. The car with the pollution-control equipment sells for $500 more than the other. If the consumer values clean air, it could be argued that he or she would choose the more expensive car to help reduce air pollution.

However, such a decision would be irrational from a strict self-interest point of view. The impact that one out of all the millions of cars on the road would have on air pollution is infinitesimal and cannot be measured. No relation exists in this kind of a decision between costs and benefits, as one would in effect be getting nothing for one's money unless one could assume that enough other people would make the same decision so as to materially affect air quality. Such actions, however, assume a common value for clean air that does not exist in marketplace transactions. Thus the market never offers consumers this kind of choice because automobile manufacturers know that pollution-control equipment will not sell in the absence of federally mandated standards.

There is another side to the coin, however, for if enough people in a given region did buy the more expensive car so that the air was noticeably cleaner, there would be a powerful incentive for others to be free riders. Again, the impact of one car would not appreciably alter the quality of the air over a given region, so one would be tempted by self-interest to buy the polluting car at a cheaper price and be a free rider by enjoying the same amount of clean air as everyone else and not paying a cent for its provision.

Because of these characteristics of human behavior and the nature of public goods and services, the market system will not work to provide them for a society that wants them. When goods and services are indivisible among large numbers of people, individual consumers' actions as expressed in the market will not lead to the provision of these goods and services.[13] Society must express its desire for such public goods and services through a political process because the bilateral exchanges facilitated by the market are insufficiently inclusive.[14] Only through the public-policy process can compromises be reached that will resolve the conflicts that are inevitable in relation to public goods and services.

Society as a whole has to decide what public goods and services it wants and is willing to pay for through taxes that it pays to government. In the case of clean air and water, for example, it would seem that these are good for everybody and are in their common interest. However, it is still up to society acting in the public-policy process to decide if they want to provide themselves with this good and incur higher taxes or more costly products as a result. In other cases, society has to decide if a particular good or service is really public or whether it should remain a private good or service. In the case of health care, we can't seem to make this decision and thus we have kind of a bastardized system of public and private involvement that no one seems to like very much. Our ideology gets in the way of designing a health-care system that responds to the health-care needs of citizens in an efficient manner.

PUBLIC POLICY

When it comes to thinking about public policy, different levels of abstraction are often confounded. Public policy is not to be equated with government even though government formulates and implements most public policies in our society. However, public policy must be considered at the same level as the market and must not be saddled with all the ideological baggage that is involved in discussing the role of government in our society. Government is an institution at the same level as business, while public policy and the market are at a different level of abstraction. Public policy is a specific course of action taken collectively by society that addresses a specific problem of public concern that reflects the interests of society as a whole.

One important issue at this level is what problems can best be addressed by the market and which by the *public-policy process*. This is a different question than asking whether business or government is the best institution to deal with a particular problem. When the market does not work in dealing with certain problems the society deems important, adjustments to corporate behavior must be made through some other process that is different from the market. These changes are simply implicit in the nature of corporations as social entities that are subject to change along with the society of which they are a part. In other words, corporations do not stand apart from society; they are embedded in society and subject to its changing values.

Over the past several decades, public policy has become an ever more important determinant of corporate behavior, as market outcomes have been increasingly altered through the public-policy process. What happens in the public-policy process has become more and more important to corporations and they have become more active in politics through lobbying, campaign contributions, and other activities of this sort. Most corporate social behavior is the result of responding to government regulations of one sort or another. These changes are making it increasingly clear that business functions in both the market system and public-policy process and both processes are necessary to encompass the broad range of decisions a society needs to make about the corporation and its role in society. The public-policy process is the means through which society as a whole articulates its goals and objectives and directs and stimulates individuals and organizations to contribute to and cooperate with them.

The term *public-policy process* refers to the various processes through which public policy is formulated and implemented in our society. There is no single process through which public policy is made in our country. Public policy can be made through legislation passed by Congress, regulations issued by government agencies, executive orders issued by the president, or decisions handed down by the Supreme Court. Not all public policies need to involve formal government action to be effective; however, most such policies do not become effective until they are adopted, implemented, and enforced by some governmental institution. Government establishes the legitimacy of public policies by making them legal obligations that command the loyalty of its citizens. Government monopolizes the use of force in seeing to it that public policies are followed by those who are affected.

The process of making public policy begins in the society as problems and issues are defined. The *public-policy agenda* is that collection of topics and issues with respect to which public policy may be formulated. There are many problems and concerns that various people in society would like to have addressed, but only those that are important enough to receive serious attention from policymakers comprise the public-policy agenda. Such an agenda does not exist in concrete form but is found in the collective judgment of society, actions and concerns of interests groups, legislation introduced into Congress, cases being considered by the Supreme Court, and similar activities.

Instead of an exchange process, values emerge with respect to particular issues on the public-policy agenda and decisions are made about the allocation of resources to address these issues through a *political process*. The political process is a complex amalgam of power and influence that involves many individuals and groups who try to persuade and influence others to adopt their point of view with respect to an issue of public concern. It is often difficult to determine who has the most power and influence in the political process because it is a very complex mixture that is impossible to describe in scientific terms.

Politics has often been called the art of the possible, which generally means that a balance of interests is necessary to resolve conflicts to arrive at a common course of action. People who participate in the process usually have to be willing to give up some of what they want to reach an agreement among all the members of the decision-making group. The usual outcome of the political process reflects the notion that no one gets everything they want and yet everyone in the process has to get something to satisfy themselves that the objective is worth pursuing. Thus compromise and negotiation are skills necessary for effective participation in the political process.[15]

The function of the process is to organize individual effort toward a collective goal or objective that individual or private groups find difficult, if not impossible, to achieve themselves. Individuals participate in the exchange process of a market system because they believe that they can better achieve their individual objectives by making some kind of trade, but the parties to the exchange do not have to share objectives or agree on a common course of action. But if some individuals in a community want to have a road built which they cannot build themselves, they must convince enough people in the community that the road should be built and that they will contribute the resources necessary to get it built. Even after this decision is made, these individuals are going to have different ideas as to the type and location of the road and other related matters. These differences must be resolved through a political process for the road to be constructed.

The task of the political process is to manage such conflicts by (1) establishing rules that all participants in the process have to follow, (2) arranging compromises and balancing interests of the various participants, (3) enacting compromises in the form of public-policy measures, and (4) enforcing these public policies.[16] The outcome of the political process is seldom under the control of a single individual or group and depends on how skillful one is at compromising and negotiating and the variety and strength of other interests involved. Decisions can be made by vote where the majority rules, by building a consensus, or by exercising raw power and coercing other members of a group to agree with one's course of action.

Individuals pursue their own interests and preferences through the political process based on the values they hold relative to the objectives being sought collectively. But these values cannot be expressed directly or precisely, particularly in a representative democracy. Individual preferences are rarely matched because of the need for compromise and the outcome is highly uncertain because of the complex interactions that take place between all the parties to a particular transaction. People are not always certain about what they are getting. They may vote for a candidate they believe will support the issues they favor and who seems to share similar values. But elected officials are a very poor store of value in this sense. They may not carry out their campaign promises, and even if they do, their vote might count for nothing in the final outcome if few others voted the same way on the issues.

Value conflicts are more pronounced in the public-policy process because of the existence of diverse value systems. There is no underlying value system into which other values can be translated; no common denominator by which to assess trade-offs and make decisions about resource allocation to attain some common objective. What is the overall objective, for example, of clean air and water, equal opportunity, occupational safety and health, and similar public goods and services? One could say that all these goods and services are meant to improve the quality of life for all members of society. But if this is the objective, what kind of common-value measure underlies all these goods and services so that benefits of specific programs can be assessed in relation to costs and trade-offs analyzed in relation to this common objective of improving the quality of life?

The costs of pollution-control equipment can be determined in economic terms. The benefits of this equipment should be positive in improving health by reducing the amount of harmful pollutants people have to breathe and making the air look and smell better. The difficulty lies in translating these benefits into economic terms so that a direct comparison with costs can be made. What is the price tag for the lives saved by avoiding future diseases that may be caused by certain pollutants? What is the value of reducing the probability that children will be born with abnormalities because of toxic substances in the environment? What is the value of preserving one's hearing because money has been spent to reduce the noise emitted by machinery in the workplace? What is the appropriate value of being able to see across the Grand Canyon and enjoy whatever benefits this view provides?[17]

The difficulty of expressing all these intangibles in economic terms so that people's individual preferences can be matched should be apparent. When people make individual choices about private goods and services offered on the market, diverse value systems present no problems. They are forced to translate these diverse values into economic terms and make choices accordingly. But making choices about public goods and services is another matter. There seems to be no way to force a translation of diversity into a common-values system that is acceptable, realistic, and appropriate. Thus the political process seems to be a reasonable way to respond to the diversity of people's values to make a decision about a common course of action. Values emerge for particular public goods and services from the interactions of the millions of people who participate in the political process.

The average person participates in the political process by voting for a representative of his or her choice, contributing money to a campaign, writing elected public officials on particular issues, and similar actions. Joining large social movements such as the civil rights movement is another way for the average person to exercise political influence. Widespread support for issues has an effect on the voting of elected public officials. People can join public-interest groups or support them with contributions and fulfill a political role in this fashion. Most citizens, however, are probably content to simply elect others to engage in the business of governing the country and go about their daily tasks with a minimum of political participation.

The vote is the ultimate power that citizens have in a democratic system and gives them a degree of sovereignty over the public-policy process. A public official can be voted out of office is he or she does not perform as the majority of citizens in his or her constituency would like. A major problem with such sovereignty, however, is the reputation that the average citizen has with regard to participation in the political system. Voter turnouts are low in many elections and most of those who do vote probably know little about the candidates and the issues that are at stake in the election. Most people are not interested in public issues much of the time, particularly those that do not affect them directly.

Taking such an interest means spending time on political concerns that might be more profitably devoted to family or leisure activities. Most citizens do not derive primary satisfactions from political participation, and unlike the marketplace, they do not have to participate to fulfill their basic needs and wants. The cost of participation in public affairs seems greater than the return. People who do not participate thus sacrifice their sovereignty and power to the minority in society who do have a strong interest in political life and choose to actively participate in the formulation of public policy for the society as a whole.[18]

Through the public-policy process the self-interest of all the participants is aggregated into a collective whole that supposedly represents the interest of society. Something of a supply-and-demand process occurs here in that if enough citizens demand something, at least in a democratic society, the system will eventually respond. But the decisions about resource allocation are visible in that certain people in the public-policy process, elected public officials and government bureaucrats, for example, can be held accountable for these decisions if they are not acceptable. The concept of the invisible hand is thus appropriate for a market system but not for the public-policy process.

The universal motivating principle in the public-policy process is the *public interest* rather than self-interest. Elected public officials often claim to be acting in the interests of the nation as a whole or of their state or congressional district. Public-interest groups also claim to be devoted to the general or national welfare. These claims make a certain degree of sense in a political context. When politicians make a decision about the provision of some public good or service, they cannot claim to be acting in the self-interest of everyone in their constituency. When goods and services are indivisible across large numbers of people it is impossible for individual preferences to be matched. Nor can policymakers claim to be acting in their own self-interest because such a claim is not politically acceptable. Some more general principle such as the public interest has to be invoked to justify the action taken.

The definition of the public interest is, however, problematical. The term can refer to the aggregation, weighing, and balancing of a number of special interests. In this definition, the public interest is the result of free and open competition between interested parties who have to compromise their differences to arrive at a common course of action. The public interest is then the sum total of all the private interests in the community that are balanced for the common good. The term *public interest* can also refer to a common or universal interest which all or at least most of the members of a society share. A decision is in the public interest if it incorporates these common values that are generally accepted in a society. Such a definition assumes a great deal of commonality and homogeneity of values in a society.

There is also an idealist perspective relative to the meaning of the public interest. Such a definition judges the alternatives facing policymakers in relation to an absolute standard of value that exists independently of the preferences of individual citizens. In this case, the public interest is more than the sum of private interests as it is something distinct from the basic needs and wants of citizens. Such a definition has a transcendent character and often refers to the preservation of abstractions such as freedom or liberty. Finally, another definition of the public interest focuses on the process through which decisions are made rather than the specification of some ideal outcome. This definition involves the acceptance of some process to resolve differences between people, and if the rules of the game have been followed, which in democratic settings means interested parties have had ample opportunity to express their views, then the outcome of the process has to be in the public interest by definition.

Whatever definition of the public interest is evoked to justify a particular decision, those who are in a position of power and influence in society and can shape public policy can never really escape their own self-interest and legitimately claim to be acting solely in the public interest or general good of society, however it is defined. Politicians want to get reelected and most often will vote for those policies that they believe will have an appeal to the majority of their constituency. Public-interest groups want to extend their power and influence in society and might more appropriately be called special-interest groups. Business organizations have their own interests to pursue and often make the claim that what is good for business is good for the country as a whole. Thus the definition of the public interest can never be entirely divorced from the self-interest of those who are making public-policy decisions.[19]

PUBLIC POLICY AND MARKETS

Many, if not most, managers see the government as intruding on what are essentially private decisions made in the interests of promoting economic efficiency. Government intrusion in any form is seen as interfering in the workings of the free-market system and is best kept to a minimum. Managers think they are operating in something called the private sector, which is judged by an efficient use of resources, while government operates in the public sector, which operates on different criteria for measuring success. The efficient use of resources is governed by natural laws that determine economic relations and is a part of the rational approach to reality than stems from the rise of modern science. As John Dewey puts it:

> Its paralyzing effect on human action is seen in the part it played in the eighteenth and nineteenth century in the theory of "natural laws" in human affairs, in social matters. These natural laws were supposed to be inherently fixed; a science of social phenomena and relations was equivalent to discovery of them. Once discovered, nothing remained for man but to conform to them; they were to rule his conduct as physical laws govern physical phenomena. They were the sole standard of conduct in economic affairs; the laws of economics are the "natural" laws of all political action; other so-called laws are artificial, man-made contrivances in contrast with the normative regulations of nature itself . . . *Laissez-faire* was the logical conclusion. For organized society to attempt to regulate the course of economic affairs, to bring them into service of humanly conceived ends, was a harmful interference.[20]

The free-market system, however, does not exist in a vacuum. It is instead embedded in a social system that can exercise control over corporate activities. The free market cannot stand alone because no society can organize all of its activities according to free-market principles. Government creates the conditions for free markets to function and without some kind of structure to regulate markets they become a free-for-all where it is all men and women for themselves and the devil take the hindmost. This was all too evident in the financial disaster in the early years of the twenty-first century when financial instruments were created in an unregulated environment that became increasingly complex and impossible to value realistically. Capital markets ceased to function and perform their role in society.

> Modern capitalist markets do not come to life simply because different parts of society are brought together and injected with money. Rather, complex trade and investment patterns occur because capital—which is the lifeblood of capitalism—is made viable by government actions that fix and guard assets . . . Injecting capital with life also includes guarding individual liberties and creating markets that support legal infrastructures so that creativity and investments pay off. It also means making sure that others in society don't have undue advantages or wield disproportionate power in markets. This prepares the conditions for market capitalism to exist and for entrepreneurs to prosper. Getting legal rights *right* is an arduous process. There are no invisible hands here.[21]

Belief in a system of natural liberty where people are free to pursue their self-interest free from outside interference is an ideological belief. In practice it takes the state with its laws and regulations to create the conditions within which people can have the liberty to function in relative freedom. Laws that respect justice and fairness are critical for efficient markets to operate and these values are not automatically protected by the natural workings of the economy. "Respect for uniform rules, the protection of private property, and the protection of civil liberties crucial for human dignity and creativity exist because states, according to Mark A. Martinez writing in *The Myth of the Free Market: The Role of the State in a Capitalist Economy*, make the effort to get the laws right."[22]

> Getting their cue from economists—who seem to understand that the state has a role in making markets function—think tanks, pundits, politicians, and their followers downplay or ignore the *dominant role* of the state in making markets work. Like readers of the Good Book who selectively quote and cite biblical passages, they pick and choose arguments from capitalism's patron saint, Adam Smith, to make their point. But unlike economists, who argue about the degree of areas in which the state must participate, political players latch onto empty, pithy maxims such as "no new taxes," "the state is the problem," or "government is inefficient." These maxims are attractive because they're quaint and they convey conviction. They are powerful because they suggest analysis and prescription. And the aura of legitimacy that they create comes from the field of economics, a discipline that has produced Nobel laureates and is considered to be the most rigorous of the social sciences. This combination helps marginalize debate about the state's role in markets in the public square.[23]

Our rhetoric has elevated the economic over the political and in the course of doing so we have lost sight of the fact modern markets do not exist in a vacuum. They rest upon political agreements which are modern liberal constitutions. These constitutions are like social contracts and give rise to political movements that propose new legislation and pass new laws and in some cases even amend constitutions. Actions such as these validate our economic arrangements and shape markets to conform with a dynamic society that changes its thinking about markets and how they should be managed.[24] Central to the market is the changing thinking about competition that has taken place over the years as market systems have evolved and new political arrangements had to be developed to respond to these changes.

COMPETITION

Competition is the most important component of the market system and essential to its functioning. In a market system companies compete with each other, products compete with other products, and people compete for the jobs that are available. Competition keeps people on their toes, so to speak, as they need to be concerned about gaining a position they do not have or about losing the position they do have to a better competitor. Competition is a regulatory device that puts constraints on individual egos and prevents any one business organization from attaining a monopoly position that would give it undue power in the market system. Such a monopoly would give a company the ability to set its prices and output based on general economic conditions rather than market forces, and would result in an inefficient allocation of resources. The company in such a position would have a strong tendency to sit on its laurels, so to speak, and not strive to introduce new and better products into the marketplace.

The ideal form of competition is pure competition where the industry is not concentrated, where there are insignificant barriers to entry, and where no product differentiation exists. In this kind of competition, the individual firm has no other choice but to meet the competition since buyers and sellers are so small that they have no influence over the market, thus ensuring that the forces of supply and demand alone determine market outcomes. In this kind of situation, competition will cause resources to be allocated in the most efficient manner, thus minimizing the cost of products and benefiting the consumer.

Markets are not perfectly competitive, however, as there are many problems with competition in the real world that have to be dealt with in order to keep the system going and make it function to the benefit of society as a whole. In practice, unregulated markets tend toward concentration because competition in any industry is never perfectly balanced. If the object of firms is to win out over competitors, the natural expectation is that eventually one or a few firms will come to dominate the industries in which they compete because they were better competitors or were lucky enough to be in the right place at the right time with the right products. Thus most industries in today's economy are oligopolistic, containing a few large firms which recognize the impact of their actions on rivals and therefore on the market as a whole.

Modern large corporations are not simply passive responders to the impersonal forces of supply and demand over which they have no control. These large firms do have some degree of economic power and some influence over the marketplace. They have some ability to control markets by the reduction of competition through merging with other firms in the industry to attain a larger market share and thus come to dominate the industry. Markets may also fail if the dominant firms in an industry are allowed to engage in collusive actions to maintain prices or interfere with the workings of supply and demand and the price mechanism in some other fashion. For these reasons the society saw fit to establish antitrust laws to deal with these problems.

The purpose of these antitrust laws is to limit the economic power of large corporations that can control markets by reducing competition through concentration. The role of these laws is to maintain something called a "workable competition" on the theory that resources are allocated more efficiently and prices are lower in a competitive system than one dominated by large corporations. Workable competition refers to a system where there is reasonably free entry into most markets, no more than moderate concentration, and an ample number of buyers and sellers in most markets. The government tries to accomplish this goal by enforcing policies that deal with the conduct of corporations and the structure of the industries in which they function.

The competitive process is not a natural process that maintains itself indefinitely through the forces of supply and demand. It is not some mechanistic process that automatically holds the economic power of corporations in check through forces that are beyond the control of any economic actor. Managers do no necessarily like competition and do everything they can to drive competitors out of business. This is the name of the game and it seems obvious that some corporations are going to be more successful than others and attain an ever-increasing market share that gives them more power to dictate the terms of the trade. Competition is something society strives to maintain because it is a commonly held value that the society views as essential for the enhancement of its welfare. The realization of this value is an achievement of society not a naturally given fact embedded in a certain kind of economic system.

Another feature of competition is that competitive behavior tends to sink to the lowest common denominator in an unregulated market system. If the object is to win in terms of market share or profits or some other economic indicator, there is always likely to be one or more competitors that will engage in predatory or questionable practices in an effort to emerge as the sole victor. If these practices allow the perpetrator to succeed, they will have to be engaged in by all competitors if they are to stay in business and remain competitive. If these practices continue long enough, they may eventually destroy the competitive system.

Perhaps a comparison with professional football would be useful in understanding this problem. If there were no rules and no one to enforce them on the field, some teams would most likely do anything they could to win games. They would hold defensive linemen to keep them from getting to the quarterback, defensive linemen would try to hit the quarterback long after the play was dead and hope to injure them, defensive backs would interfere with wide receivers any way they could to prevent them from catching the football, and other such practices. If these tactics resulted in winning football games, other teams would have to engage in the same behavior to stay competitive even if they found some of these tactics offensive. The game would then degenerate into free-for-all that nobody would want to watch. Thus there are rules to keep the game "honest" and referees and line judges to enforce them. The rules are changed from time to time to plug loopholes that develop as the game changes and to keep the game interesting for customers.

To deal with these situations the government thus passes laws that deal with corporate conduct and the structure of the industries. These laws promote fair competition by making certain forms of what are considered to be anticompetitive practices illegal and by institutionalizing a concern with the structure of certain industries by giving the government the power to file suit against monopolies if necessary and to block mergers that would reduce competition. Certain practices such as price-fixing and tying arrangements would eventually destroy the system if allowed to continue and destroy trust in the fairness of competition. Monopoly power gives a corporation the potential to abuse that power to maintain its dominant position and society does not trust this kind of power to be used in society's best interest.

A system of checks and balances is necessary to keep the free market functioning effectively just as such a system is necessary to keep a democracy functioning effectively. The business community itself has a common interest in keeping the competitive system going. No matter how strongly various members of this community may object to specific legislative and regulatory requirements and decisions by the courts, they all hold the common value of maintaining a competitive system and doing what is necessary to keep the game going. They have no interest in letting the game degenerate into a free-for-all where anything goes and the system eventually is destroyed. Determining what is necessary to keep the competitive system going is an ongoing enterprise involving the entire society.

Thus the market is embedded in a larger social and political system that can shape it to meet certain objectives the larger society deems important. Public policies are needed to address problems with the market that appear over the course of its history. The market is not some mechanical system that operates automatically to assure the best results for society. It can be manipulated by business for its own advantage with disastrous results for society as a whole. As this book was being written the government was considering new rules to regulate the financial industry to try to prevent another meltdown that occurred a few years earlier. The financial industry had gotten out of hand and brought the society down with it and this necessitated a massive government bailout. New rules were needed to keep this industry from self-destructing.

SCIENCE AND DEMOCRACY

Timothy Ferris, in his new book titled *The Science of Liberty: Democracy, Reason, and the Laws of Nature*, states that over the last two centuries two major transformations have taken place that have fundamentally altered the thinking and well-being of the entire human species. One of these transformations is scientific because the scientific revolution has enabled us to know more about how the universe operates than has been learned in all of prior history. The other transformation is democratic because this revolution has spread freedom and equal rights to half the inhabitants of the entire world and has made democracy the preference of informed people throughout the world. These two transformations are linked, according to Ferris, for by the close of the twentieth century every nation that adhered to a scientific worldview was also a liberal or at least partly liberal democracy. It must be noted, given the negative connotation attached to the word *liberal* in our society, that Ferris took the term *liberal* in its classical sense to refer to a state that guaranteed human rights to its citizens and elected its leaders.[25]

Ferris is interested in exploring the link between science and democracy because he thinks the rise of science and liberal democracy in roughly the same time period was something more than a series of coincidences. In fact, the main argument of the book was that science was the innovative ingredient without which the democratic revolution would not have occurred. The democratic revolution was sparked, says Ferris, by the scientific revolution and he believes that science continues to foster political freedom in today's world. While he hedges a bit, he does say that "caused is perhaps not too strong a word," that the scientific revolution caused the democratic revolution. Science requires openness to new ideas and discoveries, it is antiauthoritarian, and it relies on the experimental method to discover how the world operates. Science demands liberty and creates a "symbiotic relationship in which the freer nations were better able to carry on the scientific enterprise, which in turn rewarded them with knowledge, wealth, and power."[26]

The freedoms that are promoted and protected by liberal democracies are necessary so that scientific inquiry is facilitated. In fact, Ferris says " democracy itself is an experimental system without which neither science nor liberty can flourish."[27] This view is consistent with the pragmatic focus on scientific method and the experimental nature of all human experience. As was stated earlier, all human experience is experimental not in the sense that it is guided by sophisticated levels of thought as in scientific endeavors but in the sense that our ordinary way of knowing and being in the world embodies the features revealed in the examination of scientific method. Scientific endeavor as experimental inquiry is a more explicit embodiment of the dynamics that are operative at all levels of experience, and democracy facilitates this experimental approach to life in general.

However, all societies have within them something of an antiscience attitude or perspective, and sometimes this affects government policies and practices. Science can be misused by a government that manipulates scientific findings to support its policies that are based on other considerations. When science is not respected, democracy suffers. The government then becomes authoritarian and is unwilling to listen to other options and approaches to particular problems. It knows the truth and does not want to be confused by the facts because they may challenge the government's position. Such a government is not interested in openness and does much of its business in secret, shutting out all who disagree with its position and not allowing them to participate in decision making. When things go wrong, as they often do with such an approach, the decision makers circle the wagons to defend their decisions and tend to blame others or find excuses for their actions that render them blameless.

Democracy requires inclusiveness, which in turn demands tolerance of other points of view, compromise, and the ability to work with others to arrive at joint solutions to problems facing society. When one party with one worldview begins to dominate government or refuses to work with the other party, democracy begins to disappear and becomes dysfunctional. People in a democracy must constantly be on guard lest somebody or some group that claims to know the solution to every problem begins to accumulate too much political power and stifles debate about critical issues of concern to that society. This is a sure path to disaster because the wisdom of a large part of the population is shut out of decision making and the policies of government reflect a narrow worldview that not everyone shares. Absolutism and authoritarianism have no place in a democracy.

Democracy also requires a secular point of view with respect to the world and how it works. There is no place for a worldview that advocates cutting down all the trees because Jesus is coming and will turn water into wine and stones into bread.[28] Thus we won't need trees or anything else the earth provides. People can believe this if they wish, but these beliefs should not become the basis for public or foreign policy. The policies of government should reflect the best science or intelligence that can be had; the wishes of the entire populace and not just a small segment; the views of governmental leaders, and other elements. Government policy is an amalgam of many elements and should not be based on any particular worldview, religious or otherwise. We as humans do not know the truth about many things and to claim otherwise is to make oneself into a god who knows all things.

Democracy requires experimentation. The states have often been described as laboratories where solutions to problems like poverty and welfare, environmental pollution, crime, and other problems can be tried out to see what consequences result. If certain programs are successful, they may then be useful to try on a national level. No one really knows which programs are going to work or not and there are always unintended consequences. But experimentation has no place in a fundamentalist or absolutist worldview. If the truth has been revealed by God to certain people or is present in reason as claimed by certain groups, there is no need to experiment as the truth is not up for question.

Furthermore, a democracy must be open-ended with regard to the kind of society that evolves. There is so much diversity in our society that in a few years the white majority will be a minority like every other ethnic grouping. People with diverse backgrounds have many different ideas about the kind of society in which they would like to live and one particular group's vision of the good society should not be forced on others. Any group who has what they think is a clear vision of the kind of society it believes is right for all people should be feared. Society evolves over time and its goals change in response to new problems and challenges. This is what keeps society interesting and viable, not some absolutist moral vision that would stifle creativity and the flexibility society needs to cope with new problems and situations.

Finally, democracy also requires education, which is the major tool for changing irreconcilable factionalism into a growing pluralistic community. Universal education is an ideal for a democratic society and is necessary for a community to maintain itself. But this ideal means more that simply an equal opportunity to develop one's potential. It requires an understanding of the educational process as concerned with the education of the whole person. Education is not fundamentally the transmission of information but is the development of the skills of experimental inquiry vital for the ongoing expansion of the self and the institutions and practices of a democratic community. Education is the vehicle for nurturing free individuals in a free society.[29]

These five elements—inclusiveness, secularism, experimentation, open-endedness, and universal education—form a unity or sorts, and if any one of these elements begins to disappear, the others are under threat, as is democracy itself. If government becomes the exclusive purview of one segment of society, particularly a religious segment, secularism disappears and with it any chance of experimentation and open-endedness with respect to society as a whole. The society then becomes inflexible and unable to cope with change. Creativity is stifled and dissent is not tolerated, and democracy, which is something of an experiment itself, ceases to exist. This can happen very subtly and very quickly; thus democracy requires constant vigilance on the part of its adherents to keep it going for the next generation.

11 Pragmatism and Culture

Democracy is a matter of culture as many countries in postcommunist Central and Eastern Europe have come to realize. There is much more to democracy than freedom of speech, the freedom to vote, and other such institutional measures.[1] Democracy requires some sense of community in order to function effectively; a sense that people are bound together by something more than self-interested reasons; that they are part of a tradition in which there are certain core values that make a country distinctive and something to which people can give their allegiance. There has to be some sense of common interests that binds people together and creates a culture that is more than the sum of individual interests. Yet democracy in our country is undermined by a sense of individualism that is part and parcel of our economic system and thus spills over into our understanding of government and its role in society.

There is no sense of community in economic theory based on the free market as people are considered to be individual units with preferences that can be exploited by producers in the interests of selling their products. Any social reality such as a sense of community is nonexistent as scientific reductionism inherent in economic theory focuses on the individual. Our conception of society is thus reducible to the individuals who comprise the society. Competition is assumed to be the essential way that people relate to each other and this competition supposedly leads to the efficient use of scarce resources. People act rationally on the basis of economic self-interest and when they do not act in their economic self-interest they are believed to be irrational. Thus government, which may allocate resources on a different basis from economic self-interest to accomplish some more common good for the community as a whole, is considered to be an irrational interference with the workings of the free market. According to Stephen A. Marglin, writing in *The Dismal Science: How Thinking Like an Economist Undermines Community*:

> It is the importance of ties of necessity that puts community at odds with the fundamental assumptions of economics. Markets, based on voluntary, instrumental, opportunistic relationships are diametrically opposed

to the long-term commitments and obligations that characterize community. By promoting market relationships, economics undermines reciprocity, altruism, and mutual obligation, and therewith the necessity of community. The very foundations of economics, by justifying the expansion of markets, lead inexorably to the weakening of community.[2]

Community is important to a good and meaningful life. The market undermines community because it replaces personal ties of economic necessity by impersonal market transactions. Economics aids and abets the market; its very foundations make community and its virtues invisible and legitimize the focus on efficiency as the normative standard by which to judge economic outcomes.[3]

Individualism plays an instrumental role in economics because individuals are assumed to be so constituted that by their self-interested actions they produce efficient production and distribution mediated by a market system even it this if not part of their intentions. The good as far as society is concerned is an aggregation of these individual assessments of well-being and is not something that can be assessed apart from these individual judgments on the basis of some overarching theory as to what constitutes the good society. Thus attempts by government to create the good society amount to coercion of these individual choices in an attempt to create some utilitarian conception of the good. As Marglin states:

> The basic idea of individualism is that society can and should be understood as a collection of autonomous individuals, that groups . . . have no normative significance as groups, that all behavior, policy, and even ethical judgment should be reduced to their effects on individuals . . . Responsibility means that individuals have agency; their preferences—subject to constraints (like income) but not to coercion (like physical force)—determine their choices, actions, and behavior. The idea that preferences are beyond discussion implies a radical subjectivism; one set of preferences is as worthy as another. Self-interest precludes acting for the sake of others, particularly acting for others out of a sense of duty or obligation.[4]

We have an individualistic culture for the most part and the individual is considered to be the basic building block of society. There is no better example of this individualism than the Tea Party movement that appeared in 2010 and received a great deal of media attention. This movement, according to Mark Lilla, writing in the *New York Review of Books*, grew out of a populist mood inspired by a radical individualism that had been brewing in the society for decades. During the Clinton years the country moved left on issues of private autonomy such as sex and divorce, which had begun in the sixties and continued a rightward movement on economic autonomy that had started during the Reagan years with an emphasis on free markets and deregulation.[5]

The Tea Party movement, according to Lilla, appealed to individual opinion, individual choice, and individual autonomy. Their rallying cry was one of wanting to be left alone as they were tired of being told how to think about global warming, which foods they can eat, when they have to wear seatbelts and helmets, whether to insure themselves, and a host of other political grievances. The movement appealed to people who were convinced that they could do everything themselves if only they were left alone and that other people, including politicians, bureaucrats, doctors, scientists, and even schoolteachers, were controlling their lives and preventing them being autonomous individuals.[6]

These new Jacobins, as Lilla calls them, have two classic American traits: blanket distrust of institutions, particularly government, and what he calls an astonishing and unwarranted confidence in the self. People in this movement believe they can do everything for themselves and that institutions should get out of the way and let them do their thing. They are trying to remind those in power that they are in their positions to do one thing and one thing only: to protect the divine right for people to do whatever they damn well please. For half a century, according to Lilla, Americans have been rebelling in one form or another in the name of individual freedom. The Tea Party movement wants even more freedom, to be a people without rules to do whatever they want without outside interference.[7]

Such a movement, however, is completely unrealistic in today's world. Any given individual cannot even begin to provide for her- or himself in a rugged individualism kind of manner. We live in a highly interdependent world that is now global in nature. What happens in some far-off place in the world affects us in ways we do not even understand. Naturally this gives us a great deal of insecurity and a feeling that we have lost control of our lives. And indeed in many ways we have, but there is no turning back to a simpler world where we can live in relative isolation from other people and do as we please.[8] Our actions affect other people and we are affected by theirs and this must be taken into account in any realistic assessment of the responsibilities we have for each other in such an interdependent world. Zygmunt Bauman thinks that

> Indeed, globalization looks now inescapable and irreversible. The point of no return has been reached—and passed. There is no way back. Our interconnections and interdependencies are already global. Whatever happens in one place influences the lives and life chances of people in all other places. Calculation of steps to be taken in any one place must reckon with the responses of people everywhere else. No sovereign territory, however large, populous, and resourceful, can single-handedly protect its living conditions, its security, long-term prosperity, preferred form of life, or the safety of its inhabitants. Our mutual dependency is planetwide and so we are already, and will remain indefinitely, *objectively* responsible for one another. There are, however, few signs that

we who share the planet are willing to take up in earnest the *subjective* responsibility for that objective responsibility of ours.[9]

Whatever else "globalization" may mean, it means that we are all dependent on each other. Distances matter little now. Something that happens in one place may have global consequences. With the resources, technical tools, and know-how humans have acquired, their actions can span enormous distances in space and time. However local their intentions might be, actors would be ill-advised to leave out of account global factors. What we do (or abstain from doing) may influence the conditions of life (or death) for people in places we will never visit and generations we will never know.[10]

Individualism fuels a consumer society that is ever more atomistic and hedonistic trying to find meaning and purpose in buying more things on the marketplace. Individualism denies the primacy of relationships and thus goods and services become a substitute for meaningful relationships with family, friends, and community. An individualistic worldview promotes scarcity as long as commodities are a primary means of solving existential problems that stem from a lack of community. As long as we do not rethink the assumptions we are making about self and society we will never have enough stuff and a consumption-oriented society will continue. It will take a rethinking of these assumptions before we shall have enough.[11]

> The activity of consuming "has become a kind of template or model for the way in which citizens of contemporary Western societies have come to view all their activities. Since . . . more and more areas of contemporary society have become assimilated to a 'consumer model' it is perhaps hardly surprising that the underlying metaphysics of consumerism has in the process become a kind of default philosophy for all modern life.[12]

Consumption in our society is a chore that cannot be delegated to someone else to perform. It is in fact a duty and was even suggested by the president of the United States as the best strategy for the average person to deal with terrorist attacks. Whenever a sizable percentage of the population is unable for whatever reason to maintain its consumption level, the economy falters. If the output of the economy isn't substantially consumed, production levels will decline and employees will be laid off rather than hired and the economy will start on a downward spiral.[13] A high level of consumption, says Bauman, is thus necessary to keep the economy going and a satisfied consumer is anathema to the system.

> It is the nonsatisfaction of desires, and a firm and perpetual belief that each act of their satisfaction *leaves much to be desired and can be bettered*, that are the genuine flywheels of the consumer-targeted economy

... Without the repetitive frustration of desires, consumer demand would run out of steam . . . The society of consumers derives its animus and momentum from the *disaffection* it so expertly produces.[14]

The institutions of capitalism in which many people spend a majority of their lives gives people a sense of identity and belonging in addition to providing them with the means to earn an income. These institutions provide the context in which much of their social life takes place and the setting for many of their social interactions. Much of our life is focused on the economic. But we not only get the goods that we need to exist through the economy; we also live in the economy. We not only nourish our bodies in the economy; we also nourish our minds and souls through the economy. Economics must take this experience seriously and not abstract it out of existence. It must incorporate some sense of community, according to Marglin, to be consistent with these social experiences.

> First, all communities have a political structure, a system of rules and regulations and a means of enforcing those regulations on its members . . . Communities are not just about economics and politics, but about sociality as well. Members of a community celebrate together and grieve together, rejoice with one another and console one another. Communities create a common future for their members and remember a common past. A vision of the future as well as a common memory are central elements in regenerating the community, in providing continuity and connection between the generations.[15]

Thus a redefinition of the self as social and inseparably tied to community is necessary to overcome this individualism and reconceptualize capitalism as a social system that involves real people. Capitalism is not simply an organization of fictionalized atomistic commodities that can be bought and sold on the market. It is an organization of real people who are trying to make a life for themselves and their families and find meaning and fulfillment in the society in which they find themselves. These people and the institutions in which they work cannot be mathematized and plugged into abstract formulas that focus only on the economic aspects of their existence thus dehumanizing them in the process. Economics must be open to human relationships because human relationships are the keystone of community.[16]

THE SOCIAL SELF AND COMMUNITY

Changing our culture involves the development of an alternative view of selfhood that is not individualistic and that entails a conception of community that is part and parcel of the self rather than an aggregation of individuals.[17] The very definition of culture used by many anthropologists incorporates the notion of community. The term has been used to refer to the "totality of patterns of behavior that characterize a specific society," and in this sense "is sustained by and through community, the set of connections that bind people to one another economically, socially, politically, and spiritually."[18]

This view will be difficult for people to understand since most of us are rooted in an individualistic view of persons and think of community as sum of all the individuals who are involved in some kind of collective endeavor. In other words, the whole is merely the sum of the parts, and we usually break the whole down into parts that can be better understood and manipulated. This is the way science works and this is the way we tend to think of organizations. If there is a problem with organizational life, we break it down into parts to find out what is wrong.

The problem with this approach is that we lose sight of the whole by focusing so much of our attention on the parts, and when we do think of the whole, we try to put the parts back together to create the whole, forgetting that the whole is already there and is, in fact, always present and does not have to be re-created. Developing an alternative view involves focusing on both parts and wholes, and discussing then in such a way that they are integral to each other. In other words, the parts do not exist apart from the whole and the whole does not exist without the parts. Neither self nor community is prior to each other but is bound up with each other such that when one is present the other is present. It is a focus on these relationships that gives us a holistic view of society. According to Marglin again:

> "Holism," to use Lord Dumont's terminology for an organic conception of people and their relationships with one another, replaces the atomic metaphor with a subatomic view of the individual . . . Social relationships define individuals, and it is these relationships, not the individuals themselves, that are the primary matter of society . . . As an individual, one has partial and incomplete agency. Agency is a function of our relationships with other members of society rather than a given of the individual. In a holistic conception of the person, we never attain complete agency as separate persons. We cannot because interdependence is part of the human condition.[19]

The most important question concerning the self is whether the self is an isolatable, discrete entity, or is it by its very nature part of a social context. The view of the individual as an isolatable entity is firmly rooted in traditional thinking and is in fact very much taken for granted in our everyday existence. The view that singular or discrete individuals exist and have no moral ties to any associations except those they choose to form for their own self-interested purposes was the philosophical basis for the French and American revolutions and is clearly embedded in John Locke's view of property rights as well as in other social-contract theories. These presuppositions are also the basis for understanding the nature of capitalism as an agglomeration of individuals seeking their material self-interest in a competitive system that pits them against each other for the limited resources a society has to offer.

This accepted, unquestioned, presupposed view of the atomicity of the person or self is pinpointed by Charles Taylor as the common basis for positions as diverse as traditional individualistic or interest-group liberalism and traditional conservative laissez-faire economics.[20] Such an atomistic view, which sees the self as an atom separable and distinct from other atoms, pits the individual squarely against communitarian constraints such as government regulations that attempt to codify the concerns of the society as a whole. Once the individual is taken as an isolatable unit, then the individual and community become pitted against each other in an ultimately irreconcilable tension.

The movement in American philosophy known as classical American pragmatism offers a unique and helpful framework for overcoming this tension and will be used in this chapter to develop a relational understanding of the self and community.[21] The pragmatic understanding of the nature of selfhood and the relation between the self and the other and the resulting dynamics of community reject the long history of the individualistic self, which offers the choice between the collective whole at the expense of the individual and the individual at the expense of the collective whole. It offers a new way of understanding the self and community that is inherently social in nature.

According to this pragmatic view, to have a self is to have a particular type of ability, the ability to be aware of one's behavior as part of a social process of adjustment and to be aware of oneself as a social object, as an acting agent within the context of other acting agents. Not only can selves exist only in relation to other selves, but no absolute line can be drawn between our selfhood and the selfhood of others. Our own selves exist and are part of our experience only insofar as other persons exist and enter into our experience. The origins and foundations of the self are thus social or intersubjective rather than individualistic in nature. We do not grow up isolated from our surroundings but develop in a social context where we incorporate elements of that context into our own consciousness.

When cooperative action is necessary, as it is in any social context, human organisms take the perspective of the other in the development of their conduct; they have to be aware of the interests and concerns of others who are part of the cooperative entity. In incorporating the perspective, attitude, or viewpoint of the other, the developing self comes to take the perspective of others as a complex, interrelated whole. In this manner the self comes to incorporate the standards and authority of the group, the organization or system of attitudes and responses that George Herbert Mead terms "the generalized other."[22] This is the passive dimension to the self, the dimension structured by role taking in a social context, that aspect of the self which Mead refers to as the "me." This generalized other is not merely a collection of others, but an organization or structural relation of others, for the generalized other represents attitudes or perspectives which have been internalized by the self as it develops in a social context.

Mead uses the example of a baseball team as an example of a generalized other functioning in a group context. The person who plays a position on the team must understand the role of everyone else involved in the game and these different roles must have a definite relationship to each other. Any one participant must assume the attitudes of the other players as an organized unity, and this organization controls the response of the individual participant. Each one of the participant's own acts is determined by "his being everyone else on the team," in so far as the organization of the various attitudes controls his own response. "The team is the generalized other in so far as it enters—as an organized process or social activity—into the experience of any one of the individual members of it."[23]

In sum, as selves grow and develop they incorporate or internalize the standards and attitudes of the groups that comprise their social context. People internalize these standards and attitudes from their families, churches, schools, and other collective endeavors in which they find themselves. These attitudes and standards comprise the generalized other which has been formed over the years through an amalgam of the attitudes and standards of the people who comprise those collectives. This amalgam is more than just the sum of the parts, but is a unique creation of each collective entity that is concerned with its own survival and has to continue to perform a useful function in society. The group has an existence that is not separate from the individuals that comprise the group, but that is in reality more than these individuals and has the ability to shape the behavior and attitudes of individuals who are its members.

The "me," then, represents the conformity of the self to the past, to the norms and practices of a society or a group. Yet in responding to the perspective of the other, each individual responds as a unique center of creative activity; there is a creative dimension to the self which Mead refers to as the "I." The "I" represents the unique, creative dimension of the self which brings its novel reactions to present situations. By its very nature, the self incorporates both the conformity of the group perspective or group attitudes and the creativity of its unique individual perspective.

Thus the tensions between tradition and change, conformity and individuality, conservative forces and liberating forces emerge as two dynamically interacting poles or dimensions that form the very nature of selfhood.[24] Freedom does not lie in opposition to the restrictions provided by norms and authority, but in a self-direction which requires the proper dynamic interaction of these two dimensions within the self.[25] Because of this dynamic interaction constitutive of the very nature of selfhood, the perspective of the novel, "liberating" dimension always opens onto a common "conserving" perspective.

This dynamic interrelationship provides one with the ability to think of oneself in terms of the group to which one belongs and lay upon oneself the responsibilities that belong to the members of that group. This inter-relationship also bestows the ability to admonish oneself as others would and to recognize what are one's responsibilities as well as one's rights as a member of the group.[26] But these responsibilities and rights have themselves resulted not just from the internalization of the perspective of the general-ized other but from the effect on this perspective by one's own creative input. Not only is one's creative individuality not enslaved by or determined by the generalized other, but the generalized other has itself been formed in part from one's own past creative actions.

The unique individual both reflects and reacts to the common or group perspective in his or her own unique manner. Moreover, this novelty in turn changes the group attitude or perspective. This new perspective emerges because of its relation to dominant institutions, traditions, and patterns of life which conditioned its emergence, and this perspective gains its signifi-cance in light of the way it changes the common perspective. The dynamic of community is found in this continual interplay involving adjustment of attitudes, aspirations, and factual perceptions between the common per-spective as the condition for the novel perspective and novel perspective as it conditions the common perspective.[27]

To ask if a new perspective is a product of an individual or a community; to ask which comes first, the individual or the community perspective is an irrelevant question. The creativity of the individual can be contrasted with the conformity represented by the common perspective, but not with com-munity. True community occurs in the interplay between the individual and the generalized other, between the "I" and the "me," and this takes place through ongoing communication in which each adjusts to or accom-modates the other. The ongoing adjustment or accommodation between these two dimensions is essential for community. The individual and the generalized other exist only within the context of community, and without the individual and the generalized other there is no community. But with-out the ongoing interaction of adjustment or accommodations, which is the very essence of community, there is no individual or generalized other. They are an integral part of each other.

This adjustment is neither assimilation of one perspective by another nor the fusion of perspectives into an indistinguishable oneness; the adjust-ment can best be understood as an "accommodation" in which each indi-vidual creatively affects and is affected by the other through an accepted means of adjudication. Thus a community is constituted by, and develops in terms of, the ongoing communicative adjustment between the activity of the novel individual perspective and the common group perspective; and each of these two interacting dimensions constitutive of community gains its meaning, significance, and enrichment through this process of accom-modation or adjustment. Thus a free society, like a free individual, requires both the influencing power of authority as embodied in its institutions and traditions and the innovative power of creativity as expressed in individual actions. In Dewey's terms:

> No amount of aggregated collective action of itself constitutes a community . . . To learn to be human is to develop through the give-and-take of communication an effective sense of being an individually distinctive member of a community; one who understands and appreciates its beliefs, desires, and methods, and who contributes to a further conversion of organic powers into human resources and values. But this transition is never finished.[28]

The intelligence that transforms societies and institutions, then, is itself influenced by these institutions. In this sense even individual intelligence is social intelligence. And social intelligence, as the historically grounded intelligence operative within a community and embodied in its institutions, although not merely an aggregate of individual intelligence but rather a qualitatively unique and unified whole, is nonetheless not something separable from individual intelligence.

There is an intimate functional reciprocity between individual and social intelligence, a reciprocity based on the continual process of adjustment. Although the generalized other indeed represents social meanings and social norms, social development is possible only through the dynamic interrelation of the unique, creative individual and the generalized other. William James expresses this interrelation in his observation that the influence of a great man modifies a community in an entirely original and peculiar way, while the community in turn remodels him.[29]

Novelty within society is initiated by individuals, but such initiation can occur only because individuals are continuous with others and with the historically situated social institutions of which they are a part. Part of the life process is the ongoing adjustment between the old and the new, the stability of conformity and the novelty of creativity. The interrelation of continuity and novelty, stressed by virtually all the classical pragmatists, provides the conceptual tools for understanding how the uniqueness of the individual and the norms and standards of community are two interrelated factors in an ongoing exchange, neither of which can exist apart from the other. Because of the inseparable interaction of these two dimensions, goals for "the whole" cannot be pursued by ignoring consequences for the individuals affected, nor can individual goals be adequately pursued apart from concern with the functioning of the whole entity.

The development of the ability both to create and to respond constructively to the creation of novel perspectives as well as to incorporate the perspective of the other, not as something totally alien but as something sympathetically understood, is what growth of the self entails. Such growth incorporates an ever more encompassing sympathetic understanding of varied and diverse interests. This leads to tolerance of other people's perspectives, which are seen as an enlargement of the self rather than a sacrifice of one's own position. Thus to enrich, to deepen, and expand the community is at once to enrich, deepen, and expand each person involved in ongoing community interactions.

Problematic situations which arise in any and every community can be resolved through the use of social intelligence in a way which enlarges and reconstructs the situation and the selves involved, providing at once a greater degree of authentic self-expression and a greater degree of social participation. In cases where incompatibility of perspectives arise, the problematic situation must be reconstructed based on the problem situation and the history within which it has emerged. This reconstruction cannot be imposed by eliciting the standards of a past that most often does not contain a way to resolve the problem. Such reconstruction must be accomplished by calling on a more fundamental and creative level of activity.

The relation of individual selves to the generalized other requires the openness of perspectives rather than a mind closed to new ways of looking at things. The adjustment of perspectives that is necessary to reach agreement on a problem does not involve an imposition of some perspective or standards from "on high" but rather a deepening to a more fundamental level of human rapport. This deepening process involves an openness for breaking through seeming incompatibilities and situations that, on the surface at least, seem impossible to resolve. This process allows us to grasp different contexts, to take the perspective of "the other," and to participate in genuine dialogue with other people.

Characterizations of a community usually include the notion of a common goal that the community is trying to attain. The ultimate "goal" of this open-ended, dynamic process, however, is enriching growth or development, not final completion. This in turn indicates that differences between people should not be eradicated because these differences provide the necessary materials by which a society can continue to grow and develop. As Dewey stresses, growth by its very nature involves the resolution of conflict.[30] A true community which incorporates different perspectives is far from immune to conflict, but such clashes provide the material for ongoing development as these different perspectives are adjusted and accommodated by the community.

What needs to be cultivated in the community is the motivation, sensitivity, and imaginative vision needed to change irreconcilable factionalism into a growing pluralistic community. The ability to tolerate radically diverse ways of life or of making sense of things is not to be found from above by imposing one's own perspective upon such diversity, but rather from beneath, by penetrating though such differences. Different ways of making sense of the world emerge in any community, but these differences emerge from the essential characteristics of beings that are fundamentally alike that are confronting a common reality in on ongoing process of change. The diversity of responses to cope with this reality represent a strength rather than a weakness of community and is to be celebrated rather than negated.

Such a deepening does not negate the use of intelligent inquiry; rather, the deepening opens it up and frees it from the rigidities and abstractions of the past and focuses it on the dynamics of human existence. This deepening may change conflict into an increased diversity or it may lead to an emerging consensus that one of the conflicting positions is unworkable. In this way, over the course of time, incompatible perspectives are not proved right or wrong but are resolved by the weight of argument as reasons and justifications are worked out in the ongoing course of inquiry. If such adjustments do not emerge, then community has broken down and what remains is sheer factionalism.

This approach does not destroy reason but it brings reason down to earth, so to speak. What it does destroy is the belief that reason has an absolute hold on truth and values in the abstract, that scientific objectivity is the privileged domain of rationality or that the revealed truth of religious belief is absolute in some sense. Reason brought down to earth is concrete, imaginative, and deepened to operate with possibilities which have been liberated from the confines and rigidities of abstract rules and procedural steps or the confines of inculcated tradition, whether a scientific or a religious tradition.

When a community is operating within a common system of meaning and values on any one issue, then investigation of an issue will tend toward convergence. The manner of adjustment between a new perspective as a novel interpretation of the facts and the perspective of the generalized other as the previously accepted interpretation is resolved by verification of the factual evidence and a gradual acceptance of a new interpretation that makes better sense of the facts than the old interpretation. However, when a novel viewpoint brings with it a novel set of meanings and values by which to delineate facts, the process of adjustment which constitutes the dynamics of sociality within a community is not so easily accomplished.

In this case, there is no longer a question of testing varying interpretations of the facts; there are now different perceptions of what facts are available. There are now not only different interpretations to account for the facts, but there are also different facts to consider. In other words, people do not just see things differently; they see different things. Discussions to bring about an adjustment of perspectives must then stem from a generalized stance of agreement concerning what standards are to be applied in making decisions among incommensurable frameworks. Such standards may be difficult to elucidate, but because these standards are implicitly operative in the process of adjustment among divergent meaning systems, they can be elicited for clarification through reflective focus on what is operative in the process of adjustment.

Nonetheless, novel perspectives may at times emerge which are "incommensurable" not only with another way of delineating experience through the determination of what kind of facts exist in the world but which also incorporate standards and criteria related to the selection of problems that are important to be resolved that are "incommensurable" with those of another perspective. There are not only different facts, but also different methods, standards, and criteria for determining which system of facts should be accepted. In a sense, these divergent perspectives have carved out divergent worlds, the most fundamental sense of incommensurability that can be experienced. These different worlds encompass not just differing facts, but differing goals, differing problems of importance, differing criteria for resolving differences, and hence differing organs for bringing about a process of adjustment.

Such incommensurable perspectives are in a sense structuring different worlds, as, for example, exists between the religious and scientific worldviews. But they cannot be closed to rational discussion for possibilities of socializing adjustment within a given community. Diverse perspectives for delineating facts must work, for better or worse, in measuring up to the standards and criteria by which the community judges them and in solving the problems which the community decides are important. Diverse perspectives which incorporate diverse standards, criteria, and problems can be discussed in terms of the ability of these perspectives to address the problems we experience as organisms embedded in a universe in which we must learn to flourish. Such workability is reflectively incorporated in differing traditions and rituals and the emergence of differing problems that need resolution. Such diverse articulations stem from a vague, elusive, but real sense of workability embedded in the primal drive of every organism to interact successfully with its environment.

In the ongoing process of socializing adjustment, some arguments gain validity while others go by the wayside. Though none of these arguments are ultimately proved right or wrong, we eventually discard some and move on in yielding to the force of others. Such a process is based on rational discussion guided by the inescapable criteria of workability. Although abstract articulations of workability itself can be diverse and at times seem incommensurable, the primal sense of workability serves as the ineffable but inescapable and inexhaustible wellspring of vitality from which a community moves forward through rational and open discussion leaving behind reasons and arguments that have become lifeless.

The relation of the individual and the generalized other in the process of socializing adjustment within a community requires the openness of perspectives. No community need be constricted by closed horizons either in terms of the possibilities of penetrating to more fundamental levels of community or to wider breadth of community. Expansion in breadth is at once expansion in depth. As two communities recognize their openness in coming to understand the perspective of the other, there is a socializing adjustment founded on a deeper and broader community. Such a socializing adjustment involves neither assimilation of perspectives, one to the other, nor fusion of each into an indistinguishable oneness, but an accommodation in which each creatively affects and is affected by the other.

In coming to understand the pluralism and the dynamic of socializing adjustment constitutive of this kind of community, one can at the same time come to recognize the enrichment to be gained by understanding the perspective of the other. But just as important is to recognize the enrichment to be gained by understanding what is implicitly operative in one's own perspective. The pragmatic framework described here offers the foundation for a perspectival pluralism, rather than the drive towards unanimity in final knowledge.

Some may object that the novelty and diversity in this kind of perspectival pluralism leads to the view that true progress in knowledge is impossible, that there is no progress in this kind of process but only difference. However, knowledge as cumulative and knowledge as changing do not lie in opposition to each other, but rather knowledge as changing is also knowledge as cumulative, for any novel perspective emerges from a cumulative process or history of socializing adjustment which yields enrichment of intelligibility of both the old and new perspectives. Furthermore, to the extent that any perspective is reflective of its own contextual conditions, the perspective advances, for in such reflection it becomes conscious of its openness onto a deeper community and the possibilities contained therein.

RIGHTS

Pragmatism also involves a different understanding of rights that reflect a community perspective. Traditional rights theories focus on abstract, individualistic humans with rights that are inherent in the self who join together with others by entering into contracts that bind them through external ties that require they give up some of these rights or modify then in some fashion in the interests of the group they are joining. Thus any kind of community or society is always in some sense an infringement on these rights that are rooted in the individual, and a conflict between individual rights and community interests is inevitable. This view is pervasive in the literature about rights as chronicled by Alan Gewirth in his work on the interrelation between rights and community.

> In one of the main modes of interpretation, to focus on rights in moral and political philosophy entails giving consideration to individuals conceived as atomic entities existing independent of social ties, while to focus instead on community is to regard persons as having inherent affective social relations to one another . . . According to these views, rights presuppose competition and conflict, since rights are intended as guarantees that self-seeking individuals will not be trampled in their adversarial relations with one another. Community, on the other

hand, connotes the absence of such conflicts; it signifies common interests and cooperation, mutual sympathy and fellow-feeling. As a result, it is charged that the rights doctrine atomizes society and alienates persons from one another. But when persons maintain the ties of community that make for social harmony, there is no need for rights . . . The claiming of rights, then, is egoistic and antithetical to morality and community.[31]

Gewrith does point out that a more affirmative relation between rights and community has been offered by some scholars, but he doubts that they interpret "community" in the extensively cooperative, mutualistic sense that undercuts the asserted opposition between community and rights. Indeed, the author sketches the way in which the relations between rights and community developed by these scholars does not imply community in any important sense at all.[32] Thus there is a need to reconceptualize the notion of rights so that they are not in opposition to community and do not result in conflict between the individual and community.

The pragmatic reconceptualization of rights theory offers a new approach to rights and the social contracts in which they are usually rooted, a reconceptualization in which rights and community are not only compatible but are inextricably interwoven. From the pragmatic perspective, it can be said that what is more "natural" to humans is not absolute individual rights but contractual rights. However, this does not mean simply that individuals are born into societies which have been already formed, at least in theory, through a social contract involving the original participants. Nor does this view mean that rights are merely the result of government legislation or contractual agreements. Finally, it does not mean that abstract principles can be substituted for caring attunement to concrete situations and the individuals involved.

Rather, what the pragmatic view of rights intends to point out is that the "natural" state of being human is to be relationally tied to others and that apart from the dynamics of community there can be no individual rights, since individuals emerge within and develop in the context of community. Thus in the very having of rights one has community obligations. These are two sides of the same coin. There can be no absolute individual rights because the need for adjustment between novelty and constraint is built into the internal structure of the self in the form of the I-me dynamics. The self consists of a creative ongoing interpretive interplay between the individual and social perspective.

Freedom of the self, then, lies in the proper relation between these two dimensions, and as, stressed earlier, does not lie in opposition to the restrictions of norms and authority but in a self-direction which requires the proper dynamic interaction of these two dimensions of the self. Freedom does not lie in being unaffected by others but in the way one uses one's incorporation of the "other" in novel decisions and actions. As Mead states, this dynamic interrelationship provides one with "the ability to talk to oneself in terms of the community to which one belongs and lay upon oneself the responsibilities that belong to the community; the ability to admonish oneself as others would, and to recognize what are one's duties as well as one's rights."[33]

Given the dynamics of the self in pragmatic philosophy, these responsibilities have resulted not just from the internalization of the attitudes of the generalized other but from the effect on these attitudes by the past responses of one's own creative input. Not only is one's creative individuality not enslaved by or determined by the generalized other, the generalized other has been formed in part from one's own creative acts. This generalized other, as stressed previously, is neither an absolute other nor an abstract other, but the other as part and parcel of the dynamics of selfhood and the community life in which the self is enmeshed.

Individual rights are thus also social rights; rights are inherently relational. There are no purely individual rights, but there are rights relations, and all rights relations involve both entitlement and obligation. Ongoing community adjustments, then, must be understood not as pitting the individual armed with rights against the common other that limits rights, but rather as community attempts to find the proper balance between the relational poles of entitlements and obligations, neither of which can function without the other.

A free society, like a free individual, requires this balance. In this way the good of the whole is not the good of the commons or group other over against the individual. The good of the whole is the proper relation between the individual and the common other, because the whole is community and community encompasses the individual and the common other. If rights are understood as an individual possession upon which society infringes, pitting one individual against another or pitting the individual against the group, then rights will lead to self-interested factionalism and adversarial relationships rather than communal cooperation. As Dewey notes, "the principle of authority" must not be understood as "purely restrictive power" but as providing direction.[34]

The pragmatic position holds that humans are born into implicit contractual arrangements and grounds autonomy, solidarity, and fairness in the communal nature of human existence. Moreover, pragmatism recognizes the growth of each person as both a means for community development and as the end or goal of community development. Each human is neither a means to something else nor an end in itself but is both contributor and recipient in a reciprocal relationship. Means are contributions to wholes or ends in which they are ingredients, and every ending is at once a new beginning of new possibilities to be fulfilled. There is no separation of means and ends. Everything has both relational and immediate qualities, instrumental and consummatory properties. The moral worth of the flourishing of the individual is inseparable from the moral worth of the flourishing of the human community.

One of the key insights of social contract/rights theory is its voluntary nature. Thomas Donaldson, in an insightful overview of various social-contract theories and their basic differences, points out that "amid the various versions of the social contract theory a common strand exists: an emphasis on the *consent* of the parties."[35] Although humans are born into implicit contractual arrangements, the acceptance of contracts is nonetheless voluntary within the pragmatic framework; the type of reciprocal relationships which the developing self incorporates is not imposed from without but internalized by the free, creative activity of the "I" which enters into the self-structuring of the "me" and the restructuring of the generalized other. Stated differently, the nature of the self requires internalization of the perspective of the other. Obligations resulting from rule-driven abstract conceptions of external claims are very different from caring attuned relationships based on the internalization of the perspective of the other.[36] One cannot internalize any right without internalizing a corresponding obligation, for what is being internalized is inherently relational.

Thus while one cannot escape the relational nature of human existence and the rights relation which is part of its dynamics, one can escape particular rights relations including those into which one is born. Particular rights relations must be morally evaluated and will carry different moral weight depending on the role of these relations in providing enriching growth of community and the selves involved in community dynamics. Since the natural state of human existence is community existence, then the "natural rights" of the human should include the ability to participate in community. The natural rights of community existence, then, would seem to demand the right both to individual autonomy and of participation in the development of social authority. And this right of each individual is inextricably tied to the obligation of each individual to provide this right for all members of the community. The demand for freedom is the demand to move from narrow restrictive rights to those that allow for ongoing growth.

According to the pragmatic position, then, the relational nature of rights emerges within the reciprocal relation of rights and obligations inherent in community dynamics. Natural rights are natural precisely because they allow us to participate in the relational dynamics constitutive of the nature of human existence. It is the dimensions of freedom and constraint, rights and obligations, self and other, all embedded in the nature of the self and community alike, which give rise to the situational and relational nature of rights. Rather then pit one individual against another or the individual against the group, rights and their corresponding obligations can actually help tie communities together and enable them to reach the necessary compromises that contribute to ongoing community growth.

What does this view of rights mean for property rights, which are so important in American culture and help form the basis of contemporary capitalism? According to the theory of John Locke, when natural objects are taken out of a state of nature and mixed with human labor, those objects become the property of the individual. While things in a state of nature belong to everyone in common, when they are made useful the person or persons who mixed their labor with them have a natural right to possess them as their own. Government exists to protect this natural right to property and cannot take this property away without consent from the appropriate individuals involved.

However, property does not exist in a vacuum; it exists in a social and cultural context. It is the community as a whole, whether explicitly or implicitly, which decides that the best way to organize the commons to promote growth of the community is to allow individuals to have control over certain aspects of the commons and use it in the way they see fit within certain limitations. The commons is prior to the individual and can be organized in whatever way the community decides. Some cultures have no notion of property rights and what we would call stealing is called borrowing in this cultural context. In market societies, allowing individuals to have control over some aspect of the commons seems to be the best way to promote the efficient use of nature's resources and better the lot of the community as a whole.

Individuals have to pay property taxes to support functions like public education that the community deems important. Since pollution and noise do not respect property boundaries, these have to be regulated by the community in the interests of those who are adversely affected. The community can take property for public purposes, such as roads and the like, as long as the owner is fairly compensated. In a democratic society the state cannot act arbitrarily and take property without fair compensation and without giving individuals a chance to have a voice in these decisions. These notions change over time as currently municipalities can condemn property to use it for purposes that were not foreseen even a few years ago, such as allowing higher priced dwellings or commercial interests to use it, which will bring in more revenue to the municipality. The Supreme Court narrowly upheld this practice, which is a new interpretation of the "takings clause" of the constitution.

Thus the right to property is not a natural right; it is a right that arises in a community context and reflects the values of that community. It is believed that if individuals have control over property they will use if more efficiently than some kind of social ownership, and this increased efficiency will benefit the community as a whole. The abolishment of private property in socialistic systems did not lead to greater efficiency and did not benefit the community, but seemed to benefit only those who were in control of the bureaucracy that made decisions about the use of property. It was not an efficient system nor did it promote distributive justice in the allocation of the goods and services the system did produce. These systems by and large collapsed as people became less interested in ideology and more interested in their material betterment.

This view of rights has implications for our view of government and its function in society. An individualistic view thinks of the government as encroaching on the rights of the individual and thus its activities must be kept to a minimum and focus largely on securing these individual rights. The Tea Party movement mentioned earlier embodies this view of government and emphasizes the right to be left alone to do their own thing. However, we do not live in isolation from each other but are part of a larger community where we have not only rights but also responsibilities to each other. As society becomes more complex and more crowded, these responsibilities become more important as conflicts between individuals increase and the resolution of these conflicts becomes more and more difficult. According to Richard Bronk:

> All democracies have championed the freedom to participate in government, and most have also sought to enshrine in law certain individual rights which seek to secure for individuals some inalienable areas of freedom of action and thought. Progress has, in part, been defined in the liberal tradition as the gradual extension of these individual freedoms and rights. The central problem for liberal democracy, however, is that one person's right to freedom of action may clash with another person's right not to be harmed . . . But in our increasingly interconnected and congested world, many people argue that surprisingly few actions by individuals are without important consequences for others. The crucial debate has centered around what role democratic government should have in trying to ensure greater harmony of interests between members of society, and what role government should have in forging best social and environmental outcome for society as a whole."[37]

When rights are seen as stemming from an individualistic conception of self, reconciliation between clashing rights is extremely difficult. The whole notion of public policy or the public or common good is undermined by an individualistic approach where public policy represents nothing more than the aggregation of citizen preferences for public goods and services as expressed through the political process. This view is reinforced by the notion of rights that inhere in individuals and are part and parcel of their nature. Thus public policy reflects these ideas of individualism and rights that are part of the society at large and the process ends up being in irreconcilable conflict over which rights take priority as individuals and groups battle each other in pursuing their interests. What would help to make government work better is a new framework for understanding these tensions that exist within society, one that undercuts the notions of isolatable individuals with absolute rights in favor of inherently social persons that are an integral part of a larger community.

12 Pragmatism and Nature

While there has been some progress in both government and business in this country in coming to grips with environmental problems, we have not done nearly enough to develop a sustainable society. Our relationship with the environment has not really changed and we continue to view it in instrumental fashion as there to be exploited and manipulated for human purposes. We continue to think of ourselves as separate from the natural environment and do not really feel a connection with it that is something more than an objective recognition that it at least exists and needs to be taken into account. Yet humans are embedded in a natural environment and are intertwined with that environment. Everything we do as humans involves the environment in one way or another. We are part of the natural world and cannot survive apart from our natural environment. Thus we are intimately connected with it whether we like it or not, and cannot separate ourselves from the environment in which we are embedded.

The cultural history of the Western world has been one which has hindered thinking of ourselves in this manner. Spending time in nature, while helpful, is not in itself going to overcome the disconnect between humans and nature, because people can spend time hiking and camping in the most beautiful natural surroundings and still not feel connected in any real sense to that environment. They can still see nature in purely instrumental terms as offering an opportunity to test one's survival skills as in Outward Bound programs, to test one's physical strength as in mountain climbing, or as a source of pictures to be taken home and shown to family and friends. The problem is that we see nature as something to be exploited for human purposes, and this is particularly true of people living in an economic system devoted to production and consumption of material goods and services. We are not willing to accept major changes to our lifestyle to accommodate environmental concerns such as global warming.

Attempting to bridge a so-called disconnect or divide between humans and nature will not work in developing an environmental consciousness that can transform our industrial economy into a sustainable society.

Rather, we must come to recognize that there is no disconnect or divide to overcome. There is no separation of humans from nature such that humans are subjective beings that manipulate an objective nature for purposes of enhancing their material well-being. This realization involves the inculcation of a different philosophy from that which forms the foundations of a scientific worldview that separates mind and body, subjective and objective, and other such dichotomies that separate us from nature, and a religious worldview that emphasizes the supernatural as the locus of meaning and purpose for human life.

Nature cannot be dehumanized nor can humans be denaturalized. Neither human activity in general nor human knowledge can be separated from the fact that humans are natural organisms embedded in and dependent upon a natural environment with which they are continuous. Human development is connected with its biological world and the self is not something that can be viewed apart from its rootedness in nature. The human being is located in nature and emerges from and opens onto the natural world in which humans function. We are not only part of a human community but are also part of a broader community that includes the natural environment, and we have a responsibility to and for that larger community. Humans and nature must be seen in a relational context to overcome the separation between humans and nature that exists in Western culture.

Our Western tradition works against this relational understanding of nature not just in the economic realm but in all areas of Western culture. Science *dehumanizes* nature by treating nature objectively in the interests of manipulating nature to suit human interests. In doing so it abstracts nature from the relational context in which humans exist and flourish. It treats nature as something external to humans that can be exploited for self-interested purposes and views nature in instrumental terms as existing only to serve human needs and interests. The Christian religion *denaturalizes* humans by taking them out of nature with belief in the supernatural and in doing so abstracts humans from the natural world in which they live, move, and have their being. Meaning and purpose are found outside of nature and not in the natural world itself. Human origins as well as their final destiny are located outside of the natural world. Neither approach does justice to the natural world and the context in which humans and nature interact.

Neither of these two worldviews is adequate to deal with our environmental problems and overcome the separation between humans and nature. Science dehumanizes nature and Christianity denaturalizes humans, and neither worldview can change to incorporate humans and nature into an inseparable whole and remain what they are as worldviews. Thus we need a new worldview or philosophy to accomplish this task. What is needed is a revolution in the way we conceptualize our relationship to nature, a new consciousness that will allow us to see and relate to nature in a different manner. Only by some revolutionary change of this nature can the human race survive and come to live in harmony with the natural environment in which we are embedded.

ENVIRONMENTAL CONSCIOUSNESS

Nothing would seem to be more important at this juncture of human existence than the emergence of a new moral consciousness to guide the direction of production and consumption in ways that enhance the natural environment in which we are embedded. We are destroying our own habitat, but the human need to shape and develop nature to suit ourselves seems to be inexhaustible and is like a bulldozer that cannot be stopped. Sometimes it seems inevitable that we are going to build something on every square inch of the earth, exploit every last resource the earth can provide, and industrialize every last bit of wilderness. The human ego seems to have no bounds or limits, which creates a problem because the world we live in does have limits. Our refusal to live within those limits will surely lead to our demise unless we reconceptualize the relationship between humans and nature.

The problems that we face with respect to the environment and the implications these problems have for the survival of the human race point towards a major change in human consciousness regarding the place of humans in relation to the natural environment in which they exist. There have been several such shifts in thinking throughout history as people have had to come to grips with new realities that were discovered or forced on them by events. (Exhibit 1). Adoptions of these new realities never came easily because people are reluctant to change perceptions unless forced to do so by overwhelming evidence or by the magnitude of the problems that have to be solved for the human race to continue.

Exhibit 1

Changes in Human Consciousness

Theories about the Universe
    The earth is not at the center of
    the solar system let alone the
    universe.

Theories of Evolution
    Human life is the result of an
    evolutionary process that
    incorporates the principle of
    natural selection.

Theories of the Unconscious
   Human freedom is
   circumscribed by unconscious
   wishes and desires.

Theories about Nature
   Humans are a part of nature
   and must see themselves as but
   one part of a vast and
   interdependent ecosystem.

The first such change in human consciousness came with the development of science and the scientific method as it was applied to the physical world in which we exist, particularly to the nature and composition of the universe. Prior to the Copernican revolution it was accepted as an article of faith that the sun and the other planets revolved around the earth and that human beings were the center of the universe. When observations began to be made regarding movement of the planets and the sun, early scientists developed elaborate theories to explain the irregularities of their rotation based on the assumption of an earth-centered universe. When these explanations became more and more complicated and proved to be unsatisfactory, the traditional way of thinking about the universe began to change and it was recognized that the earth and the other planets revolved around the sun and the earth was not the center of the universe of even or our own solar system. The result of this change in consciousness was a humbling experience for humans as rather than being the center of everything they were now known to live on a small inconspicuous planet in a small solar system off to one side of a galaxy that is only one of billions of such entities in the vast universe with which we are surrounded.

The second change in human consciousness was triggered by theories of evolution, theories that have not been accepted by some religions even in today's world. The theory of evolution challenged the notion that human beings were created directly by God after the world had been created and that therefore they had a special status with respect to the rest of the creation. The theory of evolution, however, places human beings in an evolutionary process where the creation of plant and animal life is the result of a lengthy process of natural selection that has gone on for billions of years and will continue as far as we know as long as the world exists. Many people have not accepted this theory because they believe it degrades humans to mere animals in a long chain of evolution that has no particular purpose and therefore no meaning. Battles between creationists and evolutionists continue in our culture and show no signs of abating.

A third such challenge to human understanding that is seldom mentioned was posed by psychology and the discovery of the unconscious. Human freedom has been of particular importance in American history and culture and in the Protestant religion, which emphasizes free will and the importance of choice. Yet psychology presents a different perception of choice and places limits on free will with its theory of the unconscious. Many of our so-called choices are not really choices at all, so it is argued, in the sense in which we usually think about choice. Many of our decisions are based on unconscious wishes or desires and are not really free at all in the sense we would like to believe. It is only as these unconscious wishes or desires are brought to consciousness in psychotherapy or psychoanalysis that we can expand our degrees of freedom and make choices free of these unconscious elements.

The environment can be seen as posing yet another challenge to human self-understanding and providing yet another humbling experience for the human ego. The traditional view of humans and their relationship to nature as has been said is dualistic, that humans stand over against nature and are somehow apart from nature. The task of humans is to conquer nature and to take dominion over the animals and the natural world and use it for our purposes and shape it to serve our interests. Nature is treated as an object that has no particular value in and of itself and thus has no moral standing and can be used it in whatever way we deem necessary with no moral qualms.

There are several interesting aspects of this dualistic view of nature that deserve to be mentioned. The view that nature exists to serve human purposes can be called an anthropomorphic view of nature, which refers to the human-centered way we have traditionally approached nature. We manipulate nature to serve our own interests and our own sense of progress. Nature must be "developed" and has no value in its natural state. It has value only as it is shaped to serve some human purpose. Resources in their natural state have no utility or value until they are taken out of the ground and processed by industrial systems to make something useful that can be sold to consumers. Only then does nature have any use or value and become part of the system where economic wealth is measured. This quantification of nature then serves the purpose of guiding decisions that are made to create more wealth, which helps make humans feel secure in the world in that they have conquered nature and made it serve their purposes.

The fact that we have largely conquered nature, however, had led to a change in our relationship to nature. While once nature indeed may have been able to take care of itself and could be exploited at will, today nature is defined by human activity. While we once may have thought of nature as a collection of forces that humans reacted to as they fought for survival, it is nature's survival that is now threatened by human activity.[1] Human beings determine what lives and dies as far as plants and animals are concerned as we encroach on the habitats of more and more animal life and destroy plant life by our industrial and developmental activities. We determine the amount of ultraviolet radiation we will be exposed to through our willingness to curb production and use of ozone-destroying chemicals. We determine the kind of climate we will live in and what kind of changes in climate have to be responded to in future years.

This change led Bill McKibben several years ago to write a book entitled *The End of Nature*, which captures this change and provides a different way of viewing the present situation. While this book was mentioned in an earlier chapter, it deserves to be mentioned again. The basic thesis of the book is that nature as we have known it in the past in its pure form no longer exists. Human beings have conquered nature because the entire natural world now bears the stamp of humanity as we have left our imprint on nature everywhere and have altered it beyond recognition. We have made nature a creation of our own and have lost the otherness that once belonged to the natural world. The natural world is so affected by human technology that it is more and more becoming one or our own creations and thus is no longer the autonomous nature in which we sought refuge from human civilization.[2] According to Thomas Berry, writing in the *Dream of the Earth*:

> In our times . . . human cunning has mastered the deep mysteries of the earth at a level far beyond the capacities of earlier peoples. We can break the mountains apart; we can drain the rivers and flood the valleys. We can turn the most luxuriant forests into throwaway paper products. We can tear apart the great grass cover of the western plains and pour toxic chemicals into the soil and pesticides onto the fields until the soil is dead and blows away in the wind. We can pollute the air with acids, the rivers with sewage, and the seas with oil—all this in a kind of intoxication with our power of devastation at an order of magnitude beyond all reckoning . . . Our managerial skills are measured by the competence manifested in accelerating this process.[3]

Human activities can alter natural processes far greater than anyone could ever have imagined and nature has been subjugated and altered to serve human needs on a scale that is unsurpassed in human history. Nature can no longer take care of itself and needs humans to take better care of it in their own interests if not for the sake of nature itself. The earth has finite resources and a fragile environment which gives us a responsibility to manage the human use of planet earth. Thus far we have not done a very good job is this respect, and many people are concerned that nature will be crowded out by human interference and oppose the idea that humans should exercise their dominion over nature for the sake of material progress. They have a sense of loss because nature's independence is being destroyed.

For much of history, humans have not experienced nature as kind and gentle but harsh and dangerous, and therefore humans have felt compelled to subordinate nature in order to secure their existence. But it is now humans who are harsh and dangerous with respect to nature rather than kind and gentle, and it is nature that needs to be protected from the destructive activities of humans. Humility towards nature is now advocated, that humans should not think in terms of control or dictating to nature, but must learn to live in harmony with nature and respect nature's own rhythms and needs in its development projects and other activities.

There are many reasons behind the destruction of the environment that is currently taking place. Many of these reasons have to do with the technology we employ and how new technologies are introduced into society, the reward systems that motivate the behavior of people and organizations, and the way we measure progress in economically oriented societies. Many of these reasons are systemic in nature, having to do with the systems in which people and organizations operate. But behind these systemic problems lie deeper philosophical and religious assumptions about human beings and the world in which they live.

A new intellectual approach to the natural environment is needed, one that reconceptualizes the relationship between humans and the environment. This approach must not be human centered but must recognize that some natural objects and ecosystems have value and are morally considerable in their own right apart from human interests. Nature is not to be seen as simply a function of human interests but is important in and of itself apart from human considerations. This approach must respect each life-form and see it as part of a larger whole. All life is a sacred thing and we must not be careless about species that are irreplaceable. Particular individuals and nations come and go throughout history but nature in some form will continue indefinitely and humans must come to understand their place in nature. Each life-form is constrained to flourish in a larger community and moral concern for the whole biological community is the only kind of an approach that makes sense and preserves the integrity of the entire world.[4]

Nature itself is a source of values because the concept of value must be broadened to include far more than a simplistic human-interest satisfaction. Nature cannot be solely defined in terms of commodities that are capable of producing wealth for humans who manage nature in its own interest. Value is a multifaceted idea with structures that are rooted in natural sources.[5] It is not just a human product that is bestowed on the natural world. Values can be found in nature as well as humans and are related in some sense to natural objects themselves apart from humans and their particular valuing activities. Humans do not simply bestow value on nature when they make it into something useful, but nature also conveys value to humans. There is thus an interrelational aspect to value that emerges when humans interact with nature.[6]

When humans recognize value as an emergent property outside themselves, this need not result in a dehumanizing of the self or a diminishing of the human ego. On the contrary, it can be argued that human consciousness and status are increased when we praise and respect the value found in the natural world and this recognition results in a further spiritualizing of humans.[7] Humans find fulfillment in nature and cannot realize their full potential without interacting with nature. When nature is destroyed, we are destroying part of ourselves, and in this sense we are negating certain experiences that can be meaningful and fulfilling only in relationship to nature.

Instead of a hierarchical ordering of entities in descending order from God through humans to animals and plants, where the lower organisms are under the higher ones and ruled by them, nature needs to be seen as a web of interactive and interdependent life that is ruled by its own natural processes. These processes must be understood if we are to work in harmony with nature and preserve the conditions for our own continued existence. Protecting the rain forest is not just a matter of someone from the outside trying to preserve the rain forest as something apart from most people's existence; it is a matter of seeing oneself as part of the rain forest and acting to protect oneself from extinction.[8]

As stated by Thomas Berry, "Any diminishment of the natural world diminishes our imagination, our emotions, our sensitivities, and our intellectual perception, as well as our spirituality."[9] Human beings are integral with the entire earth and even with the universe as the larger community we belong to by the very nature of our existence. But most of us do not live within this perspective and are not in intimate communion with the natural world. We have become autistic and do not hear the voices of nature. We have been blindly pursuing more and more economic growth while replacing nature with our own view of reality and in the process have destroyed much that is good and beautiful.

> The mountains and valleys, the rivers and the sea, the birds and other animals, this multitude of beings that compose the natural world no longer share in our lives and we have ceased to share in their lives except as natural resources to be plundered for their economic value . . . We might wonder how it was that we let this fascinating world be taken from us to be replaced with the grime of our cities disintegrating the very stones of our buildings, as well as increasing the physical and emotional stress under which we live. It was, of course, the illusion of a better life, foisted on us largely through hypnotic advertising and the promise of economic enrichment.[10]

Treating nature as instrumental places the natural world in a utilitarian position with respect to humans and their relationship with nature. The natural world has value only to the extent it can serve humans. Such an approach involves an unhealthy separation between humans and the rest of nature. Humans must also ask how they can serve nature and recognize a mutual interdependence between human life and life in the natural world. Human life is a part of the natural world and the dualism and individualism that is characteristic of Western thought is no longer functional. Such thinking leads to policies and practices that undermine the conditions for supporting human life and activities by destroying the natural world on which we all depend.

If McKibben is right and nature as it once was understood no longer exists, this means that nature has been conquered and is now largely under our control. Perhaps we should even stop using the term *natural environment* since there is nothing in this environment anymore that is natural in the sense that it is unaffected by human activities. We are shaping the environment in which we and future generations will have to live and work out their existence and we need to be aware of this responsibility and take the necessary steps to enhance the environment for the benefit of the entire community of human beings, now and in the future.

For this to take place involves a reconceptualization of the relationship between humans and nature. Neither science nor religion, as has been argued, is able to accomplish this task as science has to objectify nature or it is not science and the Christian religion has to denaturalize humans or it is not Christianity. What is needed are new approaches to nature that are neither scientific nor religious in nature, or that at least redefine science and religion in way that can incorporate nature in a different manner. There have been numerous approaches to accomplish this redefinition that can fit under the general heading of environmental ethics. Something like a new environmental consciousness has been emerging over the past several decades that is based on our relation to and responsibilities for the natural environment. What is needed is a reconceptualization of humans and their relationship to nature that can place production and consumption activities in a different moral context.

TOWARD RECONCEPTUALIZING HUMANS AND NATURE

Such a reconceptualization must be based on a philosophical system that considers humans and nature in a relational context. Pragmatism offers such a possibility because it stresses that neither human activity in general nor human knowledge can be separated from the fact that humans are natural organisms embedded in and dependent upon a natural environment with which they are continuous. Human development is connected with its biological world and the self is not something that can be viewed apart from its rootedness in nature. The human person is located in nature and emerges from and opens onto the natural world in which humans function. We are not only part of a human community, but also part of a natural community and have a responsibility to and for that larger community. Gary T. Gardner describes the task as follows:

> The effort to reclaim community should include broadening our understanding of community to include the natural world on which humans radically depend. It will require an "anthropocosmic"

world-view—an understanding of humans as embedded in the cosmic order—in place of the Enlightenment view of humans as being apart from nature. It will be deeply relational, with a web as the appropriate metaphor, so that humans understand profoundly their intimate connection to all of creation. An anthropocosmic world-view would affect the way we think about everything, from law to education to the way we build economies.[11]

Humans and their environment, organic and inorganic, take on an inherently relational aspect. To speak of organism and environment in isolation from each other is never true to the actual situation, for no organism can exist in isolation from an environment, and the environment is what it is in relation to an organism. What exists is an indivisible whole and it is only within such an interactional context that humans can function and develop. The relational nature of humans and the natural world undercuts the problematics of subjective experience set over against an alien objective universe.

A deepening of reason and expansion of one's self opens up the possibility of a deep-seated harmony with the totality of the natural world to which the self is related. This involves the entire universe, for an emphasis on continuity reveals that at no time can we separate our developing selves from any part of the universe and claim that part is irrelevant. Growth involves a deepening and expansion of perspective to include an ever-widening understanding of the natural universe to which we are inseparably bound. This unity can be neither apprehended in knowledge nor realized in reflection. The totality it involves is neither a literal content of the intellect nor an intellectual grasp of nature, but is best seen as an imaginative ideal that is manifested in a deepened attunement to nature. Such an experience brings about not only a change in the intellect but also a change in moral consciousness.

Since humans exist within and are part of nature, any part of nature provides a conceivable relational context for values to emerge. The understanding we have of "human interests," of what is valuable for human enrichment, has to be expanded to incorporate a greatly extended notion of human welfare to include the natural world. To increase our experience of value is not to increase something subjective within us but to increase the value-ladenness of relational contexts within nature. Although the concept of the valuable emerges only through judgments involving human intelligence, value-related qualities such as alluring or repugnant occur at any level of environmental interaction involving sentient organisms. According to Larry Hickman relative to the pragmatic position:

Since human beings are a part of nature, their enriched experience of nature enriches nature's experience of itself . . . The self is itself a construct, and as such it is experienced neither foundationally, immediately, or privately, but just as are other parts of the built-up environment of human knowledge. It further follows that there is no objective nature to provide a foundation for knowledge. Nature is not a "thing" but a complex and fecund matrix of objects and events, experienced in part as an expanding source of novel facilities and constraints, but nevertheless constructed within the history of human inquiry.[12]

While some environmentalists may question the claim that a distinction in levels of value can be made, and that all of nature has intrinsic value that must be preserved, when push comes to shove and when all the abstract arguments have been made, is it not the case that claims of the valuable must be seen in light of its promotion of or irrepressible harm to human welfare, actual or potential. Does anyone really think that the preservation of the spotted owl and the preservation of the AIDS virus have equal moral claim? Making value judgments of this kind does not involve a reemergence of anthropocentrism as it is not the case that all value emerges only in relation to humans. Yet neither is it the case that everything in nature has equal value irrespective of its relation to the welfare of humans. Value is an emergent contextual property of situations as long as and whenever there are sentient organisms involved in our experience.

The biological egalitarianism of biocentrism cannot be maintained in practice. Value judgments have to be made relative to those parts of the natural world over which we have some control. Yet this does not mean that humans can ignore the value contexts of sentient organisms within nature. We must make judgments that provide protection for the welfare of humans, yet such judgments must consider to the largest degree consistent with this goal the value-laden contexts involving other sentient organisms. These decisions must be made in terms of conflicting claims that have to be evaluated and not exploitation of nature through egocentric disregard for the valuings of other organisms. With respect to John Dewey's position as described by Hickman:

> His [Dewey's] antitranscendentalism would have led Dewey to reject attempts by some environmental ethicists to "socialize" nature as a thing-in-itself with values, interests, or rights that are purely intrinsic to it, and independent of human interests.[13] Like many other ethicists, Dewey held that moral rights exist only in the context of a community of moral agents. This is so because of the linkage between rights and obligations. Because there cannot be obligation in the absence of choice, and because it is only with the advent of human life that choice becomes fully a part of evolutionary history, it is a mistake to attribute intrinsic rights to either nonhuman species or to individuals. To speak of nonhuman species or nonhuman individuals as possessors of intrinsic rights would in Dewey's view amount either to anthropomorphizing nonhuman nature or to opening up a chasm between human

and nonhuman nature by positing a domain of moral rights that does not involve moral agency and is therefore entirely separate from what human beings understand by the term.[14]

This position does not allow for the emergence of value in nonsentient contexts but neither does it allow for the exploitation of nonsentient entities. It is not possible to envision any aspect of nature that cannot be the object of a conceivable experience of sentient organisms. At no point can any environmental approach draw the line between human welfare and the welfare of the environment of which it is a part. Everything that can conceivably enter into human experience has the potential for being part of the relational context within which value emerges, and any value as well as any aspect of the context within which it emerges involves consequences and is therefore instrumental in bringing about something further. There is no means-end distinction but rather an ongoing continuity in which the character of the means enters into the quality of the end, which in turn becomes a means to something further.

The debate between instrumental versus intrinsic value is problematic and of no help in making decisions about nature. If everything has intrinsic value, then decisions about uses of nature become somewhat arbitrary. If, for example, every tree has its own intrinsic value and the right to exist, irrespective of its potential for valuing experiences, how can we choose which trees to cut down? Yet common sense tells us we cannot "save" them all, and decisions have to be made relative to specific situations. Value does not lie in the tree itself nor in humans themselves, but it emerges in the interactions between humans and nature, and when decisions have to be made they are made relative to the valuing experiences of human beings.

These decisions are not made by an isolated individual, abstracted from the natural context in which they are embedded. Neither individuals nor nature is the bearer of value; rather, values emerge in the interactions of individuals with nature. Nature gains its value through its interaction with individuals, but the value of individuals cannot be understood in isolation from the relationships which constitute their ongoing development and growth. Decisions must be made relative to the flourishing of humans in an environment that supports and contributes to their development in all the richness and diversity that constitutes human existence.

Managers cannot make morally responsible decisions which involve the environment based on viewing it as purely instrumental, as being there only for exploitation for human purposes. Nor can they find much guidance in holding abstractly that nature has rights or that the ecosystem supersedes the needs of individual societies or humanly structured functions. We cannot save all the trees nor can we be concerned equally with saving all species. What is needed is a recognition that the corporation has its being through its relation to a wider community that includes the natural environment and has responsibilities to that wider community.

Responsible corporate decision making, as contextually located and evaluated in terms of consequences, must include environmental considerations when these are relevant. What specific course of action should be followed in specific instances must of course emerge from the concrete situation and the unique conflicting demands it involves. But as in all moral decision making, the more deeply one is attuned to our interactions with the natural environment in which we are embedded, the more a potential exists for seeing and creating alternatives which are viable for enriching human existence.

ECONOMICS AND THE ENVIRONMENT

One major impediment to treating the natural environment in a responsible manner is the way the environment is treated in standard economic theory because this theory in large part dominates the way we behave with respect to the environment. The market does not respond very well to environmental problems and, if left to its own devices, treats the environment as something external to itself. There seems to be no way the value of the environment or any of its services can be determined through a market process since there is nothing to be exchanged or traded. People cannot take a piece of dirty air, for example, and exchange it for a piece of clean air on the market, at least given the current state of technology. The same holds true for other components of the environment.

The competitive system limits the ability of corporations to respond to environmental problems on an individual basis because if they voluntarily clean up their pollution they will most likely price themselves out of the market. Some call this inability of market systems to respond to environmental pollution and degradation a market failure, but the use of this term is not entirely accurate. Market systems were not designed to factor in environmental costs and it is not fair to blame the system for not doing something for which it was not designed. Property rights are not appropriately assigned as regards the environment and nature often lacks a discrete owner to look after its interests. Nature's interests can be violated by market exchanges and, as a common property resource, can be overused and degraded as it is subject to the "tragedy of the commons," a phenomenon that relates to property held in common for everyone.[15]

Market systems evolved to serve human needs and wants; they are not constructed to protect the environment. The environment is treated as a source of raw materials to be used in the production process and as a bottomless sink in which to dispose of raw materials. The environment has no economic value in and of itself but is worth something only as it can be used to serve some human purpose. The ecological functions of the environment have no value as far as the market is concerned. It is only their economic utility or instrumental value that is of importance in a market economy.

Thus the market fails to tell the ecological truth as it regularly underprices products and services by failing to incorporate the environmental costs of providing them.[16]

Economic growth comes at the expense of the earth's productive assets— its farmlands, forests, fisheries, aquifers, wetlands, and even its climate. The costs of this environmental degradation and pollution are external to normal market processes and are not taken into account in the price mechanism unless these costs are determined through some other process and imposed on the market system. Only then can environmental values be internalized and reflect themselves in market decisions. This is a major task facing business and society: to find some reasonable and acceptable way to factor in environmental costs along with the other costs of production.[17]

This task cannot be left to government alone because government is subject to political and ideological pressures that do not allow it to develop a consistent approach to environmental problems. Perhaps business can take the lead and work with other entities in society, including government, to develop an institutional mechanism to figure out these environmental costs and then decide on the best means of imposing these costs on the market, whether it be through standards, taxes, emissions-trading systems, or other means. People must be made aware of the environmental costs of their actions and our political, economic, and social systems must change to take into account environmental impacts in every decision. We are shaping the environment in which we and future generations will have to live and work out their existence and we need to be aware of this responsibility.

Part III

Implications for Business

13 The Corporation and Community

The social view of the self and its relation to community as described in an earlier chapter has implications for an understanding of the corporation, both in terms of an understanding of the corporation itself and its relationship to the broader society in which it functions. Within the philosophical framework that pragmatism provides, the corporation is seen as a social entity rather than strictly an economic entity that has only economic impacts and responsibilities. The corporation is a social community in itself and is also part of a larger community. These two aspects of the corporation are different from the way in which the corporation is normally understood and has implications for its role in society.

In traditional economic theory based on the scientific worldview, the corporation is abstracted out of its social context and given an independence that cuts it off from any larger social and moral purpose. The corporation is a legal device that is formed for purely economic purposes. While the corporate form of organization was first used for a public purpose such as building roads or canals in the early years of this country, in the landmark Dartmouth College decision of the Supreme Court, corporations were held to be a voluntary organization that could be used privately by people to pursue their economic self-interest without any overriding public purpose. This decision encouraged people to form corporations wherever they thought an opportunity existed that could be exploited for self-interested reasons.

The corporate form of organization enabled risk to be spread across a large number of people and made individuals who invested in the company accountable only for the amount of money they had put into the organization rather than for the whole entity. People could thus minimize their risk and yet join with others in a cooperative enterprise that needed larger sums of capital and resources than they had individually. People could share in a larger endeavor that could exploit economic opportunities that were too large and risky for any one individual to take on by himself or herself. The legal fiction called the corporation enabled this kind of an arrangement to work for the advantage of society.

The corporation was thus formed to create economic wealth by bringing together people with different skills and talents, capital resources of many different kinds, and raw material from many different locations and putting all these elements together to produce goods and services that are useful or have utility for society. In classical economic theory based on the scientific worldview, the corporation is considered to be a voluntary organization where people join together to accomplish purposes they cannot accomplish separately. Thus people in the corporation are organized to achieve a common purpose which they may not have in mind when taking a position in the organization. People band together as employees, investors, creditors, and the like because of economic self-interest. Employees are pursuing their self-interest in working to earn wages or salaries to support themselves and their families. Investors put money into the corporation because of their desire to earn an economic return on their investment. Customers buy the goods and services a corporation produces to gain personal satisfaction through their consumption activities.

Such a view, however, is again based on the understanding of individuals as *atomic* units that band together with other such individuals for certain common purposes. These individuals have no other connection except for this need to be part of the same organization for self-interested reasons. The corporation has no purpose except to generate economic wealth to serve the economic needs of these individuals and to enhance the economic wealth of the society in general. The individuals who are the parts give meaning to and comprise the whole, which is the corporation. The corporation is thus comprised of atomic individuals who work for it in some capacity and help to achieve the common purpose of producing goods and services to enhance the material well-being of society.

Since the corporation is nothing more than the people who are a part of the organization, moral agency is located in these individuals. Moral responsibility and accountability only make sense when applied to these individuals. The corporation as such does not make choices; the people in the organization make choices. People act intentionally and deliberately and it does not make sense to think of the corporation as acting intentionally. The corporation is not a moral entity; it has no conscience and no feelings of moral compulsion or obligation. The corporation cannot act of its own volition; it can only act through the people who comprise its workforce who are morally responsible for their decisions and actions.

The corporation is the primary organization in our society through which new technologies are introduced. When science makes possible the development of new technologies, these technologies will most likely be developed and employed by a corporation in order to introduce a new product into the market or improve an existing product that hopefully will be profitable. Thus technology is made to serve the aims of the corporation and the decision as to whether or not a new technology is introduced into society is primarily economic in nature. While there may be some questions asked about the potential effect of the technology on the environment and whether it is safe for society, the primary concern of the corporation is whether the technology will be profitable and serve the private interests of those who benefit from corporate activities.

The primary purpose of the corporation has become the quest for profits because managers are encouraged to maximize profits to earn the highest return they can for the shareholders. The production of goods and services has in large part become an incidental exercise in this quest for profits. The ultimate value for society resides in the profits the corporation can make rather than the goods and services it produces and the contribution it makes towards enhancing the welfare and quality of life in society. This sole focus on profits is a function of the economic value system in which corporations operate. Because the corporation is considered to be only an economic entity, measuring its economic value is the only way to determine the success of the organization. The creation of economic value is primary and other values involved in the production of goods and services are of little or no importance.

This traditional view of the corporation reflects the reductionistic and quantitative outlook that is part and parcel of the scientific worldview. *The corporation is reduced to a single purpose that can be measured by quantitative means to judge its success or failure.* This purpose is to maximize shareholder wealth, and in order to do this, the corporation must make profits or at least have the promise of doing so in the future. Shareholder wealth can be measured by looking at how well the stock price of the corporation is doing and what expectations the market has relative to its future earning potential. Profits are reported in the corporation's quarterly statements or in the annual report. This single-minded purpose enables people to develop some notion of how valuable the corporation is to society and how well it is fulfilling its purpose.

THE CORPORATION AS A COMMUNITY

From a pragmatic perspective, however, the corporation is a community and the individuals who are in such an organization are what they are in part because of their membership in the organization, while the organization is what it is because of the people who choose to become part of the organization. The corporation is a social organization and needs a certain aspect of conformity to its policies and procedures to operate, the generalized other, if you will, but at the same time needs input from the unique selves who work for it in order for it to grow and remain competitive. The unique input of individual selves over time makes up the generalized other, the personality or culture of an organization that has developed over the years and changes with new inputs, and this generalized other, in turn, shapes the behavior and attitudes of the individuals in the organization.

Nor are these individuals and their skills and abilities coordinated in some mechanical fashion to accomplish corporate objectives. Such a mechanistic view of the corporation is not consistent with the notion that people who work in the corporation should not have to sacrifice their essential humanness. Managers who treat their employees in an economic sense as just another factor of production are not treating these people as moral beings who are an essential part of the community. Moreover, treating people in a mechanical manner does not lead to an efficient or effective organization. This idea is well encapsulated in the following quote by Robert C. Solomon, writing in *Ethics and Excellence*:

> What makes a corporation efficient or inefficient is not a series of well-oiled mechanical operations but the working interrelationships, the coordination and rivalries, the team spirit and morale of the many people who work there and are in turn shaped and defined by the corporation. So, too, what drives a corporation is not some mysterious abstraction called "the profit motive." It is the collective will and ambitions of its employees, few of whom work for a profit in any obvious sense. Employees of a corporation do what they must to be part of a community, to perform their jobs, and to earn both the respect of others and self-respect. To understand how corporations work (and don't work) is to understand the social psychology of communities, not the logic of a flowchart or the organizational workings of a cumbersome machine.[1]

Pragmatism does not think of employees within the corporation as a homogeneous group working in machinelike fashion. It rejects the notions of abstract rationality with which organizations are often viewed, the idea of mechanistic conformity that represents some management ideals and other modernist views inherent in traditional theories of the corporation. Instead, it turns to the pluralistic features of community and the importance of diversity and conflict resolution in the dynamics of community growth. Even the most dissenting voice enters into the ongoing dynamics of community life with the adjustments and accommodations this requires. Corporate dynamics consists of a pluralistic community of voices in communicative interaction.[2]

Having a voice, however, is not enough. Edwin Hartman has pointed out that providing some process whereby members have some sort of voice in a business organization does not guarantee morality in the workplace any more than it guarantees it anywhere else. A good community must encourage the kind of discussion that creates cooperation, mutual support and respect, and general moral progress.[3] The "politics of community" as the embodiment of a pragmatic understanding of authentic community is by its very nature what Hartman describes as a good community that thrives in its environment. This view is opposed to a "politics of power" that is contained in many theories of the corporation where a master/slave relationship is evident in the interactions between employers and employees.

Recent trends in the workplace have undermined this sense of community, however, and are destroying the implicit contract that existed between employees and employers. Many changes have taken place in the workplace over the past several decades as employees and employers have developed new relationships that reflect changing interests and concerns. Rapid change has become more common because of global competition and rapidly developing technology. Companies have downsized by laying off many workers and eliminating layers of middle management. They have outsourced many departments and functions in order to escape paying benefits or to take advantage of much lower costs overseas. Many offices are virtually empty as employees spend their time mainly in the field or work at home. And most companies have had to cut health benefits for employees or abandon their health coverage entirely because of cost pressures. Some have even turned over their pension obligations to the federal government.

These changes in the workplace have resulted in changes in the implied contract between employees and the corporation. By and large the old contract held that employees had obligations related to satisfactory attendance at work, acceptable levels of effort and performance, and loyalty to the corporation and management. In return for these commitments, employers provided fair compensation for the work done, fringe benefits such as coverage for health care and defined benefit pension plans, the chance for advancement based on seniority and merit, and some degree of job security. Workers became primarily identified by who they worked for and found some degree of satisfaction in this relationship.

As job security has evaporated because of restructuring, downsizing, outsourcing, and other changes in the workplace, so have prospects for advancement and predictable wage and benefit increases. Management demands for individual commitment and responsibility have largely taken their place. They want people to buy into long-term visions of the company and be committed to corporate goals while at the same time expecting them to cope with an ever-present threat of termination. Such expectations seem to be one-sided and certainly have implications for employee loyalty, particularly since the effects of many of these changes are distributed bimodally. Top executives are well rewarded and are given generous job-security provisions and retirement packages while middle managers, clerical, and production workers face much greater uncertainty.

These changes in the workplace have given rise to new expectations regarding the employment relationship with corporations. These new expectations have been said to include (1) employment no longer implies job security; (2) with no lifetime jobs, corporate commitment to developing employees is on the decline as companies cannot afford to invest in employees who might be with them only a short time; (3) and with no lifetime jobs and little investment in people, it follows that more of the risk associated with a career is being pushed back onto employees. The new era of employment relations forces employees into the status of free agents, responsible for themselves and to themselves.[4]

Instead of lifelong employment, the emphasis is on lifelong employability. While employers still have something of an obligation to provide opportunity for self-improvement, employees have to take charge of their own careers and can no longer rely on a secure place in the corporate organization. They must continually acquire new skills to keep up with the development of new technologies. Employees are expected to share responsibility for their employment and in many places are gaining greater control over what they do in the workplace. Loyalty to the company is said to be dead and in its place is loyalty to one's profession or job function.[5]

Meanwhile, unions, which provided some sense of community for certain employees, have been in decline for several decades. Unions arose as industrialization took hold in this country and workers found that many problems they were experiencing in the workplace, such as long hours, poor working conditions, low wages, and arbitrary hiring and firing practices, were not being addressed. To deal with these problems they began to form unions to counter the power of management with an organized labor movement. These unions became a force to be reckoned with and won major benefits for their members in confrontations with management. During a forty-year period from 1935 to 1975, unions grew in number and bargaining power with employers.

Throughout the history of unionism, rights have been the center of controversy and have often involved intense factionalism. The rights of union workers have been pitted against the rights of management to control their employees, the rights of unions to strike against the rights of society for a smoothly functioning economy, the rights of union workers against the rights of nonunion workers. The intensity of this factionalism has manifested itself from time to time in violent situations as the rights of labor to make its case for better treatment and the rights of management to maintain control of labor have been asserted. In many, if not most, of these cases, the process has moved the relationship between labor and management away from any sense of community.

Unions, however, always had a problem of legitimacy in our society and never became an accepted part of the capitalistic system. Obviously some of this problem involved a struggle over power within the corporation as unions challenged the prerogatives of management to control its workforce. But some of this problem may also stem from the fact that unions are a collective organization and this kind of collective goes against the scientific worldview that supports atomic individualism. The corporation is not seen as a collective organization even though it is in many respects, but unions are explicitly collective and engage in collective bargaining. The scientific worldview treats employees as individuals who are supposed to bargain on an individual basis with management. They always have the option of quitting their job and moving elsewhere, at least in theory.

Because of these and other reasons, labor unions have declined as a dominant force in American society.[6] Since about 1975 the balance of power in collective bargaining has shifted back to management. Unions have been declining in numbers and power over this period of time. While there was some increase of union activity in 1994, the resurgence of management strength in collective bargaining has continued and this trend is likely to persist for some time. Thus unions are not as able to look after the rights of labor in a changing workplace and do not provide a sense of community for the labor movement that they once did in our society.

Many rights related to the workplace are now protected by state and federal legislation. Many states have laws protecting whistleblowers, right-to-know laws that require employers to identify hazardous substances used in the workplace, and laws restricting the ability of companies to close plants for economic reasons. Other states have made it illegal for companies to force retirement at any age and some have taken steps to modify the employment-at-will doctrine.[7] Federal laws include the rights to a safe workplace, the right of handicapped people to meaningful work and reasonable accommodations for their physical challenges, the right to be treated equally in the workplace, and the right to be free from sexual harassment.[8]

The forces driving changes in the workplace, such as global competition and rapid technological change, will probably continue for the foreseeable future, making further corporate adjustments necessary. The foundations of the old social contract will continue to erode, making it increasingly clear that the old social contract cannot be preserved or reestablished. The question then becomes what kind of a new contract will emerge that will be satisfactory to all parties concerned and yet deal with the new realities of the workplace. What moral issues do these changes raise with respect to the relationship between employees and employers? Do companies have a moral responsibility to provide at least some degree of job security for their employees? Can the system function effectively if employee trust and loyalty disappear and responsibility for the employee's well-being is no longer a corporate concern?

Previous administrations took the position that training is a large part of the answer and redefined job security as employment security. It was argued that workers would not accept changes that come from trade agreements, productivity gains, or technological advances unless they were confident that they could get new jobs and thus benefit from these changes. Employment security was defined as having skills and benefits that were portable. While largely unsuccessful in getting any new government-run training programs through Congress, new benefit mandates, such as the Family and Medical Leave Act, were passed, adding to an already long list of employee rights protected by federal laws and regulations. Pressure was also brought to bear on employers to take responsibility in providing the training necessary to keep workers employable.

There are some benefits to this emphasis on employment security rather than job security. What employees need in this kind of economy is opportunity rather than security, and they must have the skills to take advantage of the opportunities that come along. This calls for continual growth on the part of employees, a willingness to learn new skills, an emphasis on continual learning and creativity, and openness to change. Security in a given job or company can lead to stultification and boredom and creation of a workforce that is resistant to change. On the other hand, an opportunity society can degenerate into a free-for-all where it's every man for himself and the devil take the hindmost, as the saying goes. In this kind of environment, top management has all the security with more than adequate pension plans and severance packages and employees have all the risk and little opportunity for any kind of security.

Changes going on in the American workplace call for new understandings and new relationships between employees and employers and new roles for government and labor unions. Some of the key elements that are necessary to deal successfully with these changes are (1) the need for trust and respect between each employee and employer, (2) the need for open and honest communication within the corporation, (3) the need for participation at all levels of the organization, (4) the need to treat people as human beings rather than abstract factors of production, (5) and the need for commitment to cope with change in a manner which is not destructive for the employee or the organization.

The present situation is one in which the way in which employees and employers related to each other in the past is breaking down and new relationships must be established. But the past does not necessarily contain guidelines for the future that is emerging. This calls for creative imagination in envisioning possibilities for reconstruction of roles and responsibilities that are sensitive to the conflicting demands of different groups in the corporation and that need to be reorganized into workable relationships. Employees and employers must each strive to understand each other and their different perspectives in coming to grips with the diversity of interests to be satisfied. The working out of these new relationships cannot be mandated from on high by either employee organizations or management decrees, but will be an ongoing process that houses an opportunity for real growth on the part of all parties.

The development of a new contract calls for new relationships which can better allow the corporation to function as a true community. This explicitly requires community dialogue by recognizing all the participants as autonomous, morally responsible individuals whose creative inputs and diverse interests are vital to the adjustment necessary for the ongoing growth of the corporation. Taking everything into account, it seems that what is necessary is the recognition of individual human beings who cannot be dismembered to become a diversity of cogs in a corporate machine, but who can, in their individuality, function as diverse centers of creativity in a unified corporate community. It is the corporate community as a whole that is responsible for the success of the organization in the larger society.

THE CORPORATION IN COMMUNITY

The purpose of the corporation in traditional economic theory is to produce goods and services that contribute to the material well-being of society. If it has done things right and produced things people want to buy and find useful and has done so efficiently so that people can afford to buy the things the company produces, the company will be rewarded with profits, part of which can be paid out as dividends to stockholders. The price of its stock may also appreciate, in which case the wealth of the investors will also increase. But these economic responsibilities are not the only purpose of the corporation. Reduction of the corporation to a single purpose in society fails to recognize that the corporation is a multipurpose organization that has multiple responsibilities in society.

The business organization also exists to provide meaningful life experiences for its employees, to develop new products and technologies through research and development that can improve society as well as satisfy consumer needs, to engage in activities that enhance the environment and to minimize if not eliminate those activities that result in environmental degradation, to be a good citizen in obeying the laws of the countries in which it operates and where possible to help society solve some of its most pressing social problems. Thus the corporation is truly a multipurpose organization and many of these purposes are noneconomic in nature and cannot be measured quantitatively.

Advocates of social responsibility were trying to get at the interrelatedness of business with the broader community of which it is a part. However, this attempt remained rooted in the same individualistic and reductionistic assumptions as capitalism in general. This rootedness is indicated in the very titles used to characterize the field: "Business *and* Society" or "Business *and* Its Environment."[9] The title Business *and* Society implies that there are two separable, isolatable, and discrete entities, business and society, and that the corporation is an autonomous unit which has a choice whether or not to consider its obligations to the society which it impacts. The notion of the social responsibilities of business was problematical from the very beginning of the field and embodied implicit individualistic and atomistic assumptions that reflect the scientific worldview.

A more appropriate title for the field would have been "Business *in* Society," which reflects the relational nature of business to the society of which it is a part and for which it provides many of the meanings and values which inform the society. A corporation, as the individual pole within ongoing community dynamics, has to take the perspective of the society as a whole and incorporate the standards and authority of society, even as it remains a unique center of activity that has a creative dimension that enters into the total social experience. Corporations are entities that are embedded within society and their responsibilities are intrinsic to their very nature as social entities.

The multiple purposes of a corporation are often lost sight of in the quest for profits because managers are encouraged to maximize profits and earn the highest rate of return they can for the shareholders. Such a limited view of the corporation can only arise by severing it from the multiple environments in which corporations function. This single-minded pursuit of profits puts the cart before the horse, so to speak, for profit, while essential to the ongoing activity of the corporation, is a by-product of corporate activity and only serves as one sign that the corporation in functioning well in society. But when the economic purposes of a corporation become the be-all and end-all of its existence because of scientific reductionism, this artificially isolates the corporation from the social context which gives it its very being and destroys its relationships with the society in which it is embedded, eventually leading to a dysfunctional relationship. Profits are a means to building a thriving business, but this thriving involves the thriving of the multiple environments in which it is embedded.

William C. Frederick argues that profit is not an original business value but rather is derivative from its economizing function, which, along with growth and systematic integrity, makes up the three original business values. These three original values, rooted in the nature of the physical world, are essential for all life units, including business firms.[10] He makes the distinction between expansion as merely an increase in the size or scope of operations without improvement in economizing activities and growth as a manifestation of successful economizing. Business is embedded in a moral matrix and is a dimension of human growth and is intrinsically tied to it through its relational nature. Growth of the business is manifest not just through its economizing activities but through the many activities which enrich the relational matrix in which it is embedded.

Self-interest as a motivating factor in corporate behavior is not to be abandoned but must be understood in something other than an individualistic manner. Self-interest and community interests are inseparably intertwined, and a proper balance between these two dimensions is necessary for effective functioning of the total system. Self-interest pursued under the guidance of the proper balance is at one and the same time community interest. Self-interest becomes selfishness when the individual dimension dominates the "other"; self-interest is not only destructive of the other and destructive of the proper balance that fosters a thriving community but also destructive of the self which is engaged in selfish behavior. For the self, like the community, thrives through the properly balanced intertwining of the dimensions of the individual and the common other that constitutes its internal nature.

Growth of the corporation involves more than just economic growth, as a broader conception of growth involves the ongoing reconstruction of experience to bring about the integration and expansion of the multiple contexts in which human existence is embedded. It is a process by which individual selves and communities achieve fuller, richer, and more inclusive and more complex interactions with the multiple environments in which they are relationally embedded. The corporation in relation to the community in which it functions is the individual pole in dynamic relation to the general other, and this interaction enters into the vitality of the community.

Despite the individualistic nature of many definitions, stakeholder theory embodies in its nature a relational view of the firm which incorporates the reciprocal dynamics of community, and the theory's power lies in focusing management decision making on the multiplicity and diversity of the relationships that the corporation has with its environment. It also focuses on the multipurpose nature of the corporation as a vehicle for enriching these relationships in their various aspects. But for stakeholder theory to be a viable alternative theory of the firm and its responsibilities, it must shed itself, as social responsibility theory needs to do, of its individualistic and atomistic assumptions.

Stakeholder theory has been criticized in that it cannot be definitive as to what or who is a stakeholder and various attempts to delimit the list of stakeholders has been problematic. However, stakeholder relations are diffused throughout the community as part and parcel of the various relational networks which enter into the well-being of the community as a whole. In getting hold of the "weight" to be given to particular stakeholder claims in particular situations, what is being decided is not a list of stakeholder relations that can be balanced with some mechanical process but rather an interrelated network integral to the welfare of the community itself, and community welfare as background enters into the specific evaluation of the relative "weights" to be given various stakeholders in specific situations.

Thus there can be, not just as a practical consideration but as a theoretical necessity, no exhaustive list of stakeholders; instead, from the backdrop of community welfare the most relevant stakeholders can be given specific considerations within specific contexts. What will count as stakeholder claims is context dependent, and any decision can be only as good as the holistic moral vision of the decision- maker operating within the contours of a specific problematic context. There can be no set formula for the weighing of stakeholder claims any more than there can be a set formula for deciding what is the right thing to do from a moral and ethical standpoint.

Judgments must be made about the use of corporate resources but these judgments are made in a social context that must be taken into consideration. The corporation has multiple clients to consider in these judgments, clients whose interests will be affected in various ways by what the corporation does in society through the products it makes and the way these products are produced and marketed. Scientific inquiry is useful in making these judgments but there is no formula or flowchart that can be used to simplify the nature of the decision. It requires sensitivity to the various stakeholder interests in a given decision and imagination to come up with solutions to business problems that work in the interests of the corporation and society.

14 Business and Science

The scientific culture that dominates business schools seemed to have started in the 1950s in response to two studies that were sharply critical of business-school education as it was practiced at that time. The publication of the Gordon and Howell and Pierson reports funded by Ford Foundation and Carnegie Foundations, respectively, motivated business schools to become more analytical and rigorous in their approach to management education.[1] Both of these reports criticized business-school education as being too vocationally oriented and consequently lacking academic respectability. These reports argued that management had become more of a science with the development of decision-making tools during the war years and provided generous funding to promote reforms of teaching and research along these lines. These efforts vastly improved business-school education and helped it attain academic respectability.

Business schools began to attract better faculty and students and train them in rigorous analytical techniques to be used in solving business problems and in managing business organizations. These changes benefited business organizations and society at large through more efficient management of resources. But eventually the scientific paradigm took on a life of its own in business schools and became the dominant way to think of business-school education. The best schools, with some exceptions, came to have highly quantitative curriculums and their best faculty published in the leading management research journals. These efforts have created a scientific culture in business schools to which students are exposed. This culture shapes the way they think about business and its relationship to the society at large and is carried over into the business organizations where they eventually work.

While this approach has given business schools increased respectability in the academic community, it has also led to criticisms regarding the relevance of this academic research to the actual practice of management. If one looks at the articles published in the leading management journals, it seems that they are meant to be read by other scholars rather than a practitioner; and despite calls for more relevance and a more professional approach to management, there has been no significant change in this scientific orientation. Faculty continue to be judged primarily on their publications in scientific management journals and a highly quantitative curriculum continues to exist at many of the leading business schools in the country.

In addition to gaining academic respectability, the are other reasons for this development, not the least of which is that business education has a home discipline in economics that prescribes the role business is to play in society and how the firm functions to create economic wealth. This makes business different from the traditional professions of law and medicine, which have no home discipline that provides them with the rationale and justification for their existence. They are strictly practical activities that need no other justification beyond their duty to serve their clients' interests. While it could be argued that certain courses such as organizational behavior have their roots in sociology, this orientation is subservient to the larger economic purpose and role of the business enterprise as prescribed in economic theory.

Perhaps it is no accident that in the 1950s and 1960s, as business schools began to adopt the scientific model to promote a more rigorous curriculum, economics began to change from a political-economy orientation to the highly mathematized discipline it is today. Such changes may reflect society's fascination with science as a whole, as during this period science and technology ushered in a new age of affluence with a proliferation of new devices that made people's lives better and more comfortable. And the atomic age contained promises of unlimited sources of energy before concerns about both cost and safety entered the public arena. Science was on a roll, so to speak, and its reductionistic and quantitative orientation dominated our thinking.

Economics prescribes the role of business in our society in a scientific manner, and also provides a moral justification for its existence. Business is considered to be solely an economic institution whose purpose is to create more and more economic wealth. This purpose can be quantified and measured by the profits that a business generates and the price of its shares traded on the stock exchanges. The success of society as a whole is measured by an increase or decrease of gross national product, or gross domestic product, as it is sometimes called. Our fascination with and belief in quantification is reflected in these measures of success. As long as business schools and society as a whole continue to experience success along these lines, there is no reason to change such a scientific orientation.

Ours is a scientific and technological culture. What this means, at least in part, is that people in our society turn to science for answers as to how the world works and to technological solutions for most of their problems. Science provides us with knowledge of nature, even our own human nature, and gives us the capability of manipulating nature in our own interests. Technology involves the application of scientific findings and gives us the means to use and shape nature to accomplish the objectives of individuals and organizations. Even if we are not professional scientists, we learn to think about the world in scientific terms and are used to thinking of technological solutions to problems.

Business is dependent on science and technology for the development of new products and processes to produce those products. Scientific research has proven highly useful to business organizations in solving business problems and new technologies provide the opportunity for business to take these findings and produce new or improved products and marketing strategies. Science plays an important role in business organizations and the way it is used in these organizations is important to society. Science is employed by business organizations and business schools to attain their objectives and the way it is used can have both beneficial and adverse impacts on the society at large.

CERTAINTY

Science is used on the one hand to provide *certainty* to business-school students and managers of business organizations. Students want a formula they can use to crank out a number that will give them the "right" answer to a business problem. This then gives them a degree of certainty and they do not have to think more deeply about the problem and see it in all its complexity. The problem can be simplified to fit into a formula which will then crank out a relatively easy answer to a quite complicated problem. They do not have to reflect on the assumptions behind the formula or think about its applicability to the particular problem at hand.

As a visiting professor in one of the better business schools in the Southwest that had a highly quantitative program, I could see this process in action. The course I taught was ethics and social responsibility and was a first-year course that was usually required in the first semester of their experience as MBA students. When the course first began, I got a sense that the students had an ability to reflect on ethical issues and handle the ambiguity that ethical issues usually involve. As the semester progressed, however, this reflective ability was gradually squeezed out of them in their exposure to quantitative techniques in other courses, and they became less and less able to handle unstructured problems and became impatient with the lack of a "right" answer that could be cranked out rather quickly.

Even one of the finance professors who was also a visitor complained about this lack of reflection. All the students wanted, he said, was a formula that would give them a number, and they did not want to reflect on the assumptions embedded in the formula and ponder whether it was appropriate to use in a given situation. The quantitative program was like a crucible that molded the student's thinking. What they wanted was a hard number that they could then believe was the "right" answer, a number that gave them a sense of certainty. They had less and less tolerance for "fuzzy" stuff like ethics, which could not be expressed in a number but required more reflective thinking and analysis.

This same desire for simplicity and certainty holds true for business managers as can be seen in another personal example. While working for a Fortune 500 company, I helped develop an inventory-control system to be used by distributors of the company's products. These distributors accounted for about 25 percent of the company's business and handled the products on consignment. The marketing manager in charge of these distributors wanted a report he could send to them on a monthly basis containing order quantities for all the products they handled. The inventory-control model used for this report was a typical one in basing order quantities on past history of sales, eliminating figures that fell outside of so-called normal range so as not to distort the averages.

This model obviously assumed the future would be like the past and did not allow for any changes in the general economic conditions affecting sales of products. If general economic conditions changed that would affect what people were buying or a substitute came along for some of the company's products, these would not be reflected immediately in the order quantities on the report. The manager did not care about any of this, however; all he wanted was a report he could send out every month with numbers on it, and he wanted the system to operate more or less on autopilot. He didn't want to think about assumptions embedded in the model, assumptions that may have proven false at some time in the future because of changes that called for management judgment as to whether the order quantities on the report were realistic.

This quest for the certainty that numbers supposedly give can have disastrous consequences. During the run-up to the financial crises of 2008–2009, mortgages were pooled into different kinds of packages called collateralized debt obligations (CDOs), mortgage-backed securities that were then sold to investors all over the world. These mortgage pools were messy and unstructured as there was no guaranteed interest rate since homeowners could refinance or go into default on their homes. There was also no fixed maturity date as most homeowners sold their homes before the mortgage was fully paid. Consequently, it was difficult to rate the risk on these securities and assign a single probability to the chance of default.[2]

Many of these problems were solved through a process called tranching, which involved dividing a pool of mortgages into different risk categories. Those in the top category would be the first to be paid off and so were the most highly rated. Those in lower categories would get a lower rating but they also carried a higher rate of interest because of the higher chance of default. Thus investors could match the risk they were willing to take with the return they wanted. Tranches could be created that were triple-A rated even though none of components themselves were rated that highly. Lower rated tranches of other CDOs were also put in another pool and tranched, which became know as a CDO squared. These investment vehicles became so far removed from the underlying mortgages that no one knew what they actually included.[3]

Enter David X. Li, a mathematician who grew up in rural China in the 1960s, and after several degrees, including a PhD in statistics from the University of Waterloo in Ontario, Canada, wound up at Barclays Capital, where he was responsible for rebuilding its quantitative analysis team.[4] Quantitative people were becoming more and more popular in financial institutions to create and price the ever more complex investment vehicles that were being developed. In 2000 Li had published a paper in which he created a way to model default correlation without looking at historical data. Instead, he used market data about the prices of a financial vehicle known as a credit-default swap (CDS).[5]

CDSs are in effect insurance against a borrower defaulting so that the investor could either get interest payments by lending directly to the borrower or insurance payments. The CDS market grew rapidly as an unlimited number of swaps can be sold against each borrower. Instead of waiting to assemble enough historical data about actual defaults, Li's model used the price of these swaps as a shortcut to rate the default risk, assuming that the CDS market could price the default risk correctly. Li's formula, which was known as a Gaussian copula function because it was based on correlations between credit-default risks, was seen in the financial world as a positive breakthrough that allowed complex risks to be modeled with ease and accuracy. His method was adopted by everybody, including bond investors and Wall Street banks to rating agencies like Moodys and regulators themselves. Nobody knew or even cared what was actually in these securitization packages because they now had a number that told them what risk was involved.[6]

The market for CDSs and CDOs grew together and fed on each other. In just seven years, from 2001 to 2007, the dollar amount of credit-default swaps outstanding grew from $920 billion to more than $62 trillion. The CDO market grew from $275 billion in 2000 to $4.7 trillion in 2006.[7] People were making so much money that no one worried about the limitations of the model or the assumptions on which it was based. Foreign investors bought up huge amounts of these instruments as they promised higher returns than Treasury securities and the risk seemed manageable. After all, the rating agencies were telling what risk was involved in the various tranches and they could take on whatever risk they felt comfortable with and match that against the expected return.

Then, of course, the whole thing collapsed. Homeowners started defaulting in record numbers because they had gotten into homes they could not afford, and when their adjustable-rate mortgages adjusted to a higher rate, they could not afford to continue making payments. Nor could they refinance at a lower rate because home prices declined at the same time, making the mortgage they had taken out greater than the market price of the house. No one believed that so many homeowners would default at the same time or that housing prices would decline across the entire country. Individual homeowners might default because of loss of a job or whatever, but these individual problems would not affect the mortgage pool as a whole. And home prices might decline in some regions of the country but not in the entire country as whole. Pooling of mortgages was supposed to offset these setbacks so that the pool as a whole would still be viable.

Thus the assumptions behind the model were exposed with disastrous results for world financial markets. Who is to blame for these consequences? Li just invented the model and went back to China, heading up the risk-management department at China International Capital Corporation. The quantitative people who should have been aware of the model's weaknesses were not the ones making the asset-allocation decisions. So should we blame the bankers who misinterpreted the model and used it inappropriately? But which bankers? The problem was that everyone adopted the model, and when everybody does the same thing, it creates a classic opportunity for a financial bubble and eventual burst.[8] Numbers have a high degree of certainty in the modern world, a certainty that is perpetuated in business-school education. Numbers generated by a formula come to have a reality all their own regardless of how they are generated, and managers have come to put their faith in numbers.

> Their managers, who made the actual calls, lacked the math skills to understand what the models were doing or how they worked. They could, however, understand something as simple as a single correlation number. That was the problem.[9]

The financial numbers that managers of business organizations deal with are of a different kind than the numbers of concern to engineers and scientists. There is something out there that financial numbers represent, but that something is uncertain and imprecise. These numbers should not give us confidence that we know the true value of the thing we are concerned about. Financial numbers represent a reality that is constantly changing and cannot be quantified as precisely as a number would lead us to believe.

Numbers for an engineer refer to a physical reality, and those numbers express a precision that often go beyond what any of us can comprehend. This precision has to be adhered to in most cases for a technology to work properly. There are countless examples of problems that developed because of failure to meet precise measurements, the most well-known of which may be the primary mirror of the Hubble Space Telescope, which was faulty when the Hubble was first launched.

Financial numbers could also be said to represent a physical reality in that stock prices have some relation to physical plants and human resources. But stock prices are based more on the earning potential of a company, and represent the value of that potential expressed in financial terms. This value is not precise and changes all the time as it depends on the assessment of tens of thousands of people participating in the market.

If a company is large enough, assets can be undervalued or overvalued by hundreds of thousands of dollars in some cases and it will not lead to a catastrophe, whereas something can be off a fraction of an inch in a particular technology, resulting in failure. So the whole point of this discussion is that we should not put too much confidence in financial numbers. They are uncertain and do not necessarily convey with accuracy the underlying reality on which they are based. They are not scientific in the true sense of the word. Management involves judgment and business-school education should not convey the idea that quantitative analysis will give the "right" answer to a business problem and that what is important is to have a number. Any number must be put into perspective and the assumptions on what that number is based must be examined.

UNCERTAINTY

It is paradoxical, but business also uses the inherent *uncertainty* of scientific findings to its advantage. It is impossible to find absolute certainty about anything in the scientific community. The complexity of most environmental and medical problems makes this impossible. Even in cases where a particular substance has been well-researched there is uncertainty about having a firm knowledge of the substance's behavior under all conditions of its usage and whether it indeed can be the cause of certain unwanted and dangerous effects. Science is uncertain by nature; it is experimental and continually looks for new evidence that may challenge conventional wisdom. New theories are continually developed that may change our way of thinking about certain things that were thought to be well established. David Michaels, writing in *Doubt Is Their Product*, states the following.

> Scientists who are involved in developing public health and environmental protections recognize that we do not need (and we almost never obtain) proof beyond a reasonable doubt. Our regulatory systems call for using the best evidence available at the present time. Waiting for absolute certainty is a recipe for failure. People will die, and the environment will be damaged if we wait for absolute proof . . . Scientists do not have the truth; we seek the truth. We deal not in absolute certainties but in the "weight of the evidence." We combine and evaluate information from many sources, and we apply both quantitative and qualitative methods in order to overcome real uncertainty and gaps in scientific knowledge.[10]

Business, as well as government when it is in line with business interests, uses this inherent uncertainty to delay taking action on a problem that would cost business money. According to David Michaels, writing in *Doubt Is Their Product*, "Industry and its consultants are well aware that their use of uncertainty to challenge science exploits the very nature of science, in which knowledge is accumulated over a long period of time and the understanding of that knowledge also evolves."[11] Michaels sees a growing trend that demands proof of a scientific finding over precaution in the area of public health. Business always disputes scientific conclusions that might support regulation of a particular substance or activity. Animal data are deemed as not relevant to humans, human data are not representative of the population as a whole, and exposure data are not reliable enough to support regulation.[12] There are many ways to create doubt when it comes to scientific findings.[13]

Even though the International Panel on Climate Change (IPCC) came out several years ago with a report that blamed human activity for most of the global warming we have experienced, the Bush administration delayed taking any action on the issue, claiming more research was needed because of the uncertainty about the true causes of global warming.[14] Any attempt to limit carbon dioxide emissions, which is believed to be the major culprit, would involve major expenditures for some business organizations and hurt the economy. Thus it was important to keep the controversy going and some organizations began producing publications that questioned the science about global warming to create more uncertainty to delay taking action. Again, according to Michaels:

> Industry has learned that debating the *science* is much easier and more effective than debating the *policy*. Take global warming, for example. The vast majority of climate scientists believe there is adequate evidence of global warming to justify immediate intervention to reduce the human contribution. They understand that waiting for absolute certainty is far riskier—and potentially far more expensive—than acting responsibly now to control the causes of climate change. Opponents of action, led by the fossil fuels industry, delayed this policy debate by challenging the science with a classic uncertainty campaign.[15]

Scientific uncertainty can also be used to justify introduction of a product even though there are questions about its effect on public safety and health. Already in 1922, for example, tetraethyl lead began to be put into gasoline to reduce knock and make it possible to produce higher-compression engines for greater performance. Numerous public-health officials believed the substance was harmful and thought the use of the substance ought to be delayed and subjected to more careful study. Business argued that there was no scientific agreement about the threat this substance posed to public health, and in the absence of convincing evidence of widespread harm, which of course had not yet occurred, they had the right to proceed with using the product. The product was used for over 50 years, exposing the public and especially children to permanent brain damage as the result of exposure to lead in the air and soil in which children played.[16]

The substance was finally phased out of usage beginning in 1985, when the Environmental Protection Agency (EPA) announced a decision to cut allowable lead levels in gasoline more than 90 percent by January 1, 1986, based on evidence that airborne lead poses substantial health threats. Several studies had shown a strong correlation between high lead levels in gasoline and levels in blood resulting from airborne lead pollution. These levels could cause brain and nerve damage, mental retardation, and anemia and kidney disorders. Children were believed to be especially at risk because their brains and other organs were not as yet fully developed. By 1992, about 95 percent of all gasoline sold in the country was lead free, and over the next several years the remainder was phased out entirely. This is just one example of business using uncertainty to its advantage but there are many others.

> Because we have allowed scientific uncertainty to postpone controls on dangerous activities, we now have hazardous levels of mercury in most of the nation's fresh-water fish; the Earth's ozone shield has been dangerously depleted; global warming is upon us, with attendant droughts, fires, floods, hurricanes, tornadoes and typhoons; the ocean's major fisheries are in dangerous decline; the normal sex ratio of male-to-female babies has been changed in numerous industrialized countries, and human sperm counts have declined 50 % in 50 years; immune system disorders like asthma and diabetes are steeply rising; many of the world's coral reefs are dying; cancers of the brain, the lymph system, the blood system and the testicles are increasing; cancer in children is escalating; many species have gone extinct . . . This list of contemporary calamities could be readily extended.[17]

The limitations of science are also used to argue against its findings. The smoking controversy went on for several decades but took a major turning point when it began to be discovered that secondhand smoke was harmful to nonsmokers. This was potentially devastating to the industry as there began to be talk about banning smoking in public places to protect public health. The tobacco industry questioned the studies, arguing that none of them proved conclusively that secondhand smoke directly caused cancer.[18] Technically they were correct, but it needed to be pointed out that the technology does not exist to prove cause and effect in this situation. What cigarette smoke does to cells in the body is too complex to observe directly. All we have is correlation studies that show significant relationships between exposure to secondhand smoke and the incidence of lung cancer. As more of these correlations began to be scientifically established, it began to be believed that there had to be a cause-and-effect relationship, and smoking came to be banned in public places and airplanes all over the country.

Because of this misuse of science, it has been suggested that the precautionary principle be used to guide business decisions. In essence, the precautionary principle states that decision makers have an ethical obligation to take preventive action to avoid harm before scientific certainty has been established. As stated in the Rio Declaration from the 1992 United Nations Conference on Environment and Development: "Where there are threats of serious or irreversible damage [to the environment], lack of full scientific certainty shall not be used as a reason for postponing cost-effective measures to prevent environmental degradation."[19]

The precautionary principle shifts the burden of proof to the proponents of an activity. They have to prove that the activity being considered will not cause undue harm to human health and the environment. Those who are in a position to prevent harm have a responsibility to do exactly that. Scientific uncertainty can no longer be used as an excuse to postpone actions to prevent harm or to take actions that are potentially harmful. In lay terms, the principle can be stated in the age-old adage of "better safe than sorry." The principle tries to place scientific uncertainty in an ethical framework designed to protect public health and the environment.[20]

Business schools need to have a course that deals with the nature of science and discusses how scientific findings can be used by business in an ethically appropriate manner. Students need to understand what science can do and can't do; questions it can answer more of less definitively; and questions that are always going to have a degree of uncertainty because of their complexity. They need to learn how to deal with uncertainty and not use it inappropriately. And some acquaintance with the precautionary principle would be helpful in exploring the ethical dimensions of uncertainty and where caution is called for that will work in the best interests of both business and society.

One of the most frustrating areas of controversy in our society these days is the attempt of science to establish or substantiate the truth of claims about human health and the environment. Does smoking cause cancer? How dangerous is secondhand smoke? Are certain substances used in the workplace dangerous to workers' health? Do breast implants cause health problems for women? Is smaller particulate matter dangerous to our lungs? Is global warming for real and is it the result of human activity so that steps can be taken to reduce the emissions of greenhouse gases? There are many examples of this kind as debates about health matters and environmental concerns continue. The outcome of these debates is critical to business because of the potential expense involved in complying with regulations or responding to liability lawsuits, and to society because of the implications of these issues for human health and the environment.

One would think that science could answer these questions conclusively to the satisfaction of all concerned parties, particularly in a society where science is so dominant. But in most of these cases the "facts" are never conclusively established and the debate continues. Business comes up with its studies that show no linkage between a substance and human health, and government has its studies that show such a linkage. Who is right and which studies should be accepted as the basis of policy? How are these issues sorted out in our society in eventually arriving at a course of action?

The way these things usually work out is that after enough studies show a correlation between smoking and cancer, it comes to be believed in the general population that there is some connection and thus support builds for smoking to be restricted in public places to protect people from secondhand smoke in particular. The debate then ceases to be whether or not exposure to secondhand smoke will actually put people at risk, and focuses more on the economic impact that such restrictions will have if smoking is banned in bars and casinos, for example. Even though the relation between secondhand smoke and cancer is technically more of a hypothesis that has gained more and more support, the public begins to accept it as a fact that has emerged in the course of investigation about the effects of smoking on public health. Correlation studies prove to be relevant to the uncertain, probabilistic world in which we live where most complex issues of this nature cannot be proven conclusively by science or any other method.

Values are certainly related to what we come to believe about smoking and its effects. The values we hold about smoking as an activity enter into the judgments that are made about the validity of scientific evidence and what we finally accept as facts about this issue. These values reflect our interests that we have in the issue of smoking and a smoke-free society. Do we own stock in a tobacco company? If we are politicians, have we received contributions from the tobacco companies for our campaign? If we are smokers, do we gain satisfaction from smoking that we would like to continue enjoying? Has one of our loved ones who was a smoker died from cancer? Do we have friends whose smoking seems to have contributed to their health problems? All such interests are reflected in our values as they relate to a specific activity such as smoking and its relation to possible adverse health effects.

Several years ago there was a controversy about the safety of ethylene dibromide (EDB), a substance that was widely useful in fumigating grain-milling machinery, as a bulk fumigant in grain-storage bins, and as a soil fumigant by the citrus industry.[21] Studies were conducted that showed EDB appeared to induce cancer in laboratory animals, and on the basis of these studies and its own analysis of EDB's risk to human health, the Environmental Protection Agency (EPA) eventually banned all uses of EDB and ordered grain products to be removed from grocery shelves that contained what were considered to be harmful residues of the substance. Many reputable scientists, however, disputed the implications of these studies and argued that the results of animal studies could not be extrapolated to humans and that there were no credible studies connecting cancer in humans to trace elements of EDB in food products.[22]

In the EDB case, the EPA had the authority to make the decision about continued use of the substance and based its decision on its judgment about the validity of the scientific studies it deemed relevant and their implication for the risk humans faced from continued exposure to the substance. Its decisions about what the "facts" were in this situation reflected its mission to protect human health and the conservative values inherent in its decision-making process. If business organizations had been making the decision, they undoubtedly would have questioned the validity of animal studies and interpreted the risks involved in a much different fashion, reflecting the values of business as a profit-making institution.

Thus both facts and values emerge from our experience with nature. Facts are not these objective somethings that we observe and discover in a disinterested fashion. Most of the facts about our complex world, with its manifold and integrated system of interrelations, are disputable and changing. They are no more brutely objective and absolute than the values we hold. Descriptions of ethical reasoning processes that state at the beginning of the process that to make an ethical decision involves gathering value-free facts about the situation do not recognize this complexity. It is precisely the facts that are often in dispute, and how this dispute is eventually resolved reflects the values of the disputants.

As evidence begins to mount against a substance to which workers and/or the public is exposed, it becomes apparent to most people that the substance is harmful. But no one study is definitive in this regard and we can never be certain that the substance is harmful enough to warrant drastic measures to reduce exposure. Arguments for and against the taking of such measures embody conflicting interpretations of the relevance and significance of the data stemming from conflicting value-laden contexts. This contextual dependence of facts upon the frameworks within which they emerge as relevant is continuous with an understanding of the scientific method as understood within the philosophy of pragmatism described in an earlier chapter.

Conversely, evidence as to what the facts are influences what we hold as valuable. For years we did not pay much attention to the natural environment and used it as a source of raw materials and as a gigantic waste dump to dispose of the garbage we created. We did not value the environment in itself very highly and polluted it so badly that our quality of life was affected. Then we began to learn something about ecosystems and how our pollution was disrupting such systems on which human life depended. Eventually our values relative to the natural environment changed dramatically because evidence of what was happening to the environment began to make an impact. When we began to learn more about our environment and the nature of ecosystems, we changed our values and came to believe the environment was worth spending some money on in order to preserve human life and promote a higher quality of life for ourselves.

MANAGEMENT RESEARCH

The use of the scientific method in management research has helped a great deal in understanding business organizations and the environment in which they function. Critics of this approach do not advocate eliminating this scientific approach and going back to the days when management education consisted of a vocational approach based mainly on experience. Rather, they are saying that the scientific approach has its limitations and should not be regarded as the sole means of understanding business and what drives those who work in these organizations. Other approaches are also useful in understanding what motivates people and organizations to do the things that they do in society.

The issue of executive compensation is an ongoing problem in our society and has been in the news a good bit recently because of what some regard as excessive levels of pay many CEOs are getting whether or not their companies are returning comparable values to shareholders. It became a big issue in the financial crisis of 2007–2008, particularly in those companies that received government bailouts and yet continued to pay big bonuses to their executives and other highly paid employees. Studies have been done that attempt to discover the things that drive such compensation and approaches have been adopted that attempt to tie executive compensation more closely to actual performance. But the fact that attempts to limit the amount of compensation going to top executives, such as compensation committees composed of outside directors or linking pay and performance, have met with limited success suggests that we do not yet understand all the things that drive executive compensation.

If one wants to scientifically study this phenomenon and determine the factors that are driving executive compensation, one has to consider executive pay as a dependent variable and then identify certain independent variables that can be defended on a theoretical basis as having some potential relationship to executive compensation. Tenure on the job, for example, might be identified as having some relationship to pay because the longer one is one the job the higher the pay might be for that person. Board composition might be another variable because a board with more insiders than outsiders might be prone to grant higher pay to the CEO to whom they are beholden, while outsiders, particularly if they are independent of the corporation, might be stingier with regard to pay packages. Size of the company might also be related to pay, as might be the industry in which the company is located. Finally, there might also be some connection between the performance of the company and the pay the CEO receives.

Once these kinds of variables have been identified and a conceptual framework developed which shows all these potential determinants of executive pay, hypotheses must be developed that can be tested by statistical procedures. The researcher must state these hypotheses in a precise form that can either be verified or falsified in further analysis. For example, the researcher could state that he or she expects to find a positive relationship between performance of the company defined as rise or fall in stock price and the pay the CEO receives, i.e., the better the performance of the company the higher the compensation. The number of hypotheses depends on the number of variables that have been identified as having a potential relationship to CEO compensation.

Then decisions have to made about operationalizing these variables. What this means is that these variables have to be defined in such a way as to be quantifiable so that data can be collected and processed in a statistical procedure. None of them is simple in composition and the research can get quite messy at this point. Decisions have to be made as to how one is going to define these variables so they can be quantified in a manner that is accepted in the scientific community. The researcher has to make judgments as to the "best" way to operationalize these variables that meets scientific standards and is at the same time doable. The rubber hits the road at this point, so to speak, as data must be found that are available and accurate enough to provide the basis for a sound judgment about the hypotheses that have been formulated.

The researcher then has to choose a statistical methodology to ascertain the important relationships between these variables, particularly between the dependent variable, which in this case is executive compensation, and all the independent variables. The independent variables also have to be checked for relationships between themselves that may confound the relationship between these variables and executive compensation. For example, tenure may be related to performance because the longer a person has been a CEO the worse performance may become because of a mind-set that is not flexible enough to change with the times to keep the company competitive. These relationships have to be checked for in case they will distort the main effects between the independent variables and executive compensation.

Choice of a correct methodology is all important as it needs to be one that takes into account all extraneous factors that may confound the main effects one is checking and thus puts the pieces back together again in a legitimate fashion. After a statistical model has been developed and used to analyze the data, the results must then be interpreted as to which relationships are statistically significant. What cutoff point is valid in making this determination? After having put all this work into the design and actual conduct of the study, the researcher must guard against skewing the interpretation to get something out of the study and finding significance where perhaps none can be legitimately inferred.

The point of all this is to show how scientific reductionism works in taking some phenomenon like executive compensation and reducing it to a series of variables that can be quantified so that statistical methods can be used to show relationships between the variables. This will supposedly help in understanding what drives the level of compensation for executives, what factors are important to consider in determining the level of compensation and might be useful in predicting such levels in the future. The assumption is that executive compensation is determined by a small number of fundamental things that can be quantified. If one can get a good understanding of how these components of a phenomena like executive compensation relate to each other, then one can predict all the important properties of the phenomena as a whole. The whole is identical with the constituent parts and is not greater than these parts. The study of the parts gives meaning to the whole.

However, are tenure, size of company, composition of the board of directors, and other such factors really the important things to know about executive compensation? There may be other factors based in human experience that may have more relevance to the level of executive compensation. CEOs are in positions of power in their organizations and are able to extract a certain amount of the wealth produced by these organizations to line their own pockets. They are able to manipulate the board to approve whatever pay packages the CEO favors. Lower levels of employees cannot do this and have to be content for the most part with whatever wages and salaries are given them by the people in power to make such determinations.

What is going on here may be much more complex than a few variables can capture and more difficult to understand than a scientific study would have us believe. Executive compensation is said to be market driven, and if a particular corporation does not meet the market rates it will not be able to attract the best executive talent or keep those that it currently has in the organization. But the question of what drives this market and whether its outcomes are just is of concern to society. No scientific study on this issue can tell us anything about whether it is right and fair that executives should receive as much compensation as they do relative to the rest of the employees in the organization, all of whom make some contribution to the success or failure of the organization.

Attempts to limit the level of compensation going to top executives, whether by government or by the board of directors, are based on moral concerns and it is these concerns that are important to society. Scientific studies can help in understanding what drives compensation levels to some extent, but they must be supplemented by other knowledge based on experience with boards of directors and the way they function as well as the position CEOs hold in the corporation. If society wants to limit in some way the compensation these executives receive, all of this knowledge is useful in devising the best way to accomplish this result. Scientific research is limited in its understanding of such complex phenomena and only looks at those factors that its quantitative net can capture.

15 Financial Armageddon

The financial meltdown that occurred in 2007–2008 should put to rest several myths that have informed our understanding of the economy for decades. These myths include the myth of the free market that left to itself will result in the most efficient outcome for society, the myth that scientific laws govern the operation of the market, and the myth that the purpose of the corporation is to maximize shareholder wealth. But these myths will most probably continue to govern our behavior with respect to the economy and how we view government's role in the economy. Such myths do not die easily and we will hang onto them even in the midst of an economic crisis of unprecedented proportions.

The financial crisis brought economic adversity to millions of people in our society who were forced out of houses they recently bought, who lost their jobs and couldn't find new ones, for workers who lost their pensions in companies that went bankrupt, for people who couldn't get credit to continue their business or start a new one, and for people who lost money in a declining stock market. The financial crisis resulted in a massive increase in the federal debt because of government efforts to bail out failed or failing banks and stimulate the economy. Yet initially there was no great cry for reform of Wall Street on the part of the public or recognition that advocates of the free market that had deregulated the financial sector had deceived the public. Almost all of the anger that did exist was directed at the government itself for doing something to get the economy back on track.

The ordinary mind cannot begin to fathom the losses that occurred during this financial meltdown. During the 2008 stock-market crash, it is estimated that $7 trillion of shareholder wealth disappeared. An additional $3.3 trillion was lost in the value of homes as real estate prices fell. Globally, financial losses amounted to a staggering $50 trillion, which included a $25 trillion loss in stock values. The International Monetary Fund (IMF) estimated in April 2009 that financial institutions around the world would have to write off a total of $4.1 trillion in losses through 2010.[1] Such losses are difficult for most people to begin to comprehend.

The economy went into a nosedive as consumers and businesses cut their expenditures in response to the meltdown on Wall Street because of interruptions in the flow of credit from major financial institutions which had an impact on spending decisions and employment prospects. Consumer spending on durable goods fell 22 percent on an annualized basis in the last three months of 2008 while total private investment fell 23 percent and exports 24 percent. In the first quarter of 2009 investment fell at an annual rate of 31 percent and GDP fell at an annualized rate of more than 6 percent. The unemployment rate shot up from 6.2 percent in September 2008 to 9.5 percent in June 2009 as more than 5 million jobs were eliminated, and remained at close to 10 percent for some time is spite of the government's efforts to stimulate the economy.[2]

Banks had to hoard cash rather than lend it out to others in anticipation of the losses on the mortgage bonds that they had warehoused. Bear-Stearns alone, for example, had billions of dollars of mortgage debt on its books that was losing value every day and eventually led to the takeover of the company. The amount of illiquid mortgage debt held by these firms was so large that no amount of interest rate easing by the Fed could restore the mortgage market to health and in the late summer and early fall of 2007 it shut down completely. In past crises, the injection of massive amounts of liquidity had been able to repair the financial system as borrowing became cheaper and firms were able to make money on trades and restore their profitability. But this time the problem was too large and too widespread. Everyone learned just how important credit was to the economy because when it dried up the economy tanked.[3]

WHAT HAPPENED

It is important to understand what happened to cause the financial meltdown but such an understanding does not come easily as there are many different views as to what went wrong. One way to understand the situation is to think of it as a result of a perfect storm. The American dream is to own a home on your own piece of land with a backyard and at least a two-car garage in an area that has good schools and where it is safe to walk the streets at night and where shopping is readily available.[4] This dream has been promoted by the government in various ways with tax breaks, FHA and VA mortgages with low down payments, the creation of Freddie Mac and Fannie Mae, and through other means. As described by Adam Michaelson, a former executive with Countrywide Financial:

> In America, there have been fewer aspirations more powerful, more central, than becoming a homeowner. From the earliest days, land meant wealth, power, status, and privilege. From the new America that was founded by wealthy landowners, to the pioneering courage of Western settlers and beneficiaries of the Homestead Act of 1862, even a modest homestead meant you were an upstanding member of the community,

of society, worthy of the responsibility and *privilege* of home ownership. And if the home incurred a debt, only those worthy of such trust
would be allowed to assume such a debt. But if your credit was good,
if your word was your bond, and if the entire community knew it, you
were trusted to pay back that debt, in good faith.[5]

Perhaps there is no better example to illustrate the importance of promoting
this dream than the action of the government during the Reagan administration. This administration simplified the tax code by eliminating many
tax breaks that had been given to consumers over the years, including being
able to deduct interest on car payments and credit cards. But the one tax
break that was not touched was the ability to deduct interest payments on a
home mortgage. This was kept as an allowable deduction and was considered to be sacrosanct because it is political suicide to introduce any legislation that would take away this tax break. The home-building industry, the
real estate industry, the mortgage industry, as well as homeowners, were all
against touching this deduction.

Soon after George W. Bush took office he called on mortgage lenders
to help create an additional 5.5 billion minority homeowners by 2001 as
part of promoting what he called the ownership society. In 2003, he signed
a bill called the American Dream Downpayment Act, which made up to
$10,000 available to low-income households that had difficulty making a
down payment on a new home. During his reelection campaign, he made
homeownership a goal in stating that "American is a stronger country
every single time a family moves into a new home." The homeownership
rate hit an all-time high of more that 69 percent in early 2004, and the rate
among minorities approached 50 percent for the first time ever. By 2008,
Fannie Mae and Freddie Mac together owned about $1.5 trillion in home
loans and mortgage-backed securities and had issued another $3.5 trillion
in mortgage guarantees.[6]

In spite of such measures, however, during the last years of the twentieth
century and the beginning of the twenty-first, this dream became more
and more unreachable for American families. Incomes for most people had
stagnated even through the boom years of the 1990s because most of the
money went to the upper-income brackets through an increase in stock
prices. Inequalities grew in America and were exacerbated by the Bush tax
cuts at the turn of the century. The great majority of these cuts went to
the wealthy and the rich got richer and the poor poorer with the middle
class remaining in place for the most part. Thus there was a huge backlog
of people who wanted a house but could not afford a mortgage under the
usual conditions that were necessary to obtain a mortgage.

Enter the mortgage industry with new innovations in their mortgage
packages that included adjustable-rate mortgages (ARMs), mortgages with
no down payments, interest-only mortgages, and other innovations to
get people into houses. As a result, demand increased and housing prices

began to rise all over the country. People were encouraged to purchase houses despite the rate increases that would happen with ARMs which would adjust to higher rates in two or three years and make the payments unaffordable. By that time, it was hoped, the price of their house would be higher and they could refinance the house or simply sell it and pay off the mortgage.

After the pool of creditworthy potential homeowners had been exhausted, the subprime market developed to reach less creditworthy people and get them into homes knowing that at some time they were most likely going to default on their payments. The income these people stated on their applications as well as other financial information was taken at face value and not even checked out in many cases. In other situations this information was falsified by the mortgage companies themselves in the rush to get everyone who had a pulse into a home.

The subprime mortgage market became dominated by ARMs, which are loans with fixed rates, sometimes call teaser rates, for two years that adjust upwards every six months thereafter. These adjustments are so steep in most cases that many if not most subprime borrowers could not afford to make the adjusted payments and were forced to either refinance, sell the house, or default on the loan. No loan should force a borrower into this kind of dilemma but that is what happened all across the country. These loans were made on the basis of the value of the property, which was assumed to be forever increasing, not on the ability of the borrower to repay.

Lenders relaxed their standards and weren't too concerned about the quality of their loans because they didn't hold on to them but instead packaged them into mortgage bonds that were sold to investors. This securitization of home mortgages wasn't a new practice, but until the housing bubble it was more or less limited to what are called prime mortgages, those that involved borrowers who could make a substantial down payment and had enough of an income to be able to make their mortgage payments under normal circumstances. During the housing bubble more and more of these bonds consisted of subprime mortgages that were of dubious quality.

These bonds were then packaged into collateralized debt obligations (CDOs) that were divided into different tranches that were supposedly based on the risk involved in the underlying mortgages. These tranches were not equal in that some were more senior and had first claim on payments from the underlying mortgages. Once these claims were satisfied, then payments could be sent to the less senior tranches. This innovation supposedly made the senior tranches a very safe investment, as even if some of the underlying mortgages defaulted it was believed that not enough would default to pose problems for the senior tranches. The rating agencies were thus willing to rate these senior CDOs as AAA even if some of the underlying mortgages were of dubious quality. This opened up large-scale financing of subprime lending because there were many institutional investors, such as pension funds, that were willing to buy AAA-rated securities which gave them significantly higher returns than ordinary bonds. When not enough investors could be found, the investment banks began to keep the CDOs for themselves and warehouse them.

A typical CDO consisted of a hundred different mortgage bonds, usually the riskiest lower floors of the original tower, and used them to construct an entirely new tower and get them rerated as triple-A thereby dishonestly and artificially lowering their risk as perceived by the investor. Wall Street persuaded the rating agencies that these bonds were not exactly the same as before they were packaged but were a different, less risky diversified portfolio of assets. This was a nifty solution to the problem of selling the lower floors of mortgage bonds, and was a credit laundering service for lower-middle-class America and a machine that turned lead into gold for Wall Street investment banks.[7]

What made the process work was that the incentives were such that everyone made more money as more people bought houses and took out mortgages. The homebuilders made money by building homes. The real estate agents received more commissions the more homes they sold. The mortgage companies made more money by issuing more mortgages and collecting fees for originating these mortgages. And they did not have to take on the risk of defaults because these mortgages were packaged into mortgage derivatives that were sold to investment banks, which then sold them to their customers. These derivatives became the hot new item on Wall Street and the big investment banks made millions if not billions selling these derivatives and collecting fees for their efforts. The rating agencies had an incentive to rate these derivatives as high as possible since they were paid by the banks they were doing the rating for, and since they were more complicated than ordinary bonds, they could charge more money for their efforts.

Everyone was making more money hand over fist from top to bottom. People who thought they never had a chance to own a home were buying homes and getting in way over their head. The CEOs of the banks were getting huge pay packages because of the money their institutions were raking in without knowing or caring about the huge risks they were taking by leveraging their companies to the hilt. It was all based on the assumption that housing prices would continue to go up forever, and if there was a decline, it would never be nationwide. Thus it was also assumed that the mortgages underlying the CDOs were not correlated since they supposedly came from many different areas of the country and that if some of them defaulted the rest would hold up the value of the package.

The process included real estate agents, who did everything they could to sell houses and get people loans; mortgage lenders, who packaged the mortgage loans into mortgage bonds; the banks, which repackaged the bonds into CDOs; and the rating agencies, which blessed the process. Wall Street investment banks conned the rating agencies into blessing piles of crappy loans and this enabled the lending of trillions of dollars to people who ordinarily could not have afforded a house. These people happily complied and did what was necessary to obtain the loans, sometimes even lying on their loan applications. These risky loans were then turned into supposedly riskless securities that were so complicated that investors had ceased evaluating the risks. All of these activities created a problem that had grown so large that it was bound to have enormous social and political consequences.

It was extremely difficult to find out what was inside a CDO, and as a result most investors skipped this state of due diligence. Each CDO contained pieces of a hundred different mortgage bonds, which in turn held thousands of different loans. It was nearly impossible to find out which bonds or which loans were in any CDO. Even the rating agencies had no clue as to what was in them, yet they were bestowing ratings on them.[8] An important issue was how correlated the pieces of various subprime mortgage bonds inside a CDO might be, and possible answers ranged from zero percent, meaning their pieces had nothing to do with each other, to 100 percent ,where the prices moved in lockstep with each other. The rating agencies judged the correlation to be around 30 percent, which meant that if one bond went bad there was very little effect on the others. Yet there was very little history to go on in making this judgment.[9] The correlation among triple-B-rated subprime bonds was actually 100 percent, meaning that when one collapsed they all collapsed because they were all driven by the same broader economic forces in the country as a whole.[10]

This was all something of a Ponzi scheme, if not outright fraud, perpetrated on the American people. When defaults inevitably began to happen and housing prices began to fall, the house of cards that had been built fell with it and the results were disastrous for American society. The whole financial system collapsed and went into a deep freeze with credit drying up for everyone. Huge investment banks that were the bastion of Wall Street failed and no one knew how to stop the downward spiral. Government eventually came to the rescue by bailing out most of these banks, taking on the risk of the most toxic assets so institutions like Bear Stearns could be absorbed by Chase and Merrill Lynch by Bank of America. But they let Lehman Brothers fail while bailing out AIG with billions of dollars of taxpayer money.

WHO WAS AT FAULT

There was plenty of blame to go around because there were so many actors in the process. Companies like Countrywide Financial, a California-based lender that was one of the biggest in the country, believed they were selling the American Dream to more and more people. The goal of Countrywide as stated by Angelo Mozilo, its founder and CEO, is to "Help All Americans Achieve the Dream of Homeownership."[11] This value was instilled throughout the company and employees believed they were facilitating the realization of the oldest dream in the country, which was the dream of owning one's own home. Homeownership was believed to be one of the very core ideals of American society and constituted the bedrock of communities, civil organizations, and the family unit.[12]

Of course the company made tons of money in the process and its stock price went thought the roof making gobs of money for investors who had bought stock in the company. Everything was rosy as long as housing prices continued to increase and more people could be convinced to buy a house and take out a loan. Countrywide helped this process along by inventing new types of loans to convince borrowers that they could afford a mortgage. One such loan was the PayOption loan, which was an adjustable-rate mortgage that gave the borrower the option to pay less than owed on the loan each month. This was called negative amortization and would actually increase the amount owed on the loan as the amount a borrower was short on the interest owned each month would be rolled back into the loan.

There were several reasons for this product. Borrowers needed more exotic products that would allow them to get into more and more expensive homes and yet be able to pay only tiny payments. Countrywide made a great amount of money from these kinds of loans because borrowers would eventually need to refinance, hopefully though Countrywide, which meant more loan fees and more income for the company. The fundamental assumption behind these loans is that housing prices would continue to go up so that PayOption borrowers could always refinance their loans before the rates would adjust to a higher level beyond their ability to pay.[13]

The author of a book about Countrywide, who worked for the company in an executive position and was present at the meeting where this product was introduced, thought that this assumption was pure fantasy and that these loans could conceivably put half the country underwater when the rates adjusted to higher levels and the payments were beyond people's ability to pay, a prediction that proved to be all too true. As he stated to one of his bosses after the meeting, "I think I may have just witnessed the beginning of the end of Countrywide and maybe the entire U.S. economy."[14] Most people in the company, including his boss, paid no attention to his comments, but eventually Countrywide itself was taken over by Bank of America when it crashed, along with the country as a whole, when borrowers started defaulting on their loans and home prices declined.

Homeownership had become a right for many people and companies like Countrywide exploited this trend with exotic loan products. Mortgage companies were running out of creditworthy people they could lend to by 2003, so instead of curtailing their lending they started to look for prospects who had little hope of repaying their loans when interest rates on their ARMs adjusted. Such subprime lending went from an annual volume of $145 billion in 2001 to $625 billion in 2005, which constituted more than 20 percent of total mortgages issued. More than a third of these subprime loans were issued for 100 percent of the value of the home, and when fees were added in these loans were even greater than the home value.[15]

An array of banks and lenders were dying to give people money and offered ever-riskier and more exotic loans like the PayOption where the borrower would wind up owing more each month. Other loans would give people money even if they could not verify their income and were called no doc loans or liar loans, meaning no documentation was required. Ninja loans allowed loans to people with no income and no job. Thus one could get a loan with no down payment, no income, and no documentation. Lenders knew that these people would never be able to pay the mortgage when it reset, but were not worried because as home values increased they could always refinance or sell the house for a profit.[16]

People were buying homes that were way beyond their ability to pay, so homeowners must share some of the blame for trying to live beyond their means. For example, in Bakersfield, California, a Mexican strawberry picker with an income of $14,000 and no English was lent every penny he needed to buy a house for $724,000.[17] Such behavior is outrageous and one has to wonder how people could be convinced to buy a house under these circumstances. Where had personal responsibility gone and the ability to think rationally about one's financial situation and develop a realistic sense of what one could afford? Common sense seems to have disappeared for many of these people, who should have known better. According to Michaelson:

> To demonstrate that you could be responsible enough to be worthy of signing those promissory notes, you were *supposed* to have already struggled and succeeded in securing a good job, generating a certain level of income, and working you fingers to the bone to have saved up enough for the down payment. It showed something beyond the numbers; it demonstrated *character.* The system naturally weeded out those who either were not ready to embark on that commitment, or had demonstrated previous behaviors implying that they were not financially mature enough to keep that promise to pay the money back. The new system of loans, and Refis awarded to anyone with a pulse was, in retrospect, long-term madness driven by short-term profit.[18]

Yet lenders convinced these borrowers that they had nothing to lose in getting as large a mortgage as the bank would allow because they could always refinance as their house increased in value. Their incentives were such that larger mortgages gave them larger origination fees, so their incentives were aligned with the borrower. They both had a reason to want the largest house and the largest mortgage possible. The lender did not bear any risk if the borrower defaulted since in most cases the mortgages were packaged and sold to others. Instead of holding their mortgages the way bankers had always operated, they began to package them and sell them to outside investors. They still collected hefty fees for issuing mortgages but encumbered little, if any, of their own capital. Lending was becoming costless.[19] Thus there was a great incentive to fudge the truth about some of these subprime mortgages, and as one author put it, "This meant lying all around—lying about what the family could afford and lying about the value of the house."[20]

Thus lenders were a good bit of the problem as they took advantage of a huge subprime market that had been created over the years as the distribution of income in this country was becoming more and more skewed towards the upper-income brackets. In 1996, 65 percent of subprime loans had been fixed-rate, meaning that borrowers knew with certainty how much they owed on the loan each month until it was paid off. By 2005, however, 75 percent of subprime loans were some form of floating rate ARM that was usually fixed for the first two years and then adjusted to a higher rate.[21] These loans also got bigger and riskier. In 2001, the average value of a subprime loan was $151,000; in 2005 the average value was $259,000.[22]

In addition to getting people into new homes, lenders like Countrywide created more and more loan products that were geared to people who were in a position to refinance their existing home and use it as a personal ATM to buy things they wanted or to get into a larger home and take out a new mortgage.[23] These refinancings jumped from $14 billion in 1995 to nearly a quarter-trillion in 2005, with the great majority of them resulting in higher loan amounts from purchasing a bigger home.[24] Companies made a great deal of money from all this refinancing activity, so they did whatever they could to convince homeowners to refinance their homes and move up in the world.

The notion the home prices would continue to increase was based on what was actually happening in the housing market. Traditionally, home prices increased about 1 percent a year faster than the rate of inflation and roughly tracked the growth in real incomes. However, from 2000 through 2006, home prices increased by more than 14 percent a year, which was the fastest prolonged home price increase ever. There was no obvious demographic reason for this increase. Instead, it was prompted by a flood of financing that made it easy to buy homes at low interest rates at least for the first few years with little or no money down. By 2006, high-risk mortgages accounted for 40 percent of all mortgages issued.[25]

Between the fourth quarter of 1996 and the fourth quarter of 2006, average prices of homes increased by 129 percent. Between 1997 and 2002, the total value of real estate owned by American households went up from $8.8 trillion to $14.5 trillion and then to $21.9 trillion in the ensuing four-year period. The $13.1 trillion increase in wealth from 1997 to 2006 was roughly equivalent to $125,000 for every household in the country. Compared to the dot.com bubble at the turn of the century, the housing bubble was much larger. Between 1996 and 1999, the total value of corporate stock held by American households increased by only $5 trillion.[26]

When housing prices declined and people defaulted on their mortgages, foreclosures increased rapidly and the American Dream became an American nightmare. As one author put it, "There was no point of putting someone in a home for a few months and then tossing him out after having stripped him of his life savings. But that was what the banks were doing."[27] They kept making money by issuing more and more risky mortgages and, as long as housing prices continued to increase, everyone, including the homeowner, was happy with what was happening. When home prices started to decline, however, a different story emerged that was not too pleasant for many people.[28]

Next in line is Wall Street and the investment banks that went wild over new investment vehicles such as CDOs and bought more and more of them as they became available. One of the reasons Wall Street developed this new industry called structured finance was because its old-fashioned business had become less profitable over the years and more and more boring. The profits in stock brokering and in the more conventional kinds of bond trading had been squashed by Internet competition.[29] Thus investment vehicles that offered larger profits were too attractive to resist. In the scandals that emerged at the turn of the century involving companies like Enron, Tyco, WorldCom, and others, the problems centered on improper accounting and financial malfeasance. This time the problem involving investment banks like Bear Stearns and Lehman Brothers centered on excessive borrowing and risk taking in an overheated market.

Conventional banks that take deposits from people are part of the Federal Reserve System and operate more or less in the open and are regulated at least to some extent. The investment banks, however, are nondepository institutions and are unregulated and are far less transparent. They constitute something of a "shadow banking system" that few people realized had become so terribly important in the larger scheme of things.[30] This shadow banking system expanded to rival and even surpass conventional banking in importance, and in hindsight it seems that politicians and government officials should have realized the kind of financial vulnerability that these banks were creating by leaving them unregulated with no financial safety net to cover them in case they got in trouble.[31]

These investment banks could not resist getting more and more into the CDO market and taking on excessive risk in the process. This market exploded between 2004 and 2006 when lenders originated more than $1.7 trillion in subprime mortgages. Wall Street issued more than $1.3 trillion in subprime mortgage securities. Roughly three-quarters of all subprime loans were securitized as nontraditional mortgage lending began to rival traditional lending.[32] In the boom years of 2005 and 2006, possibly 70 percent of the mortgages in CDOs were below top grade with at least half subprime or second-lien home equity lines. By assuming low default rates, it was possible to build families of bonds where 80 percent were given triple-A or double-A ratings even though 70 percent of the assets supporting them were subprime.[33]

At first, Wall Street sold these securitized mortgages to outside investors such as pension funds and the like, but when these sources began to dry up, they kept them on their own books. Between February 2006 and September

2007, UBS, which had previously sold all of the mortgage securities it issued to outside investors, accumulated $50 billion in mortgage assets. Citigroup's investment bank greatly expanded its CDO business and accumulated more than $50 billion in senior tranches. Merrill Lynch became the leading issuer of CDOs and, when it couldn't sell all of them, built up a stockpile of more than $40 billion in mortgages and mortgage securities. Other Wall Street banks, such as Morgan Stanley and Lehman Brothers, took on smaller exposures but they were still very significant. These firms continued to market CDOs in great quantities and did not cut back on the number of subprime securitizations they were issuing, as doing so would have meant forgoing very lucrative underwriting fees and bonuses.[34]

The cheap money the Fed kept supplying created an incentive for Wall Street firms to take on more and more risk and create more and more debt such that no one could keep track of it all, not even the CEOs of these firms. There was a frenzy of buying, and with interest rates low, these banks kept these securities on their balance sheets at full value because of their triple-A ratings even though there was no market for these securities. They continued to pocket the high interest rates these securities earned and even leveraged themselves to the hilt to take on more of them.[35] During this period the leverage at Bear Stearns had gone from 20:1 to 40:1, at Merrill Lynch from 16:1 to 32:1, and Morgan Stanley and Citigroup were at 33:1. Goldman Sachs appeared to be conservative at 25:1, but it was believed that Goldman had the ability to hide its actual leverage.[36] With this kind of leverage, it would require only a slight decline in the underlying value of their assets to bankrupt any of these firms.

These banks kept some these securities in special investment vehicles (SIVs) to keep them off their balance sheets. Citigroup pioneered this practice where the SIV would borrow money by selling short-term IOUs on the market and then hiding these loans so they did not appear on the bank's balance sheets. Banks normally have to set aside capital to absorb potential losses on every loan they make and every bond they buy, but by parking the loans and securities in SIVs, Citibank and other banks that used SIVs did not have to set aside such capital, which meant that there was no capital to absorb losses. This process freed up more money, however, for the banks to take on more and more risk by buying more and more mortgage securities.[37]

As Joseph E. Stiglitz, who teaches at Columbia University and is a Nobel Prize–winning economist, put it, "The whole securitization process depended on the greater fool theory—that there were fools who could be sold the toxic mortgages and the dangerous pieces of paper that were based on them."[38] While most CEOs of these banks seemed blissfully unaware of the risks their firms were taking, at least one CEO seemed rather frank about what was happening. The CEO and chairman of Citigroup, Charles Prince, told the *Financial Times* in mid-2007 just before the bank's risky portfolio began to implode, "As long as the music is playing, you've got to get up and dance. We're still dancing."[39] Prince's reference to a game of musical chairs seemed to be a remarkably candid admission of the situation in which he was participating and an acknowledgment that a full-scale blowup in the subprime market could lead to catastrophe. But he had no intention of getting out of the market at that point but did hope to get out before the music stopped.[40]

When the music did stop rather abruptly a few months later, some of the dancers like Prince, who did not get out in time, were fired. Others were not and tended to blame people in their own firm like their bond traders, who, some CEOs claimed, did not keep them adequately informed about the risks involved. They also claimed to be victims of a system that did not have adequate safeguards or suggested that it all was out of their control despite having taken credit for the firms' success when justifying their compensation packages. The problem is that everyone, including the CEOs, was making more money than ever before and nobody wanted to get out and miss the opportunity to make more money.

Some people put a good bit of the blame for the crisis on the quants, as they were called, the math wizards who were mainly responsible for creating the tightly coupled system of complex derivatives that were the darlings of Wall Street and the superfast trading system that could shift billions of dollars around the world in an instant.[41] This system the quants had designed was supposed to make the market more efficient by allowing hedge funds to exploit small differences in pricing, but instead a monster was created that was more unstable than before as it fed on itself in a downturn. Many, including Alan Greenspan, were delusional that these quantitative programs allowed better management of risk and, according to one author, "blinded the financial world to the massive credit bubble that had been forming for years."[42]

Scott Patterson, a staff reporter for the *Wall Street Journal*, pointed out that the presence of so many quantitative people in the financial sector represented something of a "massive brain drain of mathematically gifted people who could otherwise find careers in developing more efficient cars, faster computers, or better mousetraps rather than devising clever methods to make money for the already rich."[43] The market did not allocate resources efficiently with respect to the society as a whole because there were too many quants in the financial sector when their talents were badly needed in other sectors of the economy. Yet the models these quants developed were a critical part of the whole system in giving managers confidence that they had risk under control. According to John Cassidy, writing in *How Markets Fail*:

> The very existence of the models also gave senior bankers and policymakers a false sense of security. Risk management, long an imprecise and intuitive discipline, appeared to have been converted into a hard science. A fog of acronyms and mathematical symbols obscured what should have been obvious—too many financial institutions were lending

heavily to an overheated property market. Like pilots on a modern air-liner, the regulators and Wall Street CEOs had come to rely on the computers to tell them if anything was amiss. However, the risk-management systems that had been put in place at firms such as Citigroup, UBS, and Merrill Lynch had a much shorter record than the autopilots installed on Boeings and Airbuses, and they turned out to be far less reliable. When severe turbulence hit, many of them stopped working.[44]

The rating agencies played a crucial role in this process because the super senior and senior mortgages carried AAA, AA, or A credit ratings, which made mortgage securities particularly attractive because they carried higher yields than corporate bonds with the same rating. Thus they looked like a real bargain for both investors and the investment banks themselves. The rating agencies' ratings are supposed to be objective and thus they were trusted as being reasonably accurate. The problem is that there was an inherent conflict of interest in this rating process, because the rating agencies, including Moody's, Standard & Poor's, and Fitch, were paid by the issuer of the securities themselves and earned generous fees to rate their products. Thus they had an incentive to please those who were paying them, and competition among the rating agencies only made matters worse. If one rating agency did not give the rating that was desired, the investment banks could turn to another in a race to the bottom.[45]

Since mortgage bonds were more complicated than ordinary bonds, the rating agencies could charge higher fees for their services, and as a result, structured finance became their main source of revenues. Moody's profits quadrupled between 2000 and 2007 as the structured finance market exploded. Standard & Poor's wasn't far behind and Fitch also saw its profits quadruple.[46] Thus there was a great deal of money to be made in giving the mortgage securities high ratings and these agencies were caught up in the same incentive system as everyone else. In many cases, the agencies had no idea what was in the bonds they were rating, but gave them high ratings nonetheless.

Finally there is the Federal Reserve System itself, which also shares part of the blame. The Fed's traditional function was to take away the punch bowl just as the party was getting underway to rein in excessive risk taking. Its job was to ease credit in hard times and tighten it before expansions became unsustainable. But under Alan Greenspan, the Fed kept refilling the punch bowl to make sure the party continued and refused to take it away even after the crash. Greenspan focused only on consumer price inflation and ignored signs of rampant inflation in the housing and bond markets. Some intervention would seem to be necessary when a major asset class such as housing kept going up beyond all reason indicating a major bubble was developing. Yet Greenspan refused to act and claimed it was not the Fed's job to try to determine if a bubble was indeed developing and if so to do something to make it burst.[47]

So there was plenty of blame to go around.[48] A system had been created where the incentives were such that no one wanted to question what was going on and take steps to stop it before it got so out of hand. All the major players were making money and thus thought the system had to be working. After all, making money is what it is all about and, as long as this kept going on, everyone was happy. The game of musical chairs continued and everyone did their part to keep it going, never questioning the assumptions on which the game was based. John Gillespie and David Zweig, writing in *Money for Nothing*, sort of summed up what happened and who was involved in the following manner:

[T]he Federal Reserve holding interest rates at unnecessarily low levels for too long, American consumers' debt-fueled spending binge, government encouraging home ownership by inappropriate borrowers, financial institutions ignoring risks to reap profits from complex mortgage securities, investors obsessed with short-term gains, credit-rating agencies selling inaccurate AAA ratings, coopted professional service providers failing to raise the alarm, business schools churning out executives focused on money instead of values, financial media cheerleading rather than investigating, and business organizations marshalling massive campaign contributions and lobbying efforts to deregulate the financial services industry. Two more elements should be added at the front and end of the chain leading to the economic bomb that exploded: the predominant "Chicago School" economic philosophy that championed unfettered free markets and deregulation, and, finally, the failsafe device that didn't work—the SEC. When the SEC reduced its enforcement division staff by 146 people early in 2007, a catastrophe was virtually ensured to occur.[49]

BETTING AGAINST THE MARKET

There have been hundreds of books written about this debacle and they all contain some insights about what was going on and how this happened. There is plenty of blame to go around as everyone, from the most uncreditworthy homeowner to the top management of the investment banks, was living in a dreamworld of their own making. They all wanted something for nothing and had created a house of cards that was bound to come crashing down. Michael Lewis has written one of the most interesting books about a few people who saw what was coming and bet against the derivatives market and eventually made millions.[50] But it wasn't easy and they could not believe what they were seeing.

Lewis tells the stories of four individuals who became convinced early on that housing prices would not continue to increase forever and that the mortgage market was bound to take a downturn and perhaps even collapse entirely.[51] They wanted to bet against the entire mortgage market but initially there was no way they could short the entire market. There was no way to sell a mortgage bond without owning it and profit when it falls in price as one could short stocks on the stock exchange. The instrument that eventually allowed them to do this was called a credit-default swap (CDS), something that had been invented years before to allow corporations to insure themselves against the failure of borrowers to repay their loans. Wall Street firms were at first slow to sell this kind of insurance, but Goldman Sachs and Deutsche Bank led the way by selling swaps to one of the individuals Lewis follows in his book.

A credit-default swap was an insurance policy on a bond with semiannual premium payments and a fixed term. The most you could lose was the amount paid for the insurance, but if you won, you could make as much as fifty times the money you had paid for the insurance. Credit-default swaps on subprime mortgage bonds became a trillion-dollar market and precipitated hundreds of billions of dollars' worth of losses at the big investment banks on Wall Street. With CDSs, one did not have to guess exactly when the subprime market would crash. Home prices did not even have to fall, but only stop rising at the unprecedented rate they had been for vast numbers of Americans to default on their home loans.

Some of these individuals first bought insurance on triple-B-rated bonds, which were most likely to fall in value with even a modest rise in defaults, but others bought insurance on higher-rated tranches of bonds which it was believed would fall in value almost as fast of the lower rated. The swap was, of course, much cheaper for these higher-rated tranches, something like 20 cents or so for every $100 worth of bonds. The notational value of credit-default swaps—that is, the size of portfolios covered by credit-default agreements—grew from $1 trillion in 2001 to $45 trillion by mid-2007.[52]

Eventually, credit-default swaps, filtered through CDOs, were used to replicate bonds backed by actual home loans. Wall Street was not satisfied getting unqualified borrowers to take out a huge mortgage on a house they couldn't afford. To keep the machine running, they had to create them out of whole cloth. The payments made for the CDSs were treated as the equivalent of interest payments by homeowners and bond-like vehicles were constructed out of them and given double-A and triple-A ratings by the rating agencies. These were called synthetic CDOs because they were not backed by any new mortgages. That's why the losses in the financial system were so much greater than just the subprime loans in existence.[53]

Goldman and other banks that bought credit-default swaps eventually transferred their obligations to pay off the insurance contracts, should the market collapse, to the insurance giant AIG, which sold them insurance far more cheaply than they had initially paid. In a matter of months, AIG in effect bought $50 billion in triple-B-rated subprime mortgage bonds by insuring them against default. Yet no one in the company raised a red flag and the deals by all accounts were simply rubber-stamped by the management of AIG Financial Products Division and by the top management of AIG proper.[54] In exchange for a few million dollars a year, AIG took on the risk that the bonds that it had insured would become worthless. AIG was nearly the only buyer of triple-A-rated CDOs, which were really triple-B-rated subprime mortgage bonds repackaged into triple-A-rated CDOs.[55]

AIG FP was generating almost $2 billion a year in profits and at its peak, the entire credit-default business contributed only $180 million.[56] Eventually the loans that AIG was insuring consisted almost entirely of subprime mortgages, but no one inside the company knew this as they continued to sell insurance on these mortgages at ridiculously low prices.[57] As Michael Lewis says, "In retrospect, their ignorance seems incredible—but, then, an entire financial system was premised on their not knowing, and paying them for this talent."[58] As Cassidy describes the process:

> The providers of credit insurance were effectively taking on the same default risks that banks did when they lent money, but unlike banks, they didn't set aside any capital to cover possible losses. Most CDSs were "unfunded," meaning the provider of protection didn't put up collateral. If and when a default occurred, the provider had to pay out. Until then, however, it simply collected the premiums. For any financial firm, the promise of receiving cash without locking up capital is extremely attractive: with the economy humming, and credit defaults at historic lows, it proved irresistible.[59]

If all of this seems horribly complicated, it is, and it seems as if all these complicated instruments such as CDOs and CDSs were used to hide the actual risk involved in creating derivatives based on subprime mortgages that were bound to default at some point. Enormous risk had been created for the world financial system, but as long as everyone was making money, no red flags were raised. It is difficult to see where any of these investments made a direct contribution to the real economy in which most of us live. What Wall Street did was to create a house of cards, and when this collapsed and credit dried up it was ruinous for the economy and the world as a whole.[60]

One comes away from reading Lewis's book angry at the whole process and at the major players in this fiasco. They come off as incredibly stupid in thinking this could go on forever and putting their firms, to say nothing about the country and the world financial system, at such risk. What they created was a total fiction or a massive Ponzi scheme and there is no way any of these firms should have been bailed out by the government. Taxpayers were made to pay for the stupidity of these people, who went on to get their bonuses and were never held accountable for their actions. One gets the distinct impression that Wall Street became nothing but a huge gambling casino that was rigged in such a way so that all the big players came away a winner.

The people on the short side of the subprime mortgage market had gambled with the odds in their favor. The people on the other side—the entire financial system, essentially—had gambled with the odds against them. Up to this point, the story of the big short could not be simpler. What's strange and complicated about it, however, is that pretty much all the important people on both sides of the gamble left the table rich. Steve Eisman and Michael Burry and the young men at Cornwall Capital each made tens of millions of dollars for themselves, of course. Greg Lippman was paid $47 million in 2007, although $24 million of it was in restricted stock that he could not collect unless he hung around Deutsche Bank for a few more years. But all of these people had been right; they'd been on the winning end of the bet. Wing Chau's CDO managing business went bust, but he, too, left with tens of millions of dollars—and had the nerve to attempt to create a business that would buy up, cheaply, the very same subprime mortgage bonds in which he had lost billions of dollars' worth of other people's money. Howie Hubler lost more money that any single trader in the history of Wall Street—and yet he was permitted to keep the tens of millions of dollars he had made. The CEOs of every major Wall Street firm were also on the wrong side of the gamble. All of them, without exception, either ran their public corporations into bankruptcy or were saved from bankruptcy by the United States government. They all got rich, too.[61]

The author of the book about Countrywide Financial ultimately blames materialism for the financial crisis, a distorted sense of purpose in wanting to get into bigger, more expensive homes, the pursuit of money as the only goal worth pursuing, the tendency to buy more stuff and consume more of everything and go into debt and live on credit in order to pursue these things.[62] But he also ends up blaming the forces of the marketplace and what he calls "its natural state of unrelenting self-destruction, its tendency to bubble, then to overcorrect . . . Everyone was just naturally pursuing their own self-interest," and nobody took responsibility for their actions.[63] Is the free market part of the problem? Does it tend towards such destructive consequences for society as a whole?[64]

THE FREE MARKET

The free market, left to it own devices, is supposed to assure that resources are used efficiently and that society as a whole benefits from the pursuit of individual self-interest. This belief has had a powerful hold on people, particularly in government, for several decades. It was quite apparent in the deregulation of the financial industry that took place in the Clinton and Bush administrations. In 1999 the Gramm-Leach-Bliley Act (the Financial Services Modernization Act) was signed into law and allowed commercial banks and investment banks to combine and create vast financial supermarkets. This act repealed the Glass-Steagall Act, which was passed during the Great Depression, that had prevented depository institutions such as Citigroup from engaging in investment banking activities such as selling stocks, bonds, and mortgage securities. In 1990 the Federal Reserve had allowed J.P. Morgan to become the first commercial bank to underwrite securities. Six years later it allowed banks to acquire investment banking affiliates with some restrictions that were gradually eliminated. Greenspan had declared the Glass-Steagall Act to be "archaic," adding that failure to repeal it "could undermine the competitiveness of our financial institutions, their ability to innovate and to provide the best and broadest possible services to U.S. customers, and ultimately, the global dominance of American finance."[65]

The repeal of the Glass-Steagall Act allowed banks that were supposed to be safekeeping the savings and checking accounts of average Americans to take risks that were unprecedented. It gave the ability of large financial institutions like Citigroup to combine commercial and investment banking activities and transformed what were once conservative commercial banks into what one author characterized as "gambling dens of trading increasingly exotic bonds." Since investment banks were not regulated, the massive amount of leveraging that took place during the boom years escaped serious scrutiny by the SEC despite losses that had occurred from time to time.[66] And the FDIC, or course, had no control over these banks.

This deregulatory trend with respect to the financial industry continued under the Bush administration. This antiregulatory philosophy was symbolized by a photo op held in 2003 where representatives of the various agencies that were supposed to provide bank oversight used pruning shears and a chainsaw to cut stacks of regulations. In October 2006, Bush signed the Financial Services Relief Act, which allowed banks to keep less capital in reserve than was previously required. In doing away with these reserve requirements the banks could become more aggressive in their investments and use the extra money for lucrative mortgage-backed securities and derivatives. The Bush administration also used federal power to block state-level efforts to impose some kind of oversight on subprime lending activities of the mortgage companies.[67]

The drive to deregulate the economy began during the Reagan administration, when the government was seen as the problem rather than the solution to the nation's problems. From that point on, free-market ideology has been in ascendance and an antigovernment philosophy took hold in the country at large. This drive for deregulation was nowhere more evident than in the financial sector, where lending activities were shifted more and more to nonregulated entities, until only about a quarter of all lending occurred in regulated sectors by 2006, which was a big change from twenty years before when about 80 percent of lending took place in regulated sectors of the economy.[68]

People like Alan Greenspan, who should have been worried about the fragility of the system, were instead singing the praises of all the new "financial innovation" taking place. In 2004 he declared that "Not only have individual financial institutions become less vulnerable to shocks from underlying risk factors, but also the financial system as a whole has become more resilient."[69] On another occasion he said, "In essence, prudential regulation is supplied by the market through counterparty evaluation and monitoring rather than by authorities. We regulators are often perceived as constraining excessive risk-taking more effectively than is demonstrably possible in practice . . . [P]rivate regulation generally has proved far better at constraining excessive risk-taking than has government regulation."[70] Greenspan for years had advocated an aggressive policy of deregulation and believed that investment banks, hedge funds, and the derivatives industry left to their own devices would create a more efficient financial system benefiting the entire economy.[71] As Justin Fox, writing in *The Myth of the Rational Market*, says:

> If Greenspan saw at least some of what was coming, why didn't he do anything about it? Mainly because he had taken the lesson from his "irrational exuberance" speech in 1996 that he was not smarter than the market. That, and there was a long tradition in economics that while cracking down on general price inflation was in the Fed's job description, squeezing the air out of financial market bubbles was not . . . He wouldn't try to deflate a bubble, but he would do whatever he could to ease the pain of the ensuing bust. It was a consciously asymmetric approach . . . By allowing financial markets to run rampant on the upside, while intervening to soften the impact of every ensuing crash, the Fed was encouraging irresponsible behavior that would make subsequent crashes even worse.[72]

Thus the big financial firms were allowed to monitor their own risk levels and could use any measurement tool they wanted. Most used a measurement tool called the value at risk (VAR), which was as controversial on Wall Street as it was universally accepted, according to one source. This tool could be very misleading and every analyst worth anything understood its limitations. The way it measured risk was based on historical trends which assumed that history would repeat itself forever. Common sense alone suggests that this is not the case, and the decline in housing prices across the country proved the point. But every firm that used the VAR held up its results as if it was the final word on the matter.[73]

Individual homeowners, mortgage lenders, bankers, rating agencies, and everyone else connected with the financial industry reacted to the immediate monetary incentives they faced. The macroeconomic and regulatory framework in which they were operating reflected several decades of free-market idolatry which says that self-interest plus competition spurs innovation and results in the most efficient and beneficial outcome for society as a whole. The free market is considered to be something of a godlike contraption, as one author puts it, "that takes individual acts of egocentricity and somehow transforms them into socially beneficial outcomes . . . It was a startling idea then, and it remains one today, that economic order can emerge as the unintended consequence of the actions of many people, each seeking his own interest . . . Utopian economics goes beyond a scientific doctrine: it is a political philosophy, a secular faith."[74]

What all this deregulation of the financial industry really created, according to one source, was a form of crony capitalism. The combination of a Federal Reserve System that can print money, the existence of deposit insurance for commercial banks, and a Congress that can authorize bailouts provides an extensive safety net for the big financial firms and constitutes a corporate welfare system. The gains of all the financial innovation and speculation that went on were privatized with the bulk of them going to a relatively small group of wealthy people who had positions of power in the system and were able to manipulate it to their advantage. The losses were socialized with the taxpayers not only picking up the tab but also suffering the consequences of the financial collapse caused by these same people. Such is the free market we know today.[75] As Mark A. Martinez, writing in *The Myth of the Free Market*, says:

> But providing money and political cover to collapsing industries that operate in the name of *laissez-faire*—while continuing to push the myth of "free markets"—imposes an *Alice in Wonderland* character on modern markets in America . . . Constitutional stability and political control by a state that abdicates its oversight responsibilities and permits any sector of the economy to call on the resources of the state on a regular basis. When the state permits the creation of complex investment instruments and reckless speculation, and then consents to the use of state resources to stave off bankruptcy (or to guarantee payoff), serious questions are raised . . . When the state allows the private sector to draw on the public treasury when markets break down, it also allows the private sector to act like history's tyrants, who placed their needs above those of the public.[76]

The belief that markets are self-correcting and operate according to scientific laws that assure the best outcome for society if left alone and therefore government should not interfere ironically has resulted in the largest intervention by the government in history. The government assumed a role as the bearer of risk of last resort and expanded the corporate welfare system to an entire industry. When private markets for mortgage securities went into meltdown, all the risk for the toxic assets that had been created shifted to the government. The safety net, which should focus on protecting individuals, was extended to corporations in the belief that consequences of letting them fail and go into bankruptcy would be too horrific to imagine. These large firms now know that if they are sufficiently large such that their failure represents a threat to the economy that is too difficult to comprehend and if they have significant political clout, the government can be made to bear the risk of failure. Thus they are free to speculate all over again unless meaningful reform of the financial industry takes place.[77]

Since the early 1980s state power has been used to bail out companies and stabilize market outcomes for players that have floundered for one reason or another. It has provided loan guarantees for Lockheed and Chrysler, it set up a Resolution Trust Corporation to take over failed saving and loan institutions and stabilize that industry, it dealt with the failure of Long Term Capital Management, and now it has bailed out the financial industry. The state has stepped in on numerous occasions to maintain confidence in the economy, to ensure that companies will continue in existence rather than go bankrupt, and to guarantee market results.[78] We do not have a free-enterprise system that operates according to its own dictates but a system where failure is not an option for certain firms that are deemed too big to fail. But if they are too big to fail, they may also be too big to manage effectively.

One major argument for deregulation is that regulations stifle innovation by interfering with management prerogatives and causing inefficiencies. The financial industry was certainly innovative, but in a manner that was destructive and, in effect, it innovated itself right out of existence. According to Stiglitz, these innovations were directed at circumventing regulations, accounting standards, and taxation, and mainly generated more income for the companies involved. The problems that would ultimately surface because of high default rates seemed matters for a distant future. Financial firms did not seem the least bit interested in innovations that might have helped people keep their homes and manage their finances to protect them from rises in interest rates when their mortgages adjusted.[79]

> In the Frankenstein laboratories of Wall Street, banks created new risk products . . . without mechanisms to manage the monster they had created. They had gone into the moving business—taking mortgages from the mortgage originators, repackaging them, and moving them onto the books of pension funds and others—because that was where the fees were the highest, as opposed to the "storage business," which had been the traditional business model for banks (originating mortgages and then holding on to them) . . . Their incentives were to pass on the mortgages, and the securities they had created backed by the mortgages, as fast as they could to others.[80]

Advocates of subprime mortgages tried to make the case that these innovations would enable large number of Americans to become homeowners and have the American Dream come true for the first time in their lives. While they did indeed become homeowners, in most cases it was only for a very short time and at a high cost for themselves and the economy. There were fewer homeowners at the end of the crisis than at the beginning. While expanding homeownership is a good idea, these innovations did not accomplish that objective but instead made money for the mortgage brokers and investment bankers.[81] Complicated financial stuff was being dreamed up for the sole purpose of lending money to people who could never repay it, but in the process Wall Street made billions in counterfeit money. At the end of the day, it is not clear that these "innovations" actually contributed very much to the success of the U. S. economy or the living standards of the vast majority of Americans. David Stockman, a former director of the Office of Management and Budget under President Reagan, had this to say about the crisis.

> The third ominous change in the American economy has been the vast *unproductive* expansion of our financial sector . . . the trillion dollar conglomerates that inhabit this new financial world are not free enterprises. They are rather wards of the state, extracting billions from the economy with a lot of pointless speculation in stocks, bonds, commodities and derivatives. They could never have survived, much less thrived, if their deposits had not been government-guaranteed and if they hadn't been able to obtain virtually free money from the Fed's discount window to cover their bets . . . It is not surprising, then, that during the last bubble (from 2002 to 2006) the top 1 percent of Americans—paid mainly from the Wall Street casino—received two-thirds of the gain in national income, while the bottom 90 percent—mainly dependent on main Street's shrinking economy—got only 12 percent.[82]

In sum, there is no alternative to public management in some sectors of the economy.[83] Conservative free-market types have made repeated efforts to encourage the private sector to build and run schools, provide police protection and trash pickup, manage national parks, provide low-cost housing, and provide other services. Yet governments continue to bear the responsibility to provide these services and bear the financial burden for these services.[84] Many conservative economists are willing to see the government step in when the country is threatened by another Great Depression. But that raises the question as to why anyone believed in a self-correcting free market in the first place. The miraculous supposedly self-stabilizing power of the market fails just when it is most needed. The laws of economics fail to work in crisis situations.[85] Bubbles in particular are something free markets cannot respond to effectively, according to Cassidy.[86]

> Once a bubble begins, free markets can no longer be relied on to allocate resources sensibly or efficiently. By holding out the prospect of quick and effortless profits, they provide incentives for individuals and firms to act in ways that are individually rational but immensely damaging—to themselves and others. The problem of distorted incentives is, perhaps, most acute in financial markets, but it crops up throughout

the economy. Markets encourage power companies to despoil the environment and cause global warming; health insurers to exclude sick people from coverage; computer makers to force customers to buy software programs they don't need; and CEOs to stuff their own pockets at the expense of their stockholders. These are all examples of "market failure," a concept that recurs throughout the book and gives it its title. Market failure isn't an intellectual curiosity. In many areas of the economy, such as health care, high technology, and finance, it is endemic.[87]

During the lead-up to the financial crisis, everyone was doing exactly what self-interest dictated. Borrowers kept borrowing more and more money to spend on inflated housing values because they could. Lenders created more exotic new products to entice people to borrow more and reaped huge rewards. Wall Street bought and sold mortgage derivatives because they were a big moneymaker. Rating agencies made money by giving the ratings Wall Street firms wanted. And government tried to stay out of the way because a rich and fat electorate is a happy electorate.[88] Yet all this pursuit of economic self-interest did not work out in the best interests of society, and the idea that the pursuit of individual self-interest will lead somehow automatically through an invisible hand to the best interests of society as a whole was exposed as the myth it has always been.

RATIONALITY

The scientific paradigm was adopted by economics in the 1970s as economists believed they belonged to a real science apart from psychology and sociology. Economics even had an annual Nobel Prize to call its own and place it in the same rank as the so-called hard sciences of physics and chemistry.[89] The core tenet of scientific economics was that people acted in their rational self-interest in making decisions, the so-called rational economic man. This became the foundation principle of economics as everything else followed from people acting in their self-interest and guiding the allocation of resources to produce what people wanted in a manner such that they could afford to buy what was produced.

Most early economists took a laissez-faire approach to economic policy and took their cue from a textbook published by Alfred Marshall of Cambridge University in 1890 entitled *Principles of Economics* that became the bible of the economics profession. Marshall banished equations to an appendix and developed graphs to depict supply-demand relations as well as other economic phenomena that became familiar to students for years thereafter. Scholars became enamored of Marshall and his approach became popular. There were dissidents, that became know as the institutionalists, who emphasized the role of economic institutions such as laws and customs over the role of individual decision makers, but this view was more or less marginalized.[90] Both of these approaches waned as economics became more scientific and quantitative in its approach.

In the 1950s and 1960s, economics began to change from a more political economy orientation to the highly mathematized discipline it is today. Such a change may have simply reflected society's fascination with science as a whole, because during this period science and technology ushered in a new age of affluence with a proliferation of new devices that made people's lives better and more comfortable. Science was on a roll, so to speak, and its reductionistic and quantitative orientation dominated our thinking. Even if we are not professional scientists, we learned to think about the world in scientific terms and are used to looking to new technologies to solve many of our problems.

Economics prescribes the role of business in our society in a scientific manner, and also provides a moral justification for its existence. Business is considered to be solely an economic institution whose purpose is to create more and more economic wealth. This purpose can be quantified and measured by the profits that a business generates and the price of its shares traded on the stock exchanges. The success of society as a whole is measured by an increase or decrease of gross national product, or gross domestic product, as it is often called. Our fascination with and belief in quantification is reflected in these measures of success. As long as society as a whole continues to experience success along these lines, there is no reason to question such a scientific orientation. Stephen A Marglin states the following in this regard:

> Economists claim that their discipline is part and parcel of post-Baconian science, which is to say that economics, like physics, is based on algorithmic deduction of propositions that are in turn subject to rigorous testing in a confrontation with bare empirical data. It doesn't matter for this purpose whether economic agents themselves are calculating and maximizing, but it is of signal importance that these agents are understood in terms of a rigorous, axiomatic system, and therefore that the conclusions of economics are entitled to the deference due science. Just as one would not wish the criteria for the safe capacity of a bridge to be the subject of politics, so with economic questions like inflation and unemployment: economic policymakers need not be—indeed, ought not to be—politically accountable. [91]

The claim that economics is a science provides legitimacy to the idea that economics is above politics and that economic policies are the province of economic experts the same as drug safety is the province of technical experts and neither should be the subject of political debate.[92] But just as in decisions about drug safety, economic policies are very much involved with politics and reflect the prevailing ideologies and thinking of the times. Value judgments are present and are "hidden in the foundational assumptions that social well-being consists of satisfying the rational, calculating individual's self-interested pursuit of consumption."[93]

The first serious attempt to use reason and science to understand the way the financial markets work came in the early decades of the twentieth century. Irving Fisher, an economics professor at Yale University, published *The Nature of Capital and Income* in 1906, in which he advocated a more rational and quantitative approach to the market. He recommended that stock-market players adopt a more scientific approach, but his efforts were rendered to the ash heap of history after he missed the stock-market crash of 1929 and asserted that stock prices had reached a "permanently high plateau," blowing his entire fortune in the process.[94]

Despite this setback, finance eventually became more scientific and quantitative in its approach. The corollary of the principle of the rational economic man in the financial world is that financial markets are rational rather than haphazard and unpredictable. Quantitative models began to be developed based on this assumption. The capital asset pricing model (CAPM), portfolio theory, and in particular the efficient market hypothesis became the core of the new quantitative approach to finance. The fundamental assumption was that market forces invariably pushed security prices toward their correct, fundamental values.[95] It was believed that there was some intrinsic value to all the entities traded in the financial system. As John Cassidy, a journalist for the *New Yorker* and author of a book entitled *How Markets Fail*, says:

> The efficient market hypothesis, which Eugene Fama, a student of Friedman popularized, states that financial markets always generate the correct prices, taking into account all of the available information . . . For somebody lacking the benefit of a higher degree in economics or finance, it may be difficult to accept that the daily lurches of the Dow and the S&P 500 reflect a calm and rational processing of new information on the part of investors; that the tripling of home values in some parts of the country between 1996 and 2006 was nothing untoward; and that crude oil was correctly priced at roughly $50 a barrel in January 2007, was equally reasonably valued at $140 a barrel in June 2008, and was also accurately priced at $40 a barrel in February 2009. But such is the message of the efficient market hypothesis.[96]

For many years, as Cassidy points out, Alan Greenspan and other economists had argued that the development of complicated and little-understood financial products such as subprime mortgage-backed securities, collateralized debt obligations, and credit-default swaps had actually made the financial system safer and more efficient. The idea that informed this view was that by putting a market price on risk and selling it to investors who were willing to take on this risk, these complex securities greatly reduced the chances of a systemic crisis.[97] That this was a false view is now a part of history, but the crisis that shouldn't have happened but did calls into question the scientific approach to financial markets according to Scott Patterson:

> Physics, because of its astonishing success at predicting the future behavior of material objects from their present state, has inspired most financial modeling. Physicists study the world by repeating the same experiments over and over again to discover forces and their almost magical mathematical laws ... It's a different story with finance and economics, which are concerned with the mental world of monetary value. Financial theory has tried hard to emulate the style and elegance of physics in order to discover its own laws ... The truth is that there are no fundamental laws in finance.[98]

What did happen was the best example of what one author calls rational irrationality that one could hope for.[99] It was perfectly rational from an economically self-interested point of view for borrowers to take advantage of the products that were offered by lenders to buy a house they really could not afford in the hopes of benefiting from continually rising housing prices. It was perfectly rational for lenders to develop these products and sell then to willing customers and make lots of money in the process. It was perfectly rational for Wall Street investment banks to trade in hot new products such as CDOs because they were moneymakers. It was perfectly rational for rating agencies that were paid by the banks whose securities they were rating to give high ratings and make more money than they had ever made in the process. As Gillespie and Zweig describe the process:

> Since the agencies are paid by the bond issuers (who could essentially shop for the highest ratings) and the fees are higher based on the size and complexity of the transactions, the agencies have powerful incentives to produce those quality assurances. The issuers needed them because many of their institutional investor customers had high ratings-based requirements on what they could buy. The ratings agencies charged double or triple the fees for rating subprime mortgage-based debt than for plain vanilla corporate bonds ... The rating agencies' analytical models were based on assumptions that were fundamentally flawed and historical data that proved inapplicable. Very few financial services CEOs and directors had any real understanding of how these unimaginable complicated securities worked, but as profits skyrocketed from selling and trading them, these same leaders didn't ask questions. Many now say they relied on the ratings to assess their risks.[100]

People made choices based on an assessment of their economic self-interest and these choices were supposedly rational from an individual perspective. Managers of the investment banks on Wall Street would have been taken to task for not investing in CDOs and reaping the profits from the sale of these financial instruments. Executives at institutions like Countrywide Financial would have been amiss to their shareholders if they had not offered exotic mortgages to try to beat the competition. It is only in hindsight that some of these executives like Michaelson can see how crazy some of the things they were doing really were, but at the time they seemed like the perfectly rational thing to be doing.

> Corporations' self-interest was to return value to shareholders as fast and as profitably as possible, by giving the marketplace what it wanted to buy. In Countrywide's case, they provided easy access to money and reaped the fees and revenue rewards of that service. But common sense says that to give anyone a loan with a "no documentation" review process is madness. To allow people to pay *less than* their mortgage demands every month is lunacy. To give anyone a loan who has a substantial history of poor repayment and bad credit, dumb—no matter how high the interest rate.[101]

From the standpoint of society, however, such rationality was a disaster from which the country has not yet recovered. An unregulated market made such an irrational outcome possible because it provided incentives that were perverse from society's perspective. The same thing happens in other areas such as health care. From the perspective of an individual insurer it is perfectly rational to refuse to insure someone with preexisting conditions and cancel policies for sick people. That's the way insurance has to work in order to remain profitable. But from the perspective of society such practices are inhumane and inefficient. Sick people without insurance, who don't get treated when they should, get worse and eventually end up in the emergency room, which is much more expensive. They then have to be treated and somebody has to pay for their care.[102] Rational irrationality is the term used to refer to situations where the application of rational self-interest results in an inferior and socially irrational outcome.[103]

The rational herd is a term also used to refer to the way people act in such situations. The basic idea is that while you may be doing something dumb, if everybody else is doing the same dumb thing at the same time, people will not think of you as stupid and your reputation will not be harmed.[104] Investment banks continued to buy CDOs even as their value began to be questioned because everyone else was doing the same thing. Then when it became apparent that they might not be such a good investment, everyone tried to sell them at the same time but there were no buyers and their value crashed. There were no buyers because everyone was trying to sell, having made the same stupid assumptions.

As pointed out by Justin Fox, a columnist for *Time* magazine and author of *The Myth of the Rational Market*, the development of the efficient market hypothesis, the Black-Scholes option-pricing model, and all the other major elements of the rational scientific approach to financial markets took place during the end of a long period of market stability that was characterized by tight government regulation. As this author states, "These theories' reliance on calmly rational markets was to some extent the artifact of a regulated, relatively conservative financial era—and it paved the way for deregulation and wild exuberance."[105] The idea of an efficient and rational market was given far more credit than it deserved.

WEALTH

One estimate puts global losses by investors in the stock market at $30 trillion, a staggering sum that is beyond comprehension.[106] Again, the question is where did all this wealth go and what did it initially represent? A case could be made that all the so-called economic wealth generated by Wall Street and other institutions based on mortgage-backed securities was counterfeit wealth; it was not real and was pure fiction that was bound to collapse as soon as subprime buyers started to default on their mortgages and housing prices started to decline. This was indeed the gamble that those who bet against the mortgage market took and won huge sums of money in the process. The goal was not maximization of shareholder wealth but maximization of wealth for most active players in the game including CEOs.

The issue of executive compensation has been around for some time and has been written about extensively in the management literature. Throughout the last several decades CEO pay has continued to grow despite efforts to rein it in and tie executive pay more closely to performance. In 2006, according to an analysis by The Corporate Library, the average CEO of a Standard & Poor's 500 company earned $14.78 million in total compensation. This represented a 9.4 percent increase from the previous year. According to some estimates, the ratio between the compensation of top executives and the average pay of workers increased from 42 in 1980 to more than 400 in 2005, a ratio that is unprecedented, particularly when compared with that of other countries.[107] According to Gillespie and Zweig:

> Data from the Economic Policy Institute show that CEO compensation in the United States has since risen to become about 10 percent of all corporate profits—twice what is was in the mid-1990s. The average CEO in 2007 was paid $275 for every dollar paid for a typical worker, up from a ratio of 24 to 1 in 1973. Over the past twenty years, CEO pay has grown more than 16 times as fast as the average worker's and American CEOs now earn 2.25 time the average of CEOs in other wealthy countries.[108]

These figures alone suggest that the real purpose of the corporation over the past several decades has been to maximize the wealth of top management and has relatively nothing to do with maximizing shareholder wealth. There have been many efforts to tie CEO pay more closely to actual performance but very few of these efforts have been successful. In most cases, CEO pay continues to increase year after year whether or not the company is profitable and the returns to shareholders are positive. Typical is the case of General Motors, which was eventually bailed out by the government, and its CEO, who lost his job as a result, walked away with wealth that for most of us is beyond comprehension.

On June 6, 2000, Richard Wagoner was appointed CEO of General Motors. The company's stock price fell some 95 percent during his tenure and lost more than $85 billion. Nonetheless, the board had elected him to also be chairman of the board in 2003 and increased his compensation by 64 percent in 2007, a year the company had lost $38.7 billion. In August of 2008 GM announced another quarterly loss of $15.5 billion. Wagoner was finally forced out of office in March 2009 as part of the federal bailout plan for the company. By that time the stock had dropped to the $2 range and the company had already gone through $13.4 billion in bailout money. The company had failed to address key strategic questions about the future of the automobile industry and the kind of cars it should produce. Because of this and other failures the stockholders lost $52 billion.[109]

But if people were not convinced that maximization of shareholder wealth had become a myth, the financial meltdown should provide the final nail in the coffin. Stanley O'Neal held the titles of chairman, CEO, and president for most of his nearly six years at the top of the ladder at Merrill Lynch. He proclaimed 2006 as the most successful year in the company's history and was paid $48 million in salary and bonuses for that year, which was one of the highest compensation packages in all of corporate America. Only ten months later, however, the company suffered a third-quarter loss of $2.3 billion and an $8.4 billion write-down on failed investments, which was the largest loss in the company's ninety-three-year history. These losses exceeded all of the 2006 net earnings. Its exposure to subprime mortgages and collateralized debt obligations has soared from $1 billion to $40 billion in just eighteen months. O'Neal was finally relieved of his duties in October 2007 with an exit package worth $161.5 million on top of the $70 million he was awarded during his time as CEO and chairman. Merrill Lynch was eventually sold to Bank of America. The shareholders lost more than $60 billion in the process.[110]

Richard Fuld had joined Lehman Brothers in 1969, and since 1994 had been both CEO and chairman of the board. From 2000 to 2007 he had received $484 million in salary, stock, options, and bonuses. The board continued to support its CEO even after it reported a loss of $3.9 billion in the 2008 third quarter. Four days later, the company declared bankruptcy after the government failed to come to its rescue, the largest bankruptcy in the history of the nation. The shareholders lost more than $45 billion in the process, and while Fuld saw his wealth decline because of the bankruptcy, he did not retire in poverty.[111]

Countrywide Financial, which was acquired by Bank of America in July 2008, was one of the worst offenders related to its abusive sales practices for subprime loans. Its CEO, Angelo Mozilo, wanted the company to become the nation's largest mortgage lender, and it plunged into the subprime loan market with a frenzy. It implemented innovations like an 80–20 loan program which allowed a buyer to pay the entire cost of a house with two separate subprime mortgages. This was said at the time to be the most toxic product in existence because it allowed people to get into houses that had mortgage payments they could not hope to meet and were only hoping to refinance as housing prices continued to increase. By 2006, Countrywide financed nearly one in five mortgages throughout the country.[112]

In 2004, Mozilo made more than $70 million from salary, bonuses, and gains from exercising stock options and had a net worth of half a billion dollars. In 2006, he made $48 million not including gains on stock options. In June 2009, he was charged by the SEC with fraudulently selling stock that gained him $140 million while he allegedly knew the company was in serious trouble while promoting the stock to the public and repurchasing his own shares using shareholder's money. The shareholders lost $22 million and communities throughout the country were devastated as homeowners defaulted on their mortgages and were forced out of their homes.[113]

Similar stories could be told about Citigroup, Bear Stearns, Morgan Stanley, Goldman Sachs, Bank of America, and most of the other companies involved in the financial meltdown.[114] The taxpayers either bailed out the company or it merged into some other entity with government support. Stockholders bore the brunt of the losses and top management came away with most of their wealth intact. If this doesn't suggest that the purpose of the corporation has changed from maximization of shareholder wealth to maximization of top management wealth, I don't know what more evidence is needed.

These CEOs justified their huge salaries and bonuses by arguing that they were generating huge returns to their shareholders as the stock prices of their companies increased. Indeed, that was true for a time but the shareholders as well as some of these CEOs had little or no idea how shaky the foundations on which this wealth had been built really was. In some cases the CEOs knew little of how exposed their firms were to the mortgage market and how all these complex financial products really worked. It seems as if they were paid for their ignorance. According to Gasparino:

> In one of the great ironies of the era, CEOs such as Jimmy Cayne [at Bear Stearns] and Stan O'Neal at Merrill had been paid historically high bonuses in 2006 because of gains largely from the selling, trading, packaging, and carrying of mortgage-related debt, yet as they delved deeper into their mortgage holdings they realized that they had no idea of how the business really worked and how much of the stuff they were now carrying on their books.[115]

In any event, the imperial CEO is alive and well in corporate America, as the rich get richer and the poor poorer, hardly indicative of a system that works for the benefit of the entire society.[116] The American dream of getting ahead and every generation being better off than the one before is fading for many citizens. One study finds that males in their thirties are worse off than their fathers' generation, which is a reversal of fortunes from just a decade ago. The typical family's income has lagged far behind the growth of productivity, also a reversal from most of the period since the Second World War. Between 2000 and 2005 productivity rose 16 percent while median income fell 2 percent, challenging that notion that a rising tide lifts all boats. Some people don't have a boat and if they do it is leaking badly.[117]

These trends of ever-increasing executive compensation and declining incomes for many workers will keep this issue on the agenda for some time. CEOs have become a symbol for the inequalities that have increased in the society as a whole as the middle class loses more and more ground. Corporations have outsourced many jobs, leaving Americans unemployed, opted out of their pension programs, and shed their health-care coverage for employees while all the time rewarding their top executives ever-increasing compensation packages. Compensation committees have been unable to control executive pay and it is not clear at this point how this issue is going to be resolved.[118]

For much of the last century, chief executives of large corporations have held unilateral power over their companies with unquestioned authority to do whatever they wanted with the resources at their disposal. Boards rarely oppose the will of management even at poorly performing companies; and institutional investors and activist shareholders, while effective at times in pursuing objectives at odds with management in some companies, have not mounted an effective overall challenge to management control. Top management determines how corporate resources are used and enjoy increasing levels of pay and benefits that enable them to live a lifestyle that most people cannot even imagine. They became a new class of royalty, if you will, that is able to extract huge sums of money from corporations for their services.

The new reform bill that passed Congress, called the Dodd-Frank bill, requires that companies disclose the difference in pay between the chief executive of the company and the lowest-paid workers. Many corporate executives and corporate lawyers opposed this requirement, claiming that it would be a "logistical nightmare" for their companies to compile this information. Rana Foroohar, writing in *Newsweek*, thinks this should not be too onerous a requirement and that the real issue is that companies don't want the public to see this information because it will show how egregious, as she puts it, the pay gap has become. She thinks this rule is a good one that if nothing else "could be the starting point of a conversation in which America's business leaders explain, to their shareholders and to the wider public, exactly why they need so much money to get the job done."[119]

REFORM

In the aftermath of the financial meltdown, many people in the financial sector as well as in government lamented what had happened and questioned whether anyone could have predicted such a devastating crash and taken steps to prevent it from happening. Yet there were many critics that had made such predictions and, as mentioned earlier, took steps to profit from it, but their dire warnings were an inconvenient truth, to use a phrase Al Gore made famous with his predictions about global warming. As stated by one author, "Too much money was being made by too many people for their warnings to be heard."[120] The boom in mortgage-backed securities made money for just about everyone involved, from the homeowner who purchased a subprime mortgage, to the bank that issued the mortgage, to the investment banks that created complex securities that no one understood, to the rating agencies that profited from unjustified high ratings, and to the investor who profited from higher interest rates on these securities. According to Martinez:

> Peter F. Drucker saw this happening as far back as 1986 and described a new "symbolic" economy in which capital and wealth creation are separated from the real economy. Rather than look toward history for clues as to what happens when market players focus on wealth extraction and creating paper empires tied to debt, policymakers and market players largely ignored Drucker's observations because of the new wealth that was created. This allowed financial instruments and financial assets around the world to become increasingly separated from the production of real goods and services. This explains why the U.S. government was reluctant to allow financial institutions that were deemed "too big to fail" to collapse. There was simply too much nervousness about what would happen if the opaque world of debt-laden financial instruments began to unravel.[121]

While there were imitators and fellow travelers, as one author put it, the global financial crisis was made in America. A new class of superrich had been created in America "who had invented nothing and built nothing, except intricate chains of paper claims that duller people mistook for wealth."[122] The financial sector channeled too much money into real estate and in particular to people who could not repay their debt. It had failed to allocate money where the returns to society were highest. The financial sector was centered on profits for itself and had come to see their business as an end in itself rather than a means to the end of prosperity and efficiency for the society as a whole.[123]

Capitalism cannot exist without capital and yet at one point the credit markets seized up and credit was not available and banks were afraid to lend to anyone or any other institution. Trust is important for an economy to operate. People have to have trust that the products they are buying are safe to use as directed. Creditors have to trust that the company they are lending money to is a viable institution that will be able to pay off its debts at some time in the future. During the financial crisis of 2008–2009, trust was lacking and the banks and other financial institutions would not lend any more money because they did not believe the debt would be paid. The government had to restore that trust with a bailout package to get credit moving again.

The bailout package was called the Troubled Asset Relief Program (TARP), and while it was very unpopular in the country as a whole and ended the careers of several politicians, it proved to be successful in preventing a total collapse of the financial system. Originally set at $700 billion and eventually lowered to $475 billion, most of the money was repaid and the final cost to taxpayers was estimated to be around $50 billion. Even American Insurance Group, which was given $70 billion, might even make money in the final analysis, although that was speculative at best and a loss of around $10 billion was thought to be more realistic.[124] Banks were given $250 billion but the bulk of these funds had been repaid and the government expected to make a profit from these payments.[125]

However, even the $700 billion TARP bailout program was insufficient to deal with the troubled assets that had been acquired by Wall Street firms. The Federal Reserve had to step in and buy bad subprime mortgage bonds directly from the banks. By early 2009 losses associated with more than a trillion dollars of bad investments had been transferred from Wall Street to the American taxpayer.[126] Even as the government (taxpayers) provided banks with money to recapitalize and ensure a flow of credit, some of this money was used to pay themselves record bonuses. According to Stiglitz, nine lenders that together had nearly $100 billion in losses received $175 billion in bailout money from the government and paid out nearly $33 billion in bonuses. They also used some of this money to pay dividends, which in this case came from government handouts rather than profits.[127]

Such a bailout sends a signal to the banks that they do not have to worry about lending practices that get them in trouble. The government will always pick up the pieces and will not let them fail because such failure would be too damaging to the economy as a whole. They can do whatever they want with this bailout money. This practice does the exact opposite of what the market should do in enforcing discipline on the banks by rewarding those that had been prudent and letting fail those that had been foolish and taken on more risk than they could handle. The bailout gave the banks that did the worst in risk management the biggest gifts from the government.[128] This is not the way the system is supposed to work to benefit the entire society. As Michaelson says:

> When government rescues, bails out, helps—whatever you call it—those who acted financially *irresponsibly*, engaged in reckless speculation,

or otherwise made their own mess, government potentially rewards that behavior, ensuring its perpetuation, enabling its proliferation into greater levels of nuttiness, and motivating even greater levels of risk-taking . . . There is extreme danger for the future in rewarding bad decisions, yes, but a foreclosed home also does not pay property taxes, which is already beginning to cripple state and local government budgets. It is arguable, but it may actually be *less* expensive overall to bail people out than to let the system self-correct. Whether or not the math favors either action may come down to the final scale of the damage, which is, as yet, frighteningly undetermined. But the point is, the moral issue is very complex.[129]

According to Stiglitz again, these actions of the government only strengthened the too-big-to-fail banks and worsened the problems of moral hazard. Future generations of Americans were saddled with a legacy of debt that increased the possibility of inflation in the future and put the US dollar at risk on world markets. These actions also strengthened many Americans' doubt about the fundamental fairness of the system. If you were big enough, such that failure would threaten to bring the entire financial system down, you did not have to worry about taking on risky investments. But if you are an average citizen, the government would not necessarily come to your aid with a big enough aid package to make a real difference.[130]

To mention just one example of a bank that was too big to fail, Citigroup stock fell more than 97 percent by early March of 2009 and $263.8 billion in shareholder value had disappeared. At the time, this was the largest loss in corporate history. To be able to continue operations, the bank required $45 billion of taxpayer funds and a further guarantee for $301 billion of its most dubious mortgage-related securities.[131] The bank was rewarded for making risky investment decisions at society's expense. Other banks, such as Morgan Stanley and Goldman Sachs, which were the last freestanding investment banks still in business, became members of the Federal Reserve System to gain some protection and come under the purview of the FDIC and deposit insurance.[132]

Greed is a given on Wall Street. The problem was the system of incentives that had channeled the greed in a self-destructive manner and allowed a huge bubble to occur that no one wanted to burst. As one author points out, the problem wasn't that Lehman Brothers had been allowed to fail. The problem was that it had been allowed to succeed based on such risky investments. Without government intervention, every one of these investment banks would have failed and the world's most highly paid financiers would have been entirely discredited.[133] Yet no one wanted the music to stop and it kept going until the entire system collapsed, and when it did the government had to step in to save the system. As Michaelson again says:

Bubbles like this occurred because the motion of housing and mortgages was bubbling, and there was no external force to stop it—until, of course, it burst or collapsed under its own weight, from the "surface tension" of over-inflated prices. But why is America continually prone to such bubbles? What is it about our world culture that pushes us to continue with financial frenzies—from gold, to railroads, to dot.coms, to housing and mortgages, even going back to the Dutch tulip craze in the early-seventeenth century—every few decades, like clockwork? We never seem to learn. When will we learn to see the signs of irrationality and correct them before it is too late? . . . The bubble began to feed on itself when a too-easy supply of exotic loans collided with rabid consumerism gone hog wild, and when housing values skyrocketed because everyone demanded a house. By thinking we were doing *good*, by allowing much greater, and nutty, access to homeownership, we inadvertently deluged the marketplace with never-before-seen demand from many people who were not ready for the responsibility of ownership.[134]

Creating a financial system that actually works and fulfills the functions that a financial system is supposed to perform is the first priority of reform. A better regulated financial system would actually be more innovative, according to Stiglitz, and direct the creative energy of financial markets to develop products that enhance the well-being of society rather than line the pockets of financiers.[135] Any institution that has to be rescued during a crisis situation because it plays such an essential role in the financial system should be regulated when there is no crisis to be sure it does not take on excessive risk that jeopardizes its integrity and ability to continue in business.[136]

The legislation that eventually came out of Congress to reform the financial system and protect investors hoped to do this, but there were many skeptics who had serious doubts.[137] The law creates a new agency, called the Consumer Financial Protection Bureau, to protect consumers in their financial transactions. This agency will be housed within the Federal Reserve System and consolidates several other consumer agencies dealing with financial transactions. The law also creates a council of regulators to monitor the financial system for overly risky practices that threaten the financial system and increases the government's power to liquidate failing firms whose collapse could threaten the financial system. In addition, it imposes limits on complex derivative contracts requiring that they be routed through exchanges, electronic trading platforms, and clearinghouses to create more transparency. Finally, it bans certain predatory lending practices on the part of the mortgage industry and requires lenders to assess borrowers' ability to pay off their mortgages.[138]

The bill, however, is ambiguous with respect to many of its provisions. It is not clear, for example, that it preserves the so-called Volcker rule, named after a former Treasury secretary.[139] This rule established a separation between commercial and investment banking that was eliminated with repeal of the Glass-Steagall Act by barring commercial banks from speculating in the markets and from operating and investing in hedge funds and private-equity funds. Commercial banks need government protection in case things go wrong because business organizations and consumers depend on them for credit, but in exchange for this protection they should refrain from risky practices such as proprietary trading and sponsoring hedge funds. The new law, however, allows banks to invest up to 3 percent of their capital in hedge funds or private-equity funds but does not explain how this rule will be enforced and does not create a firm line between commercial and investment banking.[140]

The bill was 2,300 pages in length, but despite this length some critics called it a shell bill leaving most of the critical details of enforcement to unelected regulators. Thus there is no way to tell at the moment how far these regulators will penetrate into the market. As stated by the *Wall Street Journal*, "The rule-making possibilities are endless." Others were skeptical that more regulation would prevent another financial meltdown, pointing out that the SEC and FDIC did not do their job in stopping banks from feeding off what they called a "speculative mortgage frenzy."[141] Thus whether the new law will be effective or not depends on who is appointed to do the regulating and only time will tell how all this turns out and if another financial Armageddon will be prevented.[142]

16 Management and an Ethic of Service

The scientific worldview was very much operative in the financial Armageddon described in the previous chapter. Government officials and financial executives alike came to believe in the quantitative models that were used by financial institutions and thought these models allowed these institutions to measure and control the risk they were taking on so that the system was deemed safe and beyond crashing. That this was a misplaced belief is now all too evident, but at the time it seemed a reasonable approach and was part and parcel of the worldview that prevailed with respect to financial activities. Quantitative models gave investors and financial institutions a sense of certainty and confidence they knew what they were doing.

Yet these models were no better than the assumptions that went into their creation. With respect to the financial house of cards that had been built regarding housing, these assumptions included the belief, and it was a belief not a certainty, that housing prices would continue to increase with no end in sight, that even if a downturn happened it would be limited to only one or a few regions of the country and would not be nationwide, and that the mortgages underlying collaterlizeddebt obligations were not correlated, i.e., that while some of the mortgages within the tranche might go bad they would not all go bad at the same time and the good ones would keep the CDO a viable investment. All of these assumptions were wrong and came back to haunt all those involved—from the homeowner who saw housing prices decline to the point where the mortgage was greater than the value of the house to the financial firms whose stockpile of CDOs became relatively worthless.

Years and years of quantitative education in business schools had convinced its graduates that good business judgments are based on quantitative measures and that this alone is enough to make sound business judgments. Things like intuition, imagination, emotion, experience, and all the other aspects that go into decisions are relegated to the sidelines as factors that are not important enough and too fuzzy to consider. Stephen Marglin calls this algorithmic knowledge, which became the dominant way of thinking about economic issues in our society and in making business decisions. Yet he argues that the uncertainty inherent in most business decisions forces decision makers to rely on other forms of knowledge that do not involve rational calculation and maximizing behavior.

> Contrary to the economic conception of knowledge, my assertion is that under conditions of uncertainty, decision makers do not and cannot mobilize the apparatus of calculation and maximization. Without something to peg probabilities on, individuals necessarily fall back on quite different methods—on intuition, conventional behavior, authority—in short, on a different *system of knowledge* from that which drives maximizing behavior. This is a system of knowledge that is embedded in community, in the nexus of relationships that bind people to one another.[1]

The author goes on to say that business knowledge is largely experiential knowledge that is necessarily embedded in community While algorithmic knowledge is held to be universal and applicable to all times and places, experience is contextual and closely allied to time and place. It is by its very nature specialized and reveals itself only through practice and exists for a particular purpose and is geared to creation and discovery rather than to falsification and verification. Within experiential knowledge "one knows with and through one's hand and heart as well as with one's head."[2] However, the notion that real knowledge resides in algorithmic knowledge and that knowledge of experience is trustworthy only insofar as it is validated by algorithm has undermined the knowledge of experience to the point that it has lost value with regard to business decision making as well as in society as a whole.[3]

What would it take to change this scientific view of management and management education and develop a view that is less tied to science and incorporates other aspects of experience that are important to management decision making? Referring again to the Bennis and O'Toole article mentioned in the introduction, which forms the basis of this book, it is argued there that to change the dominant scientific paradigm in business schools would require a view of management as a profession. Management is not an academic discipline like the traditional sciences but is a profession. The scientific model that is currently dominant should be replaced by a model that is more appropriate to the requirements of a profession.

In my previous book I traced the implications of viewing management as a profession and argued to treat management as a profession would involve no less than a rethinking of capitalism, which I argued was based on a philosophy of individualism and rights.[4] This philosophy would have to be broadened to include community and responsibility for management to become a true profession. In this book I have tried to show how the scientific worldview contributes to and is intertwined with this traditional philosophy of capitalism, and that a different view of science is necessary to change this view of capitalism and the role of the corporation in society. This has implications for management and business-school education that are similar to what I developed in my previous book. This book simply looks at these implications from a different perspective.

MANAGEMENT

The corporate system is currently geared toward making a profit and maximizing shareholder wealth. Nothing else really matters, including corporate social responsibility, ethics, ecology, or any other subject not directly related to the central objective of meeting the financial goals of the organization. Once in the corporation one has to play the game to get ahead, and the game consists of meeting financial goals, not being socially or environmentally responsible or making a contribution to society. This view of the corporation informs business-school education as well. As Rakesh Khurana states in his insightful book on business-school education: "Notions of sustained effort to build companies that create useful products and services, provide employment, and contribute to their communities are less and less a part of the aspirations American business school students." [5]

The emergence of management as an identifiable function within the corporation was congruent with the rise of the modern corporation. These enterprises grew in size and complexity by combining the various stages of production within a single industrial establishment. The integration and synchronization of these stages allowed output to be controlled and managed in a manner that was not possible in an economy composed of many smaller enterprises. Thus the economy changed after the Civil War from one composed mostly of small organizations in competition with each other to one dominated by the large corporations we see in today's economy that operate in a different kind of competitive environment.

The management of this kind of organization involves a great many administrative tasks, such as directing the labor force, organizing the production process, defining procedures to get the work done, and numerous tasks of this nature. The performance of these tasks fell to an emerging function within the corporation called management that was not identified as either labor or capital, but that over time came to control the modern corporation. This managerial class did not derive its legitimacy from ownership of stock, but from its ability to administer and coordinate the tasks that needed to be done in large and complex organizations. It took over the authority that entrepreneurs had who may have started the business and from the owners of the corporation who had certain property rights. Managers controlled the corporation and called the shots and their authority within the corporation was unquestioned. Their legitimacy, however, was always in question, and the argument that they derived their authority from stockholders through the board of directors was largely fictional.

This legitimacy question continued to haunt management because they needed to find some basis for the authority they exercised over the use of corporate resources. One of the ways this was attempted, according to Khurana, was the establishment of business schools within the American university. The primary purpose of these schools at their inception, according to Khurana, "was to legitimate and institutionalize the new occupation of management."[6] The achievement of this purpose was attempted by presenting management as an emerging profession like the traditional professions of medicine and law and thus dedicated to serve the broader interests of society rather than the more narrowly defined interests of either capital or labor.

Khurana calls this effort to establish business as a subject of professional education the professionalization project and was at the center of concerns for business schools for several decades.[7] This professionalization project, however, began to be abandoned after the end of World War II and was accelerated with the publication of the Gordon and Howell and Pierson reports, funded by Ford Foundation and Carnegie Foundation, respectively, both of which were extremely critical of business-school education as being too vocationally oriented and consequently lacking academic respectability. These reports argued that management had become more of a science with the development of decision-making tools during the war years and provided generous funding to promote reforms of teaching and research along these lines.[8]

These efforts were based on the notion of a science-based professionalism, but this notion contained a contradiction that eventually led to the demise of the professionalization project. For if management is truly a science that can be reduced to a set of fundamental scientific principles, what need is there for management to be viewed as any kind of a profession with broader responsibilities to society? Typical of this view is a book by Oliver Sheldon entitled *The Philosophy of Management*, in which he argued that the aim of those who are practicing the management profession should be to develop a "Science of Industrial Management" which would involve the development of standards to guide managerial practice that can be determined by the analytical and synthetical methods of science.[9]

What finally ended the professionalization project for good was the emergence of what Khurana calls investor capitalism as a replacement for managerial capitalism. Managers were seen as standing in the way of the efficient operation of competitive markets and were accused of mismanaging corporate assets. Takeovers were justified on this basis and to ward off hostile takeovers managers had to improve performance of their companies by divesting themselves of unrelated businesses, cutting out layers of middle management, outsourcing noncore functions, downsizing, and other measures to improve their economic situation. Loyalty to workers, products, communities, and the like went out the door because the only thing that mattered was the creation of shareholder value.

According to Khurana, the rise of agency theory supported this change to investor capitalism and ended any concern about the professionalization of management. Agency theory holds that managers serve merely as agents of shareholders and are bound to manage corporate assets in their interests. They were in a sense nothing more than hired hands (hence the title of the book) and had no permanent responsibilities to any collective interests such as society. Agency theory is clearly based on an atomistic view of reality and does not incorporate any notion of a collective responsibility, but instead views managers as discrete individuals dissociated from one another that have no responsibilities to any collective entity including the organization itself. The organization is simply a nexus of contracts among individuals with no sense of community. Such a view is opposed to any notion of professionalization.

> The promise that business schools would socialize managers into a culture of professionalism—thereby legitimating managerial authority in the face of competing claims to corporate control from the socially disruptive forces of capital and labor—. . . gave rise to the university business school in the first place. The autonomy and authority of professional managers would be rooted not only in expert knowledge but in their obligation not to represent the interests of either owners or workers—much less of themselves—but to see that the corporation contributed to the general welfare. Agency theorists, however, dismiss any such framing of managerial work as tenderhearted do-gooding. Agency theory also excludes from consideration any notion of collective identity—a fundamental attribute of professions in any sociological framing of the phenomenon—let alone collective responsibility. On the contrary, it frames managerial agents as distinct and dissociated from one another, defining an organization as simply a nexus of contracts among individual agents.[10]

Khurana goes on to say that managers were thus cut loose from any moorings to the organizations they led and to the communities in which these organizations were embedded. In the final analysis, they were cut loose from shareholders themselves as shareholders were unable to prevent these managers from taking a greater and greater share of corporate wealth to enrich themselves at the expense of shareholders and other employees of the corporation regardless of their performance. It also opened the door to a series of corporate scandals involving misstatement of earnings, backdated stock options, and a host of other malpractices in a number of companies, all of which undermined public trust in the integrity and fairness of the capitalistic system.

Managers have become loose individuals who do not feel constrained by any social values such as fairness or equity and have no allegiance to anyone else but themselves. When relationships are anchored only in utilitarian self-interest they can play fast and loose with other individuals in relationships that involve trust and responsibility. This attitude was certainly present in the financial meltdown because financial executives felt no responsibility to anyone but themselves and did whatever was necessary to keep making money for themselves and their companies. They felt no responsibility to others or the society as a whole, which depended on a viable financial system to keep the economy growing.

AN ETHIC OF SERVICE

To counter these trends, Khurana advocates reviving the notion of professionalism as it applies to management, as professions are a vital part of the economic and social order, and when they are compromised or corrupted society is harmed. However, the problem with a professional model for business, as was stated by William A. Levi in a most perceptive article on business ethics, is the conflict between the professional demand for service and the exclusively business demand for profits.[11] The true professional is committed to serve his or her client, and while profits are necessary for lawyers and doctors to continue to serve their clients, profits are not the overriding objective as they are for business. The businessman has to keep his eye on the reward and the overriding objective of business is to make a profit and maximize shareholder wealth. Whatever goods business produces or services business provides are secondary to this objective. Levi thinks this is largely a matter of emphasis, a kind of mentality that pervades the business community; it is not necessarily a function of the capitalistic system itself.

Levi did not seem too optimistic that a change in this mentality would ever take place because it would go against the way Western civilization thinks of business activity and would require a rethinking of the purpose of business as well as society. It is not just business that has this kind of mentality; it is pervasive throughout the entire society. As Levi states, the ethical behavior of any segment within society is generally not without roots in the more general aspiration of that society as a whole.[12] The notion that wealth is primarily if not exclusively economic in nature is widely shared in Western industrialized societies. The creation and acquisition of material wealth are what these societies are all about and money is what an acquisitive society values above everything else.

Money can be counted, it is quantifiable, and it is therefore considered to be a measure of economic wealth. Individuals and households can determine how much they are worth and what income they have to support themselves. Assets can be evaluated in terms of money and added up to determine economic wealth. The nation as a whole adds up the goods and services that are produced in the entire economy to determine if the economy is growing and getting richer in terms of economic wealth. Money is the measure of all things good and bad and is used as an indicator to determine how well the economy is doing.

Business managers are, of course, a part of this money-oriented society and it is not surprising that they should seek profits as the overriding goal of their organization. Money is the measure of their success and the success of the organization. Profits are taken to be an indicator of how well the company has contributed to the well-being of society even if those profits come at the expense of people's health and the environment. If a company is profitable it is generally taken that the organization has performed a useful role in society and is given society's blessing to continue in existence. It is believed to have served the public good. But profits in themselves are not necessarily the problem; it is the profit motive that must be given consideration and looked at more closely.

What is the difference, for example, between a for-profit and not-for-profit organization? The latter has to make a profit of some kind or at least have more income than expenses to continue in existence. The difference, then, has to be whatever motivates people in the organization. Managers of a for-profit organization are motivated by the desire for profit while managers of not-for-profit organizations are supposedly motivated by other objectives. But isn't it time we grew out of this idea that profits are what motivate managers to use resources efficiently which results in the best outcome for society? The financial crisis should put to rest this idea and enable us to see beyond this self-serving motive. Managers who work only to increase the profits of the organization and maximize their own incomes are cutting themselves off from more rewarding and satisfying goals related to doing something that goes beyond mere profit making.

To be a profession in the true sense of the word, management must put profits in a broader context, and recognize that their major objective is to *serve* all the clients of the organization, not just the stockholders.[13] This broader perspective includes the people who consume their products, who work for it, and who depend on it for various things in the community. Serving the clients' interests also involves giving consideration to the moral, economic, political, cultural, and natural environments in which these clients live. To be part of a profession, managers must change their focus to one of putting service to the client foremost in their decisions. If they do this and produce products that truly enhance people's lives and provide good jobs for their employees with adequate wages and are concerned about their impact on the environments in which people live, profits will follow in a society that keeps money in its proper perspective.

Business, then, has multiple clients, which is actually no different from the traditional professions. Hospitals and doctors have patients to satisfy as well as the many nurses and clerical personnel that work for them. Private hospitals also have stockholders to satisfy. Lawyers have clients to keep happy as well as staff. Every decision they make will affect all of these clients to some degree. Management must then be concerned with producing goods and services that are going to better the lives of consumers and provide them with enriching experiences, with providing its employees with meaningful experiences and the opportunity to grow and develop as human beings during the time they spend working for the corporation, and in providing stockholders with an ample return on their investment. It is not a matter of balancing these various interests against each other, but of giving all of them attention at the same time. They are all part of the same holistic nexus and these interests are tied together in seeking a better life with more enriching experiences. This is what an *ethic of service* is all about.

THE PROFESSIONALIZATION OF BUSINESS SCHOOLS

What would it take for the professionalization project to be revived in business schools? Currently the business-school curriculum reflects all the characteristics of a scientific worldview, as the stated or unstated purpose of most courses is still the maximization of shareholder wealth despite many years of social responsibility, ethics, and stakeholder management. There has been no significant change in the economic, social, and moral philosophy that informs the courses that are taught in the traditional business school. Even business ethics, to the extent that it is based on the "good ethics is good business" idea, reflects this traditional philosophy. The goal of most ethics courses is to promote the making of profits in an ethical manner, but when push comes to shove, the bottom line takes precedence and the creation of economic wealth remains the paramount goal of the corporation.

If management is no longer considered to be a profession and managers are nothing more than hired hands, then in what sense can business and management schools be considered professional schools at the same level as schools of law and medicine? Have they become nothing more than highly sophisticated trade schools to prepare students for careers in organizations whose sole purpose is to create wealth for themselves as agents and for shareholders as principals?[14] Is one of the primary purposes of gaining a business-school education to develop a social network that can give access to a job in one of the top companies in the country if not the world? Is the MBA program more like an exclusive fraternity or country club that gives students an advantage in the labor market, as Khurana suggests?

> If academic credentialing and providing a social network are now the primary functions of business schools, then the role of the institution is that of a gatekeeper rather than a transmitter of knowledge and values . . . a student invests in higher education simply to purchase a signal that is received by prospective employers as an indication of the likelihood that he or she is committed to a business career and will perform productively.[15]

If business schools are nothing more than sophisticated vocational schools, then what on earth are they doing in a university setting? The university is supposedly dedicated to the search for knowledge for its own sake, not for the sake of profit, and educates people so they can become better citizens, not so they can make more money for themselves. If universities want a business school because it is a cash cow, i.e., it brings in a lot of money, then they may have sold their soul in the process and have become just another commercial enterprise that trains its students for some utilitarian purpose.[16] The goals of a university and the goals of a business school can only be aligned if business schools are training true professionals to perform a service in society.

The place to begin this alignment would seem to be in the business schools themselves where business-school students are trained and enculturated. Change has to start somewhere, it will not happen by magic, and the educational process is one place where students can be encouraged to think differently about their lives and occupation and adopt values that they come to believe will lead to a more fulfilling and enriching life for themselves and society. Reviving the notion of management as a profession that makes managers the primary link between the narrow concerns of business and the broader concerns of society is seen by Khurana to be essential for business schools to gain respectability within the university and regain a sense of mission and purpose that goes beyond that of a trade school.

> If university business schools . . . are to continue to play any role in the education of managers that could not be filled equally well by corporate training programs or for-profit, purely vocational business schools, they belong in the forefront of the discussions now taking place among informed and thoughtful citizens all around the globe about the shape that capitalism should take in the twenty-first century.[17]

To effect this change and regain a sense of professionalism, business schools must change their worldview. According to Giacalone and Thompson, "We teach students to perpetuate business' importance and its centrality in society, to do so by increasing wealth, and to assume that by advancing organizational interests, they advance their own and society's overall best interests."[18] According to these authors the corporation must be decentered and placed in the context of society at large. Business exists to serve society and enhance the well-being of the members of that society; the society does not exist to serve business and its interests. This entails the adoption of a different worldview on the part of business schools, which tend to think of the business organization as being at the core of the universe.[19]

This idea that society and all its elements exist to serve corporate interests has to change in order for business to be seen as a profession. Managers of these organizations have to broaden their perspective to think of society in their decisions and how the corporation can enhance the well-being of society's members in ways that involve more considerations than just the creation of economic wealth. Economic wealth is something of an illusion and a fiction and merely reflects the value society places on economic entities. Business must serve a wider spectrum of values and interests than just economic ones and this broader perspective must be considered when managers formulate business policies and practices.

What would have to change to reflect a different worldview is not so much a matter of content but is rather a matter of emphasis.[20] The rationale or objective of courses would have to be restated and taught with a different focus. An ethic of service would have to permeate the entire curriculum. For example, marketing courses would have to focus on how products could be sold in such a way as to focus on consumer satisfaction and take into account the interest of consumers of bettering their lives rather than an exclusive focus on how the consumer can be persuaded to purchase the company's products so that a profit can be made for the company. Advertising would have to focus on providing the consumer with the information needed to make an informed decision that will work to make lives better rather than trying to manipulate the consumer to buy things he or she may not want or need in order to better the company.

Likewise, strategy courses would have to focus on how the company can do better things to enhance the entire society rather than focus on how to beat the competition and attain a greater market share. Finance courses would focus on using financial resources efficiently and effectively in bettering society rather than on maximization of shareholder wealth. Organizational-behavior courses would have to be concerned with providing experiences in the workplace that enhance workers lives rather than on how to make them more productive. And accounting courses would have to broaden their perspective to focus on accounting for the use of society's resources as whole, not just on financial concerns, and develop means for reporting on the use of human and physical resources in a meaningful and accurate manner that could be audited in the way financial information is audited.[21]

Other courses that are not now a part of most business schools could be added, such as a course in science and technology to give business students a better understanding of how science works and the importance of technological concerns in decision making. An important course would be one that deals with ecology and environmental concerns to provide an understanding of the way in which nature is connected with human well-being and how corporate activities affect the environment. While liberal arts courses are important to broaden a student's perspective, these kinds of courses would show the relevance of science and technology and the environment to business concerns. While ethics should be a part of every course where appropriate, a separate course that focuses on conflicts of interest, fraud and deception, and other strictly ethical issues is a necessity.[22]

The final course to be added, if it is not already in the curriculum, is a leadership course that should come in the final semester. This course could focus on the qualities of leadership and stress how leadership is different from just managing a corporate organization. It could look at how leaders in business, politics, and other areas have used their power to effect change in the organization and society. The most important project in this course would be to require a paper that would make students articulate their philosophy of management. Every student in an MBA program graduates with some kind of philosophical understanding of management, but in most cases this is unarticulated. This project could serve as kind of a capstone to the entire MBA experience and would give students the opportunity to reflect on their business education and set down on paper what it all means. This could be the most important project in the entire curriculum.

Such a curriculum would most likely have little appeal to MBA students who are currently in the program or to faculty currently teaching who see maximization of shareholder wealth as the overriding objective of business organizations and profits as their major responsibility. But over time such a curriculum could appeal to different people who have an interest in serving society and devoting their lives to something more than just making profits for the organization in which they spend the majority of their lives and thereby gaining more power and economic wealth for themselves. This curriculum should have an appeal to more socially minded students who want to do something more fulfilling for themselves and recognize that their well-being is tied up with the well-being of society as a whole.

The change to an ethic of service in business-school education could not be more important. We are at one of those times in our nation's history when change seems to be inevitable. The financial and economic crisis brought about by defaulting on subprime loans has resulted in an unprecedented involvement of government in bailing out financial institutions and taking an ownership interest in private companies. Unregulated capitalism is being questioned and a new administration has pressed for new regulations on the financial industry in particular and the economy in general. The era of free-market capitalism seems to be over and something else is emerging and what that something is may not be in the best interests of the society as a whole.

Since the election of Ronald Reagan we have been in an era of bashing government and praising the virtues of the free market. There was an emphasis on deregulation, particularly of the financial markets, and Wall Street went wild as private enterprise is prone to do when completely unregulated. Many oppose a new regulatory effort, but something needs to be done to prevent such upheavals in the future. The question is whether an ethic of service and the changes in thinking about capitalism it involves represents a viable alternative to increased government involvement or whether it is hopelessly utopian. The answer to this question has important implications for the future of our society and the future of capitalism.

Notes

NOTES TO THE INTRODUCTION

1. Rogene A. Buchholz, *Rethinking Capitalism: Community and Responsibility in Business* (New York: Routledge, 2009).
2. Warren G. Bennis and James O'Toole, "How Business Schools Lost Their Way," *Harvard Business Review*, 83 (2005): 96–104.
3. Kelley Holland, "Is It Time to Retrain B-Schools? *New York Times*, March 15, 2009, BU1. In response to this last criticism, there has been some effort to professionalize management to make it more like law and medicine with the development of a code of conduct, a certification examination, and continuing education. The dean of Thunderbird's School of Global Management, Angel Cabrera, has been working with the United Nations Global Compact, which promotes standards for worldwide business practices, and has led a task force to develop a set of "Principles for Responsible Management Education" that are said to follow a similar philosophy. Thus far about 200 business schools worldwide, including Thunderbird, have adopted them, although there is considerable skepticism that these principles will have a major impact on business-school education. Ibid., BU2. For a statement of these principles, see *ISBEE Newsletter*, March 2009, 8. For other assessments of business-school education, see "Issue of the Week: Rethinking Business Education," The Week, June 12, 2009, 46; and Roger Martin, "What We Learned from the Crash," *Bloomberg Businessweek*, November 15–21, 2010, 82.

NOTES TO CHAPTER 1

1. David Filkin, *Stephen Hawking's Universe: The Cosmos Explained* (New York: Basic Books, 1997), 26–27. "Ptolemy's model of the universe was founded on Aristotle's dictates, coupled with what the Alexandrian knew about the actual behavior of the heavenly bodies based on years of careful observation. A troubling conundrum that he had to explain was 'retrograde motion'—the concept that the wandering stars during their annual rotation around the earth appeared to stop and then actually go in reverse before stopping again and then resuming their proper course. Ptolemy cleverly solved this mystery. In his conception, the planets revolved around the earth by being attached to one of two spheres. Each planet had two spheres. The main sphere, the one that had the earth at its center, was called the 'deferent.' The second, smaller sphere, to which the planet was attached, was called the 'epicycle.' The epicycle revolved around a point on the deferent. So the

construct was a sphere whose center was on the edge of a much larger sphere: Picture (in two dimensions) a tambourine and one of the round cymbals attached to it; the perimeter of the tambourine is the deferent, and the small cymbal is the epicycle." There were other complications as well that had to be addressed. Since it was observed that the earth was not quite the center of the universe, Ptolemy created a point near the earth called the "eccentric," which was the center of all the planetary deferents. The planets did not move at a consistent and uniform speed either, necessitating the creation of another point called the "equant" (equalizing point), on the other side of the eccentric, which was the point around which the planets revolved at a consistent and uniform speed. The complexity and cumbersomeness of this model should be apparent. Jack Repcheck, *Copernicus' Secret: How the Scientific Revolution Began* (New York: Simon & Schuster, 2007), 14–15.

2. In a memorandum that Copernicus drafted sometime before 1514, he states, "Yet the planetary theories of Ptolemy and most other astronomers, although consistent with the numerical data, seemed likewise to present no small difficulty. For these theories were not adequate unless certain equants were also conceived; it then appeared that a planet moved with uniform velocity neither on its deferent (main orbit) nor about the center of its epicycle (second orbit). Hence a system of this sort seemed neither sufficiently absolute nor sufficiently pleasing to the mind. Having become aware of these defects, I often considered whether their could perhaps be found a more reasonable arrangement of circles, from which every apparent inequality would be derived and in which everything would move uniformly about its proper center, as the rule of absolute motion requires." Repcheck, *Copernicus' Secret*, 54. "The great success of Ptolemy's model represented both the best and worst of ancient Greek science. On the positive side, the model gained acceptance because if made predictions that agreed reasonably well with reality, and insistence on such agreement remains at the heart of modern science today. On the negative side, the model was so convoluted that it's unlikely that anyone, including Ptolemy himself, thought it represented the true nature of the cosmos. Indeed, the model was not even fully self-consistent, as different mathematical tricks needed to be used to calculate the positions of the different planets. Today, these negatives would weigh so heavily against any scientific idea that people would go immediately back to the drawing board in search of something that worked better. But in Ptolemy's time, these negatives were apparently acceptable, and it was another 1,500 years before they were revisited." Jeffrey Bennett, *Beyond UFOs: The Search for Extraterrestrial Life and Its Astonishing Implications for Our Future* (Princeton, NJ: Princeton University Press, 2008), 31.

3. See Thomas S. Kuhn, *The Structure of Scientific Revolutions*, 3rd ed. (Chicago: University of Chicago Press, 1996), for his view of how scientific revolutions and paradigm shifts take place.

4. Copernicus's magnum opus, *On the Revolutions*, was published as he was dying. There is reason to believe that a copy of the publication arrived at his house the last day of his life, so that he saw it before he died. See Repcheck, *Copernicus' Secret*, 167, 171.

5. Ibid., 194.

6. Filkin, *Stephen Hawking's Universe*, 38–47.

7. See Thomas S. Kuhn, *The Copernican Revolution: Planetary Astronomy in the Development of Western Thought*, revised edition (New York: MJF Books, 1985).

8. Ibid., 2.

9. Steven Shapin, *The Scientific Revolution* (Chicago: University of Chicago Press, 1996), 13.

10. Ibid., 85.
11. Ibid., 92.
12. Ibid., 105.
13. Timothy Ferris, *The Science of Liberty: Democracy, Reason, and the Laws of Nature* (New York: HarperCollins, 2010), 4.
14. Shapin, *The Scientific Revolution*, 116.
15. Ibid., 159. Italics in original.
16. Ibid., 159–161. Descartes postulated that this connection took place in the pineal gland, a small organ located in the middle of the brain. This gland was supposedly well adapted to transfer movements from the body to the mind and from the mind to the body. This explanation, however, proved to be unsatisfactory.
17. See Lucretius, "Does Neuroscience Refute Ethics?" *Mises Daily Article*, August 24, 2005, 1–7; Sharon Begley, "The Biology of Love—Not," *Newsweek*, February 18, 2008, 53; Jeffrey Kluger, "Why We Love," *Time*, January 28, 2008, 55–60; Carl Zimmer, "Romance Is an Illusion," *Time*, January 28, 2008, 98–99; Paul J. Zak, "The Neurobiology of Trust," *Scientific American*, June 2008, 88–95; and Christof Koch and Susan Greenfield, "How Does Consciousness Happen?" *Scientific American*, October 2007, 76–83.
18. Shapin, *The Scientific Revolution*, 36.
19. ". . . a universe whose essential characteristic is fixed order and connection has no place for unique and individual existences, no place for novelty and genuine change and growth." John Dewey, *The Quest for Certainty* (New York: Capricorn Books, 1960), 209.
20. "The rise of new science in the seventeenth century laid hold upon the general culture in the next century. Its popular effect was not great, but its influence upon the intellectual elite, even upon those who were not themselves engaged in scientific inquiry, was prodigious. The enlightenment . . . testified to the widespread belief that at last light had dawned, that dissipation of the darkness of ignorance, superstition, and bigotry was at hand, and the triumph of reason was assured—for reason was the counterpart in man of the laws of nature science was disclosing." John Dewey, "Time and Individuality," in *The Later Works, 1925–1953*, Vol. 14, ed. Jo Ann Boydston (Carbondale and Edwardsville, IL: Southern Illinois University Press, 1988), 100.
21. Matthew Fox and Rupert Sheldrake, *Natural Grace: Dialogues on Creation, Darkness, and the Soul in Spirituality and Science* (New York: Doubleday, 1997), 15–19.
22. Sandra Rosenthal, "Reductionism," *The Encyclopedia of Business Ethics and Society*, ed. Robert W. Kolb (Thousands Oaks, CA: Sage Publications, Inc., 2008), 1784–1785.
23. Ibid.
24. By the time this book is published, the Large Hadron Collider, located at CERN, is likely to be operational. With the energies produced by this collider, scientists hope to discover new particles, including the elusive Higgs particle, which is thought to provide mass for other particles. See "The Future of Physics," *Scientific American*, February 2008, 38–53; Joel Achenbach, "At the Heart of All Matter: The Hunt for the God Particle," *National Geographic*, March 2008, 90–105.
25. Charles Barber, "The Brain: A Mindless Obsession," *The Wilson Quarterly*, 32 (Winter 2008), 42. Some research questions whether there is such a thing as free will that drives our behavior or whether we are actually mechanistic creatures and what we claim to be self-aware consciousness is actually an illusion. Studies have shown that our unconscious brains are active in influencing our decisions milliseconds before a subject made what he or she

thought was a "spontaneous" decision. See "Health & Science: Is Free Will a Myth?" *The Week*, May 2, 2008, 19.

26. Paul Oppenheim and Hilary Putnam, "Unity of Science as a Working Hypothesis," in Janet A Kourany, ed., *Scientific Knowledge*, 2nd ed. (Belmont, CA: Wadsworth Publishing Co., 1998), 270.

27. Ibid., 271.

28. Ibid., 269.

29. "Atomism," *Catholic Encyclopedia*, ed. Kevin Knight, http://www.newadvent.org/cathen/02053a.htm (accessed August 23, 2008).

30. John Dewey, "Time and Individuality," 103. See also John Dewey, *The Quest for Certainty*, 188–120.

31. Zeno's paradox involves getting from one place to another. For example, to get from where you are to the nearest door, you first have to cover half the distance. Then you have to cover half the remaining distance and so on ad infinitum, meaning you never can reach the door because you will always have an ever-decreasing infinitesimal distance that remains to be covered. Yet in experience we do reach the door, so this phenomena is simply the result of breaking space into discrete elements that can't be put back together into some continuous whole.

32. Christopher Dawson, *Progress and Religion: An Historical Inquiry* (London: Sheed & Ward, 1929), 219.

33. John Dewey, *The Quest for Certainty*, 201–202.

34. Carl Hofer, "Causal Determinism," *Stanford Encyclopedia of Philosophy*, http://plato.stanford.edu/entries/determinsim-causal/ (accessed July 9, 2008).

35. John Dewey, *The Quest for Certainty*, 231–232.

36. Charles Flowers, *A Science Odyssey: 100 Years of Discovery* (New York: William Morrow and Company, 1998), 27–29.

37. See Charis Anastopoulos, *Particle or Wave: The Evolution of the Concept of Matter in Modern Physics* (Princeton, NJ: Princeton University Press, 2008).

38. See Henry J. Folse, *The Philosophy of Niels Bohr: The Framework of Complementarity* (Amsterdam: North-Holland, 1985), for a philosophical treatment of Bohr's attempt to reconcile wave-particle duality with his theory of complementarity.

39. Flowers, *A Science Odyssey*, 29–30.

40. Werner Heisenberg, *Physics and Philosophy: The Revolution in Modern Science* (New York: Harper Perennial, 1958), 32.

41. Anastopoulos, *Particle or Wave*, 186.

42. Flowers, *A Science Odyssey*, 31–33.

43. John Dewey, *The Quest for Certainty*, 208.

44. Ibid., 24.

45. Frank Capra, *The Web of Life: A New Scientific Understanding of Living Systems* (New York: Anchor Doubleday, 1996), 31.

46. Fox and Sheldrake, *Natural Grace*, 15–19.

47. Roger Lewin, *Complexity: Life at the Edge of Chaos* (Chicago: University of Chicago Press, 1999), x.

48. Ibid., 21.

49. Edward Lorenz, who developed chaos theory, died in 2008. His paper, entitled "Predictability: Does the Flap of a Butterfly's Wings in Brazil Set Off a Tornado in Texas?" published in 1972, became one of the most referenced scientific papers in modern history. When he received the Kyoto Prize for earth and planetary sciences in 1991, the committee said he had "brought about one of the most dramatic changes in mankind's view of nature since Sir

Isaac Newton." See "Obituaries: The Meteorologist Who Formulated Chaos Theory," *The Week*, May 2, 2008, 35.
50. Ibid., 23–24.
51. For example, Capra argues that conventional social science is based on an outdated mechanistic paradigm of natural science that calls for objective analysis of discrete building blocks to aid in the erection of conceptual frameworks that allow for prediction and control of natural and social phenomena. See Capra, *The Web of Life*, 30.
52. Fox and Sheldrake, *Natural Grace*, 20.
53. Ibid., 26.

NOTES TO CHAPTER 2

1. Jeremy Bentham, *Introduction to the Principles of Morals and Legislation*, ed. W. Harrison (Oxford: Oxford University Press, 1948).
2. John Stuart Mill, *Utilitarianism*, ed. Oskar Piest (Indianapolis: Bobbs-Merrill, 1957). What is being presented here is the "standard" interpretation of Bentham and Mill. It has been argued that Bentham did not ignore the fact-value distinction but had a very sophisticated theory of how moral judgments could be made that is grounded in his theory of language. For details, see Ross Harrison, *Bentham* (London: Routledge and Kegan Paul, 1984). Also there is a large body of literature on the question of whether Mill's famous "proof" in Chapter II of *Utilitarianism* does in fact fail in attempting to derive the ought from the is. Moore's charge that Mill commits a fallacy has been challenged. This chapter, however, is not the place to discuss various scholarly defenses of either Bentham or Mill but rather to take them, as well as other scholars to be discussed, in terms of the general understandings of their positions which dominate the renderings they receive in the literature.
3. David Hume, *Essays Moral, Political, and Literary* (London: Longmans, Green & Co., 1875); *A Treatise of Human Nature* (Oxford: Clarendon Press, 1896).
4. G. E. Moore, *Principia Ethica* (Cambridge, UK: Cambridge University Press, 1903).
5. A. J. Ayer, *Language, Truth and Logic*, 2nd ed. (New York: Dover Publications, 1936).
6. Sandra Rosenthal, "Fact-Value Distinction," in Robert Kolb, ed., *Encyclopedia of Business Ethics and Society* (Thousand Oaks, CA: Sage Publications, 2008), 848–851.
7. Those who hold to a source of knowledge other than sense experience can maintain a general type of distinction between facts and values without falling into relativism, for this other source of knowledge provides awareness of the "ought." Kant's position makes moral duty or obligation expressed in prescriptive or ought claims totally independent of our desires and totally devoid of any reference to facts, especially the facts of human nature and its inclinations. The categorical imperative is a prescriptive statement that Kant regards as a moral law by which all reason must be bound because it is self-evidently and universally true for all human beings in all circumstances. The source of morality, according to Kant, is reason, not empirical observation. See Immanuel Kant, *Foundations of the Metaphysics of Morals*, trans. L. W. Beck (Indianapolis: Bobbs-Merrill Company, 1959). But what is self-evident to Kant is not necessarily self-evident to another person, let alone to all human beings.
8. For a fuller description of these two approaches, see Linda K. Trevino and Gary R. Weaver, "Business ETHICS/BUSINESS Ethics: One Field or Two?", *Business Ethics Quarterly*, 4 (1994): 113–128.

9. Gary R. Weaver and Linda K. Trevino, "Normative and Empirical Business Ethics: Separation, Marriage of Convenience, or Marriage of Necessity?", *Business Ethics Quarterly*, 4, (1994): 129–143.
10. Diane L. Swanson, "Toward an Integrative Theory of Business and Society: A Research Strategy for Corporate Social Performance," *Academy of Management Review*, 24 (1999): 506–521.
11. B. Victor and C. W. Stephens, "Business: A Synthesis of Normative Philosophy and Empirical Social Science," *Business Ethics Quarterly*, 4 (1994): 145–155.
12. Thomas Donaldson and Thomas Dunfee, "Toward a Unified Conception of Business Ethics: Integrative Social Contracts Theory," *Academy of Management Review*, 19 (1994): 252–284. See Thomas Donaldson and Thomas W. Dunfee, *Ties That Bind: A Social Contracts Approach to Business Ethics* (Boston: Harvard Business School Press, 1999) for a fuller development of their approach.
13. Tom Donaldson and Patricia Werhane, *Ethical Issues in Business: A Philosophical Approach*, 4th ed. (Englewood Cliffs, NJ: Prentice Hall, 1993), 17. Italics mine.
14. Manuel Velasquez, *Business Ethics: Concepts and Cases* (Englewood Cliffs, NJ: Prentice Hall, 1992), 104–106. Italics mine. Other books note the same problem. John R. Boatright, for example, states: "The difference between theories should not lead us to despair of resolving ethical issues or to conclude that one resolution is as good as another. Nor should we be discouraged by the fact that agreement on complex ethical issues is seldom achieved. Unanimity in ethics is an unreasonable expectation. The best we can do is to analyze the issues as fully as possible, which means getting straight on the facts and achieving definitional clarity, then to develop the strongest and most complete arguments we can for what we consider to be the correct conclusions." John R. Boatright, *Ethics and the Conduct of Business* (Englewood Cliffs, NJ: Prentice Hall, 1993), 25.
15. J. B. Callicott, "The Case Against Moral Pluralism," *Environmental Ethics*, 12 (1990): 115.
16. Dennis Collins and Thomas O'Rourke, *Ethical Dilemmas in Business* (Cincinnati: Southwestern, 1994).
17. See John Rawls, *A Theory of Justice* (Cambridge: Harvard University Press, 1971).
18. John Dewey, *The Quest for Certainty: A Study of the Relation between Knowledge and Action* (New York: Capricorn Books, 1960), 40–41
19. Ibid., 53.

NOTES TO CHAPTER 3

1. Adam Smith, *The Wealth of Nations* (New York: Modern Library, 1937), 423.
2. "For Smith, the promotion of national wealth through the market was a goal worthy of the attention of moral philosophers because of its place in his larger moral vision. Smith valued commercial society not only for the wealth it produced but also for the character it fostered. He valued the market in part because it promoted the development of cooperative modes of behavior, making men more gentle because more self-controlled, more likely to subordinate their potentially asocial passions to the needs of others. In his own way, *The Wealth of Nations*, like Smith's *The Theory of Moral Sentiments* (1759), was intended to make men better, not just better off." Jerry

Z. Mueller, *The Mind and the Market: Capitalism in Modern European Thought* (New York: Knopf, 2002), 52.

3. Justin Fox, writing in *Time*, claims that the reason the invisible hand emerged as the one idea from Smith's work that everyone remembers is because it is so simple and powerful. "If the invisible hand of the market can be relied on at all times and in all places to deliver the most prosperous and just society possible, then we'd be idiots not to get out of the way and let it work its magic. Plus, the supply-meets-demand straightforwardness of the invisible-hand metaphor lends itself to mathematical treatment, and math is the language in which economists communicate with one another." Justin Fox, "What Would Adam Smith Say?" *Time*, April 5, 2010, 18.

4. Richard Bronk, *Progress and the Invisible Hand* (London: Warner Books, 1998), 90.

5. Adam Smith, *The Theory of Moral Sentiments* (New Rochelle, NY: Arlington House, 1969), 265–266.

6. Bronk, *Progress and the Invisible Hand* , 7

7. Julie A. Nelson, *Economics for Humans* (Chicago: University of Chicago Press, 2006), 22.

8. Thomas Michael Power, "Trapped in Consumption: Modern Social Structure and the Entrenchment of the Device," ed. Eric Higgs, Andrew Light, and David Strong, *Technology and the Good Life* (Chicago: University of Chicago Press, 2000), 271–293.

9. See Karl Polayni, *The Great Transformation* (Boston: Beacon Press, 1944).

10. Bob Goudzwaard, *Capitalism and Progress: A Diagnosis of Western Society* (Toronto: Wedge Publishing Foundation and Grand Rapids, MI: William B. Erdmans Publishing Co., 1979), 214.

11. There are many criticisms of using economic indicators to measure the well-being of the nation. See Jon Gertner, "The Rise and Fall of the G.D.P.," *The New York Times Magazine*, May 16, 2010, 60–71; and Megan McArdle, "Misleading Indicator," *The Atlantic*, November, 2009, 36–38.

12. The European Union created a market to control carbon dioxide emissions in 2005 by establishing a cap and issuing tradable allowances based on this cap. At the time of writing, Congress was considering seven proposals to set up a similar program in this country. See Bret Schulte, "Putting a Price on Pollution," *U.S. News & World Report*, May 14, 2007, 37–39.

13. United States Environmental Protection Agency, *Environmental Progress and Challenges: EPA's Update* (Washington, DC: U.S. Government Printing Office, 1988), 28.

14. United States Environmental Protection Agency, Office of Air and Radiation, *The Plain English Guide to the Clean Air Act* (Washington, DC: EPA, 1993), 15.

15. "Pollution Swap," *Time*, May 25, 1992, 22.

16. Jeffrey Taylor, "CBOT Plan for Pollution-Rights Market Is Encountering Plenty of Competition," *Wall Street Journal*, August 24, 1993, A8.

17. United States Environmental Protection Agency, Acid Rain Program 2003 Progress Report, *Clean Air Markets—Progress and Results*, 2005, www.epa.gov. (accessed September 11, 2008).

18. See T. H. Watkins, "The Worth of the Earth," *Audubon*, September–October 1997, 128; Donella H. Meadows, "How Much Is Nature Worth?" *Business Ethics*, 11 (July/August, 1997): 7.

19. Watkins, "The Worth of the Earth," 128.

20. Ibid.

21. Robert Nadeau, "The Economist Has No Clothes," *Scientific American*, April 2008, 42.

22. See David Michaels, *Doubt Is Their Product: How Industry's Assault on Science Threatens Your Health* (New York: Oxford University Press, 2007); Chris Mooney, *The Republican War on Science* (New York: Basic Books, 2005).
23. Robert C. Solomon, *Ethics and Excellence: Cooperation and Integrity in Business* (New York: Oxford University Press, 1993), 149.
24. Neil W. Chamberlain, *The Limits of Corporate Responsibility* (New York: Basic Books, 1973), 4, 6.
25. William C. Frederick, one of the founders of the field of business and society and a leading proponent of corporate social responsibility, concludes the following: "This much we can conclude about the social responsibility movement in the United States: both external and internal advocates of corporate social action have been, and remain, highly constrained in what can be accomplished through the corporate structure. Corporate philanthropy, while part of a life support system for many important community activities, cannot begin to serve many of the community's most urgent social needs. Corporate social responsiveness appears mainly as a defensive tactic utilized by an elite group of socially aware companies; it is not generally perceived or treated as a broad-scale societal strategy capable of leading humanity to a resolution of its most severe problems." William C. Frederick, *Corporation, Be Good!: The Story of Corporate Social Responsibility* (Indianapolis, IN: Dog Ear Publishing, 2006), 62.
26. Archie B. Carroll, *Business & Society: Ethics and Stakeholder Management* (Cincinnati: Southwestern, 1996), 74.
27. Andrew C. Wicks, Dan R. Gilbert, and R. Edward Freeman, "Feminist Reinterpretation of the Stakeholder Concept," *Business Ethics Quarterly*, 4 (October 1994): 479.
28. See Melvin Anshen, *Managing the Socially Responsible Corporation* (New York: Macmillan, 1974).
29. See Milton Freidman, "The Social Responsibility of Business Is to Increase Its Profits," *New York Times Magazine*, September 13, 1970, 122–126.
30. Committee for Economic Development, *Social Responsibilities of Business Corporations* (New York: CED, 1971), 12.
31. See Thomas Donaldson, *Corporations & Morality* (Englewood Cliffs, NJ: Prentice Hall, 1982); Thomas Donaldson, *The Ethics of International Business* (New York: Oxford University Press, 1989).

NOTES TO CHAPTER 4

1. *The Basic Works of Aristotle*, ed. Richard McKeon (New York: The Modern Library, 2001), 1127.
2. Alasdair MacIntyre, "Is Patriotism a Virtue?" Lindley Lecture (Lawrence, KS: University of Kansas, 1984), 19–20.
3. John Hospers, *Libertarianism* (Los Angeles: Nash, 1971), 4–5.
4. Amitai Etzioni, *The Moral Dimension: Toward a New Economics* (New York: The Free Press, 1988), 5.
5. Michael J. Sandel, *Democracy's Discontent: America in Search of a Public Philosophy* (Cambridge, MA: Belknap Press, 1996), 3–4.
6. Ibid., 4. Michael Lerner makes the same point in the following quote: "A just society, according to liberalism, does not seek to promote any substantive aims of its own, but rather enables its citizens to pursue their own ends. Rather than having goals that it wants to implement, the liberal state refuses to choose in advance among competing purposes that exist in society. The

highest value for the liberal state is to promote the individual's right to pursue his or her own wants and desires, unimpeded by others. These rights ought not to be sacrificed for the sake of the general good . . . By giving highest priority to individual choice, liberals have seemed to suggest that there could be no possible basis for an objective ethical standard from which that choice could flow. Moreover, liberals have seemed to suggest that the welfare of the individual must always take precedence when making judgments or facing difficult choices." Michael Lerner, *The Politics of Meaning: Restoring Hope and Possibility in an Age of Cynicism* (Reading, MA: Addison-Wesley, 1996), 92–93. It should me mentioned that both Sandel and Lerner are using liberalism in its classical sense, not in its modern sense as being identified with government solutions to social and economic problems as opposed to conservative market solutions.

7. Ibid., 5.
8. Ibid., 8.
9. Ibid., 6.
10. See Robert B. Reich, "Everyday Corruption: The Policy-Making Process Has Become an Extension of the Market Battlefield," *The American Prospect*, July/August, 2010, 25.
11. Lerner, *The Politics of Meaning*, 17.
12. See Joe Klein, "Democracy's Discontent: The Debate over Health Reform Is a Case Study of How Special Interests Trump the Common Good," *Time*, August 10, 2009, 34–35.
13. *The Basic Works of Aristotle*, 1185.
14. Jeffrey D. Sachs, "Flying Blind in Policy Reforms: Health Care, Climate Change, and Other Complex Topics Demand More Expert and Public Debate," *Scientific American*, May 2010, 32. See also Ryan Lizza, "As the World Burns," *The New Yorker*, October 11, 2010, 70–83, for the story of what happened to climate-change legislation.
15. See David Bohm, *Wholeness and the Implicate Order* (London: Routledge & Kegan Paul, 1980).
16. John Locke, *Two Treatises of Government* (Cambridge: Cambridge University Press, 1988).
17. Kenneth Minogue, "The History of the Idea of Human Rights," in Walter Laqueur and Barry Rubin, eds., *The Human Rights Reader* (Philadelphia: Temple University Press, 1979), 14–15.
18. Richard Bronk, *Progress and the Invisible Hand* (London: Warner Books, 1998), 59.
19. Nicholas Lemann, "Conflict of Interests," *The New Yorker*, August 11 & 18, 2008, 86–92.
20. Barack Obama focused on lobbying on his first day in office by issuing an executive order to restrain lobbyists after the scandals of the Bush administration. This order stated that if you had been a registered lobbyist in the past two years you could not work for the administration on any issue in which you were involved. Also, after you left government you couldn't lobby the administration at all unless a special waiver was obtained from the White House budget director. These rules, however, created problems of their own by placing limits on legitimate advocacy. See Jacob Weisberg, "All Lobbyists Are Not Created Equal," *Newsweek*, April 27, 2009, 35.
21. Michael Tomasky, "Washington: Will the Lobbyists Win?" *The New York Review*, April 9, 2009, 20.
22. Steven Brill, "On Sale: Your Government. Why Lobbying Is Washington's Best Bargain," *Time*, July 12, 2010, 29–35. Goldman Sachs alone, which was charged with civil fraud for some of its practices during the financial

meltdown, spent $1.2 million on lobbying during the first three months of 2010, which amounted to a 72 percent increase over the same period of time the previous year. The firm also hired two former influential senators to lobby Congress on its behalf. "Noted," *The Week*, May 7, 2010, 18.

23. Ciara Torres-Spelliscy, "Spending on Politics? Tell Shareholders," *Business Week*, November 2, 2009, 80.

24. Dan Eggen, "PACs Gone Wild: New Groups Up Ante," *The Denver Post*, September 28, 2010, 9A. The article points out that one such PAC, American Crossroads, which was founded with the help of Karl Rove, who was an influential adviser in the George W. Bush administration, spent more than half of this money. American Financial Group, a publicly held company, donated $400,000 to this group. Another source claims that these PACs spent $98 million between September 1 and October 17, 2010, on House and Senate races. The great majority of this money was spent supporting Republican candidates. Jonathan D. Salant and Kristin Jensen, "The Many Ties That Bind GOP Fundraisers," *Bloomberg Businessweek*, October 25–October 31, 2010, 34–38.

25. Ciara Torres-Spelliscy, writing in *Business Week,* argues that US securities laws should be rewritten to protect shareholder interests because they do not necessarily profit from a corporation's political donations. She cites a study that showed corporate political expenditures were typically linked with lower shareholder value. The study suggested that these donations were based, at least in part, on the political preferences of managers and not on what might benefit the business. See Ciara Torres-Spelliscy, "Spending on Politics?"

26. See Robert G. Kaiser, *So Damm Much Money: The Triumph of Lobbying and the Corrosion of American Government* (New York: Knopf, 2010).

NOTES TO CHAPTER 5

1. Michael Lerner, *The Politics of Meaning: Restoring Hope and Possibility in an Age of Cynicism* (Reading, MA: Addison-Wesley, 1996), 35.

2. Max Weber, *The Protestant Ethic and the Spirit of Capitalism* (New York: Charles Scribner's Sons, 1958).

3. Ibid., 35–40.

4. David C. McCelland, *The Achieving Society* (New York: Free Press, 1961), 48.

5. Richard LaPiere, *The Freudian Ethic* (New York: Duell, Sloan and Pearce, 1959), 16.

6. Gerhard W. Ditz, "The Protestant Ethic and the Market Economy," *Kyklos*, 33 (1980): 626–627.

7. Bob Goudzwaard, *Capitalism & Progress: A Diagnosis of Western Society* (Toronto, Canada: Wedge Publishing Foundation; Grand Rapids, MI: William B. Eerdmans Publishing Co., 1979), 61. In a related passage, Michael Lerner states: "A materialist worldview emerged that validated only that which could be experienced by the senses. And in place of any ethical concerns of the community, this new social order insisted that the ultimate reality was the pleasure and satisfaction of each individual. The lone individual became the center of the universe, and if we built families and communities, it was only because the lone individual had found it in his or her interest to do so. All connections between human beings hereafter would be based on contract: free individuals choosing to make a connection with others. The sole goal of the state, in this scheme, was to ensure that there was a realm

of free contracts in which no one would interfere." Lerner, *The Politics of Meaning*, 37.

8. John Gilchrist, *The Church and Economic Activity in the Middle Ages* (London: Macmillan, 1969), 123. Protestantism, as an institution, could never exercise the kind of control and domination over secular forces as did the medieval Catholic Church. The nature of the Protestant principle did not allow for this kind of control. The revolution it introduced encouraged political and economic forces to establish their own ground and authority. The challenge the Protestant movement presented the Catholic Church in questioning its claim to universal and eternal truth, and the revolutionary philosophy that informed it, did not allow Protestantism to then turn around and exercise the same kind of domination and control in the nature of a universal authority. Protestantism as an institution and a movement could not exercise a universal constructive approach to the ordering of life and still be true to the critical principles that informed its emergence. Economic forces had to be given their own course and develop secular sources of meaning and purpose. See Richard Niebuhr, *The Kingdom of God in America* (New York: Harper and Row, 1937), 28–30.

9. Goudzwaard, *Capitalism & Progress*, 22.

10. Christopher Lasch, *The Culture of Narcissism: American Life in an Age of Diminishing Expectations* (New York: Norton, 1978), 52–53.

11. The University of Michigan Survey Research Center asked 1,533 working people to rank various aspects of work in order of importance. Good pay came in a distant fifth behind interesting work, enough help and equipment to get the job done, enough information to do the job, and enough authority to do the job. See "Work Ethic," *Time,* October 30, 1972, 97. See also *Editorial Research Reports on the American Work Ethic* (Washington, DC: *Congressional Quarterly*, 1973); Harold L. Sheppard and Neal Q. Herrick, *Where Have All the Robots Gone* (New York: The Free Press, 1972); Special Task Force to the Secretary of Health, Education, and Welfare, *Work in America* (Cambridge, MA: MIT Press, 1973); and Judson Gooding, *The Job Revolution* (New York: Walker & Co., 1972).

12. Clyde Kluckhohn, "Have There Been Discernible Shifts in American Values During the Past Generation?" *The American Style: Essays in Value and Performance*, ed. Elting E. Morrison (New York: Harper & Bros., 1958), 207.

13. Ibid., 184.

14. Ibid., 207

15. Ibid., 192.

16. Daniel Bell, *The Cultural Contradictions of Capitalism* (New York: Basic Books, 1976), 70.

17. Ibid., 21.

18. Ibid., 64–65.

19. Ibid.,71–72.

20. Ibid.,75.

21. Lasch, *The Culture of Narcissism*, 53.

22. Ibid.

23. Ibid., 68–69.

24. Robert H. Tawney, *Religion and the Rise of Capitalism* (Gloucester, MA: P. Smith, 1962), 228–229.

25. Clarence E. Ayres, *Toward a Reasonable Society* (Austin: University of Texas Press, 1961), 280.

26. Donella H. Meadows, Dennis L. Meadows, Jorgen Randers, and William W. Behrens, III, *The Limits to Growth: A Report for the Club of Rome's Project on the Predicament of Mankind* (New York: Universe Books, 1972).

27. Mihajlo D. Mesarovic, *Mankind at the Turning Point: The Second Report to the Club of Rome* (New York: Dutton, 1974).
28. William C. Clark, "Managing Planet Earth," *Scientific American*, September 1989, 48.
29. Alan Durning, *How Much Is Enough?* (New York: W.W. Norton, 1992), 13.
30. Ibid., 25.
31. Goudzwaard, *Capitalism and Progress*, 66.
32. Ibid., 137.
33. Zygmunt Bauman, *Does Ethics Have a Chance in a World of Consumers?* (Cambridge, MA: Harvard University Press, 2008), 148–149.
34. Ibid., 169–170.
35. Michael Lerner made the following observation: "Every aspect of our personal lives is decisively shaped by the deprivation of meaning. Alienation at work and the absence of opportunities to serve the common good, an economy that rewards selfishness and materialism while encouraging us to think of others as objects for manipulation and control, and a society that preaches looking out for number one, all contribute to the dissolution of relationships and ethical values in civil society and in private life. The triumph of mechanistic thinking and the de-spiritualization of daily life further intensify our hunger for meaning and our vulnerability to substitute forms of gratification." Lerner, *The Politics of Meaning*, 86.
36. See Theodor Adorno and Max Horkheimer, "The Concept of Enlightenment," in *Critical Theory: The Essential Readings*, ed. David Ingram and Julia Simon-Ingram (St. Paul, MN: Paragon House, 1991), 49–56; and Theodor Adorno and Max Horkheimer, "The Culture Industry: Enlightenment as Mass Deception," in Theodor Adorno and Max Horkheimer, *Dialectic of Enlightenment*, trans. John Cumming (New York: Continuum, 1990), 120–167. Most of the material for this section on instrumental reason was taken from Axel Honneth, "The Turn to the Philosophy of History in the Dialectic of Enlightenment: A Critique of the Domination of Nature," in Axel Honneth, *The Critique of Power*, trans. Kenneth Baynes (Cambridge, MA: MIT Press, 1991), 32–56.

NOTES TO CHAPTER 6

1. Jim McNeill, "Strategies for Sustainable Economic Development," *Scientific American*, September 1990, 155.
2. Robert A. Forsch and Nicholas E. Gallopoulos, "Strategies for Manufacturing," *Scientific American*, September 1990, 144.
3. Erik Assadourian, "The Rise and Fall of Consumer Cultures," *The State of the World 2010: Transforming Cultures* (New York: W.W. Norton, 2010), 4.
4. McNeill, "Strategies for Sustainable Development," 156. " If the global economy grows at 3 percent a year, it will expand from an output of $29 trillion in 1997 to $57 trillion in 2020, nearly doubling. It will then more than double again by the year 2050, reaching $138 trillion. Yet even in reaching $29 trillion, the economy has already overrun many or the Earth's natural capacities." Lester R. Brown and Jennifer Mitchell, "Building a New Economy," *State of the World 1998* (New York: W.W. Norton & Company, 1998), 168.
5. Ibid., 155–156.
6. Lester R. Brown, Christopher Flavin, and Sandra Postel, "Outlining a Global Action Plan," *State of the World 1990* (New York: W.W. Norton & Company, 1990), 173–174.
7. Ibid., 174–175.
8. McNeill, "Strategies for Sustainable Development," 156.

9. Ibid., 157.
10. Ibid.
11. Ibid., 158–163.
12. Bill McKibben, *The End of Nature* (New York: Random House, 1989).
13. Roderick Frazier Nash, *The Rights of Nature: A History of Environmental Ethics* (Madison, WI: University of Wisconsin Press, 1989), 125.
14. Peter Singer, "The Place of Nonhumans in Environmental Issues," in *Moral Issues in Business*, 4th ed., William Shaw and Vincent Barry, eds. (Belmont, CA: Wadsworth, 1989), 471.
15. Ibid., 74.
16. Nash, *The Rights of Nature*, 140–141.
17. Ibid., 126.
18. Christopher D. Stone, "Should Trees Have Standing?—Toward Legal Rights for Natural Objects," in *Moral Issues in Business*, 4th ed., William Shaw and Vincent Barry, eds. (Belmont, CA: Wadsworth, 1989), 475–479.
19. Nash, *The Rights of Nature*, 128–129. Oftentimes, rights given to animals are used as surrogates to protect other aspects of nature that are not given moral consideration. For example, the Endangered Species Act gives rights to species that are threatened with extinction. In the controversy over the spotted owl, which took place in the northwest part of the United States, the rights given to the owl when it was placed on the endangered species list were used to prevent logging of old-growth forests. Protecting the species means protecting its habitat. The same thing may be happening with regard to the polar bear in the Arctic region. Placing it on the endangered species list may be a way to force the US government to deal with climate change in order to protect the bear's habitat.
20. Kenneth E. Goodpaster, "From Egoism to Environmentalism," *Ethics and Problems of the 21st Century*, in Kenneth E, Goodpaster and K. M. Sayer, eds. (Notre Dame, IN: University of Notre Dame Press, 1979), 21–33.
21. Nash, *The Rights of Nature*, 152.
22. Ibid., 153.
23. Ibid., 160.
24. Holmes Ralston III, "Just Environmental Business," in *Just Business: New Introductory Essays in Business Ethics*, Tom Regan, ed. (New York: Random House, 1984), 325–343.
25. Holmes Ralston III, *Philosophy Gone Wild: Essays in Environmental Ethics* (Buffalo, NY: Prometheus Books, 1987), 121.
26. Ibid., 141.
27. Ibid., 103–104.
28. Sara Ebenreck, "An Earth Care Ethics," *The Catholic World: Caring for the Endangered Earth*, 233 (July/August 1990): 156.
29. Nash, *The Rights of Nature*, 10.
30. Ibid., 150.

NOTES TO CHAPTER 7

1. Maurice Merleau-Ponty, *The World of Perception*, trans. Oliver Davis (New York: Routledge, 2008), 43.
2. John Dewey, *The Quest for Certainty* (New York: Capricorn Books, 1929), 221.
3. John Dewey, "Time and Individuality," *The Later Works*, Vol. 14, 1939–1944, ed. Jo Ann Boydston (Carbondale and Edwardsville, IL: Southern Illinois University Press, 1988), 105.

4. Steven Shapin, *The Scientific Revolution* (Chicago: University of Chicago Press, 1996), 53.
5. John Dewey, "Theories of Knowledge," *The Middle Works*, Vol. 9, 1916, ed. Jo Ann Boydston (Carbondale and Edwardsville, IL: Southern Illinois University Press, 1980), 344.
6. See Stephen Hawking and Leonard Mlodinow, "The (Elusive) Theory of Everything," *Scientific American*, October 2010, 69–71.
7. Larry Hickman, for example, argues that Dewey's thinking represents advances beyond the positions taken by some of the authors who are commonly identified as postmodernists. He identifies some of the problems postmodernism leaves unresolved and shows how Dewey had already dealt with them in his writings. In this sense Dewey is a post-postmodernist and will be waiting for them when they reach the end of the road they are traveling. See Larry Hickman, *Pragmatism as Post-Postmodernism* (New York: Fordham University Press, 2007), 13–14.
8. Sandra B. Rosenthal, *Speculative Pragmatism* (LaSalle, IL: Open Court, 1986), 2–5.
9. Ibid., 8.
10. Social-science research based on statistical analysis presents particular problems given the many choices that have to be made relevant to how the research is conducted. Given the different ways such research can be conducted, it is inevitable that the conclusions that are based on this research will be different on any given issue. There is no such thing as the "definitive" study in most of these areas because scientific procedures are so different in these instances. No one procedure can be defended as the "correct" one to use with respect to a given study. Granted some procedures are better than others, but no single procedure can be taken as definitive so that its results are the last word in the matter. Thus different scientists come to different conclusions with respect to the issue under investigation.

Researchers, in fact, may not want to have a definitive study because that would close off an area of research to further study and possible funding. In the area of management and its social and ethical responsibilities, for example, countless studies have been done trying to find some kind of link between the social performance of companies or their ethical behavior and some measure of economic performance. In performing these studies there is the problem of defining social or ethical performance and operationalizing this variable so it can be quantified and measured in some fashion. And choosing a measure of economic performance is not straightforward either, as stock market performance, profits, return on equity, or other measures can be used for this purpose.

Nonetheless, numerous studies have been done on this issue, and as might be expected, different conclusions have been reached. Some studies have shown a negative relationship between social or ethical performance and economic performance, some have shown no relationship, and others have shown a positive relationship. No single study can be taken as definitive, however, so the area remains open for further research. Thus there will be more studies of this nature appearing in management journals where the researcher will review the existing studies, which gets to be more and more of an arduous task, point out the deficiencies of these studies from the researcher's point of view, and then go on to perform a new study that the researcher will claim is superior to the others. If the study is well done and receives favorable reviews, it will get published in a journal to be referred to at some later time by another researcher interested in the same topic.

11. Hickman, *Pragmatism as Post-Postmodernism*, 118–119.
12. Stephen A. Marglin, *The Dismal Science: How Thinking Like an Economist Undermines Community* (Cambridge, MA: Harvard University Press, 2008), 132–134. This last statement has implications for the case method of instruction. It is difficult to draw generalizations form a particular case that are relevant to other situations. One must be careful about doing this because other situations take place in a different context. Nonetheless, one can learn how to approach situations and analyze them that may be useful in other situations.
13. Hickman, *Pragmatism as Post-Postmodernism*, 216.
14. Ibid., 193.
15. George Herbert Mead, *The Philosophy of the Present* (La Salle, IL: Open Court, 1959), 98.
16. It has been argued elsewhere that the positions of the five major American pragmatists form a systematic and unified movement. See Sandra Rosenthal, *Speculative Pragmatism* (Amherst, MA: University of Massachusetts Press, 1986); paperback edition (Peru, IL: Open Court, 1990).
17. Hickman, *Pragmatism as Post-Postmodernism*, 95–196, 257, n7.
18. See George Herbert Mead, "The Definition of the Physical," *Mead: Selected Writings*, ed., A. J. Reck (New York: Bobbs-Merrill Co., 1964); John Dewey, "Experience and Nature," *The Later Works*, Vol. 1, ed. Jo Ann Boydston (Carbondale and Edwardsville, IL: Southern Illinois University Press, 1981).
19. See William James, "The Principles of Psychology," *The Works of William James*, Vol. 2, ed. Frederick Burkhardt (Cambridge: Harvard University Press, 1981), 1232–1234; John Dewey, "The Quest for Certainty," *The Later Works*, Vol. 4, ed. Jo Ann Boydston (Carbondale and Edwardsville, IL: University of Southern Illinois Press, 1984), 163–165.
20. Rosenthal, *Speculative Pragmatism*, 12–13.
21. John Dewey, "The Quest for Certainty," *The Later Works*, ed. Jo Ann Boydston (Carbondale and Edwardsville, IL: Southern Illinois University Press, 1984), 163.
22. Rosenthal, *Speculative Pragmatism*, 11.
23. James, "The Principles of Psychology," 1232–1234.
24. Linda Simon, *Dark Light: Electricity and Anxiety from the Telegraph to the X-Ray* (New York: Harcourt, Inc., 2004), 199.
25. James, "The Principles of Psychology," 961.
26. Charles Peirce, *Collected Papers*, Vol. 7, ed. Arthur Burks (Cambridge: Harvard University Press, 1958), 7.498.
27. Charles Peirce, *Collected Papers*, Vol. 5, eds. Charles Hartshorne and Paul Weiss (Cambridge: Belknap Press of Harvard University, 1931–1935), 5.384.
28. Rosenthal, *Speculative Pragmatism*, 14.
29. See John Dewey, "The Seat of Intellectual Authority," *The Middle Works*, Vol. 4, ed. Jo Ann Boydston (Carbondale and Edwardsville, IL: Southern Illinois University Press, 1984), 137–138; John Dewey, *Essays in Experimental Logic* (New York: Dover Publications, 1916), 86; George Herbert Mead, *Philosophy of the Act* (Chicago: University of Chicago Press, 1938), 251; and C. I. Lewis, *Mind and the World Order* (New York: Dover Publications, 1929), 395–397.
30. Rosenthal, *Speculative Pragmatism*, 15.
31. John Dewey, "The Objectivism-Subjectivism of Modern Philosophy," *The Later Works*, Vol. 14, 1939–1941, ed. Jo Ann Boydston (Carbondale and Edwardsville, IL: Southern Illinois University Press, 1988), 196.
32. Rosenthal, *Speculative Pragmatism*, 15.

33. George Herbert Mead, "The Definition of the Psychical," *Mead: Selected Writings*, ed. A. J. Reck (New York: Bobbs-Merrill Co., 1964), 34; George Herbert Mead, *Philosophy of the Act* (Chicago: University of Chicago Press, 1938), 32.

34. John Dewey, "Experience and Nature," *The Later Works*, Vol. 1, 1925, ed. Jo Ann Boydston (Carbondale and Edwardsville, IL: Southern Illinois University Press, 1981), 37.

35. Peirce, *Collected Papers*, 3.527.

36. C. I. Lewis, "Replies to My Critics," *The Philosophy of C. I. Lewis*, ed. P. A. Schilpp, Library of Living Philosophers Series (La Salle, IL: Open Court, 1968), 660.

37. Charles Peirce, Microfilm edition of the Peirce Papers, Sect. 647, 8.

38. Hickman, *Pragmatism as Post-Postmodernism*, 39.

39. Ibid., 159.

40. Lee Smolin, "Cosmological Evolution" and "Loop Quantum Gravity," in John Brockman, ed., *Science at the Edge* (New York: Sterling Publishing Co., Inc., 2008), 156–157, 426.

41. John Dewey, "The Crisis in Culture," *The Later Works*, Vol. 5, 1929–1930, ed Jo Ann Boydston (Carbondale and Edwardsville, IL: Southern Illinois University Press, 1984), 107.

42. Robert B. Laughlin, *A Different Universe: Reinventing Physics from the Bottom Down* (New York: Basic Books, 2005), 208–209.

43. Ibid., 31.

44. John D. Barrow, *New Theories of Everything* (New York: Oxford University Press, 2007), 163.

45. The relationship of nonlinear thinking to holism is captured in the following quote: "Thus, if a situation is linear or dominated by influences that are linear, it will be possible to piece together a picture of its whole behavior by examining it in small pieces. The whole will be composed of the sum of its parts ... The output of a linear operation varies steadily and smoothly with any change in its input. Non-linear problems are none of these things. They amplify errors so rapidly that an infinitesimal uncertainty in the present state of the system can render any future prediction of its state worthless after a very short period of time. Their outputs respond in discontinuous and unpredictable ways to very small changes in their inputs. Particular local behaviors cannot be added together to build up a global one: a holistic approach is required in which the system is considered as a whole." See Ibid., 225.

46. "Reductionism virtually destroys the meaningful wholes associated with our traditional understanding of humans and the world in which they live. For example, religion is reducible to some nonreligious origin such as the human psyche, human drives, or brain constitution. Human action as purposive or goal-oriented activity by which we relate to the meaningful world in which we live is reduced to neurophysiological behavior, with humans becoming nothing more than the object as studied by various disciplines such as physiology, neurology, anatomy, behavioral psychology, and so forth. Human values that direct action and the course of cultural development become identified with physiological or psychological drives and needs. Mental activity is reduced to biological or computational functions; mental phenomena are nothing more that neurophysiological functions. Human freedom is but a myth, with human actions governed by the laws of physiology, and with enough information, human actions could be predicted. At its extreme, physical objects themselves become nothing more than experienced sensations in

our brain. In sum, the concrete fullness of humans and the qualitatively rich, value-laden, goal-directed contexts in which they have their being are all ultimately identical with, or reducible to, the systems of mathematical physics and physiology . . ." Sandra Rosenthal, "Reductionism," *Encyclopedia of Business Ethics and Society*, Vol. 4, ed. Robert W. Kolb (Thousand Oaks, CA: Sage Publications, 2008), 1784–1785.

47. "Holism," http://abyss.uoregon.edu/~js/glossary/holism.html, accessed August 23, 2008.

48. Charis Anastopoulos, *Particle or Wave: The Evolution of the Concept of Matter in Modern Physics* (Princeton, NJ: Princeton University Press, 2008), 341.

49. John Dewey, "Democracy and Education," *The Middle Works*, Vol. 9, 1916, ed. Jo Ann Boydston (Carbondale and Edwardsville, IL: University of Southern Illinois Press, 1980), 4–5.

50. The qualities of objects did pose a problem for the rise of modern science. Scientific descriptions and definitions are framed in terms that made the qualities of objects superfluous. Science penetrated into the inner being of objects and the existence of qualities like colors, sounds, texture, etc., was a problem. What status did these qualities have in a scientific view of nature? The usual way of dealing with them is to consider these qualities as merely subjective, existing only in the consciousness of individuals. They thus have no objective status. See John Dewey, "Essays: I Believe," *The Later Works*, Vol. 14, 1942–1948, ed. Jo Ann Boydston (Carbondale and Edwardsville, IL: University of Southern Illinois Press, 1988), 105.

51. John Dewey, "Essays: Has Philosophy a Future?" *The Later Works*, Vol. 16, 1949–1952, ed. Jo Ann Boydston (Carbondale and Edwardsville, IL: Southern Illinois University Press, 1989), 370–371.

52. John Dewey, "Qualitative Thought," *The Later Works*, Vol. 5, 1925–1930, ed. Jo Ann Boydston (Carbondale and Edwardsville, IL: Southern Illinois University Press, 1984), 251.

53. Barrow, *New Theories of Everything*, 63–65.

54. Ibid., 66.

55. John Dewey, "Essays: Inquiry and Indeterminateness of Situations," *The Later Works*, Vol. 15, 1942–1948, ed. Jo Ann Boydston (Edwardsville and Carbondale, IL: Southern Illinois University Press, 1989), 39.

56. John Dewey, "The Naturalization of Intelligence," *The Later Works*, Vol. 4, 1929, ed. Jo Ann Boydston, (Carbondale and Edwardsville, IL: Southern Illinois University Press, 1984), 167.

57. Ibid., 166.

58. Ibid., 165. Italics in original.

59. Dewey has this to say about the idea of universal laws. "It displaced once for all the notion of a world in which the unaccountable and the mysterious have the first and last word, a world in which they constantly insert themselves. It established the ideal of regularity and uniformity in place of the casual and sporadic. It gave men inspiration and guidance in seeking for uniformities and constancies where only irregular diversity was experienced. The ideal extended itself from the inanimate world to the animate and then to social affairs. It became, it may fairly be said, the great article of faith in the creed of scientific men." Ibid., 166.

60. Ibid., 168.

61. Ibid., 162–163.

62. Ibid., 163.

63. Hickman, *Pragmatism as Post-Postmodernism*, 53.

64. Ibid., 140.

NOTES TO CHAPTER 8

1. John Dewey, *The Quest for Certainty: A Study of the Relation between Knowledge and Action* (New York: Capricorn Books, 1960), 255.
2. Steven Shapin, *The Scientific Revolution* (Chicago: University of Chicago Press, 1996), 162.
3. "Scientific inquiry seems to tell us one thing, and traditional beliefs about ends and ideals that have authority over conduct tell us something quite different. The problem of reconciliation arises and persists for one reason only. As long as notions persist that knowledge is a disclosure of reality, of reality prior to and independent of knowing, and that knowing is independent of a purpose to control the quality of experienced objects, the failure of natural science to disclose significant values in its objects will come as a shock. Those seriously concerned with the validity and authority of value will have a problem on their hands . . . If they are forbidden to find standards in the course of experience they will seek them somewhere else, if not in revelation, then in the deliverance of a reason that is above experience." Dewey, *The Quest for Certainty*, 44.
4. Larry A. Hickman, *Pragmatism as Post-Postmodernism: Lessons from John Dewey* (New York: Fordham University Press, 2007), 157.
5. William C. Frederick questions the validity of this dichotomy between fact and value or normative and empirical business ethics. The suggestion is made that all of the authors who debate this dichotomy accept as fact that this distinction is valid as a descriptive category. In other words, this distinction is posited as a real one that then needs to be discussed. They overlook the possibility that they have posed a false dichotomy. What such distinctions may represent is merely a sociocultural reality and an institutional history. See William C. Frederick, "Are SIM and Business Ethics Different Fields?" Paper presented at a joint session of the Society for Business Ethics and Social Issues in Management Division of the Academy of Management, Dallas, Texas, August 14, 1994, 2.
6. "Scientists often refer to universal statements—or rather to what is expressed by such statements—as 'facts'. They forget that the word *fact* was originally applied (and we shall apply it exclusively in this sense) to singular, particular occurrences . . . Facts are particular events . . . When we us the word *fact* we will mean it in the singular sense in order to distinguish it from universal statements. Such universal statements will be called 'laws' . . . science begins with direct observations of single facts. Nothing else is observable. Certainly regularity is not directly observable. It is only when many observations are compared with one another that regularities are discovered. These regularities are expressed by statements called 'laws.' " Rudolf Carnap, "The Confirmation of Laws and Theories," ed. Janet A. Kourany, *Scientific Knowledge: Basic Issues in the Philosophy of Science*, 2nd ed. (Belmont, CA: Wadsworth Publishing Company, 1998), 165–166.
7. Thomas S. Kuhn, *The Structure of Scientific Revolutions*, 3rd ed. (Chicago: University of Chicago Press, 1996).
8. Hickman, *Pragmatism as Post-Postmodernism*, 139.
9. Patricia H. Werhane, "The Normative/Descriptive Distinction in Methodologies of Business Ethics," *Business Ethics Quarterly*, 4 (April 1994): 175–179.
10. William C. Frederick, "The Virtual Reality of Fact vs. Value: A Symposium Commentary," *Business Ethics Quarterly*, 4 (April 1994): 171–173.
11. William James, "A Pluralistic Universe," in *The Works of William James*, ed. Frederick Burkhardt (Cambridge: Harvard University Press, 1975), 131.
12. See John Dewey, "The Quest for Certainty," in *The Later Works*, Vol. 4, 1925–1953, ed. Jo Ann Boydston (Carbondale and Edwardsville, IL: University of Southern Illinois Press, 1984), for an in-depth discussion of this issue.

13. "If the physical terms by which natural science deals with the world are supposed to constitute that world, it follows as a matter of course that qualities we experience and which are the distinctive things in human life, fall outside of nature. Since some of these qualities are the traits that give purpose and value, it is not surprising that many thinkers are dissatisfied with thinking of them as *merely* subjective; nor that they have found in traditional religious beliefs and in some elements of the classic philosophical tradition means by which these traits can be used to substantiate the being of a reality higher than nature, one qualified by the purpose and value that are extruded from natural existence." John Dewey, "The Supremacy of Method," in *The Later Works*, Vol. 4, 1929, ed. Jo Ann Boydston (Carbondale and Edwardsville, IL: Southern Illinois University Press, 1984), 186.

14. Sandra B. Rosenthal, *Speculative Pragmatism* (La Salle, IL: Open Court, 1990), 174.

15. Hickman, *Pragmatism as Post-Postmodernism*, 174.

16. Rosenthal, *Speculative Pragmatism*, 191.

17. Hickman, *Pragmatism as Post-Postmodernism*, 166.

18. Rosenthal, *Speculative Pragmatism*, 176–177.

19. Mead stresses that the life process is such that it must "confer its characteristics within its whole field of operation." George Herbert Mead, *The Philosophy of the Present* (La Salle, IL: Open Court, 1959), 36.

20. Hickman, *Pragmatism as Post-Postmodernism*, 45.

21. Rosenthal, *Speculative Pragmatism*, 175.

22. John Dewey, "Ethics," in *The Middle Works*, Vol. 5, 1899–1924, ed. Jo Ann Boydston (Carbondale and Edwardsville, IL: University of Southern Illinois Press, 1978), 173.

23. John Dewey, "Reconstruction in Philosophy," in *The Middle Works*, Vol. 12, 1899–1924, ed. Jo Ann Boydston (Carbondale and Edwardsville IL: University of Southern Illinois Press, 1982), 180.

24. Rosenthal, *Speculative Pragmatism*, 192.

25. Robin Derry and Ronald M. Green, "Ethical Theory in Business Ethics," *Journal of Business Ethics*, 8 (1989): 521.

26. Dewey, *The Quest for Certainty*, 278.

27. John Dewey, "Human Nature and Conduct," in *The Middle Works*, Vol. 14, 1899–1924, ed. Jo Ann Boydston (Carbondale and Edwardsville, IL: University of Southern Illinois Press, 1983), 35.

28. Dewey, "Reconstruction in Philosophy," 181–182.

29. George Herbert Mead, *Mind, Self, and Society*, ed. Charles Morris (Chicago: University of Chicago Press, 1934), 386.

30. Dewey, "Reconstruction in Philosophy," 181, 186.

31. Dewey, "Ethics," 327.

32. Rosenthal, *Speculative Pragmatism*, 191.

33. Dewey, "Ethics," 287.

34. Dewey, "Human Nature and Conduct," 150.

35. John Dewey, "The Theory of Inquiry," in *The Later Works*, Vol. 12, 1925–1953, ed. Jo Ann Boydston (Carbondale and Edwardsville, IL: University of Southern Illinois Press, 1986), 76.

36. Rosenthal, *Speculative Pragmatism*, 192.

NOTES TO CHAPTER 9

1. John Dewey, "The Democratic State," in *The Later Works*, Vol. 2, 1925–1927, ed. Jo Ann Boydston (Carbondale and Edwardsville, IL: Southern Illinois University Press, 1984), 291.

2. Bob Goudzwaard, *Capitalism and Progress: A Diagnosis of Western Society* (Toronto, Canada: Wedge Publishing Foundation and Grand Rapids, MI: William B. Eerdmans, 1979), 26–27.

3. John Dewey, "Search for the Public," in *The Later Works*, Vol. 2, 1925–1927, ed. Jo Ann Boydston (Carbondale and Edwardsville, IL: Southern Illinois University Press, 1984), 240.

4. John Dewey, "The House Divided against Itself," in *The Later Works*, Vol. 5, 1929–1930, ed. Jo Ann Boydston (Carbondale and Edwardsville, IL: Southern Illinois University Press, 1984), 46.

5. See Francis Fukuyama, *The End of History and the Last Man* (New York: Free Press, 1992).

6. Robert Gilpin, *The Political Economy of International Relations* (Princeton, NJ: Princeton University Press, 1987), 15.

7. The existence of economics points to another major difference between business and the traditional professions of law and medicine. These latter professions have no home discipline that provides them with the rationale and justification for their existence. They are strictly practical activities that need no other justification beyond their duty to serve their clients' interests. Business, however, does have a home discipline in economics that prescribes the role business is to play in society and describes how the firm functions in a capitalistic society to create economic wealth.

8. Goudzwaard, *Capitalism and Progress*, 214.

9. Mark Sagoff, "What Is Wrong with Consumption?" Paper presented at the Ruffin Lectures, The Darden School, University of Virginia, Charlottesville, VA, April 1997.

10. Durning, *How Much Is Enough?* (New York: W.W. Norton, 1992), 13.

NOTES TO CHAPTER 10

1. Henry David Thoreau, "Civil Disobedience," in *Walden, and Civil Disobedience*, ed. Owen Thomas (New York: Norton, 1996), 224, as quoted in Garry Wills, *A Necessary Evil: A History of American Distrust of Government* (New York: Simon & Schuster, 1999), 15.

2. Wills, *A Necessary Evil*, 300.

3. John Dewey, "Civil Society and the Political State," in *The Middle Works*, Vol. 5, 1899–1924, ed. Jo Ann Boydston (Carbondale and Edwardsville, IL: Southern Illinois University Press, 1978), 425.

4. Wills, *A Necessary Evil.*, 320.

5. Michael J. Sandel states that a minimal state that is compatible with libertarian thinking involves one that only enforces contracts, protects private property, and keeps the peace. The libertarian rejects (1) any kind of paternalism, i.e., laws that protect people from harming themselves, (2) morals legislation that promotes certain kinds of virtue or expresses the moral convictions of the majority, and (3) any attempt to redistribute income and wealth. See Michael J. Sandel, *Justice: What's the Right Thing to Do?* (New York: Farrar, Strauss & Giroux, 2009), 60–61.

6. See Sandel, *Justice,* for an exposition of this same criticism in regard to notions of justice.

7. Stephen A. Marglin, *Dismal Science: How Thinking Like an Economist Undermines Community* (Cambridge, MA: Harvard University Press, 2008), 28.

8. John Dewey, "Creative Democracy—The Task Before Us," in *The Later Works*, Vol. 14, 1925–1953, ed. Jo Ann Boydston (Carbondale and Edwardsville, IL:

Southern Illinois University Press, 1988), 226–228. The importance of community as a counter to individualism will be extensively discussed in the next chapter, which deals with the social self. It should be noted here that community is also important for Aristotle as he holds that politics is "about learning to live a good life. The purpose of politics is nothing less than to enable people to develop their distinctive human experiences and virtues—to deliberate about the common good, to acquire practical judgment, to share in self-government, to care for the fate of the community as a whole." Sandel, *Justice*, 193–194.

9. Sandra B. Rosenthal and Rogene A. Buchholz, "Pragmatism as a Political Philosophy for Emerging Democracies," in Leszek Koczanowicz and Beth Singer, eds., *Democracy and the Post-Totalitarian Experience* (New York: Rodopi, 2005), 194.

10. In the economics literature, pollution is generally considered to be an example of an externality which is defined as either a beneficial or detrimental (pollution is detrimental) effect on a third party such as a homeowner who lives close to a polluting factory who is not involved in the market transaction between the principals (customer and producer) who caused the pollution because of their activities in the marketplace. The results of pollution control, which in this example would be clean air and water, are more properly called public goods because they are entities with beneficial physical characteristics for human health that are widely shared in different amounts by the citizens of a society.

11. John Rawls, *A Theory of Justice* (Cambridge, MA: Harvard University Press, 1971), 266.

12. Something like health care, for example, is divisible in that each individual has different needs and tries to match those needs through the health-care system. But the value of health care is still not determined through a market process even if it is privatized. People do not shop around for doctors as they do other products and do not know what different doctors charge for their services so they could pick the least costly. Thus competition doesn't exist in the health-care system the same way it exists elsewhere and does not operate to hold down the costs of health care. Most of us pick an internist that we trust and then go to the specialist he or she recommends if one is needed. We do not shop around for the least costly alternative. We want the best care we can afford, or if on Medicare or Medicaid, the best care they will cover.

13. Gerald Sirkin, *The Visible Hand: The Fundamentals of Economic Planning* (New York: McGraw-Hill, 1968), 45.

14. James Buchanan, *The Demand and Supply of Public Goods* (Chicago: Rand McNally, 1968), 8.

15. Interest-group pluralism works as long as politicians are willing to compromise and negotiate with each other to reach a decision about addressing a problem in society. But when politics is seen as warfare, compromise is impossible because it is seen as selling out to the enemy. See Robert J. Samuelson, "How Politics Became Dysfunctional," *The Week*, November 5, 2010, 18.

16. Thomas R. Dye, *Understanding Public Policy*, 3rd ed. (Englewood Cliffs, NJ: Prentice Hall, 1978), 23.

17. See Michael J. Mandel, "How Much Is a Sea Otter Worth?" *Business Week*, August 21, 1989, 59, 62.

18. Aaron Wildavsky, *Speaking Truth to Power: The Art and Craft of Policy Analysis* (Boston: Little, Brown, 1979), 253–254.

19. There is a school of thought called public-choice theory that looks at government decision makers as rational, self-interested people who view issues from their own perspective and in light of personal incentives. While voters, politicians,

and bureaucrats may desire to reflect the "public interest" and often advocate it in support of their decisions, this desire is only one incentive among many with which they are faced and is likely to be outweighed by more powerful incentives related to self-interest of one sort or another. See Steven Kelman, "Public Choice and Public Spirit," *The Public Interest*, 87 (Spring, 1987), 80–94, for an interesting critique of the public-choice school of thought.

20. John Dewey, "The Naturalization of Intelligence," in *The Later Works*, Vol. 4, 1929, ed. Jo Ann Boydston (Carbondale and Edwardsville, IL: Southern Illinois University Press, 1984), 169.
21. Mark A. Martinez, *The Myth of the Free Market: The Role of the State in a Capitalist Economy* (Sterling, VA: Kumarian Press, 2009), xv.
22. Ibid., 26.
23. Ibid., 4.
24. Ibid., 12.
25. Timothy Ferris, *The Science of Liberty: Democracy, Reason, and the Laws of Nature* (New York: HarperCollins, 2010), 1.
26. Ibid., 4–7.
27. Ibid., 2. Thomas Jefferson wrote the following in 1804: "No experiment can be more interesting than that we are now trying, and which we trust will end in establishing the fact, that man may be governed by reason and truth." As quoted in Michael Shermer, "Democracy's Laboratory," *Scientific American*, September 2010, 34. In this article Shermer states that liberal democracies progress ever closer to finding the right balance between individual liberty and social order. This statement reflects the same problem with much of American thought in pitting individuals against the community. Liberty is found in a social order and is not something that has to be balanced over against that order. The next chapter will deal with the self and community in an attempt to overcome this dichotomy.
28. The first secretary of the Interior for the Reagan administration, James Watt, was very influential in shaping the overall environmental policy of that administration. He advocated easing strip-mining rules, opening up more offshore land to oil and gas exploration over the objection of state and local interests, and unlocking many acres of onshore federal lands for mining, drilling, and timber harvesting. These policies were based on very explicit theological assumptions that grew out of his faith as a born-again fundamentalist Christian. He was quoted as saying that his "responsibility is to follow the scriptures which call upon us to occupy the land until Jesus returns." Thus the federal government's role was to use the country's natural resources to ensure that "people are provided for until He does come." Regarding preservation of some of these resources for future generations, Watt remarked, "I do not know how many future generations we can count on before the Lord returns." See Andy Pastzor, "James Watt Tackles Interior Agency Job with Religious Zeal," *Wall Street Journal*, April 15, 1981, 1.
29. Rosenthal and Buchholz, "Pragmatism as a Political Philosophy for Emerging Democracies," 200.

NOTES TO CHAPTER 11

1. Emil Visnovsky, Review of *Democracy as Culture: Deweyan Pragmatism in a Globalized World*, *Transactions of the Charles S. Peirce Society*, 46 (Spring 2011): 321–326.

2. Stephen A. Marglin, *The Dismal Science: How Thinking Like an Economist Undermines Community* (Cambridge, MA: Harvard University Press, 2008), 27.
3. Ibid., 56.
4. Ibid., 45–46.
5. Mark Lilla, "The Tea Party Jacobins," *The New York Review of Books*, May 27, 2010, 53.
6. Ibid.
7. Ibid., 56.
8. See Andrew Romano, "America's Holy Writ," *Newsweek*, October 25, 2010, 33–37. Also see Jacob Weisberg, "A Tea Party Taxonomy," *Newsweek*, September 27, 2010, 33.
9. Zygmunt Bauman, *Does Ethics Have a Chance in a World of Consumers?* (Cambridge, MA: Harvard University Press, 2008), 26. Italics in original.
10. Ibid., 71.
11. Marglin, *Dismal Science*, 222.
12. Bauman, *Does Ethics Have a Chance in a World of Consumers?*, 58–59.
13. George P. Brockway, *The End of Economic Man: An Introduction to Humanistic Economics* (New York: W.W. Norton, 2001), 201–202.
14. Bauman, *Does Ethics Have a Chance in a World of Consumers?*, 170–171. Italics in original.
15. Marglin, *Dismal Science*, 27–28.
16. Ibid., 153.
17. There has been a movement in existence for several years that goes by the name of communitarianism that challenges the primacy of the unfettered individual and tries to temper the excesses of American individuality in the interests of the larger society. According to this movement, the rights of the individual must be balanced with responsibilities to the needs of the community. An understanding of the general welfare of the common good must take group interests and identities into account while standing apart as more than their aggregate. In the words Amitai Etzioini, the founder of this movement: "The term highlights the assumption that individuals act within a social context, that this context is not reducible to individual acts, and most significantly, that the social context is not necessarily or wholly imposed. Instead, the social context is, to a significant extent, perceived as a legitimate and integral part of one's existence, a We, a whole of which the individuals are constituent elements." Amitai Etzioni, *The Moral Dimension: Toward a New Economics* (New York: The Free Press, 1988), 5.
18. Marglin, *Dismal Science*, 245.
19. Ibid., 68–69.
20. Charles Taylor, *The Ethics of Authenticity* (Cambridge, MA: Harvard University Press, 1991), esp. 95 and 117.
21. Classical American pragmatism incorporates the writings of its five major contributors, Charles Peirce, William James, John Dewey, George Herbert Mead, and Charles I. Lewis. That these philosophers provide a unified perspective on self and community is assumed in this chapter, but this claim is defended at some length in Sandra Rosenthal, *Speculative Pragmatism* (Amherst, MA: University of Massachusetts Press, 1986).
22. George Herbert Mead, *Mind, Self, and Society*, ed. Charles Morris (Chicago: University of Chicago Press, 1994), 154.
23. Ibid.

24. John Dewey, "Authority and Social Change," in *The Later Works*, Vol. 11, 1925–1953, ed. Jo Ann Boydston (Carbondale and Edwardsville, IL: University of Southern Illinois Press, 1987), 133.
25. Ibid.
26. George Herbert Mead, *Movements of Thought in the Nineteenth Century*, ed. Merritt Moore (Chicago: University of Chicago Press, 1936), 375–377.
27. Ibid., 353–354. A person may be a member of more than one community, for there are diverse levels and types of communities. Any community consists of many subgroups, and although individuals may feel alienated from a particular society, they cannot really be alienated from society in general, because this very alienation will only throw them into some other society.
28. John Dewey, "The Public and Its Problems," in *The Later Works*, Vol. 2, 1925–1953, ed. Jo Ann Boydston (Carbondale and Edwardsville, IL: University of Southern Illinois Press, 1984), 330, 332.
29. William James, "Great Men and Their Environment," in *The Will to Believe and Other Essays, The Works of William James*, ed. Frederick Burkhardt (Cambridge, MA: Harvard University Press, 1979), 170, 170n, 171.
30. John Dewey, "Ethics," in *The Middle Works*, Vol. 5, 1899–1924, ed. Jo Ann Boydston (Carbondale and Edwardsville, IL: University of Southern Illinois Press, 1978), 327.
31. Alan Gewirth, *The Community of Rights* (Chicago: University of Chicago Press, 1996), 1–2.
32. Ibid., 2–3.
33. Mead, *Movements of Thought in the Nineteenth Century*, 375–377.
34. John Dewey, "Authority and Social Change," in *The Later Works*, Vol. 11, 1925–1953, ed. Jo Ann Boydston (Carbondale and Edwardsville, IL: University of Southern Illinois Press, 1987), 133.
35. Thomas Donaldson, *Corporations and Morality* (Englewood Cliffs, NJ: Prentice Hall, 1982), 41. Italics in original.
36. As an example, envision on the one hand a person taking care of a sick spouse because of an intellectualized "external" sense of duty and, on the other hand, a person taking care of a sick spouse because of the internalization of a caring and attuned relationship to that person.
37. Richard Bronk, *Progress and the Invisible Hand* (London: Warner Books, 1998), 59.

NOTES TO CHAPTER 12

1. Peter A. A. Berle, "How Do We Define Nature?," *Audubon*, May 1991, 6.
2. Bill McKibben, *The End of Nature* (New York: Random House, 1989).
3. Thomas Berry, *The Dream of the Earth* (San Francisco: Sierra Club Books, 1988), 7.
4. Holmes Ralston, "Just Environmental Business," in *Just Business: New Introductory Essays in Business Ethics*, ed. Tom Regan (New York: Random House, 1984), 325–343.
5. Holmes Ralston III, *Philosophy Gone Wild: Essays in Environmental Ethics* (Buffalo, NY: Prometheus Books, 1987), 121.
6. Ibid., 103–104.
7. Ibid., 141.
8. Sara Ebenreck, "An Earth Care Ethics," *The Catholic World: Caring for the Endangered Earth*, 233 (July/August 1990): 157.

9. Thomas Berry, "Spirituality and Ecology," *The Catholic World: Caring for the Endangered Earth*, 233 (July/August 1990): 159.
10. Ibid., 161.
11. Gary T. Gardner, *Inspiring Progress: Religion's Contribution to Sustainable Development* (New York: W.W. Norton, 2006), 147.
12. Larry A. Hickman, *Pragmatism as Post-Postmodernism: Lessons from John Dewey* (New York: Fordham University Press, 2007), 136–137.
13. Ibid., 135.
14. Ibid., 147.
15. See Garret Hardin, "The Tragedy of the Commons," *Science*, 162 (December 13, 1968): 1243–1248.
16. See Lester R. Brown, *Plan B: Rescuing a Planet Under Stress and a Civilization in Trouble* (New York: W.W. Norton, 2003), especially 199–222.
17. See Matt Jenkins, "Mother Nature's Sum," *Miller-McCune*, October 2008, 44–53.

NOTES

1. Robert C. Solomon, *Ethics and Excellence: Cooperation and Integrity in Business* (New York: Oxford University Press, 1992), 150.
2. Some contemporary theories of the organization see organizational dynamics in terms of power tensions and creative confusions. These tensions between empowerment and disempowerment are necessary in order for organizations to sustain themselves. This approach represents the "politics of power" as opposed to the "politics of community" involved in pragmatic theory. See John Hassard, "Postmodernism and Organizational Analysis: An Overview," in *Postmodernism and Organizations*, eds. John Hassard and Martin Parker (London: Sage Publications, 1993), 20–22.
3. Edwin Hartman, *Organizational Ethics and the Good Life* (New York: Oxford University Press, 1996), 174–176.
4. Allan A. Kennedy, *The End of Shareholder Value: Corporations at the Crossroads* (Cambridge, MA: Persus, 2000), 94.
5. Ibid., 95.
6. As private-sector unionism declined, the public sector became more unionized as teachers, firefighters, police, etc., organized to bargain collectively with state administrations. In 2011, however, several states, such as Wisconsin and Ohio, took legislative action to deprive state employees of their right to bargain collectively. See "A Battery of Elected Ideologues Opens Fire on Those Who Serve the Public," *The Hightower Lowdown*, Vol. 13, No. 5 (May 2011): 1–4.
7. In 2007, some states were even considering laws that would make bullying in the workplace an "unlawful employment practice" and give victims of such bullying the right to sue an employer who does not take steps to prevent bullying from happening. See Michael Orey, "Legal Notes," *Business Week*, May 14, 2007, 14.
8. With all these laws it is hard to find an American worker who does not fall into at least one and sometimes several of these protected categories. This trend is something of a countertrend to the threat of termination leading to less job security as the threat of litigation makes employers less likely to terminate even problem workers. See Michael Orey, "Fear of Firing," *Business Week*, April 23, 2007, 52–62. Such a situation, however, is hardly conducive to the creation of a true community.

9. This point is developed in some detail in Sandra B. Rosenthal and Rogene A. Buchholz, "Business and Society: What's in a Name?" *The International Journal of Organizational Analysis*, 5 (1997): 180–201.

10. These values make up his first cluster of values listed under the general category of "economizing values" or those which support prudent and efficient use of resources. These are intertwined with the other two sets of values fitting into the respective categories of "ecologizing" and "power-aggrandizing." The tensions and conflicts between and among the three sets of value clusters, economizing, ecologizing, and power-aggrandizing, are seen as evolutionarily inevitable. See William C. Frederick, *Values, Nature and Culture in the American Corporation* (New York: Oxford University Press, 1995).

NOTES TO CHAPTER 14

1. R. Gordon and J. Howell, *Higher Education for Business* (New York: Columbia University Press, 1959); Pierson et al., *The Education of American Businessmen* (New York: McGraw-Hill, 1959).

2. Felix Salmon. "A Formula for Disaster," *Wired*, March 2008, 77.

3. Ibid., 79.

4. See also Scott Patterson, *The Quants: How a New Breed of Math Whizzes Conquered Wall Street and Nearly Destroyed It* (New York: Crown Business, 2010), 192.

5. Salmon, "A Formula for Disaster," 78.

6. Ibid., 76, 78.

7. Ibid., 79.

8. Ibid., 112.

9. Ibid.

10. David Michaels, *Doubt Is Their Product: How Industry's Assault on Science Threatens Your Health* (New York: Oxford University Press, 2007), 60.

11. Ibid., 60.

12. Ibid., x.

13. See Michelle Hijhuis, "The Doubt Makers," *Miller-McCune*, June/July 2008, 27–35; Sharon Begley, "Whitewashing Toxic Chemicals," *Newsweek*, May 12, 2008, 39; Chris Mooney, "A Dirty Business," *The American Prospect*, October 2010, 38–39. In the latter publication, Mooney states that "Cynically using science to stall policy is the research equivalent of filing frivolous legal motions."

14. See Chris Mooney, *The Republican War on Science* (New York: Basic Books, 2005).

15. Michaels, *Doubt Is Their Product*, xi.

16. GE-Rachel #657: The Uses of Scientific Uncertainty, http://www.gene.ch/info4action/1999/Jul/msg00019.html, accessed March 24, 2009, 2.

17. Ibid.

18. According to David Michaels, "Tobacco has manufactured more uncertainty over a longer period and more effectively than any other industry." Michaels, *Doubt Is Their Product*, x. Another author states that "The essential tactic of the tobacco strategy is to ignore the big picture and attack the details. Tobacco executives, after all, 'didn't deny the reality of the hazard . . . They simply said that they needed more evidence and that both sides needed to be considered.' " See Hijhuis, *The Doubt Makers*, 29.

19. GE-Rachel #657: The Uses of Scientific Uncertainty, 3.

20. Ibid., 4–5.

21. See Rogene A. Buchholz et al., "The EDB Controversy," *Management Responses to Public Issues: Concepts and Cases in Strategy Formulation,* 3rd ed. (Englewood Cliffs, NJ: Prentice Hall, 1994), 100–121.
22. See Robert Bernstein, "Traces of Pesticide Found in Food Products," *The San Antonio Light,* January 4, 1984, 1. See also American Council on Science and Health, *Ethylene Dibromide* (New York: ACSH, May 1984), 12.

NOTES TO CHAPTER 15

1. John Gillespie and David Zweig, *Money for Nothing: How the Failure of Corporate Boards Is Ruining American Business and Costing Us Trillions* (New York: Free Press, 2010), 44. Other estimates put the total loss of household wealth at more than $13 trillion. See Charles Gasparino, *The Sellout: How Three Decades of Wall Street Greed and Government Mismanagement Destroyed the Global Financial System* (New York: Harper Business, 2009), 492.
2. John Cassidy, *How Markets Fail: The Logic of Economic Calamities* (New York: Farrar, Straus and Giroux, 2009), 332.
3. Gasparino, *The Sellout*, 280.
4. This dream of homeownership and its benefits may well be a fantasy according to some sources. See Barbara Kiviat, "The Case against Homeownership," *Time*, September 6, 2010, 40–46. See also Froma Harrop, "Redefining the American Dream," *Denver Post*, December 2, 2010, 11B; and Christopher Caldwell, "The Way We Live Now," *The New York Times Magazine*, November 7, 2010, 19.
5. Adam Michaelson, *Foreclosure of America: Life Inside Countrywide Home Loans and the Selling of the American Dream* (New York: Berkley Books, 2010), 95–96.
6. Cassidy, *How Markets Fail*, 242.
7. Michael Lewis, *The Big Short: Inside the Doomsday Machine* (New York: W.W. Norton, 2010), 73.
8. Ibid., 130.
9. Ibid., 207–208.
10. Ibid., 214.
11. Michaelson, *Foreclosure of America*), xxvii. Mozilo was the first prominent chief executive to be held accountable for questionable business practices that contributed to the housing bubble. He was accused of touting Countrywide's stock in public while privately stating that much of its portfolio was "toxic," while collecting an estimated $521 million as chief executive officer. On the eve of this trial he agreed to settle these charges by paying $47.5 million in penalties and forfeited profits. Bank of America, which took over Countrywide in 2008, will pay an additional $20 million. See "Investigations: Mozilo Pays to Settle Fraud Charges," *The Week*, October 29, 2010, 38; Gretchen Morgenson, "How Countrywide Covered the Cracks: Angelo Mozilo's Public Bravado and Private Doubts," *New York Times*, October 17, 2010, BU1; Frank Rich, "What Happened to Change We Can Believe In?" *New York Times*, October 24, 2010, WK10. In February 2011, the criminal charges against Mozilo were dropped by federal prosecutors who determined that his actions in the mortgage crisis did not amount to criminal wrongdoing. See E. Scott Reckard, "U.S. Probe of Mozilo Dropped," *Denver Post*, February 23, 2100, 9B.
12. Michaelson, *Foreclosure of America*, 143.
13. Ibid., 10–13.

14. Ibid., 25.
15. Charles R. Morris, *The Two Trillion Dollar Meltdown: Easy Money, High Rollers, and the Great Credit Crash* (New York: Public Affairs, 2008), 69.
16. Michaelson, *Foreclosure of America*, 131, 298.
17. Lewis, *The Big Short*, 97.
18. Michaelson, *Foreclosure of America*, 132–133.
19. Morris, *The Two Trillion Dollar Meltdown*, 60.
20. Joseph E. Stiglitz, *Free Fall: America, Free Markets, and the Shrinking of the World Economy* (New York: W.W. Norton, 2010), 88.
21. Lewis, *The Big Short*, 23.
22. Cassidy, *How Markets Fail*, 258.
23. Michaelson, *Foreclosure of America*, 152.
24. Morris, *The Two Trillion Dollar Meltdown*, 67.
25. Ibid., xvii–xviii.
26. Cassidy, *How Markets Fail*, 238.
27. Stiglitz, *Free Fall*, 11.
28. See Michaelson, *The Foreclosure of America*, 25–32, for a typical story of the American Dream that turned into a nightmare.
29. Lewis, *The Big Short*, 172.
30. Paul Krugman, *The Return of Depression Economics: And the Crisis of 2008* (New York: W.W. Norton, 2009), 160.
31. Ibid., 163.
32. Cassidy, *How Markets Fail*, 256.
33. Morris, *The Two Trillion Dollar Meltdown*, 78.
34. Cassidy, *How Markets Fail*, 273.
35. Gasparino, *The Sellout*, 219.
36. Lewis, *The Big Short*, 228.
37. David Wessel, *In Fed We Trust: Ben Bernanke's War on the Great Panic* (New York: Crown Publishing Group, 2009), 104.
38. Stiglitz, *Free Fall*, 91.
39. Gillespie and Zweig, *Money for Nothing*, 27.
40. Cassidy, *How Markets Fail*, 297–298.
41. On May 6, 2010, the Dow slid 1,000 points in less than an hour due to computerized trading. See Nina Mehta, Lynn Thomasson, and Paul M. Barrett, "The Machines That Ate the Market," *Bloomberg Businessweek*, May 24–May 30, 2010, 49–55; "Wall Street's Secret Advantage," *The Week*, July 2–9, 2010, 11; Peter Coy, "What's the Rush?" *Bloomberg Businessweek*, November 15–November 21, 2010, 10–12; Tim Fernholz, "The End of Capitalism!" *The American Prospect*, July/August 2010, 6–9.
42. Scott Patterson, *The Quants: How a New Breed of Math Whizzes Conquered Wall Street and Nearly Destroyed It* (New York: Crown Business, 2009), 290.
43. Ibid., 305.
44. Cassidy, *How Markets Fail*, 269–270. See also Steve Lohr, "Wall Street's Math Wizards Forgot a Few Variables," *New York Times*, September 13, 2009, BU3.
45. Stiglitz, *Free Fall*, 92. The rating agencies received a good deal of criticism and were even sued in the aftermath of the crisis. See Kathleen Casey and Frank Partnoy, "Downgrade the Rating Agencies," *New York Times*, June 6, 2010, WK11; and David Segal, "Suddenly, the Rating Agencies Don't Look Untouchable," *New York Times*, April 23, 2010, BU1.
46. Gasparino, *The Sellout*, 201.
47. Morris, *The Two Trillion Dollar Meltdown*, 62–63.
48. See Hanna Rosin, "Did Christianity Cause the Crash?" *The Atlantic*, December 2009, 39–48, for an interesting twist on the cause of the financial crisis.

49. Gillespie and Zweig, *Money for Nothing*, 36–37.
50. Michael Lewis, *The Big Short*. A reviewer of the book had this to say: "So powerful is the tale Lewis tells of self-interest run amok that perhaps it will help awaken the nation to the basic truth that some individuals were indeed responsible for what happened, and had they been stopped by adequate regulation and enforcement, the speculative fires could have been brought under control. Lewis has written the best book I know about the financial catastrophe by bringing us close to the deluded and duplicitous minds that caused it." Jeff Madrick, "At the Heart of the Crash," *The New York Review*, June 10, 2010, 37–39.
51. See Gregory Zuckerman, *The Greatest Trade Ever* (New York: Broadway Books, 2009), for a similar story about John Paulson and his bet against the market that made financial history.
52. Morris, *The Two Trillion Dollar Meltdown*, 75.
53. Lewis, *The Big Short*, 143.
54. Ibid., 71.
55. Ibid., 83.
56. Ibid., 89.
57. Because of lack of evidence, the SEC declined to file charges of fraud against the former AIG financial products chief, Joseph Cassano, who insisted that he had been "prudent" in selling billions of dollars in credit default swaps. Michael Hirsh, "Tough Case," *Newsweek*, 41.
58. Lewis, *The Big Short*, 88.
59. Cassidy, *How Markets Fail*, 282.
60. See James Surowieki, "Too Clever by Half?" *The New Yorker*, May 17, 2010, 40.
61. Lewis, *The Big Short*, 256–257.
62. Michaelson, *Foreclosure of America*, 306–308.
63. Ibid., xxx.
64. See Stephen Gandel, "How Goldman Trashed a Town," *Time*, July 5, 2010, 32–35, for a good description of the effects of the crisis on a small city in the Midwest.
65. Cassidy, *How Markets Fail*, 229.
66. Gasparino, *The Sellout*, 196–197.
67. Krugman, *The Return of Depression Economics*, 164.
68. Morris, *The Two Trillion Dollar Meltdown*, 54.
69. Krugman, *The Return of Depression Economics*, 164.
70. Cassidy, *How Markets Fail*, 283.
71. Patterson, *The Quants*, 264.
72. Justin Fox, *The Myth of the Rational Market: A History of Risk, Reward, and Delusion on Wall Street* (New York: Harper Business, 2009), 318–319.
73. Gasparino, *The Sellout*, 197–198.
74. Cassidy, *How Markets Fail*, 32–33.
75. Ibid., 234.
76. Mark A. Martinez, *The Myth of the Free Market: The Role of the State in a Capitalist Economy* (Sterling, VA: Kumarian Press, 2009), 243–244.
77. Stiglitz, *Free Fall*, 145–146.
78. Martinez, *The Myth of the Free Market*, 243–245.
79. Stiglitz, *Free Fall*, 8, 13.
80. Ibid., 14.
81. Ibid., 104–105.
82. David Stockman, "Four Deformations of the Apocalypse," *New York Times*, August 1, 2010, WK5. Italics mine.

83. Richard Posner, who is said to be a libertarian and adherent of the Chicago school of economics, had this to say in a new book entitled *A Failure of Capitalism: The Crisis of '08 and the Descent into Depression*, published by Harvard University Press: "Some conservatives believe that the depression is the result of unwise government policies. I believe it is a market failure. The government's myopia, passivity, and blunders played a critical role in *allowing* the recession to balloon into a depression, and so have several fortuitous factors. But without any government regulation of the financial industry, the economy would still, in all likelihood, be in a depression; what we have learned from the depression has shown that we need a more active and intelligent government to keep our model of a capitalist economy from running off the rails. The movement to deregulate the financial industry went too far by exaggerating the resilience—the self-healing powers—of laissez-faire capitalism." As quoted in Robert M. Solow, "How to Understand the Disaster," *The New York Review*, May 14, 2009, 4.
84. Cassidy, *How Markets Fail*, 134.
85. Ibid., 334.
86. See also Gary Stix, "The Science of Bubbles & Busts," *Scientific American*, July 2009, 78–85.
87. Cassidy, *How Markets Fail*, 9.
88. Michaelson, *Foreclosure of America*, 333.
89. Fox, *The Myth of the Rational Market*, 107.
90. Ibid., 30
91. Stephen A. Marglin, *Dismal Science: How Thinking Like an Economist Undermines Community* (Cambridge, MA: Harvard University Press, 2008), 169–170.
92. Ibid., 172.
93. Ibid., 180.
94. Fox, *The Myth of the Rational Market*, 3–5.
95. Paul Krugman states that "The belief that financial markets always set the right price blinded many if not most economists to the emergence of the biggest financial bubble in history." See Paul Krugman, "How Did Economists Get It So Wrong?" *The New York Times Magazine*, September 6, 2009, 36–43.
96. Cassidy, *How Markets Fail*, 86–87.
97. Ibid., 13.
98. Patterson, *The Quants*, 294.
99. See John Cassidy, "Rational Irrationality," *The New Yorker*, October 5, 2009, 30–35.
100. Gillespie and Zweig, *Money for Nothing*, 210–211.
101. Michaelson, *Foreclosure of America*, 306.
102. Cassidy, *How Markets Fail*, 138.
103. Ibid., 142.
104. Ibid., 177.
105. Fox, *The Myth of the Rational Market*, 320.
106. Zuckerman, *The Greatest Trade Ever*, 2.
107. AFL-CIO, "2006 Trends in CEO Pay," www.aflcio.org. According to another source, CEO pay averaged $10.8 million in 2006, 364 times the average worker's pay. This was down from 411 in 2005 and below the all-time high of 525 times the average pay set in 2000. See "The Bottom Line," *The Week*, September 14, 2007, 36.
108. Gillespie and Zweig, *Money for Nothing*, 35–36.
109. Ibid., 10–13.
110. Ibid., 6–10.

111. Ibid., 13–17.
112. Ibid., 54–58.
113. Ibid.
114. See Cassidy, *How Markets Fail*, 289.
115. Gasparino, *The Sellout*, 271. Former top executives of Bear Stearns, including James Cayne, the former CEO, told government officials investigating the financial crisis that they could not have foreseen the meltdown and that there was little they could have done to head off the company's failure. Paul Davidson, "Bear Stearns Execs Blame 'Market Forces,' " *USA Today*, May 6, 2010, 3B.
116. "The top-earning 20 percent of Americans—those making more than $100,000 annually—received 49.4 percent of all income generated in the U.S. in 2009. The 14.3 percent of Americans living below the poverty line received 3.4 percent of income, the Census Bureau says. The disparity between those at the top and those in poverty is the widest recorded since the Census Bureau started tracking household income in 1967." "The bottom line," *The Week*, October 8, 2010, 44.
117. Greg Ip, "Not Your Father's Pay: Why Wages Today Are Weaker," *Wall Street Journal*, May 25, 2007, A2.
118. See David Owen, "The Pay Problem," *The New Yorker*, October 12, 2009, 58–63; Jessica Silver-Greenberg and Alexis Leondis, "How Much Is a CEO Worth?" *Bloomberg Businessweek*, May 10–May 16, 2010, 70–71; James Surowiecki, "The Financial Page: Board Stiff," *The New Yorker*, June 1, 2009, 34.
119. Rana Foroohar, "Stuffing Their Pockets," *Newsweek*, September 13, 2010, 20. One author blames the governance structure of corporations for allowing top executives to plunder the corporation for their own purposes. This governance structure was created by the government, it did not develop through the free market, and it could be changed by the government in ways that would return control to the shareholders. See Dean Baker, "Ending the Myth of Market Fundamentalism," *Dissent*, Spring 2010, 61.
120. Stiglitz, *Free Fall*, 18.
121. Martinez, *The Myth of the Free Market*, 232.
122. Morris, *The Two Trillion Dollar Meltdown*, x.
123. Stiglitz, *Free Fall*, 36.
124. See James Sterngold and Hugh Son, "AIG's Declaration of Independence," *Bloomberg Businessweek*, June 7–June 13, 2010, 73–76.
125. Amy Schoenfeld, "Rolling Up TARP, Though the Cleanup Isn't Over ," *New York Times*, October 3, 2010, BU8; Rebecca Christie with Hugh Son and James Sterngold, "Love It or Hate It (Most Do), TARP Didn't Bust the Bank," *Bloomberg Businessweek*, October 4–October 10, 2010, 29–30.
126. Lewis, *The Big Short*, 261.
127. Stiglitz, *Free Fall*, 80.
128. Ibid., 135.
129. Michaelson, *Foreclosure of America*, 310–311.
130. Stiglitz, *Free Fall*, 145.
131. Gillespie and Zweig, *Money for Nothing*, 183.
132. In July 2010, Goldman Sachs settled a lawsuit filed by the SEC alleging that the company helped structure a mortgage security that was designed to fail and then sold it to unwitting clients. The company agreed to pay $550 million to settle the case but admitted to no wrongdoing. This amount represented a mere two weeks' worth of the company's first-quarter profits. See "Issue of the Week: Did Goldman Get Off Easy?" *The Week*, July 30, 2010; Marcy Gordon and Daniel Wagner, "Goldman Settles Civil Fraud Charges,"

The Denver Post, July 16, 2010, 9B; Stephen Gandel, "The Case against Goldman Sachs," *Time*, May 3, 2010, 30–37; Jonathan Weil, "Goldman Slapped," *Bloomberg Businessweek*, April 26–May 2, 2010, 13–14.

133. Lewis, *The Big Short*, 262.
134. Michaelson, *Foreclosure of America*, 307–308.
135. Stiglitz, *Free Fall*, 182.
136. Krugman, *The Return of Depression Economics*, 189–190.
137. John Cassidy states that "Taken overall, the reform effort amounts to tinkering with the existing system rather than fundamentally reforming it." See John Cassidy, "The Economy: Why They Failed," *The New York Review*, December 9, 2010, 27–29. See also Christine Harper, "Will Reforms Be Too Late?" *The Denver Post*, August 15, 2010, 6K; Michael Lewis, "Shorting Reform," *New York Times*, May 30, 2010, WK9; and "Still at Risk," *The American Prospect*, June 2010, A1–A23. Some argued that we did not need new financial regulations and that what the financial world needs is radical transparency. See Daniel Roth, "The Road Map for Recovery, *Wired*, March 2009, 81–113.
138. Jim Kuhnhenn, "Finance Reforms Pass," *The Denver Post*, July 16, 2010, 5B.
139. See Louis Uchitelle, "Volcker, Loud and Clear," *New York Times*, July 11, 2010, BU1; and Paul Volcker, "The Time We Have Is Growing Short," *The New York Review*, May 25, 2010, 12–14, for a good review of all Volcker's recommendations.
140. John Cassidy, "The Volcker Rule," *The New Yorker*, July 26, 2010, 25–30.
141. "A New Era of Financial Regulation," *The Week*, July 30, 2010, 5. See also Zeke Faux, "Individual Investors Duped by Derivatives," *Bloomberg Businessweek*, October 4–October 10, 2010, 43–44.
142. In 2010 a new problem emerged as some banks had to suspend their foreclosure activities because of paperwork problems. During the boom years many banks apparently got sloppy and as loans were turned into securities many of the trusts that were supposed to hold the documents related to the underlying mortgages had neither the actual promissory notes nor the liens that give a lender the right to foreclose on the property. Thus the banks could not prove that they actually owned the mortgage loans on which they were foreclosing. See Robert Kuttner, "The Next Banking Crisis," *The American Prospect*, January/February 2011, 17–18.

NOTES TO CHAPTER 16

1. Stephen A. Marglin, *Dismal Science: How Thinking Like an Economist Undermines Community* (Cambridge, MA: Harvard University Press, 2008), 128.
2. Ibid., 132.
3. Ibid., 159–160.
4. See Rogene A. Buchholz, *Rethinking Capitalism: Community and Responsibility in Business* (New York: Routledge, 2009).
5. Rakesh Khurana, *From Higher Aims to Hired Hands: The Social Transformation of American Business Schools and the Unfulfilled Promise of Management as a Profession* (Princeton, NJ: Princeton University Press, 2007), 380.
6. Ibid., 6.
7. Ibid., 19.
8. Ibid., 271.
9. Oliver Sheldon, *The Philosophy of Management* (London: Pitman Publishing Ltd., 1923).

10. Khurana, *From Higher Aims to Hired Hands*, 324–325.
11. William A. Levi, "Ethical Confusion and the Business Community," *Ethics and Standards in American Business*, ed. J. W. Towle (New York: Houghton Mifflin, 1964), 20–29.
12. Ibid., 27.
13. This change of focus has legal implications because shareholders have the right to file lawsuits based on the duty of managers to seek the highest possible financial return for the shareholders of the corporation. But a new Maryland law allows for the creation of a new kind of company called a "benefit corporation" and gives it greater protection from such lawsuits. This kind of company would be created to attract investors with a social agenda. The states of Vermont and California were considering similar measures. See John Tozzi, "Is There More to Business Than Profits?" *The Week*, May 7, 2010, 42.
14. Khurana, *From Higher Aims to Hired Hands*, 331.
15. Ibid., 352, 348.
16. Martha Nussbaum, in a new book, argues that the United States has increasingly treated education as though its primary goal was to teach students how to become economically productive, a utilitarian goal, rather than teaching them to think critically and become knowledgeable and empathetic citizens. See Martha C. Nussbaum, *Not for Profit: Why Democracy Needs the Humanities* (Princeton, NJ: Princeton University Press), 2010.
17. Khurana, *From Higher Aims to Hired Hands*, 366.
18. Robert A. Giacalone and Kenneth R. Thompson, "Business Ethics and Social Responsibility Education: Shifting the Worldview," *Learning and Education*, 5 (September, 2006): 267.
19. A similar view is expressed by Marcus et al. in an article in *Business and Society*, where they describe the embedded view of the business-society-nature interface where business is seen to exist within society and society within the broader natural environment. The business and societal systems do not merely overlap, but the business system is completely enveloped within the societal sphere and is not considered to be equal to society but is rather a component nested within the larger social system. See Joel Marcus, Elizabeth C. Kurucz, and Barry A. Colbert, "Conceptions of the Business-Society-Nature Interface: Implications for Management Scholarship," *Business and Society*, 49 (September 2010): 402–438.
20. The content of courses in the curriculum of business schools could still be science based depending on the nature of the course itself. Bennis and O'Toole, while critical of the scientific orientation of business schools as a whole, do not advocate throwing the baby out with the bathwater. Science would still be important in providing rigor to an analysis of business problems. But the scientific base would have to be placed in the context of business as a profession and broadened to include other aspects of human and organizational behavior. Agency theory and a strictly economic view of the firm overlook such organizational phenomena as power, coercion, exploitation, discrimination, conflict, and other such issues and relieve a manager of any meaningful responsibility to other members of the organization or to society as a whole. But people are not just contracting agents; they relate to coworkers in the organization and to society in a variety of ways and have a nexus of responsibilities for which the disciplines of sociology, political science, and psychology are just as important as economics and agency theory in understanding how people behave in organizations and the behavior of organizations in society.
21. It is interesting to note that the current accounting curriculum in schools of business and management is geared towards helping the accounting student

meet CPA requirements so that he or she can become a Certified Public Accountant and attain the professional status that goes with this certification. Thus these students have some exposure to professionalism that other students in the business school do not have and have to engage in continuing education to maintain this certification, including exposure to the American Institute of Certified Public Accountants (AICPA) code of ethics. Yet accounting research is dominated by the agency model, which prevents a full measure of professionalism from being imparted to these students. See Dann G. Fisher and Diane L. Swanson, "Accounting Education Lags CPE Requirements: Implications for the Profession and a Call to Action," *Accounting Education: An International Journal*, 16 (2007): 345–363.

22. A campaign was mounted in 2002 called Campaign AACSB. It took aim at the Association for the Advancement of Collegiate Schools of Business (AACSB), which is the accrediting agency for the nation's business schools. This campaign sought to upgrade and strengthen ethics accreditation standards and charged that the AACSB's weak ethics standards unwittingly contributed to corporate crime and corruption by failing to mandate a required ethics course as a condition of accreditation. See Diane L. Swanson and William C. Frederick, "Campaign AACSB: Are Business Schools Complicit in Corporate Corruption?" *Journal of Individual Employment Rights*, 10 (2001–2002): 151–165; Diane L. Swanson, "The Buck Stops Here: Why Universities Must Reclaim Business Ethics Education," *Journal of Academic Ethics*, 2 (March 2004): 43–61; and Diane L. Swanson and Dann G. Fisher, "Business Ethics Education: If We Don't Know Where We're Going, Any Road Will Take Us There," in *Advancing Business Ethics Education*, eds. R. A. Giacalone and C. L. Jurkiewicz (New York: Information Age Publishing, 2008), 1–23.

Selected Bibliography

Anastapoulos, Charis. *Particle or Wave: The Evolution of the Concept of Matter in Modern Physics*. Princeton, NJ: Princeton University Press, 2008.

Ayre, A. J. *Language, Truth and Logic*, 2nd ed. New York: Dover Publications, 1936.

Ayres, Clarence E. *Toward a Reasonable Society*. Austin TX: University of Texas Press, 1961.

Barrow, John D. *New Theories of Everything*. New York: Oxford University Press, 2007.

Bauman, Zygmunt. *Does Ethics Have a Chance in a World of Consumers?* Cambridge, MA: Harvard University Press, 2008.

Bell, Daniel. *The Cultural Contradictions of Capitalism*. New York: Basic Books, 1976.

Bennett, Jeffrey. *Beyond UFOs: The Search for Extraterrestrial Life and Its Astonishing Implications for Our Future*. Princeton, NJ: Princeton University Press, 2008.

Bentham, Jeremy. *Introduction to the Principals of Morals and Legislation*, ed. W. Harrison. Oxford: Oxford University Press, 1948.

Bohm, David. *Wholeness and the Implicate Order*. London: Routledge & Kegan Paul, 1980.

Borgmann, Albert. *Technology and the Character of Contemporary Life*. Chicago: The University of Chicago Press, 1984.

Brockman, John, ed. *Science at the Edge: Conversations with the Leading Scientific Thinkers of Today*. New York: Union Square Press, 2008.

Brockway, George P. *The End of Economic Man: An Introduction to Humanistic Economics*. New York: W.W. Norton, 2001.

Bronk, Richard. *Progress and the Invisible Hand*. London: Warner Books, 1998.

Brown, Lester R. *Plan B: Rescuing a Planet Under Stress and a Civilization in Trouble*. New York: W.W. Norton, 2003.

Buchan, James. *The Authentic Adam Smith: His Life and Ideas*. New York: W.W. Norton, 2006.

Buchanan, James. *The Demand and Supply of Public Goods*. Chicago: Rand McNally, 1968.

Buchholz, Rogene A. *Rethinking Capitalism: Community and Responsibility in Business*. New York: Routledge, 2009.

Capra, Frank. *The Web of Life: A New Scientific Understanding of Living Systems*. New York: Anchor Doubleday, 1996.

Cassidy, John. *How Markets Fail: The Logic of Economic Calamities*. New York: Farrar, Straus and Giroux, 2009.

Chamberlain, Neil W. *The Limits of Corporate Responsibility*. New York: Basic Books, 1973.

Chandler, Alfred. D. Jr. *The Visible Hand: The Managerial Revolution in American Business.* Cambridge, MA: Belknap Press, 1977.

Cortright, S. A., and Michael J. Naughton. *Rethinking the Purpose of Business.* Notre Dame, IN: University of Notre Dame Press, 2002.

Dawson, Christopher. *Progress and Religion: An Historical Inquiry.* London: Sheed & Ward, 1929.

Dewey, John. *Essays in Experimental Logic.* New York: Dover Publications, 1916.

Dewey, John. *The Quest for Certainty: A Study of the Relation between Knowledge and Action.* New York: Capricorn Books, 1960.

Dewey, John. *The Middle Works, 1899–1924,* Vols. 1–15, ed. Jo Ann Boydston. Carbondale and Edwardsville, IL: University of Southern Illinois Press, 1976–1983.

Dewey, John. *The Later Works, 1925–1953,* Vols. 1–16, ed. Jo Ann Boydston. Carbondale and Edwardsville, IL: University of Southern Illinois Press, 1981–1989.

Donaldson, Thomas. *Corporations & Morality.* Englewood Cliffs, NJ: Prentice Hall, 1982.

Donaldson, Thomas. *The Ethics of International Business.* New York: Oxford, 1989.

Donaldson, Thomas, and Thomas Dunfee. *Ties That Bind: A Social Contracts Approach to Business Ethics.* Boston: Harvard University Press, 1999.

Durning, Alan. *How Much Is Enough?* New York: Norton, 1992.

Etzioni, Amitai. *The Moral Dimension: Toward a New Economics.* New York: The Free Press, 1988.

Ferris, Timothy. *The Science of Liberty: Democracy, Reason, and the Laws of Nature.* New York: HarperCollins, 2010.

Filkin, David. *Stephen Hawking's Universe: The Cosmos Explained.* New York: Basic Books, 1997.

Flowers, Charles A. *A Science Odyssey: 100 Years of Discovery.* New York: William Morrow & Company, 1998.

Folse, Hanry J. *The Philosophy of Niels Bohr: The Framework of Complementarity.* Amsterdam: North-Holland, 1985.

Fox, Justin. *The Myth of the Rational Market: A History of Risk, Reward, and Delusion on Wall Street.* New York: HarperCollins, 2009.

Fox, Matthew, and Rupert Sheldrake. *Natural Grace: Dialogues on Creation, Darkness, and the Soul in Spirituality and Science.* New York: Doubleday, 1997.

Frederick, William C. *Values, Nature and Culture in the American Corporation.* New York: Oxford University Press, 1995.

Frederick, William C. *Corporation Be Good!* Indianapolis: Dog Ear Publishing, 2006.

Fukuyama, Francis. *The End of History and the Last Man.* New York: Free Press, 1992.

Gardner, Gary T. *Inspiring Progress: Religion's Contribution to Sustainable Development.* New York: W.W. Norton, 2006.

Gasparino, Charles. *The Sellout: How Three Decades of Wall Street Greed and Government Mismanagement Destroyed the Global Financial System.* New York: HarperCollins, 2009.

Gewirth, Alan. *The Community of Rights.* Chicago: University of Chicago Press, 1996.

Gilchrist, John. *The Church and Economic Activity in the Middle Ages.* London: Macmillan, 1969.

Gilpin, Robert. *The Political Economy of International Relations.* Princeton, NJ: Princeton University Press, 1987.

Gillespie, John and David Zweig. *Money for Nothing: How the Failure of Corporate Boards Is Ruining American Business and Costing Us Trillions.* New York: Free Press, 2010.

Gordon, R., and J. Howell. *Higher Education for Business.* New York: Columbia University Press, 1959.

Goudzwarrd, Bob. *Capitalism & Progress: A Diagnosis of Western Society.* Toronto: Wedge Publishing Foundation; Grand Rapids, MI: William B. Eerdmans, 1978.

Gray, John. *False Dawn.* New York: The New Press, 1998.

Greider, William. *The Soul of Capitalism: Opening Paths to a Moral Economy.* New York: Simon & Schuster, 2003.

Griswold, Charles L. Jr. *Adam Smith and the Virtues of Enlightenment.* Cambridge, UK: Cambridge University Press, 1999.

Hartman, Edwin. *Organizational Ethics and the Good Life.* New York: Oxford University Press, 1996.

Hassard, John, and Martin Parker, eds. *Postmodernism and Organizations.* London: Sage Publications, 1993.

Hausman, Daniel M., and Michael S. McPherson. *Economic Analysis, Moral Philosophy, and Public Policy,* 2nd ed. New York: Cambridge University Press, 2006.

Heisenberg, Werner. *Physics and Philosophy: The Revolution in Modern Science.* New York: Harper Perennial, 1958.

Hickman, Larry A. *John Dewey's Pragmatic Technology.* Bloomington and Indianapolis: Indiana University Press, 1992.

Hickman, Larry A. *Pragmatism as Post-Postmodernism.* New York: Fordham University Press, 2007.

Higgs, Eric, Andrew Light, and David Strong, eds. *Technology and the Good Life?* Chicago: University of Chicago Press, 2000.

Hospers, John. *Libertarianism.* Los Angeles: Nash, 1971.

Hume, David. *Essays Moral, Political, and Literary.* London: Longmans, Green & Co. 1875.

Hume, David. *A Treatise of Human Nature.* Oxford: Clarendon Press, 1896.

James, William. *The Will to Believe and Other Essays: The Works of William James,* ed. Frederick Burkhardt. Cambridge, MA: Harvard University Press, 1979.

Kaiser, Robert G. *So Damn Much Money: The Triumph of Lobbying and the Corrosion of American Government.* New York: Knopf, 2010.

Kant, Immanuel. *Foundations of the Metaphysics of Morals,* trans. L. W. Beck. Indianapolis: Bobbs-Merrill Company, 1959.

Kennedy, Allan A. *The End of Shareholder Value: Corporations at the Crossroads.* Cambridge, MA: Perseus, 2000.

Khurana, Rakesh. *From Higher Aims to Hired Hands.* Princeton, NJ: Princeton University Press, 2007.

Koczanowicz, Leszek, and Beth Singer, eds. *Democracy and the Post-Totalitarian Experience.* New York: Rodopi, 2005.

Krugman, Paul. *The Return of Depression Economics and the Crisis of 2008.* New York: W.W. Norton, 2009.

Kuhn, Thomas S. *The Copernican Revolution: Planetary Astronomy in the Development of Western Thought.* New York: MJF Books, 1985.

Kuhn, Thomas S. *The Structure of Scientific Thought,* 3rd ed. Chicago: University of Chicago Press, 1996.

Kuttner, Robert. *The Squandering of America.* New York: Knopf, 2007.

LaPiere, Richard. *The Freudian Ethic.* New York: Duell, Sloan and Pearce, 1959.

Laqueur, Walter, and Barry Rubin, eds. *The Human Rights Reader.* Philadelphia: Temple University Press, 1979.

Lasch, Christopher. *The Culture of Narcissism: American Life in an Age of Diminishing Expectations.* New York: Norton, 1978.

Laughlin, Robert B. *A Different Universe: Reinventing Physics from the Bottom Down.* New York: Basic Books, 2005.

Lerner, Michael. *The Politics of Meaning: Restoring Hope and Possibility in an Age of Cynicism.* Reading, MA: Addison-Wesley, 1996.

Lewin, Roger. *Complexity: Life at the Edge of Chaos.* Chicago: University of Chicago Press, 1999.

Lewis, C. I. *Mind and the World Order.* New York: Dover Publications, 1929.

Lewis, Michael. *The Big Short: Inside the Doomsday Machine.* New York: W.W. Norton, 2010.

Lewontin, Richard. *The Triple Helix: Gene, Organism and Environment.* Cambridge, MA: Harvard University Press, 2000.

Locke, John. *Two Treatises of Government.* Cambridge: Cambridge University Press, 1988.

Marglin, Stephen A. *The Dismal Science: How Thinking Like an Economist Undermines Community.* Cambridge, MA: Harvard University Press, 2008.

Martinez, Mark A. *The Myth of the Free Market: The Role of the State in a Capitalist Economy.* Sterling, VA: Kumarian Press, 2009.

McCelland, David C. *The Achieving Society.* New York: The Free Press, 1961.

McKeon, Richard, ed. *The Basic Works of Aristotle.* New York: The Modern Library, 2001.

McKibben, Bill. *The End of Nature.* New York: Random House, 1989.

Mead, George Herbert. *Movements of Thought in the Nineteenth Century,* ed. Merritt Moore. Chicago: University of Chicago Press, 1936.

Mead, George Herbert. *Philosophy of the Act.* Chicago: University of Chicago Press, 1938.

Mead, George Herbert. *The Philosophy of the Present.* La Salle, IL: Open Court, 1959.

Mead, George Herbert. *Mind, Self, and Society,* ed. Charles Morris. Chicago: University of Chicago Press, 1994.

Merleau-Ponty, Maurice. *The World of Perception,* trans. Oliver Davis. New York: Routledge, 2008.

Michaels, David. *Doubt Is Their Product: How Industry's Assault on Science Threatens Your Health.* New York: Oxford, 2007.

Michaelson, Adam. *The Foreclosure of America: Life Inside Countrywide Home Loans and the Selling of the American Dream.* New York: Berkley Books, 2010.

Mill, John Stuart. *Utilitarianism,* ed. Oskar Piest. Indianapolis: Bobbs-Merrill, 1957.

Mitchell, Lawrence E. *The Speculation Economy: How Finance Triumphed over Industry.* San Francisco: Berrett-Koehler Publishers, Inc., 2007.

Mooney, Chris. *The Republican War on Science.* New York: Basic Books, 2005.

Moore. G. E. *Principia Ethica.* Cambridge, England: Cambridge University Press, 1903.

Morris, Charles R. *The Two Trillion Dollar Meltdown: Easy Money, High Rollers, and the Great Credit Crash.* New York: Public Affairs, 2008.

Morrison, Elting E., ed. *The American Style: Essays in Value and Performance.* New York: Harper & Bros., 1958.

Mueller, Jerry A. *The Mind and the Market: Capitalism in Modern European Thought.* New York: Knopf, 2002.

Muller, Jerry Z. *Adam Smith in His Time and Ours.* Princeton, NJ: Princeton University Press, 1993.

Nash, Roderick Frazier. *The Rights of Nature: A History of Environmental Ethics.* Madison: University of Wisconsin Press, 1989.

Nelson, Julie A. *Economics for Humans.* Chicago: University of Chicago Press, 2006.

Nussbaum, Martha C. *Not for Profit: Why Democracy Needs the Humanities.* Princeton, NJ: Princeton University Press, 2010.

Patterson, Scott. *The Quants: How a New Breed of Math Whizzes Conquered Wall Street and Nearly Destroyed It.* New York: Crown Business, 2010.

Phillips, Kevin. *Bad Money: Reckless Finance, Failed Politics, and the Global Crisis of American Capitalism.* New York: Viking, 2008.

Pierson et al. *The Education of American Businessmen.* New York: McGraw-Hill, 1959.

Polanyi, Karl. *The Great Transformation.* Boston: Beacon Press, 1944.

Posner, Richard A. *A Failure of Capitalism: The Crisis of '08 and the Descent into Depression.* Cambridge, MA: Harvard University Press, 2009.

Posner, Richard A. *The Crisis of Capitalist Democracy.* Cambridge, MA: Harvard University Press, 2010.

Ralston, Holmes III. *Philosophy Gone Wild: Essays in Environmental Ethics.* Buffalo, NY: Prometheus Books, 1987.

Rawls, John. *A Theory of Justice.* Cambridge: Harvard University Press, 1971.

Regan, Tom, ed. *Just Business: New Introductory Essays in Business Ethics.* New York: Random House, 1984.

Reich, Robert B. *After-Shock: The Next Economy and America's Future.* New York: Alfred A. Knopf, 2010.

Repcheck, Jack. *Copernicus' Secret: How the Scientific Revolution Began.* New York: Simon & Schuster, 2007.

Rosenthal, Sandra B. *Speculative Pragmatism.* La Salle, IL: Open Court, 1986.

Sandel, Michael J. *Democracy's Discontent: America in Search of a Public Philosophy.* Cambridge, MA: Belknap Press, 1996.

Sandel, Michael J. *Justice: What's the Right Thing to Do?* New York: Farrar, Strauss & Giroux, 2009.

Shapin, Steven. *The Scientific Revolution.* Chicago: University of Chicago Press, 1996.

Sheldon, Oliver. *The Philosophy of Management.* London: Pitman Publishing Ltd., 1923.

Sirkin, Gerald. *The Visible Hand: The Fundamentals of Economic Planning.* New York: McGraw-Hill, 1968.

Solomon, Robert C. *Ethics and Excellence: Cooperation and Integrity in Business.* New York: Oxford, 1993.

Smith, Adam. *The Theory of Moral Sentiments.* New York: Arlington House, 1969.

Smith, Adam. *The Wealth of Nations.* New York: Bantam Dell, 2003.

Stiglitz, Joseph E. *Free Fall: America, Free Markets, and the Sinking of the World Economy.* New York: W.W. Norton, 2010.

Tawney, Robert H. *Religion and the Rise of Capitalism.* Gloucester: MA: P. Smith, 1962.

Taylor, Charles. *The Ethics of Authenticity.* Cambridge, MA: Harvard University Press, 1991.

Weber, Max. *The Protestant Ethic and the Spirit of Capitalism.* New York: Scribner's Sons, 1958.

Wessel, David. *In Fed We Trust: Ben Bernanke's War on the Great Panic.* New York: Crown Business, 2009.

Wildavsky, Aaron. *Speaking Truth to Power: The Art and Craft of Policy Analysis.* Boston: Little, Brown, 1979.

Wills, Garry. *A Necessary Evil: A History of American Distrust of Government.* New York: Simon & Schuster, 1999.

Yankelovich, Daniel. *New Rules: The Search for Self-Fulfillment in a World Turned Upside Down.* New York: Random House, 1981.

Zuckerman, Gregory. *The Greatest Trade Ever: The Behind-the-Scenes Story of How John Paulson Defied Wall Street and Made Financial History.* New York: Broadway Books, 2009.

Index

Printed in the United States
by Baker & Taylor Publisher Services